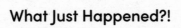

What Just Happened?!

Marina Hyde

What Just Happened?!

DISPATCHES FROM
TURBULENT TIMES

First published by Guardian Faber in 2022
Guardian Faber is an imprint of Faber & Faber Ltd,
Bloomsbury House, 74–77 Great Russell Street,
London WC1B 3DA

Guardian is a registered trade mark of
Guardian News & Media Ltd,
Kings Place, 90 York Way, London N1 9GU

Typeset by Ian Bahrami
Printed and bound by CPI Group (UK) Ltd, Croydon CR0 4YY

A CIP record for this book
is available from the British Library

ISBN 978-1-78335-259-3

2 4 6 8 10 9 7 5 3 1

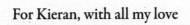

For Kieran, with all my love

CONTENTS

INTRODUCTION

Hello to you, dear reader!

If you are holding this book in your hands, you have set your sights on adventure. Not for you the elective comfort of simply forgetting that any of the past few years happened in the mind-boggling way that they did. No. Instead, you have opted to clamber inside the news simulator and relive every inspirationally chaotic moment all over again. You have chosen to be reminded that the path to the sunlit uplands goes right through shit creek. You're all 'Oooh, what's a Wuhan wet market? It sounds fun!' You have chosen to reload the concept album *Chris Grayling*. You have said yes to all this. I don't pretend to understand it – but I *do* respect it.

In case you skipped the cover, it's called *What Just Happened?!* – like I have the first fricking clue. That's what the exclamation mark is for. It says: this is the opposite of a rhetorical question. Guys, I genuinely have no idea! And, encouragingly, I discovered when going through the 47 trillion words I've written since 2016 that I often don't even have a memory of writing half of them. It felt like I had written a book I hadn't read. A bit like Katie Price – only instead of not having even skimmed a single one of my seven autobiographies, I was completely in the dark about other stuff. Take the whole week of daily columns focusing on something called 'indicative votes'. What in the name of sanity were they? I've heard of past-lives therapy; maybe I need past-columns therapy. Just as distinguished Hollywood crazy Shirley MacLaine is convinced she previously walked the earth as Charlemagne's Moorish peasant lover, so I could be assured that I really did once turn out 1,100 words on how Boris Johnson had *literally* swapped bodies with his dog. I mean, it sounds like something I might have done? And I don't think I have an alibi for it?

In the end, these pages are just my record of an era in which so many of us – but not all! – felt the news had become stranger than fiction. Here follows a series of contemporaneous dispatches from a period when it often seemed like the UK had tumbled down a rabbit hole. Or gone through the looking glass. Or maybe got trapped in the ancient curse – 'May you live in interesting times.' Things seemed to become permanently 'interesting'. For instance, in the space of a very short time in early 2019, Tory MP Mark Francois and novelist Will Self had a spat about the size of Mark's penis on a midday politics TV show; a Ukip leader wrote to the Queen and informed her she had committed treason when she signed the Maastricht treaty; and a Conservative MP stood up in the Commons and intoned to the House: 'This is a turd of a deal, which has now been taken away and polished, and is now a polished turd. But it might be the best turd that we've got.'

Let's face it, you had to laugh. Indeed, I hope you got several belly cackles in the bank, because within a year we would be in the midst of a deadly global pandemic. Very, very interesting times indeed.

*

At this point, I should say something about the whole idea of a book of columns. Can I confide in you? It worries me. In the olden times, anything written in a newspaper mercifully and quite rightly disappeared within a day of it being published, ideally ending up wrapped round your fish and chips. (And, yes, newspapers *have* turned out to be even less sustainable than cod.) These days, of course, newspaper content lives on seemingly for ever, acquiring rather more permanence than many of us journalists deserve. Particularly someone like me. In fact, I often feel that if I wrote my column in the afternoon, it would say something completely different to whatever I'd ended up writing that morning. 'Do you still think this, six years on?' 'Oh my God – I probably didn't even think it by tea THAT DAY.'

I know some people like to think of column-writing as an art, but for me, it's definitely not. It's a trade. You get up, you write something to fill a space, and you hope it's not one of your worst shots and that readers enjoy it. Maybe some people are out there imagining they're writing the first draft of history, but I feel like I'm just sticking a pin in a moment. All of which is a long way of saying that I cringe at quite a few bits in the earlier columns in this book. (You, however, may wish to reserve your shudders for the later efforts.) When I was putting together this selection, I read a couple of them and just thought, 'Oh, do get OVER yourself, luv. Do you have any idea how histrionic you sound?'

Clearly I didn't. But time's a great teacher, and on reflection I thought it was best not to airbrush all of those little embarrassments out. Like I say, they're just a record of a moment in time – perhaps some howl of entitled despair that liberals like me had to work through. After all, as was made abundantly clear from 2016 onwards, we were no longer flavour of the century. Yup, we'd got home to our ivory tower to find the locks had been changed. We had, in the immortal words of Chris Morris to Peter O'Hanraha-hanrahan in *The Day Today*, LOST THE NEWS.

Other potential potholes? If there are any predictions in here, please forgive them, because in recent years I have tried to steer clear of all that. I can't remember exactly when it hit me, but at a certain point I noticed how often political journalism was about predicting what was coming. We were suddenly awash with discussions about how the various stories were going to play out. Don't get me wrong, I read and very much enjoyed most of it. But with the best will in the world, I'm not totally sure it's the job of a journalist to tell you what's going to happen next, as opposed to what's just happened. Let's be clear: the stuff that actually was occurring was wild enough. Even so, increasing amounts of content seemed to be a kind of futurology, with speculation about potential scenarios occasionally crowding out analysis of existing developments. I think it comes back to that thing of having lost the news. There was almost a cargo cult element to it. If we just lay out the flowchart, if we just set out our logical case for how things SHOULD develop, then somehow – somehow! – the old familiar certainties will be airdropped back to us.

They haven't been yet – but soon, no doubt. Any day now . . .

*

To talk briefly about the format: I thought about doing all the politics in themes, before realising I don't have anything so highfalutin as those. What I do have – and what we've all had – is characters. So this book doesn't just have politicians; it has a queen, various princes and duchesses, celebrities, wicked advisers, reality TV monsters, billionaires, philanthropists, fauxlanthropists, Hollywood sex offenders, judges, media barons, populists, police officers and all kinds of other heroes and villains. The full fairy tale, in fact. Sometimes pretty Grimm. In the end I've grouped the political columns together, with each year given its own chapter. And I've broken those years up with columns about things like sport or celebrities, because we all need an interlude/respite.

Ideally it'll all be a deeply unpleasant and staggeringly unwelcome reminder of how the news felt to some of us as we were put through it, seemingly on a permanent wringer cycle. The Americans got Trump; UK citizens got the seemingly interminable Brexit wars. Everyone got plunged into a pandemic. How would you rate your satisfaction at your news journey, on a scale of one to the survivors of the USS *Indianapolis*? Those sailors survived one of the worst naval disasters in US history, when their ship was torpedoed by the Japanese in 1945, and were then left bobbing in the Pacific Ocean. Subsequently, and over several days, they were subjected to the worst shark attack in history.

So it seems that when it comes to interludes/respite, there weren't a whole lot of them in real life. And in the month I'm typing this, horrifyingly, war has broken out in Europe. Unimaginable scenes that seem plucked from the darker parts of the 20th century are playing out live on our TV screens. Elsewhere, Donald Trump is once again the favourite to win the Republican nomination.

Things will calm down. Won't they? Any day now . . .?

*

A non-scientific 'most' people in the UK had absolutely had enough of politics by about six months after the Brexit vote in 2016. On the other hand, had we? Had we *really*? We supposedly hated it, but couldn't stop rubbernecking at it. The BBC Parliament channel had never rated so highly. Westminster seemed to reach far beyond its bubble. A friend of mine was doing a comedy tour in September 2019, and I remember going to Worcester to see his show there. Having put my bag down in my hotel room, I went downstairs to the bar and beheld a selection of people at separate tables completely and utterly glued to the Sky News feed from the Supreme Court, where arguments on the lawful or otherwise prorogation of Parliament were being heard. It was 3pm on a Tuesday afternoon. Without wishing to go out on a limb, it was difficult not to conclude that something quite odd had happened to the UK.

Having said that, I do have one small theory about what has happened both here and beyond. I think that reality television – the overwhelmingly dominant and highest-rating entertainment genre of the early 21st century – became reality politics. Instead of sitting back and having entertainment done to them, audiences in the reality TV heyday were given buttons to press and voting lines to call, and were invited to change the narrative themselves. They loved it. *The X Factor* had 'kind of given democracy back to the world', its supremo, Simon Cowell, noted mildly. At the height of his light-entertainment powers in 2009, Cowell was convinced that his next big will-of-the-people format would be 'a political *X Factor*', a 'referendum-type TV show' in which viewers would vote on hot topics. No. 10 would then be challenged to phone in to the studio and explain its position. Well, now . . . Be careful what Simon Cowell wishes for.

And as shows like *X Factor* and *Strictly* matured, a new phenomenon could be observed: people were taking increasing delight in voting for talentless or disruptive candidates, convinced they were sticking it to the experts. 'We don't care if some respected twat in London thinks we shouldn't like these candidates,' they seemed to be saying. 'Indeed, the fact the respected twat doesn't like them makes us like them all the more.' Muscles were being flexed. Control was being taken back.

Meanwhile, just as *Big Brother* or *Survivor* bookers once had, day-time TV shows started picking guests from the extremes because it made for better 'conflict'. And in fairly short order the news pro-grammes decided they wanted in on the drama too. Adversarial punditry was in. Katie Hopkins started off as an *Apprentice* can-didate, then moved on to the *This Morning* sofa to insult children with 'common' names, eventually graduating to alt-right politics like it was the most seamless journey in the world. I don't believe it's a coincidence that the biggest reality TV star of the era eventu-ally ended up in the White House – and, of course, social media sent the ratings of reality politics into the stratosphere.

*

Any other business? Well, I almost feel bad admitting it, but I should say that in general I have found writing about these turbulent years rather cathartic. Instead of having what we might call 'unresolved news issues', I have simply had to sit down, open a blank document and – on a good day – try to work out a way of making people laugh about some current events. The routine is pretty therapeutic.

It's also helped that I've never thought of myself as a proper journalist or political writer or anything grand and professional like that. I started out in journalism entirely by accident, when the secretarial temping agency I worked for sent me to answer the phones on the *Sun*'s showbiz desk for a few days. I loved it – it was so much more hilarious than answering the phone in a bank, which is what I'd been doing before – but maybe because of that odd entry path I've never felt entirely 'formal' on the old hackery front. After a long while in the trade, I finally realised this could be an asset. Or at least I gained the confidence to treat it as such. I stopped trying to emulate other people's voices and found my own.

The first column I think I managed that with was a celebrity one I started in the *Guardian*, called Lost in Showbiz. The mid-2000s were an amazing time to be writing about celebrity culture. I also had a sports column, which I'm afraid to say was vanishingly rare for a woman back then, and would go and cover live things like the World Cup and the Olympics and so on, where that male–female imbalance became even clearer. (It's much better now!) So I always felt rather outsidery on the sports pages too, and gradually realised that this actually gave me a lot of leeway. I didn't have to cover things in some 'expected' way, so I learned, on the job, to do my own thing.

In fact, I can now see it was covering the showbiz and sport beats in that particular way that helped me to find a way of writing about politics that I hoped would be more accessible. I tend to think very associatively, so for me the reflexive way of making sense of a lot of things is by using references to other things. I'm forever internally analogising. When it came to applying that to politics, I found drawing comparisons with political history and philosophy less amusing than drawing them with stuff like pop music or movies or football. I just thought there might be a fun way of writing about politics that filtered it through the prisms of things people actually *liked*, given how many of them seemed to dislike politics itself.

Even now, I always feel like more of an old-style blogger (albeit one lucky enough to be paid). I don't really have any special access – once a year I might do something mad and masochistic like go to the party conferences – but in general I watch it all from the sofa at home, just like everyone else. Or, to put it another way, as far as political writing goes, I'm a cook, not a chef. So over the past few years I've tried above all to be a companion to any reader – to be a sympathetic friend, as opposed to an expert or educator. The latter is *definitely* a job for finer minds than mine. I can, however, do you fellow-feeling and a few jokes. Just watched Michael Howard casually threaten war with Spain (April 2017)? Come and sit down next to me, and we'll have a slightly deranged laugh about it together.

But – and with apologies to all the serious-minded big hitters out there – the companionable laughter space is a pretty great one to be in. As the past few years have gone by, more and more people have been kind enough to read my columns. And when a new one gets published, I've noticed an increasing number of readers saying that they're saving it to read with a cup of tea or glass of wine. And that, honestly, is THE nicest thing I can possibly imagine. Talk about a personal pinnacle. If anything I write can be a brief but pleasurable part of someone's downtime or relaxation, then that is my absolute honour. Saving me for a drink? Yes please! Yes please to being an accompaniment! More than anything else in this entire crazy world, I want to be the journalistic equivalent of a chocolate digestive or packet of salt and vinegar crisps.

Quite heavy on the vinegar. Obviously.

2016: BINFIRE OF THE VANITIES

Having successfully persuaded the British electorate to avoid 'chaos with Ed Miliband' at the previous year's general election, Conservative prime minister David Cameron is about to hold a referendum 'to settle the issue of Europe for a generation'. Yet instead of making a remain win the formality he appears to expect, the battle is quickly mired in divisive rhetoric and accusations of misinformation. One week before polling day, the Labour MP Jo Cox is brutally murdered on her way to hold a surgery in her Batley and Spen constituency. She was 41.

So, Britain, are you ready to enter the United Kingdom of Ukip?

17 June 2016

Nigel Farage is about to achieve everything he wants. That alone should make leavers think again

Right now, in the Ukip bunker, there is a search going on. It is urgent. It is probably desperate. It is the search for a tone. The emotional Rolodex of Nigel Farage is being riffled through in the hope it might throw up something usable. Top presentational aides have been dispatched on a vital quest to find the outer limits of his range. The journey is unlikely to detain them very long. Yet at the most recent reckoning Farage stands a few disputed percentage points away from being acclaimed – like it or not – the most extraordinarily successful British politician of a generation. Globally, he may soon be seen as reflecting us.

A man who yesterday morning was standing in front of a poster eerily similar to genuine Nazi propaganda is today in seclusion, his campaign suspended – like all the official referendum efforts – 'out of respect'. And, presumably, out of uncertainty as to what the hell he does next.

Yesterday morning, Farage was playing dog-whistle politics. Forgive me: he was playing whistle politics. Understanding the import of the words 'BREAKING POINT' across a snaking queue of stricken brown-skinned people does not require ultrasonic capabilities. You can stand down, Lassie. You're not needed today, girl.

Yesterday afternoon, the MP Jo Cox was killed in the street in her Batley and Spen constituency. That her alleged killer had suffered years of mental health issues seems likely. That he is alleged to have shouted, 'Britain first' – perhaps a reference to an organisation with which Ukip were last year forced to deny an electoral pact – is a matter of acute sensitivity. If the party barkers were a hundredth as careful about anything else as they are about that alleged 'Britain first' cry, then they would have moderated themselves into retirement years ago.

'We are not won by arguments that we can analyse,' the great liberal supreme court justice Louis Brandeis observed, 'but by tone and temper; by the manner, which is the man himself.'

Character is not always destiny, but tone matters. As we head towards polling day, all eyes must be on the man himself, Nigel Farage, who did more to bring about this referendum than anyone else, and whose artless, divisive bait-and-switch has felt like its governing spirit. How bound up Britain's destiny has seemed with the character of this rather small man. Where does Britain's-most-successful-politician-in-waiting go from here? Cometh the hour, whence cometh the tone?

Farage will, of course, have to find some words that address the utter loathsomeness of where we find ourselves, and the shame and despair it makes many people feel. Like him or not, David Cameron can do this. Like him or not, Jeremy Corbyn did so on Thursday. Together in Birstall, they found the bearing. And then . . . Well, it ought to be noted mildly that Thursday's repulsive poster was merely the first in a planned series. Will we see the rest? At this moment of national and personal destiny, will Farage manage to be the politician of stature he assures us he is?

Hitherto, Farage has had a tried and tested shtick for Serious Moments. I notice it all the time now, but I first saw it when I asked him with sledgehammer flippancy whether Nelson Mandela was one of his political heroes. Immediately, Farage lowered his voice and opened his eyes very wide. 'He's a human hero,' he intoned. 'That day he came out of Robben Island' – it wasn't Robben

Island, but anyway – 'and stood there and forgave everybody, I just thought: "This is Jesus."' Hugely idiosyncratic for a man on the right of the Tory party at the time, considering most of his political soulmates had only just given up wearing 'Hang Mandela' badges, but there you go. 'I don't regard him as a political hero,' Nigel went on very quietly, and with his eyes still open very wide. 'I think he's on a rather higher plane than that.'

Drop the voice, widen the eyes. He'll probably do it this weekend. He certainly does it when anyone accuses him of borderline racism. Down goes the voice, as though he is personally trying to smother their insinuation in the appalled hush it deserves. I have to confess the Farage mind trick doesn't work on me. Instead, every time Nigel deploys it, it makes me think of a Truman Capote line from *In Cold Blood*: 'The quietness of his tone italicised the malice of his reply.'

That the political atmosphere was febrile and fetid before Jo Cox's death hardly needs stating. 'How foul this referendum is,' wrote the novelist Robert Harris this week. 'The most depressing, divisive, duplicitous political event of my lifetime. May there never be another.' Boris Johnson's sister Rachel has since retweeted the observation.

So many of the things that have felt bizarre or even vaguely comic at one Atlantic Ocean's remove have suddenly alighted on our shores. Lies are knowingly painted on buses; previously unsayable things have been said on platforms that lend them a hideous legitimacy; the word 'expert' has become as dirty as the word 'Westminster'; and the shift to post-factual political discourse feels rapidly under way. No one is more post-fact than Farage. Asked why he was back on the cigs again this week, he replied: 'I think the doctors have got it wrong on smoking.'

Don't get me wrong on Nigel – he's fine for a fag, a pint, some jolly japes on the Thames. The entire campaign's only moment of levity came on Wednesday, as his flotilla did battle with Bob

Geldof's. In fact, it was while aboard Farage's boat that I saw two children on one of the small remain dinghies and wondered who they were. They looked the same age as my eldest two – about five and three – and I thought how hilarious and exciting mine would have found the whole spectacle. I smiled and waved at them, because there is obviously a law stating that people in or aboard funny forms of transport should always wave at children. I only found out the next day that those children were Jo Cox's. Her husband Brendan had tweeted: 'Kids seriously disappointed there isn't another flotilla today.'

My God, the horror. Lying in wait, the unthinkable horror. Twenty-four hours later, Brendan Cox was issuing a statement on his wife's murder. That he was able to find the words and tone that I am sure I never could in such unimaginable circumstances has been a thing of marvel to so many. We know the heights of humanity when we see them.

And I'm afraid we know when we don't. I'm not sure I've ever heard humanity emanate from Nigel Farage, certainly not convincingly. On the eve of what he hopes will be his finest hour, he must rise to the challenge now. People expect. Britain expects. If you haven't the words and the deportment for this sort of horror, and the politics that the timetable dictates will have to be conducted while it is still so fresh, then you are not fit for office or the sniff of it.

There are many people I respect and admire voting leave – there are people in my family voting leave. I understand their reasons. But they must stomach the reality that a vote for leave will be taken by Farage and countless others as a vote for him, a vote for his posters, a vote for his ideas, a vote for his quiet malice, a vote for his smallness in the face of vast horrors. Is it worth it?

The leavers have taken control.
No wonder things are unravelling

24 June 2016

In the moment of triumph the victors began walking away from their promises – and further disappointments await their disciples

Wanting your country back turns out to have been a zero-sum game. Waking up this morning, about 52% of voters felt they'd got it back, and about 48% felt they'd lost it. Yet perhaps in the long reckoning both sides will find they had, in the unspeakably tragic phrase of the hour, more in common than that which divides us. Maybe it'll be like Clint Eastwood says at the end of *The Outlaw Josey Wales*, as he stares that thousand-yard stare: 'I guess we all died a little in that damn war.'

For now, the victory belongs to Boris Johnson and Michael Gove, and to Nigel Farage. This is their triumph. Either celebrate it or attempt not to choke on it. They have 'taken back control'. They have 'got their country back'.

What else did we get back? Definitely our financial arse, which was being handed to us way before the FTSE 100 even opened. David Cameron's much-remarked-upon political luck has finally run out, and a campaign whose guiding spirit was a mendacious short-termism has produced the ultimate long-term result.

Whichever way you slice it, this feels like a significant moment for trust in politics. Before the result was even formally declared, Farage had rubbished the idea of the extra £350m for the NHS as a 'mistake', while the MEP Dan Hannan had talked down the idea of a reduction in immigration. What a magical mystery tour it will be for people, then, to discover what it was in fact they were actually voting for. And who will be blamed for things now the EU bogeyman is slain? The history of the continent offers a series of chilling answers to that inquiry.

Doubtless a coherent plan of action will emerge. For now, Farage has one idea for the credit column: 'June 23 needs to become a national holiday,' he declared. 'And we will call it INDEPENDENCE DAY!' (Come, friendly aliens...)

To watch him bluster about a win against 'big politics' and 'getting on with the job' was to be struck by an old conviction: there is little so dangerous in politics as people who regard complex things as being incredibly simple.

As for Johnson and Gove, who have spent the best part of eight weeks joyfully telling whoppers and making mind-boggling Nazi comparisons, they deployed their extra-special slow and quiet voices to address the nation. Gove in particular came off like a ham actor seconds from segueing into John Hannah's 'Stop all the clocks' reading from *Four Weddings and a Funeral*.

As for Boris, never forget that the only untruth the prime ministerial favourite-in-waiting corrected in the entire campaign was the *Sunday Times*'s misapprehension that he dyes his hair.

'This does not mean that the United Kingdom will be any less united,' he intoned this morning, suggesting he must have been watching the day's events on catch-up. Before breakfast the SNP had declared it sees Scotland's future as part of the EU, while Sinn Féin called for a referendum on Irish unity. Boris was proud we were the fifth-largest economy, he went on, apparently unaware that Events had already bumped us down to number six.

For those who had voted to remain . . . morning had broken. Broken irreparably. Four hours before the official leave campaign mounted their podium, Nigel Farage arrived triumphantly in front of the Houses of Parliament, to which he has failed to get elected seven times, and which may ultimately only be visible protruding from the sand, to be stumbled upon by a latter-day Charlton Heston. (Ask your grandparents, millennials. Because really, even by their own exacting standards, this result was the baby boomers' finest hour.)

What would the Ukip leader say? Cometh the hour, what man would come? When Margaret Thatcher arrived in Downing Street in 1979, she famously addressed 'all the British people – howsoever they voted' with the attributed words of St Francis of Assisi: 'Where there is discord, may we bring harmony. Where there is error, may we bring truth. Where there is doubt, may we bring faith. And where there is despair, may we bring hope.'

Finally required to find his own words for the moment towards which he had been building all his political life, statesminnow Farage dismissed half the country as indecent, ruling: 'This is a victory for ordinary people, for decent people.' Where there was harmony, let him bring discord. 'Mass immigration is the issue that ultimately won this election.' Where there was faith, let him bring doubt. 'And we did it all without a single bullet being fired.' Where there was hope, let him bring despair.

Yes, this is his victory. Fascinatingly, he seemed psychologically incapable of accepting it. I must confess to always having suspected that a man of Farage's Partridgean stature would become overwhelmed in his hour of personal destiny, and was struck by his decision to pull out of the final referendum TV debate merely an hour before he was due to appear. Vote night itself saw him concede early, only to unconcede, then reconcede, then re-unconcede.

What insecurities tug beneath the surface of the leader of the United Kingdom Independence party? Or rather, the leader of the Kingdom Independence party, given the various schisms opening up seemingly by the hour. As for what sort of country Farage believes himself to have taken back control of, there were heavy clues, not just in that infamous poster but in the film he narrated at his final rally on Wednesday morning.

A work of suitably nostalgic, sub-Pearl & Dean production values, this depicted a place of Spitfires and the Battle of Britain and the Queen's coronation. Most jarring (for this viewer at least) was a section in which Farage explained that Britain was 'a country of sporting greatness'. Bizarrely, this was illustrated only with footage of Ian Botham from the 1981 Ashes series.

Why? You'd think there'd have been something slightly more *au courant* – the London Olympics were pretty epic, for instance. What precisely is it about so much of the British sporting success that has followed Botham's Ashes, a full 35 years ago, that makes it unsuitable for a Ukip rally film? Perhaps we'll put our collective finger on it as he becomes more emboldened by this stunning victory.

Each of us can speak only as we find. For my own part – with a political wishlist that has always included progressivism, tolerance, universal human rights, openness, truthfulness and an outward-looking national state of mind – I can't help feeling 2016's wave of famous demises finally makes sense. All those cool people died just in time.

Farage is now Britain's face at the EU: petty, unlovable, essentially terrified

28 June 2016

The Ukip leader's boo-winning European parliament rant shows he isn't going anywhere – but will 'Shitfinger' drag us all down in a race to the bottom?

In a crowded field, I think it was the flag that was the killer. The absolute state of that flag. Nigel Farage's desktop Union Jack, with its little sucker pad leeching obnoxiously on to the unlovely beech of the European parliament chamber. Part of the genius of the TV series *The Office* was its ability to distil all human life down to a series of recognisable archetypes most people had encountered at work. To see Farage there with his desktop flag was to suddenly and irrevocably understand it: the UK is the Gareth Keenan of Europe. This is how we must look to those still condemned to share continent space with us: petty, unlovable, essentially terrified, our workplace set up in a show of cod-martial defiance, which in fact only flags up our raging insecurity.

Farage has been building up to this moment his entire political life, as he tells everyone at every single opportunity. In which case, how is it humanly possible that his speech to the European parliament today could be so artless, so crass, a scarcely refined version of some England fans' infamous recent chant at the Euros: 'Fuck off, Europe, we voted out'? To couch it in the sort of imbecilic historical inaccuracy which is the only language Farage understands: this speech was so bad that they're now quits with us for saving them in the second world war.

You may disagree with this reading of the war; Nigel would regard it as hugely overcomplicated. This, he repeated once more, was a victory against 'big politics'. 'Virtually none of you', he bellowed at the MEPs, 'have ever done a job in your lives.'

Watching him was like watching the live abortion of Churchill's oratorical legacy. As the latter's grandson Nicholas Soames observed: 'Appalling ghastly performance by that dreadful cad Farage in the European parliament. #hownottoinfluence.' Agreed. There is soft power, and then there is politics as erectile dysfunction.

Indeed, it is becoming increasingly difficult not to speculate as to the psychological underpinnings of the Farage condition. 'When I came here 17 years ago,' he shouted, failing to hide his nervous elation, 'you all laughed at me. Well, I have to say: you're not laughing now, are you?' He made it, you losers! He got out. He's in the big leagues now. He's the guy who just turned up to his school reunion in a white limo with two dead-eyed escorts on his arm.

Above all, the performance offered a reminder that Farage makes everything in which he is involved a race to the bottom. The opposite of a Midas, he may as well be nicknamed Shitfinger. His excruciatingly aggressive display eventually drew boos from the chamber. 'Ladies and gentlemen, I understand you're emotional,' urged the assembly president. 'But you're acting like Ukip.'

Farage was loving it, just as his financial backer in the provisional wing of the leave campaign is revelling in their legitimisation. Arron Banks has spent much of his time since the weekend laughing at reports of racist and xenophobic incidents on Twitter. Two weeks ago, he couldn't even book 75% of Bucks Fizz for his Brexit concert; now he's taking a triumphalist dump on 50 years of race relations policy.

Meanwhile, presumably in a doomed attempt to own it – certainly out of an inability to transcend it – Farage embraces his smallness. The victory against 'big politics', he stressed again to the European parliament, was for 'the little people'. Incidentally, during the general election campaign last year I was in a Grimsby pub where Farage's supporters were waiting for his long-scheduled visit. He blew these 'little people' out to go and have fish and chips with reality television star Joey Essex. Foot soldiers of Ukip, they were crestfallen and couldn't understand it. Yes, Farage is as elitist as the rest of them. Even the central London victory party for his senior referendum campaign staff was stratified, featuring a VIP snug into which he retreated for most of the night.

And still he rises. This time, the political leader who's had more farewell tours than Kiss isn't going anywhere. Whenever I touched on Farage's malevolent guiding spirit during the referendum campaign itself, I was pleased to take all sorts of optimistic correspondence explaining that as soon as a successful leave vote was achieved, Farage's work would be done, and he would retire triumphantly into the sunset.

How's that working out for ya? As reports of racist and xenophobic incidents across Britain intensify, Farage appears on *Channel 4 News* to warn ominously against what he detects as 'backsliding' in the leadership of the official Vote Leave campaign. My suspicion is that these two strands of post-referendum fallout will come together in what we might call 'ever closer union'. All sides of leave know they can't deliver all they promised – even most of what they promised – and the coming anger will serve as Farage's greatest recruiting sergeant. Indeed, he may seem like the cuddly option compared with some.

Still, don't take it from me. Let's play out with the UK's second-biggest cheerleader in the European parliament, Marine Le Pen, leader of the French National Front. Turning to Farage after his speech, she smiled, and declared: 'Look at how beautiful history is!'

Bye bye, Boris, the man who wouldn't clear up his own mess

30 June 2016

Thanks to the scheming Gove, we're not going to find out in this leadership contest how much of a #massivelegend Boris Johnson is outside London and the home counties

Here comes Boris Johnson, half an hour before the deadline closes. He's going to chuck his hat into the ring like *Blackadder*'s Lord Flashheart, isn't he? 'I've got a plan, and it's as hot as my pants!'

Except he isn't. Standing at a podium bearing not a soaring campaign slogan, but the rather more prosaic 'ST. ERMIN'S HOTEL', the leading political bounder of the age announced that he had thought about the individual needed to take the country out of the mess he's dumped it in (I paraphrase) and 'concluded that person cannot be me'.

Where did it all go right? Normally, Johnson is so selfish he doesn't even fly by the seat of his own pants. Unfortunately for him, his wingman recently decided he isn't willing to offer up his undergarments any longer. Michael Gove, fresh from destroying his friend David Cameron, is going for the accumulator by announcing his surprise Tory leadership bid. As Gove put it this morning: 'I have come, reluctantly, to the conclusion that Boris cannot provide the leadership or build the team for the task ahead.' It sounds like a tragic conflict of disloyalties, with which Gove has wrestled for perhaps 24 hours.

Even before Johnson took to his hotel podium, you could hear the offstage crash of defections to Gove. Dominic Raab was now off, despite having written a piece for this very morning's *Sun* headlined 'Why Boris Has the Heineken Effect'. To which the only rejoinder can be: 'If Carlsberg Did Political U-Turns ...'

Even so, and however inevitable it might feel after some reflection, this was a shock. We did know a schism might be on the House of Cards, as it were, thanks to yesterday's accidentally leaked email from Gove's wife Sarah Vine. Think of her as Claire Blunderwood. The pisser for Boris is that he now can't even contemplate having Michael beaten up, like he did that troublesome little journalist back in the day, because many people have one eye on the news at the mo and would probably notice.

Perhaps there were other signs of uncertainty. Friends of Johnson have spent much of the week briefing that his 'private polling' shows he is 'the only Tory leadership candidate with enough public support to ensure the Conservatives win the next general election'.

Herein, perhaps, lies the paradox of Boris. Front of house, his brand has him as the era's most off-the-cuff and confidently charismatic politician. Backstage, he was sufficiently insecure and calculating to be running up private polling bills. Alan Clark once remarked snobbishly that the trouble with one colleague 'is that he had to buy all his furniture'. I can't help feeling there is something rather nouveau frit about Johnson having to buy his own polling.

So now we will not discover how much of a #massivelegend Johnson is outside his London and home counties heartlands. Quite how he'd go over in Sunderland in the event of Hitachi pulling out of the area, for example, must remain a known unknown.

His surprise non-running speech played much on the need for unity, for uniting those who come from opposing sides. I don't know if you've read *Team of Rivals*, but try and picture it with Johnson in the chair instead of Abraham Lincoln. Gove's statement could scarcely have been more pointed about Johnson's weakness in this area: 'I respect and admire all the candidates running for the leadership. In particular, I wanted to help build a team behind Boris Johnson so that a politician who argued for leaving the European Union could lead us to a better future. But . . .' Cos you know Michael loves the players. And Boris loves the game.

Reading the writing on the wall, perhaps the former London mayor decided he was damned if he was going to play Monopoly and settle for the Community Chest card reading 'You have won second prize in a beauty contest'. It remains to be seen how his public – all those wonderful people out there in the dark as to his real nature – will take Johnson's decision.

Where does this leave them? On spying Baldrick, Lord Flashheart declares: 'You look like a decent British bloke. I'll park the old booties on you, if that's OK.' 'It would be an honour, my lord,' replies Baldrick. Hard lines for Britain, then, which will now not be offered the golden opportunity to be Johnson's bootrest.

In the Tory laundry basket,
Michael Gove is the dirtiest item

1 July 2016

No one bidding for the leadership of the Tories is unsoiled. But Gove's weapons-grade treachery makes rivals such as Theresa May look squeaky clean

In the notorious words of Michael Gove: 'People in this country have had enough of experts.' But have they had enough of expert shits? Shares in kitchen companies fell sharply this morning as Gove launched his bid for No. 10. Firms hoping for a post-Brexit boost from Gove's wife, Sarah Vine – who famously regarded Ed Miliband's kitchen design as the most useless thing about him, and would be only too happy to rip out her former friend Samantha Cameron's stainless-steel effort at No. 10 – may well be disappointed.

Early days, of course, but Gove's behaviour looks to have been judged as simply too unpleasant and distasteful for the Conservative party. High praise indeed. It has certainly caused the *Daily Mail* – which employs Vine as a columnist – to press its hanky to its nose.

'With the best will in the world,' ran a leader column dripping with anything but, 'we cannot see Mr Gove as a prime minister for these turbulent times.' Not the most unexpected of positions, given that yesterday's *Mail* website led for most of the afternoon with the headline 'THAT C*** SET THIS UP FROM THE START!'

For his campaign slogan, Michael has decided against 'Welcome to politics, bitch!' Instead, he stood before the media with a claim so preposterous it must have been included in his speech as a dare: 'I stand here not as the result of calculation.' Funny old turn of events, then.

24

But there was more – so much more. A gazillion-word speech more. 'Whatever charisma is, I don't have it; whatever glamour may be, I don't think anyone could ever associate me with it.' Consider us up to speed on that front. But if you need help identifying your current personal brand, it's weapons-grade treachery.

Sarah had not urged him to run, he conceded wryly, 'but she did say she'd support me'. Gove wanted to talk a lot about the things that have made the country of Britain 'the greatest in the world'. Unfortunately, everyone else wanted to talk about the things that have just made Britain the greatest laughing stock in the world.

But do go on, Michael.

One of his proudest moments, we learned, was 'seeing our party conference rise and give thunderous applause to a former violent criminal who had turned his life around'.

Yes, bravo to Boris, who did pull it together and go straight after discussing having that journalist beaten up. And so to Boris: how come Gove didn't ring him to tell him he was standing? 'I tried repeatedly to ring Boris.' You could have texted. Maybe he couldn't find the right words, though apparently Apple is fast-tracking the Brutus emoji for their next software update.

And there was plenty more where that act of tough love came from. Would a putative Prime Minister Gove give a job to his much-reviled yet long-time special adviser, the leave strategist Dominic Cummings? The answer was stark: 'No.'

Is there anyone left whom Michael hasn't done over? That said, Cummings has operated at the heart of Gove's empire without an official job before. He doesn't require a Downing Street pass to gain access; he could just slide through a haunted mirror.

Maybe Gove deliberately scheduled this launch against the Somme commemoration service so he'd have an excuse as to why the MP quota in the room was somewhat thin. Either way, the sense of gathering poignancy has been a long time building. Two years ago, *Game of Thrones* fan Michael was making sledgehammer

25

Tyrion Lannister analogies about himself. 'You see there that this misshapen dwarf,' he mused, 'reviled throughout his life, thought in the eyes of some to be a toxic figure, can at last rally a small band of loyal followers. And at the last moment he suddenly hears the noise of the relief column coming.'

Mmm. Unfortunately, it doesn't work like that. It's not for you to say, Michael. Just as no one in the England dressing room ever called Paul Ince the Guv'nor – except Paul Ince – no one apart from Michael Gove has ever thought of Michael Gove as Tyrion Lannister.

Asked to reassign himself today, Gove said he didn't want to unleash any spoilers for those not up to speed with the series. Allow me to fill in the gaps: following the events of the past 24 hours, Gove has been placed in a holding pile labelled Ramsay Bolton/Joffrey and will be formally classified in the coming weeks or even days.

A week has always been a long time in politics, but this one appears to have torn the space–time continuum a new one. It feels as if we are operating in a fifth dimension of news. It would not be especially outrageous, for instance, to learn that Cthulhu has chucked his tentacles into the Tory contest. Over in the Labour party, you could certainly see the aforementioned dark lord being worshipped by The Mandate (the collective noun by which people keep referring to Jeremy Corbyn's supporters).

But Conservative leadership-wise, it still feels far-fetched to imagine 'gay cure'-linked Stephen Crabb emerging as the Fortinbras in all this (though he might well take the role next time round).

As for the Goves, their 12-hour status as the SW1 Macbeths appears to be rapidly oxidising. Much was made of that leaked email from Sarah Vine, but its battleaxe nannyish tone may yet cast the pair as a sort of metropolitan elite version of Christine and Neil Hamilton.

When it went tits-up for the Hammies, of course, there was 'Christmas theatre' to fall back on. Neil's Baron Hardup was, I believe, well received in Kettering. But the sense must be that Michael would be less suited to the demands of this role, while Sarah – for all her faux homespun ordinariness – looks likely to be less of a joiner-in than Christine.

Which leaves us with Theresa May, whose draft-dodging in the Great Referendum War looked cynical, but not as horrendously cynical as rather a lot of things that have happened since. In a column about domestic slapdashery, the great Katharine Whitehorn once asked: 'Have you ever taken anything out of the dirty-clothes basket because it had become, relatively, the cleaner thing?' There is something of this to Theresa May's leadership bid. A week ago, she was the reluctant remainer. Why would anyone think she would fight for Britain when she didn't even fight for remain? But now . . . well, for many, Theresa seems to have become, relatively, the cleaner thing.

So farewell then, Michael Gove. You were right about one thing

7 July 2016

Wielding the traitor's knife again and again, you certainly achieved your repeatedly stated ambition of not wanting to be prime minister

The Conservative party doesn't do carriage clocks for people like Michael Gove. They just get a note reading 'You have outlived your usefulness' and a five-minute head start on the hounds.

Still, let's fire up 'Walkaway' by Cast and watch a montage of Gove's best bits. First, Michael positioned himself as the man who had put his country before his friend David. Next, he was the man who'd put his country before his friend Boris. Then he was the man who'd put his country before his long-time special adviser. Finally, he graduated to being the man who'd put his country before what he apparently deemed the socially backward Conservative membership.

The trouble was that each time Michael did this, everyone else popped him back in the file marked 'disloyal shit'. Just walkaway, walkaway, walkaway...

Yes, the results are in: Theresa May 199, Andrea Leadsom 84, Michael Gove 46. Without wishing to stick my neck out here, it seems his parliamentary colleagues have had enough of the expert-slasher Michael Gove. He has emerged from the Houses of Parliament to salute the assured advent of a 'female prime minister' and explain how proud he was to have spent the past week contributing to the debate by arguing 'for the most vulnerable'. Unfortunately, the most vulnerable has now been eliminated from the contest.

Even in the final hour, Gove was vainly trying to make the leap from character actor to leading man. A *Spectator* interview found him glossing the Boris knifing thus: 'I compare it to a group of people standing outside a collapsing building, wondering who is going to rescue a child inside. I thought: well, I don't think I've got either the strength or the speed for this, but as I looked around, I thought, God, I'm at least as strong and at least as fast as the others. I've got to try to save the child.' Spoken like the world's creepiest arsonist.

Laughing from the upstairs windows of the inferno, we must assume, are the psychopathic babysitters Theresa May and Andrea Leadsom, only one of whom will emerge from the burning temple as the mother of dragons. All then shall kneel.

Still, at least Gove has achieved his repeatedly stated ambition of not wanting to be prime minister. It looked touch-and-go for a bit, what with there being one key group Michael had yet to formally alienate in the course of his treachery accumulator: namely, Conservative party members.

Fortunately, they were hosed down with some of that Gove magic in a text message sent on the eve of Thursday's ballot by his campaign manager, Nick Boles. 'I am seriously frightened about the risk of allowing Andrea Leadsom on to the membership ballot,' this ran. 'What if Theresa stumbles? Are we really confident that the membership won't vote for a fresh face who shares their attitudes about much of modern life? Like they did with IDS.'

Can't help but agree with Nick. And yet, his decision to commit all this to a text message suggests he has the potential to be outstrategised in a game of Connect Four against a chimp. It even allowed the aforementioned Iain Duncan Smith – a Leadsom backer, natch – to essay a zinger when he was shown the message. He sniffed: 'People with knives will end up stabbing themselves,' which sounds like something Iain's mother might have told him when he was 13 to explain why he was still using a spoon to eat his lunch.

So where now for Gove? Michael has put it all on red, only to have to watch Leadsom collect her winnings, smiling her terrifying smile. It doesn't end there, of course. Michael and his wife, Sarah, will have to send her goddaughter, little Florence Cameron, birthday presents via a lawyer or other third-party intermediary.

His wife's emailed suggestion that the support of both Rupert Murdoch and Paul Dacre was in his gift might save the latter a trip to an employment tribunal, while the former is unlikely to invite Michael to his fifth wedding, shortly after Jerry Hall dies of disappointment in 2036.

Not only has he killed the matinee idol of the Tory shires, Boris Johnson, but he has insulted the membership. The upshot for Gove – who was already polling among Tory members as slightly less trustworthy than Marshal Pétain – is that he should probably never visit the countryside again.

Andrea Leadsom is the leader of an am-dram peasants' revolt

9 July 2016

In this golden age of post-fact politics, who are we to doubt Leadsom's chances of becoming the next prime minister?

As a ferociously keen Bible student, Andrea Leadsom will know whether she is predicted in the Book of Revelation. For those of us operating on a lower plane, condemned to pick through the entrails of the past fortnight, the portents are not hugely encouraging. On the basis that most things that could have gone wrong have, there is absolutely no reason to think that Andrea doesn't have an excellent chance of nicking this.

Before we go on, however, congratulations are in order for the sensationally misguided generation of politicians, from Gordon Brown to David Cameron, who were always going on about wanting 'an *X Factor* politics'. They have finally got their wish. I'm not sure if the official psephological study confirming this is out yet, but the referendum result was the exact equivalent of series seven of Simon Cowell's apocalypse-beckoning karaoke show, in which Essex decorator Matt Cardle beat One Direction. One Direction! Don't get me wrong, I'm sure Matt is perfectly sufferable. I'm sure you can get through him, one way or another. But last year One Direction were the world of celebrity's fourth-largest economy.

And so to the act many can only hope is the Jedward in all this. On Thursday morning Andrea Leadsom delivered her promised 'major speech' on the economy like she'd just won a competition to deliver a major speech on the economy. All the eye-catching endorsements had been pouring in for Leadsom. Nigel Farage. Nick Griffin. Katie Hopkins. There had been rumours that fellow backer Boris Johnson would introduce her, but the former leadership favourite presumably regarded the chance to play Spinal Tap to Andrea's Puppet Show as simply too much perspective.

'I am an optimist,' Andrea began. Indeed, her CV lists her as a former Director of Optimism Compliance at the Bank of Unicorns for All. Please don't regard the developing row over Andrea's CV as in some way detrimental to her prospects, incidentally. We are very much not in Kansas any more. It is already being suggested that the 'confusion' over Andrea's career in finance will keep the media returning handily to her City background and life beyond politics. As one of her key supporters put it delightedly to *The Times*: 'This will turn out to be her £350m claim – the embellishment (if that is what it turns out to be) that works.'

I don't know about you, but I'm psyched that we're already in the second golden age of post-fact politics – the time when an 'embellishment' is regarded as so brilliant that it harks back to the great 'embellishments' of the first golden age (which was last month).

'I want to speak to the markets,' Leadsom smiled, with the air of someone who imagines you can negotiate with gravity. There was absolutely nothing to fear, she went on, smiling that smile again. Andrea Leadsom's smile is terrifying. It is the smile of the school careers adviser telling you flatly that the school is looking for a night caretaker. It is a smile that is powered by the extinguishing of your future. You can't escape Andrea's smile. And it'll certainly come for you if you try.

The address ended with her supporters being instructed by Leadsom backer Penny Mordaunt to march up to parliament to impress upon the Tory MPs voting that day the need to do their duty. Andrea took a car herself, but it's the thought that counts. To watch them make their way up Millbank was to picture the Walking Dead on the Countryside Alliance march. There was drill sergeant Tim Loughton MP. 'What do we want?' he demanded.

'Leadsom for leader!' they shouted back. 'When do we want it?' he enquired. 'NOW!'

There were T-shirts over suits. There was perennial Stupidest Backbencher contender Peter Bone, several non-party members, a brachiosaurus with fairly eye-watering views on civil partnerships, and a few prematurely tweeded need-to-belongers, who – had they been born under other stars – would probably have ended up trying to set fire to their trainers in an aisle seat on a plane. The entire event was an am-dram peasants' revolt metaphor against whichever section of the establishment former banker Andrea is pretending not to be part of. Perhaps it will play brilliantly with the membership.

As for the rest of us, it's hard to imagine where we were before Andrea was deemed a breakout star of the referendum campaign. Yet we still know so tantalisingly little about her. After all, as a junior minister in Her Majesty's government, Andrea enjoyed the sort of anonymity you'd hope for in one of the better witness protection programmes.

Even the verdicts of her friends tend towards the confusing. 'She has steel,' blethered Iain Duncan Smith, 'but there is a velvet glove of compassion.' Oh, Iain! God knows I've learned to manage my expectations as far as IDS is concerned. But I would like a secretary of state who understood a basic despot metaphor before he accidentally deployed it.

Other points of intrigue? Andrea's the passionate advocate of attachment theory who wants to abolish maternity rights. If you're one of those people who imagines that the two positions are in some way contradictory, you are strongly urged to let go of your rational brain and experience Andrea as an idea, a feeling, a repository for thousands of subclinical Thatcher fixations which are less an indicator of her calibre than they are of the stigmatisation of asking for help among a particular stripe of Tory rank and file.

At least 50% of her public statements sound as if they were said for a dare. 'Let's banish pessimists.' 'Boris Johnson is a lovely man.'

The rest sound like she's assembling end times magnetic fridge poetry. 'As a mum', Leadsom would like her hands on the nuclear codes. She likes to retreat to cooking the Sunday roast, which – contrary to what you may have heard – is not always a homosexual. This homespun hard-arse stuff is pushed with sledgehammer deliberateness – an attempt to position her as Brexit's Oxo mum.

Which leaves us with Theresa May. Has it really come to this? Yes. Yes, I'm afraid it has. There are few neater indicators of quite how far we've travelled over the past 14 days than to find so many people, particularly non-Tory voters, now actively *yearning* for it to be Theresa May. 'Christ', muttered one friend with wry despair, 'I now want this more than I did Obama.' Yup, we're all realpolitikos now. Stick a fork in my dreams. They're done.

That final David Cameron PMQs in full: everything is awesome!

13 July 2016

This really was vintage Cameron: cracking gags while Britain burns. Mind you, all we seem to care about is that bleeding cat

'As I leave today', reflected David Cameron, 'I hope that people will see a stronger country.' And I hope to open the batting for England in the first Test against Pakistan at Lord's tomorrow.

He certainly leaves behind a country that has voted to leave the European Union, in which he wanted it to remain, whose own union is imperilled, which is beset by the grimmest economic warnings, which is moving close to a one-party state, and which is staring down the barrel of a Sam Allardyce managerial era. Technically, the last two aren't his fault. But when you're hot, you're hot.

This wasn't the precise summary the outgoing prime minister went with, deciding to play out with a tribute to the House of Commons. 'I will miss the roar of the crowd, I will miss the barbs of the opposition. But I will be willing you on – willing all of you on.' His last line was a soaring hymn to accomplishment that glossed over the fatal political nosedive he'd just taken. 'Nothing is really impossible if you put your mind to it,' Cameron claimed. 'After all, as I once said, I was the future once.' Mm. Unfortunately, you can't fit 48% of the country in a DeLorean.

Later, he would stand outside Downing Street with Samantha Cameron and his three children behind him, promising them no more red boxes and declaring that he had always been struck by 'a quiet but prevailing sense that most people wished their prime minister well'.

Still, let all farewell montages be soundtracked with 'Everything Is Awesome'. Cameron always has a masterful line in wry faux self-deprecation, and his final prime minister's questions was the usual genial cockabout. There were walk-ons for a couple of classic Cameron ordinary folk. An employee in Downing Street who wasn't remotely interested in politics but who'd thanked him for 'your lot' passing legislation allowing him to marry his partner. A man in New York who'd apparently said to him, 'Hey – *Prime Minister's Questions* – we love your show.' These should be among your favourite real-life characters to be showcased by Cameron since the TV debate shortly before he first came to power in 2010, in which he described meeting 'a 40-year-old black man' who'd 'served in the Royal Navy for 30 years'.

He was mostly thanked by the house. Even the leader of what is currently euphemised as 'the opposition' had some praise. Jeremy Corbyn, who always delivers jokes like he's chewing a wasp, asked Cameron to pass on his thanks to his mother for the advice on smartening up his business attire and inquired if he was going to take up the newly vacant seat on the *Strictly* judging panel. Do they film it in a seven-star hotel in the Maldives? If not, probably best to rule him out.

So what now? In answer to the traditional question about his engagements, Cameron had begun by observing wryly that his diary for the rest of the day was 'remarkably light', other than a meeting with Her Majesty. Ah yes, this afternoon's appointment to see the Queen – the 12th prime minister to take their leave in her reign. There's always speculation as to what she says at these moments. I assume that today, HM will just adapt the words of the police chief in *Point Break*: 'You were a real blue-flame special, weren't ya? Young, dumb and full of . . .'

Fun? He was full of fun while it lasted, wasn't he? We must hope Cameron's resignation honours will reflect this aspect of his personality. A peerage for his friend Jeremy Clarkson. A knighthood for the former police horse he couldn't remember riding at the height of the phone-hacking scandal.

His other task today will be to leave a letter for his successor. And as a prime minister who spent most of the last election campaign holding up Liam Byrne's joke note reading 'I'm afraid there is no money', I'd like to think he went with some black humour of his own when dashing something off to Theresa May. Something like: 'I'm afraid there is no future.' The other thing he leaves May is Samantha Cameron's naff chrome kitchen, which she'll be too waste-conscious to rip out.

In the end, though, perhaps you shall know a country by the boggling displacement activity in which it engages in its hour of greatest crisis. The prime minister was at pains to address one of the dominant news preoccupations over the past 48 hours. To wit: the future of Larry, the Downing Street cat. Honestly, this bleeding cat. There is no better illustration of the thousand-yard stare of British repression than the worry, time and concern that has been lavished on this cat, even as Britain hurtles deeper into the shitstorm. How will the cat handle a new person in charge of the people who are in charge of the people who put food in its bowl? Is the cat pining? Would it be best to give the cat to the Cameron children? Or will the cat take Brexit as an opportunity and seize it with both paws? What is the optimal way to help the cat through this?

Sling another chair leg on the fire and accept that this is your reality. For Queen and country we must do our duty to the cat, just as Anthony Hopkins in *Remains of the Day* must serve dinner while his father is dying upstairs.

Boris Johnson, David Davis and Liam Fox as the Three Brexiteers? Dream on

16 July 2016

Extracting ourselves from the European Union could take up to six years, and the trio in charge are a joke

Another week in Brexit, another seven days in which the tickers along the bottom of the news channels' screens may as well have been changed to a continuous loop of the inquiry 'WHAT JUST HAPPENED?????'

Matters that would have added to the gaiety of the nation for days are relegated to news-in-brief items that really are far too brief. Gay-cure-linked biblical moraliser Stephen Crabb has left the government 'in the best interests of my family'. Iain Duncan Smith must be sanctioned for failing to get back into work again. Michael Gove's analogy, in which he was well placed to save a child from a collapsing building, has ended with the child taking out a restraining order against him.

But it is the news of appointments actually made that has felt more deranged, with Theresa May's reshuffle of government widely described as 'root and branch'. Typically in the UK, jobs that are utterly thankless and unworkably exhausting are left to migrants. For whatever reason, Theresa May didn't feel she had that option when she had to appoint her troika of senior ministers to handle the UK's graceless exit from the EU. So it is that Boris Johnson, David Davis and Liam Fox will be hopping inside the Jean-Paul Sartre simulator and testing the theory that hell is other fatally flawed Tories. A bold branding initiative is trying to cast them as the Three Brexiteers, but you'll probably be less disappointed if you see them as Aramis, Werritys and Takethepiss.

Nobody knows anything, runs William Goldman's ever-versatile verdict on Hollywood, and that motto is being metaphorically chiselled into the stone lintel above Whitehall's newest department. Take our new secretary of state for exiting the European Union, David Davis. It has emerged that as recently as May, Davis had believed it would be possible for Britain to negotiate trade deals directly with each EU member state, as opposed to the reality, which is that member states are only permitted to negotiate as a bloc.

Frankly, there hasn't been as masive a misreading of a trade situation since the Jedi master Qui-Gon Jinn judged: 'These federation types are cowards. The negotiations will be short.' See ya 37 hours of tedious CGI politicking later, buddy! Or as Philip Hammond, the incoming chancellor of the exchequer, observed earlier in the week, extracting ourselves from the European Union could take six years, reminding dreamers that Brexit will be like living in an even crappier version of *The Phantom Menace* for more than half a decade.

That David Davis was last seen suing Theresa May's Home Office over surveillance, in the European Court of Justice, is just another of those boggling quirks of the new order which are – like the deaths of Spinal Tap drummers – best left uninvestigated. The judgment is pending, so let's hope both parties are shameless enough to claim it as a win for the ministerial top table, whichever way it goes.

Perhaps the best that can be said for Davis thus far is that his boss has yet to undermine his negotiating skills publicly. As we know from her 30-minute Tory leadership campaign, Theresa May has a benchmark for buffoonish negotiation, and it's that loser who went to Europe to do a deal and 'came back with three nearly new water cannon'. Which she wouldn't let him use.

Anyhow, that loser is now the foreign secretary. Sham marriages have longer honeymoon periods than May, who enjoyed a couple of hours after her nice speech in Downing Street before handing Boris Johnson the Foreign Office. Much of the reaction to the news was probably best summarised by the member of the public who hung a sign on the railings outside Boris's London home reading simply 'SORRY WORLD'.

There has been a welter of speculation on the thinking behind the decision. Maybe May was worried that foreigners were too stupid to read the message of Brexit, and consequently made the appointment to underscore the point. After all, having the insult-happy Johnson as our outward face to the world sends the clearest message possible, short of spraying 'BOTHERD WHAT YOU LOT THINK' in 50-metre-high letters on the White Cliffs of Dover.

As for the third of our ministerial band of brothers, it is a pleasure to welcome back former disgraced former minister Liam Fox, now secretary of state for international trade. Liam is a guy I always feel like I go back years with, on account of the fact that in the very first week of my employment at the *Guardian*, he was the star of the best item in the Diary column on which I worked. Certainly the only thing approaching a story. Liam had attended a reception in Westminster, where he had enchanted fellow guests with a brilliant joke. Question: 'What do you call three dogs and a blackbird?' Answer: 'The Spice Girls.'

Yup, that guy's now secretary of state for international trade. The Spice Girls are currently trading with just Mel B, Geri and Emma involved, so Liam might want to adjust his numbers when wheeling out the old gag as an icebreaker with the Canadians. Always start with a joke, secretary of state. Heaven knows your boss did.

Bending reality like a spoon: the week Labour entered *The Matrix*

28 September 2016

Endless meetings about anti-Semitism, Jeremy Corbyn fan poetry and a plot arc straight out of Hollywood – this year's Labour party conference was in a world of its own. Roll up for the progressive future!

'A queer experience, always, that conference,' wrote Virginia Woolf of a visit to the Labour party annual gathering at Hastings in 1933. 'The door opened into a buzzing bursting humming perfectly self-dependent other world.'

Were Woolf to be reanimated and transported to this year's Labour conference in Liverpool, you sense the hermetically sealed new politics might not have looked quite so new to her. Then again, there do seem to have been certain . . . developments since 1933. As an on–off antisemite, for instance, Virginia may have welcomed this year's bogglingly increased number of opportunities to discuss 'the Jewish question'.

By way of illustration, consider this snapshot of about three hours on the first evening of the conference. At 7.15, there was a Jewish Labour Movement rally against racism and antisemitism. At 7.30, there was an event organised by Jewish Socialists for Justice, entitled 'Anti-Zionism is not Anti-Semitism'. By this stage, a chap manning the Labour Friends of Israel stand in the conference auditorium had revealed that he had been approached by another chap asking, rhetorically, 'But wasn't there a Jewish plot to oust Jeremy

Corbyn?' following up with the inquiry, 'But it was organised by Jewish MPs, wasn't it?' and continuing in this vein until his attempt to confirm that Angela Eagle's 'husband' is Jewish caused the LFI volunteer to curtail the discussion.

A few minutes' walk away, at Momentum's concurrent conference, the hours between 5pm and 7pm were given over to a debate featuring the movement's vice chair, one Jackie Walker, whose chief claim to fame was previously being briefly suspended from the Labour party for an allegedly antisemitic social media post (though today it was revealed she had enlivened a conference antisemitism training session by declaring it would be 'wonderful' if Holocaust Memorial Day was not just for the Jews). On Sunday, however, she took the opportunity to judge that her claim to Jewish identity had been questioned by Jewish publications 'because I'm a black person and that's it'.

Fellow panellist and Jewish Labour chair Jeremy Newmark was rebuked from the floor for comments about the Holocaust, the speaker referencing the current 'police holocaust' against black people. Newmark cited a poll showing just 8% of British Jews supported Labour; an audience member demanded, 'Whose fault is that!?' The event's title: 'Does Labour have an Antisemitism Problem?' To which the only possible answer seems to be: what does it effing look like? I'm sure there were party conferences in the year 1933 at which the Jews were discussed this much. But not, perhaps, in this country.

Still, roll up for the progressive future. These days, party conferences – for all of the parties – have about as much cut-through as minor fluctuations in the bale price on the Karachi cotton exchange. When I was young, the BBC daytime schedules were cleared for live screening of all the speeches from the podiums, allowing viewers to really get inside the action of a plenary session on NEC constitutional amendments. I don't know what they rated then, but now they'd struggle even to rate at all. To watch someone bellowing from the podium about this being the most exciting moment in socialism in decades is to know more powerfully than you have ever known anything that it would get murdered by a *Jeremy Kyle* repeat.

Did shadow defence secretary Clive Lewis punch a wall or didn't he? It's unconfirmed, but unless he had somehow contrived to punch a wormhole right through the backdrop of the Trump–Clinton debate, political attention was largely concentrated a few thousand miles west of here this week.

Still, there were some diversions. This year the conference bubble has a precocious off-Broadway rival in the form of Momentum's own festival, which goes under the banner of 'The World Transformed' and sports amusing innovations, such as an 'actor in residence'. I particularly enjoyed the series of three giant artworks pointing out diffidently that 'Advertising Shits in Your Head'. The Momentum fringe is unquestionably far more vibrant and jolly than the conference proper, but the comparison feels like a discussion about which occupant of a morgue would perform best on *Strictly*. I feel I have to challenge the assertion one Momentum attendee made to Paul Mason: namely that 'the whole city's buzzing'. But perhaps I was plodding round the wrong bits of it.

Anyway, the festivities began last Saturday with the Labour party renewing its vows with Corbyn. 'Genuinely the best moment of my life,' a very nice and enthusiastic young Momentum member told me. 'An even worse idea than when my parents got back together for the second time,' shuddered my husband. I believe the modern way past this division is to observe vaguely that everyone can only live their truth. For some, that means operating on a higher plane of politics. You might have heard about Tom Watson's eye-catching speech praising the achievements of the Blair/Brown years, during which I imagine the autocue cable was simply cut in paragraph three. When Watson got to a line declaring that 'We need to win elections', there were several boos from the floor.

Wherever you stand on this slightly idiosyncratic version of enthusiasm and energy, though, to be among it for a few days is to be reminded anew of its essential draw. I know those on the centre left think Corbyn has stolen everybody's future and whatnot, but watching him take the podium stronger than ever, they have to concede that part of the excitement of the past year for Corbynistas is that they are basically involved in a plot that's straight out of the movies. An anonymous guy is suddenly – by an extraordinary series of events – catapulted on to the big stage. Vast crowds mass to hear him speak; his iconic image is plastered on everything. It all becomes increasingly intoxicating, in a quasi-religious type of way, and almost frighteningly unmanageable before he has even had a chance to change his jacket.

I would say we are now at the end of Act One. If you are asking me how this type of movie usually progresses, it eventually becomes clear that it could have been him, but it could have been anybody. As the plot thickens, it turns out that our hero is utterly expendable to the wider machine, and potentially a minor inconvenience down the line when They have to sideline him to keep his legacy alive for The Cause (not that one, just a generic Cause). But it's altogether simpler for Them if he can just fall off something and get martyred. Of course, he won't.

Traditionally, this all sets up a great Act Three, in which the hero can go full training montage and show what he is really made of by bringing down the whole edifice/getting crushed and sent to live in disappointed exile. Who stars? Hanks, if you can get him, or a young Jimmy Stewart, obviously. Costner would ruin it, though not as badly as the signs suggest Corbyn will.

A year in to his leadership, and despite his best major speech performance yet, Corbyn still comes across as someone all this is happening *to*, as opposed to *because of*. Monday morning found him touring and posing among the official conference stands. When he came to the one run by the Labour Campaign for Mental Health, he smiled and dutifully held up their placard reading 'Bring Back the Shadow Cabinet Minister for Mental Health' – a post he himself scrapped in July. Perhaps he is so used to decades of ineffectually waving protest banners that he didn't realise this was one campaign he alone had the power to fix.

Whether the alarm bells ring for him as he tours Momentum stands selling £10 books of fan poetry about himself is unclear. He doesn't let on, though I don't know if he has specifically read, say, 'Someone Happened' by Abigail E. O. Wyatt: 'Someone crept in / and lit a candle in our hearts / that someone happened / to be him.' Either way, I have been to Madonna tours with less merchandise featuring the star. Alan Partridge's reaction when faced with similarly T-shirted and enshrined levels of fandom was to run for the hills, screaming, 'You're a mentalist!' but Corbyn seems more relaxed about this aspect of his role than any other.

It's not just doggerel and JC singlets, though. Wares available in the main Labour conference venue ranged from the gently self-parodic – £2 beard comb, anyone? – to remnants from the besuited, Mandelsonian era of City style. One stall sold ties and cufflinks and socks in a tin, though a brisk trade did not seem to be happening. Over at Momentum, a man had set out a table offering anti-army merchandise. 'Join the army,' enticed the cover of a pamphlet. 'Free prosthetic limbs!' That one was competitively priced at £10.

Away from the retail opportunities, the moral relativism is striking. At a Momentum event discussing the menace of media bias, there were loud cheers and applause for the notion that 'the BBC's treatment of Jeremy Corbyn has been a much bigger disgrace than the *Daily Mail*'s'. All visitors to 'The World Transformed' were handed a document calling for 'a democratic media' which contains what you might think would have been a real warning sign of a quote: 'Of course,' this runs, 'the only media we can really rely on is our own.' Spoken like all the good guys of history, right there.

One speaker from the floor solved the problem of Jeremy and the media via recourse to a discussion in *The Matrix* on spoon-bending. It is explained to Neo that 'It is not the spoon that bends, it is only yourself.' What this showed very clearly, the woman concluded, was that 'Jeremy Corbyn should not bend to the media; the media should bend to Jeremy Corbyn.' Mmm. I have always had a weakness for those great 1968 graffiti slogans ('Do not adjust your mind – there is a fault in reality'). But with the best will in the world, there actually is a spoon. There are lots of spoons. Experience – bitter or otherwise – suggests Corbyn's Labour are going to have to make their peace with the notion of spoons.

Finally, as someone who has been spared conference attendance for what I think must be 10 years, one of the most striking aspects was the almost total lack of security. In the run-up to the event, there was a faintly embarrassing saga, when it looked like Labour couldn't get any firm to provide security services. My instinct at that moment was that they should have got the Hells Angels to do it, like the Rolling Stones did at the Altamont festival in 1969, but perhaps the fatalities put them off. In the end, Labour went with another firm (albeit one criticised for its use of zero-hours contracts).

But this week you basically just walked in with a wave of your pass. The contrast could barely have been more marked with the 40-minute queues to get anywhere near the event that were such a maddening feature of the Blair/Brown era. On the one hand, the absence of that hysterical self-importance was more than welcome. On the other, given the desiccated nature of the event inside and the enduring notion that you are nothing in public life if people can't manufacture a security threat around you, it did rather give the impression of the Labour conference being something too irrelevant to even dream of attacking. You'd have had more trouble getting into a Football League ground. A conference headed for the Conference? I leave it to you to decide. You can only live your truth, after all.

Ladies, please tell – how do you resist the hardmen of Ukip?

7 October 2016

Now that they've got the Brexit they wanted, Ukip's leading lights are behaving like drunks at the end of a stag weekend

Of all the political mysteries we'll never get to the bottom of, the most unfathomable is surely Ukip's own admission that it lags so significantly behind with female voters. At the last count, over two-thirds of the party's support was male, while the 2015 election saw the Tories post majority female support, at 56%. Ladies, what is wrong with you? We know you're irrational, but this just proves it. How can it be that Ukip is such a thrusting and potent political force, but still struggles to break through to anything like the same degree with womankind – even when it acts like a party whose motto is the Latin for 'Sorry, luv, I'm too big for condoms'?

I once saw a TV dating show in which a contestant was asked what she looked for in a partner, and she said: 'I like men who fight in bars.' So the potential support base must be out there. As resignation-resistant superbug Nigel Farage is always saying: it's up to us to reach it and build on it. Or get it to hold our jacket while we lamp some twat. Whatever. Among the metaphorical dating show contestants that are Ukip's elite, then, who is your favourite hardman? There's certainly an embarrassment of choice. Do join me as we review the options.

First up is Steven Woolfe, the polished and modern wannabe leader who writes terrible poetry, yet who offered a colleague outside during a 'clear the air' meeting of Ukip MEPs. Precisely what happened next appears to be a matter of debate, though no one disputes the fact that Steven later suffered two seizures and was taken to hospital, where he spent much of the afternoon reportedly fighting for his life with suspected bleeding on the brain. That grim diagnosis has thankfully not come to pass, and Woolfe is now much recovered. Or, as another Ukip MEP, Nathan Gill, put it: 'Steven is sick of croissants and ready for a full English.' I like how even this comment smacks of resentment at foreigners (they're still technically foreigners, even though it's their own country, aren't they?). A dim view appears to have been taken of the hospital, which had not only the temerity to treat Woolfe without charge, but then to offer him a continental breakfast.

Anyway, if you're not taken with Steven, how about the fella who allegedly nearly gave him a brain haemorrhage, Mike Hookem? Mike, who is Ukip's defence spokesman, says that what happened was that Steven walked into a door or something. On Friday he thought carefully about what he wanted to say about the slurs and declared he was going to 'fight my corner'. Mike reminds me a lot of the bit in *Hard to Kill* where Steven Seagal says: 'I'm going to take you to the bank, Senator Trent. To the blood bank!'

If Mike doesn't do it for you, maybe you're a lesbian, but not the hot kind? Or maybe you have your eye on Neil Hamilton – memba him? – who on Thursday showed how political office, no matter how obscure, can even make guys who were picked last for sport at school imagine themselves to be slightly harder than Dirty Harry. While reports still had Woolfe fighting for his life, Neil busted on to the BBC to declare, like a man of the world, that Woolfe had 'picked a fight and come off worse'. Yeah – out here, men are men. Welcome to the Strasbourg frontierland! Furthermore, Neil chuckled like one who knows, the alleged punch-up was the kind of thing that happens when 'passions run high'. To which the only reasonable reply is: dude! That means a lot from a man whose signature streetwear is a spotty bowtie.

Still, if Neil doesn't stuff your brown envelope, maybe you're the demographic that would be psephologically excited by Arron

Banks. As the chief Ukip financier, Arron had to buy his way in to the gang, but that doesn't stop him styling himself as the Chuck Norris of insurance firms. Having at first declared himself 'utterly disgusted' by Hamilton, Arron soon decided he'd prefer to be disgusting than ignored. He took to Twitter to announce: 'I once punched my Oz business partner after a row but I asked permission. He sat through dinner with a bag of frozen peas on his chin.' 'Odd men,' one tweeter observed rather mildly. 'You wouldn't understand,' shot back Arron, who always tweets like he's doing 97mph in a Vauxhall Cavalier with a suit jacket hung up in the rear window. 'It's called a competitive spirit! It's why some people are winners . . .'

Of course, if Banks isn't your bag, ladies, you are left with covert-coated caretaker leader Nigel Farage, who is trying to rise above this illegal *kumite* by summarising it as 'something that happens between men'. It really says something about our leading males that Farage has become the stylish sophisticate in all this. He's basically Ukip's Cary Grant now, if not its Clooney. The minute he's set up this latest inquiry, he's got his eye on a Nespresso ad.

So there you have it. Perhaps a certain amount of bloodsport is inevitable, given that Ukip has always disported itself in the Strasbourg parliament like Brits on a stag do. Various of their number have mugged off the foreigners in excruciatingly boorish speeches, formally denied pissing in hotel plant pots, got sensationally drunk, posted pictures with a stripper and run up taxpayer bills only slightly less than the outgoing EU rebate. Now that they've got what they wanted out of the referendum, we are in the final stages of this jolly – which is to say, that bit where the best man punches the groom and you end up having to bellow 'Speak English!' at some Dr Dipstick in A&E. It's time to go home, lads. But will anyone still be speaking as they wait for Ryanair to airlift them out?

While we've yet to find out, perhaps it's time to ask whether Ukip's brave gender experiment has delivered for the party or is becoming even more of a liability than a business hiring a woman who might get knocked up in a couple of years? Put simply: Ukip has made amazing and admirable strides in promoting men. But let's be realistic: that has resulted in an elite that clearly has a tendency to become too emotional, that acts highly irrationally and that frequently comes off as a bit crazy. I know Ukip hardmen want to have it all. But are they up to it?

It's winner takes all on Brexit island, because the audience demands it

4 November 2016

Politics has become a non-stop TV reality show. Pity the judiciary – it's been voted off this week

Like so many of the biggest formats in the golden era of reality TV, Brexit is set on an island. Back in the early years of the millennium, you were nothing in unscripted programming unless you were marooned on an island or in a McMansion, then forced to fight your way to the prize by scheming, screaming, demeaning, and not forgetting the lyrics to 'Dance with My Father'. The transatlantic spirit of the age was Simon Cowell, a populist whose love of plebiscites did little to disguise his totalitarian ambition. When he declared, 'No one is ever going to publish a book called *Simon Cowell, My Struggle*,' I wept for the loss of the German edition.

The holy grail of reality formats was conflict, as orchestrated by cynical, unseen producers, who manipulated participants into degrading themselves and the public into voting – at financial cost – for the result. Absurd props and esoteric MacGuffins were spoken of as solemnly as if they were articles of a country's constitution. Tribal Council. The Diary Room. Bushtucker Trials. The £350m

Bus. Judges' Houses. Unelected Judges' Houses. Hang on – a couple of those have ended up in the wrong list. Still, you get the idea.

As any number of dystopian fictions, from *Rollerball* to *The Hunger Games*, have long warned us, the future is a televised contest played for the highest stakes. So we must have known the current shitshow was in the post. Either way, it turns out all those who used to tut, 'How low can reality TV go?' were totally asking the wrong question. Look how high it's gone! Never mind history repeating itself as farce – reality TV is repeating itself as history. On the other side of the Atlantic, arguably the biggest reality star of that golden era is currently the Republican nominee for the presidency. Over this side, to many narcotised by two decades of the genre, the uncomplicated certainties of its voting are regarded as less of a conspiracy than judicial process.

With the exception of *The X Factor*, where the hostility was more covert, reality-TV voting was always disapproval voting. You voted off. You voted out. And that was that. A significant section of the population believe the EU was voted off on 23 June and now are beginning to openly dismiss the rule of law, as though it were Jedward or a *Survivor* contestant who disparaged the Ulong tribe's plans for a shelter with an awesome sex crib attached. Who does Cayla even think she is? What even is the rule of law? Who made it queen of everything? Tory MP David Davies doesn't believe in it; half the papers don't believe in it; others have already taken their lead without encouragement. Maybe the rule of law's 'journey' on the show has come to an end, and we should crank up 'Everybody Hurts' and bid it farewell with a montage of its best bits.

Today's *Daily Express* front page likened the 'threat' of a high court ruling on the triggering of Article 50 to that of Hitler. Guys, if you hate Hitler so much, stop publishing front pages that read like future exhibits in a museum show called 'Before the Militias'. The second most WTF-laden intro was in the *Daily Mail*, which assigned Ark of the Covenant-like qualities to a leaflet whose only prior claim to fame was being dismissed as a biased disgrace in the *Daily Mail*. As Friday's paper had it: 'MPs last night accused judges of failing to read the £9m taxpayer-funded publicity leaflet that stated the referendum result would be followed directly by ministers.' Wait – MPs accused judges of failing to read a leaflet? Did they also accuse them of failing to follow the rules of Bootcamp? Can we settle this with an immunity task/a sing-off in the karaokosseum/a catfight between the leaflet and the bus? Also, didn't the *Daily Mail* watch the shows? The mean judge is always a Brit – and in this case, there are three of them. Can't at least one of these leaflet-shunners be replaced by *X Factor* judge – and Brexiteer – Sharon Osbourne?

Having banged on about their failure to remotely understand what they were asking for at the time, I do have to offer another slow handclap for the generation of politicians such as Gordon Brown – a man so obsessed with *The X Factor* that he once wrote personal letters to the finalists – who were forever on about wanting 'an *X Factor* politics'. Newsflash, Gordon: this is what *X Factor* politics looks like. Try not to choke on it!

Now his ratings are on the slide, Cowell can at least take comfort that his plan to 'give politics the X factor' has come to pass. 'The fact we're allowing the public to make the decisions most of the time is a really good thing,' Cowell once mused of his various shows. 'The great thing is when you start seeing it in places like China and Afghanistan. It's democracy. We've kinda given democracy back to the world.' Man, he had it all figured out, didn't he?

A bit like his best mate Philip Green – whose report into government efficiency concluded that running the vast and complex machinery of the state was akin to retail – Cowell's reputation as a man with the answer to everything is likely to oxidise rapidly. At one stage he punted the idea of a TV show where the public voted every week on a political issue – and perhaps Simon passed on this faith in frequent referendums to David Cameron, whom he backed in a major *Sun* splash on the eve of the 2010 election. Cameron, he reckoned, was a man of 'substance' with 'the stomach to navigate us through difficult times'.

In the end, it's amazing – considering how histrionic and uncivilised many found it at the time – quite how rule-abiding and righteous reality TV now looks compared with actual reality. There were parameters on the shows, even on many of the ghastlier ones. I mean, at least soundstages were frequently equipped with lie detectors. Imagine how much better this US election would have been with a polygraph. Imagine how much better the referendum campaign would have been with a polygraph. Imagine how much better both would have been if politicians had been bleeped and called into the producers when they said something racist.

Please don't take all this as the view from above. It is hardly a matter of pride, but I suspect I am as unwittingly, hopelessly addicted to the horrifyingly debased dramas of today's politics as many others. I used to watch lots of reality shows, but they haven't done it for me for years now. Maybe the hit I used to get off their dramas and conflicts – was it dopamine? – requires a bigger stimulus. In the mad fever dream of the US election and the increasingly frightening divisions of Brexit, both amplified by social media, maybe I and countless others have found it. This used to be the way we watched. Now it's the way we seek to govern; the way we govern; the way we live.

CELEBRITIES, AND OTHER THOUGHT LEADERS

The minute a Kardashian uses a Pepsi commercial to teach us about civil rights protests is the minute we understand the essential thing about some celebrities: they're like humans – but better. From Gwyneth Paltrow's Goop (a rolling satire on late capitalism) to *MasterChef*'s Gregg Wallace (a rolling satire on late Gregg Wallace), humanity remains super-blessed in the entertainment department. Nobody, but nobody, works harder than celebrities. And you know how we know that? Because celebrities keep on telling us.

Gregg Wallace falls out of the spotlight and into the deep-fat fryer

1 September 2016

The MasterChef *presenter has given* Great British Bake Off's *Mary Berry a light battering as the cooking-show rivalry heats up*

Lost in Showbiz has had a particular weakness for stories involving the television cooking-show judge Gregg Wallace, ever since he was contacted on Twitter by a member of the public. 'Hi Greg,' ran the message. 'I am cycling just over 180 miles in 2 days for Macmillan Cancer Support. Any chance of a retweet?' The *MasterChef* star's retort was as heartwarming as it was lengthy, and ran simply: 'Gregg?' 'No worries mate,' shot back the charity bike rider. 'It's only people with cancer. You worry about your extra G.'

However, Twitter has been a place of ups as well as downs for Gregg. He had met his third wife, Heidi, on the platform when she contacted him to ask him a question about celery. Alas, the marriage foundered after 15 months, despite the fact that Heidi ran his household for him, looked after his two teenage children and was charged with running his diary to a level of micromanagement that can certainly be described as eye-catching. His daily list would need to include instructions to eat breakfast, brush his teeth, check BBC News . . . 'Then it'll say Twitter,' explained Gregg blithely, 'because I want to tweet twice a day.'

Alas, Heidi seems to have fallen behind on her own marital to-do list. 'I want to be out on the town,' Gregg eventually lamented to the newspapers. 'I crave company. I want to take my sexy, elegant wife to smart restaurants dressed up in her heels on my arm. She likes the local Italian. I spent a lot of time doing things to please Heidi and it was bothering me.'

Poor Gregg. Yet it wasn't him who called time on the union. In fact, Heidi's request to end things on the basis that he was 'needy' was entirely unfathomable to him. 'It is weird, isn't it?' he wondered rhetorically to the *Daily Mail* at the time. 'I find it all weird. I mean, she came up to the flat in London last week to change my sheets. I honestly can't get to the bottom of it.'

Amazing.

Anyway, back to the present day. It is little known that every morning for some years, Gregg would stare into his enchanted mirror and inquire: 'Mirror, mirror on the wall, who's the most cooking judge of all?' And every morning the mirror would beam his own visage back at him and reply: 'YOU ARE, GREGG.' Gregg Wallace has long known that he bestrides the world of awarding-points-to-food like a Colossus. He looms over a plate like he's invading its personal space, and the public loves him for it. He strongly suspects his iconic catchphrase – 'Cooking doesn't get tougher than this' – will soon be given listed status.

One day last week, however, this morning ritual was cataclysmically disrupted, and it was not Gregg's face that he saw in the looking glass. But who is this? Who is this lady biting into a *Sachertorte* with a critical tooth, before pronouncing it 'really very accomplished'? Over to the mirror, which doesn't mince its words: 'MARY BERRY IS THE MOST COOKING JUDGE!' it informs him. '*MASTERCHEF* HAS BECOME A SECOND-TIER COOKING SHOW.'

Once he's stopped screaming and swept up the mirror shards and spittle, Gregg has two options. A poisoned apple tart with a brûlée glaze. Or an outing in the *Sun on Sunday*, in which he goes to war with Mary over some passing comment she's made about deep-fat fryers. He chooses the latter. Indeed, he chooses batter.

But first, a recap of Mary's comment – made to *Good House-keeping* – in which the *Great British Bake Off* star poured scorn on the smell and health risks of fryers, declaring: 'I don't think any household should have one.' Dear Mary! I suspect she is one of those national treasures whose results on the Political Compass test I'd be much happier not knowing. A bit like Joanna Lumley.

For Gregg, however, this was nothing less than a culinary invasion of Poland. As he thundered in the *Sun*: 'Every household down my road in Peckham, south-east London, stunk of deep-fat frying and I'm sure every working-class home around the country was the same. How would you have done chips and Spam fritters without a deep-fat fryer? It really does beggar belief. Our nation was built on chips and Spam fritters.'

Mirror, mirror on the wall . . . But there was more. Much more. 'The smell of deep-fat frying was universal back then, wasn't it?' inquired Gregg, again rhetorically. 'It brought families and friends together. To suggest getting rid of it isn't just an assault on the deep-fat fryer but on the traditional British psyche. I love Mary dearly but this is an attack on our British way of life.'

If those sound to you like the words of someone who'll say anything, and with any amount of confected feeling, just to get *Bake Off* out of the headlines, then you have simply failed to understand the centrality of the fryer to this island race. It is existential. Happily, Gregg, now on his fourth marriage – they met after she asked him a question about rhubarb on Twitter – understands all about gathering round the fryer like the Waltons. Not that he didn't write the book on moderation too. 'I've lost three stone in the past couple of years,' he finds space to point out, 'so I know about it.'

Lest the sledgehammer nature of his shade-throwing be missed, though, Gregg ends with a reminder that certain glass-house dwellers are no better than they should be. 'The main thing to remember,' he points out, 'is that things like deep-fat-fried foods, or the delicious sugary buttery cakes like Mary Berry bakes, are treats.'

As are you, Gregg. As are you. Indeed, we look forward to hearing much more from you at your very earliest convenience, and as frequently as possible while this record-breaking series of *Bake Off* continues.

Shia LaBeouf, Tom Hiddleston and Daniel Craig reveal the toll of the role

8 September 2016

It's a tough life being an actor – just ask the American Honey *star, Taylor Swift's ex and the reluctant Bond*

It was cinema's Gerard Butler who once observed: 'There's no one in this world I think works harder than me.' It's true. Although a UN report found their daily toil sufficiently backbreaking and hazardous to rank them as among the very poorest of the poor, there are Filipino fishermen who come home and almost collapse after 18 hours on the waters, only to rally themselves when their wives sniff: 'Tough day? Do me a favour – you're not Gerard Butler. Gerard's been in his trailer since 7am and he's still waiting for the light.'

The fact is, movie acting is *the* toughest profession, and anyone who feels moved to query that has simply never shot a really intense scene about being on welfare with Kristen Stewart, much less had to bang her afterwards. People who endure that go fishing to relax, you know what I mean? That's how tough the gig is.

And so to another week in which the role, and the toll of the role, has been diversely discussed by those forced to weather it. We begin with returning character Shia LaBeouf, whose tireless attempts to get everyone to forget he was once a Disney star mark him out as a Proper Celebrity. Shia understands his responsibility to add to the gaiety of the nations, and consequently has torn through various breakdown-effect public poses in the past few years. Ways in which he has 'given back' include – but are by no means limited to – doing acid in front of Ron Weasley; a plagiarism scandal he sought to defuse by hiring a skywriting plane; wearing a paper bag reading 'I Am Not Famous Anymore' to a premiere; staging an art installation in which he sat for five days in an LA gallery and allowed the public to join him in short shifts; revealing he was raped by a woman during the latter performance; a majestically irksome motivational speech on YouTube; filming himself binge-watching his own movies in a cinema for three days. (He walked out of *Transformers: Revenge of the Fallen*, fact fans, but managed to stay for *Indiana Jones and the Kingdom of the Crystal Skull*.)

Anyway, Shia's latest outing is a lengthy interview in *Variety*, in which he announces: 'I'm learning how to distil my "crazy" into something manageable, that I can shape and deliver on the day.' I must say I like the sound of his new film, director Andrea Arnold's *American Honey*, a lot. 'For *American Honey*, Arnold never gave LaBeouf a script,' we learn, 'just a black-and-white picture of a forest for inspiration.' Very much hoping that one doesn't come out the same week as *Rogue One*.

The movie concerns 'a gang of nomad thieves and misfit kids selling magazine subscriptions on a cross-country road trip'. And in keeping with today's theme, it appears to be a shoot of a rare order, during which the cast slept in motels and were encouraged to replicate their fictional relationships. 'You do whatever is required for it to be true, for it to be honest,' explains Shia. 'I had to run this group, sort of like a pimp.' He acquired 12 new tattoos during the shoot, including a matched pair of Missy Elliotts on his knees. He doesn't like Missy Elliott that much, apparently – it was just 'peer pressure'.

Other interview highlights? Mugging off Mister Spielberg – 'He's less a director than he is a fucking company' – and *Variety*'s deadpan parenthesis 'Spielberg declined to comment'. And there's a reminder that actors can always find new variations on the old fib 'I don't act for trophies. But you know, it would be nice to be nominated.' Or, as Shia puts it: 'The Oscars are about politics. I got to earn my way back. It's not about who is the best. I'm not that guy for a long time – for a long, long time. I'm good with that, though. Sometimes that shit is a curse.'

Elsewhere in acting, though, there is a horrendous – if tenuously credible – dilemma for Daniel Craig. Does he or does he not take the rumoured $150m he is being offered to commit to two further James Bond movies? At first look, this would seem to be a gimme, but remember: even among movie acting gigs, Bond is one of the absolute toughest. As Craig put it after the last one, he'd rather 'slash my wrists' than go through it again. In fact, reading his frequent discourses on Bond's demands, it seems desperately wet of Björk to have vowed never to act again after making *Dancer in the Dark* with Lars von Trier in 2000. Man up, love! I honestly think it would have finished Björk off if some gender alchemy had required her to shag around in an edition-of-10 Aston Martin between various luxury spa locations, all the while trying to retrieve important nanotechnology from some intriguingly scarred foreigner.

Then again, while we're on the subject of Bond, does this week's reported split with Taylor Swift put Tom Hiddleston back in the frame for the role? As previously discussed, Lost in Showbiz has grave reservations about the suitability of Hiddleston for Bond, particularly on the basis of an interview he once gave, in which he explained that as an actor, 'I can't turn off my intelligence.' But following his high-profile three-month relationship with Taylor . . . well, things have merely crystallised. No offence, but I don't go to the movies to watch my country being covertly defended by someone who'd wear an 'I Love TS' singlet. You might as well give Isis our nuclear codes or make Boris Johnson foreign secretary.

I speak, of course, of the photos of Tom cavorting in the sea with Taylor, wearing a customised vest. Clearly, his outfit was a joke, some impenetrable Fourth of July japery between new lovers. But it's out there now, and for all the briefing and counter-briefing over who dumped whom, I can't help feeling one of the sundered parties is going to swim forward faster and more lethally. Oh, Tom, Tom, Tom! Why did you think it was safe to go into the water?

Enter Shirley MacLaine – the words we've been longing to write since Oscar-chaos night

2 March 2017

The sister of Warren Beatty has stepped in to stick up for him after his involvement in envelopegate, which saw La La Land *accidentally named as Best Picture instead of* Moonlight

Oh God, will it ever not be funny? Will the Oscars catastrophe ever stop unfurling new petals of merriment to us, like a mysterious orchid that blooms eternally? Not if Warren Beatty's sister has anything to do with it. Yes, days after the cock-up that amused the world, Lost in Showbiz is finally able to type the words it has been longing for: ENTER SHIRLEY MACLAINE.

'I think we're all processing the horror of it,' says Shirley, with typical local understatement. 'I'm still dealing with it. I'm concerned with how [Warren] must have felt, being so close to him. I'm three years older and I'm protective. We know how difficult it was for him, but it was also for me.' A reminder that we may never know the full tally of victims.

Even so, any corporeal intervention from Shirley is always welcome – 93% of the time this Proper Celebrity is detained in another dimension, conveyed there by whichever fringe therapies she is currently espousing. Psychic surgery, radionics, a past-lives catchment area that stretches from the Ottoman empire to Atlantis

– has anything prepared her for what happened in the Dolby theatre on Sunday? 'I'm basically a mystic,' Shirley tells *USA Today*. 'And I'm wondering what that was all about. And I am not sure yet. I'll have to think about it some more.'

It says something of the historical magnitude of the incident that there is nothing in Shirley's vast repository of quackery to handle what went down when her little bro was flummoxed by the wrong envelope. Stay with this, because I'm just giving free voice to nagging energy currents in my aura, but is it perhaps explained by something Warren himself did in a past life? It certainly sits at odds with most of what he did in this life. Look, I love him and stuff, but Beatty's behaviour as the mistake became clear is best described as persona-aborting. Admittedly, there's often something rather narcissistically doomed about his characters. But, honestly, half a career spent in wistful exultation of the ideals of Frank Capra, and what does he do when the chips are down? He pushes his way to the microphone and explains that this had nothing to do with him. He wasn't trying to be funny; he gave it to Faye; it wasn't him. It wasn't him! Thanking you, Warren. You've stood up and asked NOT to be counted.

As for what happens next, who can say? Hollywood is a town that takes being made to look silly about as well as Kim Jong-un does. The consequent show of strength could be horrifying, and you are advised to gird your loins accordingly.

Diet Woke: how Pepsi's ad backfired for Kendall Jenner

6 April 2017

The soda company missed the mark with its protest promo. But will no one think of how it soured the Kardashian brand too?

To the repository of cultural treasures taken from us far too soon, we must add Pepsi's latest commercial, 'The Woke-ing of Kendall Jenner'. Released on the anniversary of Martin Luther King's assassination, it seemed the perfect marriage of model and material. Wherever we were before it made the civil rights movement look like a totally transformative hair serum, we are now back there again, somehow knowing the place for the first time.

The day after its release, Pepsi pulled the ad, tacitly conceding that its attempt to 'project a global message of peace, unity and understanding' would be scaled back in order to concentrate on its core business: selling soft drinks. It was a hugely courageous attempt at market entry, but the global injustice space is notoriously competitive, and Pepsi found that out the hard way. The hardest way, if you don't count being shot dead by a police officer. And I sense they don't.

Look, I'd love to be able to say with confidence that the final straw for the ad was a tweet from Dr Martin Luther King's daughter, Bernice King, which featured a picture of her protesting father being restrained by police, with the caption: 'If only Daddy would have known about the power of Pepsi.' But looking at the apology Pepsi issued, Lost in Showbiz detects the influence of someone else's parent. After some opening lines in which they blather about 'miss[ing] the mark', the firm gets down to the serious business of damage limitation, concluding pointedly with the words: 'We also apologise for putting Kendall Jenner in this position.'

Mmm. In some ways, I'm glad Bernice's daddy never knew about the power of Kendall's mother, Kris Jenner. Either way, to read that final sentence is to detect a sulphurous whiff of Kardashian materfamilias Kris, who will have regarded the furore engulfing her daughter as a major injustice. As for Pepsi, they clearly deem it entirely unnecessary to apologise to Black Lives Matter – or anyone who might feel their imagery was co-opted in the cause of shifting aspartame. Yet it is a matter of the utmost commercial and political importance to grovel, as far as the Kardashians are concerned.

Think of it this way: Black Amexes Matter. We are now back in a realm wherein anyone with any power in this saga will feel much more comfortable: a place where extremely rich white people argue via lawyers about the level of financial reparations now due. And reparations are certainly on the table, considering Kendall would have been paid every time this ad aired.

According to various reports, Kris is more than unhappy about the horrendous position in which Kendall has been placed by her decision to accept unspecified millions of dollars to participate in a Pepsi advert whose concept she will have approved. Her mother fears this unfortunate association has rendered Kendall less attractive as a brand-face to other firms – and may even cause firms with whom she already has contracts to consider not renewing their association. It wouldn't be anything personal; it's just whether or not they want the image of silly Kendall solving racism with a fizzy drink drifting into consumers' thoughts at the point of purchase.

Alas, owing to TV scheduling, earthlings only really understand the 30% of their culture owned by the Kardashian family on a time lag. It was months after the event by the time Kim was shown discussing her Paris robbery on *Keeping Up with the Kardashians*, and it will be many moons before the family are shown going through Kendall's Pepsi horror show to the requisite level of detail.

Still, if you truly can't wait, just picture several minutes of the family staring in mounting shock and fury at their phone screens as the row develops. In the end, a large part of any given *KUWTK* episode involves watching the Kardashians react to things they're looking at on their phones. It's like a showbiz version of Sky's *Soccer Saturday*, where, instead of watching Paul Merson losing his shit about a disallowed goal at Turf Moor that you can't see, you watch the ladies' faces lit up by bad news from the internet that you can't see.

Anyhow. Elsewhere in the intersection between canned soft drinks and global injustice, there is more news of Lindsay Lohan. It wasn't so long ago, you might recall, that Lindsay was herself coming under fire for the glib deployment of soda, following reports that she had been handing out cans of the energy drink that sponsors her to Syrian refugees, on visits the firm had organised to a camp in Turkey. The brand drew itself up to its full height to deliver a response: 'Lindsay, as brand ambassador, of course has a certain quantity of cans at her disposal. She is free and welcome to give those cans to refugees she is meeting.'

Oof. The beverage also retails at the Athens nightclub bearing Lindsay's name, at the opening of which madam was keen to stress the snowballing synergies her involvement brings.

'There's bigger things to be done with the LOHAN club,' she told reporters. 'There is spas, there is refugee camps . . .' You know, the full range of venues.

'We have to help people,' she goes on, 'and if we can do it with a nightclub, or with a spa, or with refugee camps, or with containers . . .'

I never did find out what containers she was on about – and, it must be said, things have gone a little quiet on the refugee camp front too. Instead, Lindsay is very much ramping up the Islam-curious aspect of her output. Not only did she claim to have been 'racially profiled' at Heathrow recently – she was asked to remove her scarf – but she has posted a headscarved photo of herself, promising a 'new fashion line'.

It all seems loosely connected with Lindsay's long-mulled conversion to Islam. This week has found her posing for a full series of pictures on a Thai beach while wearing a burkini. What does it all mean? I haven't the foggiest. But the minute Lost in Showbiz has clear eyes on Lindsay's spiritual, political and commercial coordinates, so will you.

Who let Brad Pitt's fashotainment shoot happen?

4 May 2017

The troubled star's GQ Style *cover story is the most excruciating interview of 2017*

Call off the search. The high-water mark of excruciating celebrity magazine interviews has already been reached for 2017. It is – it will forever be – *GQ Style's* 'BRAD PITT IN AMERICA'S NATIONAL PARKS'. That is literally the coverline for the latest edition of the fashion quarterly. It's as if the editor was given a pile of actors' names and a pile of auto-parodic location ideas and told to pick one from each deck. 'BRAD PITT IN AMERICA'S NATIONAL PARKS'. 'GEORGE CLOONEY BENEATH THE CASPIAN SEA'. 'TOM CRUISE ON THE ARCTIC SHELF' (hair by Ken Paves). The entire feature has been conceived by the last three people connected with fashotainment publishing not to have seen *Zoolander*.

Before we proceed with the exposing horrors of the accompanying interview, which is predicated on the notion that performative recovery and fashion advertorial need not be mutually exclusive, I should say this: I am very sorry for Brad Pitt that he is getting divorced, or rather being divorced by Angelina Jolie when he really doesn't want to be. It must be completely, heartbustingly horrible, and he could hardly look more drawn. But I would like to ask his agent/manager/ publicist/anyone remotely responsible for pastoral guidance: what the hell happened here? Do you understand that you should now carry the stain of 'BRAD PITT IN AMERICA'S NATIONAL PARKS' like the mark of Cain for the rest of your natural life? I am looking at pictures of Brad in the foetal position at White Sands (socks by Brunello Cucinelli), Brad brimming with tears at White Sands (suit jacket $2,250, sweater $1,380, both by Bottega Veneta), Brad in the Everglades, looking like he could have six burgers and still weigh out for the 2,000 Guineas, and it is impossible not to wonder: where were you, guys, you bunch of massive arses, other than slyly reckoning that open-heart surgery (patient's gown: Rick Owens SS17) is probably the quickest route back to box office?

At one point, Brad explains to the interviewer, Michael Paterniti: 'I went through two therapists to get to the right one.' Yes, the right therapist is so important, and I am thrilled he burned through a couple of duds before apparently settling on one who would green-light his decision to discuss the intimate details of his private life while hawking Ralph Lauren in a dank cavern. 'Yes, yes, Brad – I think this is a really positive move for you – but I would like final approval on the knitwear.'

The other thing to concede is that I am afraid this stuff is really what we want from our celebrities. We don't want prudent periods of reticence. We don't want them to hide the fact they are working with the healing medium of clay – more of this shortly – because it might sound radioactively affected. We don't want them to think that the best way through pain probably *isn't* standing knee-deep in the Everglades and talking about court-ordered visitation rights for the readers of *GQ Style*. We want this.

So, without further ado, let's have it. On with the show. And it's clear pretty much from the get-go that this is going to turn out to be of the horror variety. The standout quotes from Brad are too numerous to reproduce the full range, but here is a flavour. 'I grew up in caves.' 'Genuinely, I just felt like Brad was a misnomer, and now I just feel like fucking Brad.' 'I've never heard anyone laugh bigger than an African mother who's lost nine family members. What is that? I just got R&B for the first time. R&B comes from great pain, but it's a celebration. To me, it's embracing what's left. It's that African woman being able to laugh much more boisterously than I've ever been able to.'

Where. Is. Your. Agent.

I mean, to adapt Mickey in *Rocky III*, they're killing ya to death out there. At least 70% of the questions initially appear to have been asked as a dare – 'What is pain, emotional and physical?' – but, as time wears on, it's impossible not to conclude the interviewer really is this much of a dick. Consider the bit where he simply says to Brad: 'Metaphors are my life.' And then decides to include that statement in the final copy.

At no point is anyone permitted to escape the hilariously ghastly *GQ*-ness of it all, with references to decor dropped as signposts for some poignant pretension to come. In the opening paragraphs describing the interior of Brad's house, the interviewer casually mentions 'the sideboard, with its exquisite inlay'. Much later, Brad says of his children: 'They won't give a shit about that inlay, but somewhere down the road it will mean something – I hope that it will soak in.'

Oh God, poor Brad. This is awful. Why can't we just go back to the time you were giving it to Geena Davis on a motel sideboard, or being released from desert prison into the arms of the type of girlfriend who remembers to bring a pair of Levi's with her (and was about to get it on a motel sideboard)? No one cared about the inlay then.

As for making the majesty of America's national parks the backdrop to all this, that seems especially wicked, like getting Ansel

Adams to do a shoot with Mariah Carey. Here's a picture of Brad making a windswept prayer gesture in the Everglades that couldn't even have been redeemed by a *Gentle Ben* reference, wearing a $485 shirt that just screams: 'Come, friendly gators.' Here he is sprawled brokenly in the dunes of White Sands National Monument (necklace by David Yurman). Here is a stalagmite desperately trying to erode itself out of shot in Carlsbad Caverns. And here is Brad back in the Everglades, demanding answers of the sky in what seem to be $875 Emporio Armani waders. I do think they missed a trick by not picturing him on the vast extended arm of the Crazy Horse Memorial in South Dakota, gesturing in a wordless scream towards the inscription declaring 'MY LANDS ARE WHERE MY DEAD LIE BURIED'.

Still, we do get to hear about sculptural projects of his own, as Brad reveals: 'I'm working with clay, plaster, rebar, wood. Just trying to learn the materials. You know, I surprise myself.' A digression that reminds me of something Chazz Michael Michaels said in *Blades of Glory*: 'Before a big competition, I like to work with leather. The Native Americans always said that working with hides and pelts releases your soul.'

But back to sculpture. 'It's a very, very lonely occupation,' says Brad. 'There's a lot of manual labour, which is good for me right now. A lot of lugging clay around, chopping and moving and cleaning up after yourself. But I surprise myself.' Hang on, there's more. 'Right now I know the manual labour is good for me,' he repeats of sculpting, which I always think of as the coalmine of the visual arts, 'getting to know the expansiveness and limitations of the materials. I've got to start from the bottom, I've got to sweep my floor, I've got to wrap up my shit at night, you know?'

'Is the sculpting a Sisyphean thing,' wonders the interviewer, who must have an exceptional gastric constitution to have been able to transcribe his own interjections from the tape: 'rolling the rock up the hill, action obliterating all thoughts?' Of course, that wasn't the point of the king's eternal punishment . . . But given this guy doesn't seem to have watched *Zoolander*, I guess we can't expect him to have googled Sisyphus.

Anyway. That, perhaps mercifully, is all there is room for. All we can do is wish for Brad to feel better as soon as he is able. And if part of that is seeking new representation, then I don't think any of us would begrudge him it for a minute.

Juicing, workouts and monetised self-obsession – acting ain't what it used to be

14 September 2018

Hollywood was once all about insouciance. But not any more, as Mark Wahlberg's hilariously intense daily schedule makes all too clear

When the famously dissolute movie star John Barrymore died, having spent much of the last year of his life passed out at Errol Flynn's house, the brilliant character actor Peter Lorre bribed the funeral home's director to loan him the corpse for a night. Lorre, Humphrey Bogart and a couple of others sneaked into Flynn's Mulholland Drive home while he was shooting late, arranged the body in a chair near the bar, then hid and waited. When Flynn returned home from set, he nodded at Barrymore, and continued to walk over to fix himself a drink. After a few steps, Flynn froze. He went back to the chair, touched Barrymore's ice-cold body, then shouted: 'All right, you bastards, come on out!'

I know what you're thinking. This is all very well, but did any of these ill-disciplined men make *Daddy's Home 2*, Mark Wahlberg's highly called-for sequel to his turn in *Daddy's Home*? Alas not. At the time of this late-night incident, Bogart was shooting some little picture called *Casablanca*, and though we'll probably never know his workout schedule for the movie, I guess we can say for sure that he could bench-press at least a quarter of John Barrymore. But only after tipping-out time at the Cocoanut Grove.

And so to the much-remarked-upon daily routine of Wahlberg, which is here reproduced in full:

2.30am wake up
2.45am prayer time
3.15am breakfast
3.40–5.15am workout
5.30am post-workout meal
6.00am shower
7.30am golf
8.00am snack
9.30am cryo chamber recovery
10.30am snack
11.00am family time/meetings/work calls
1.00pm lunch
2.00pm meetings/work calls
3.00pm pick up kids @ school
3.30pm snack
4.00pm workout #2
5.00pm shower
5.30pm dinner/family time
7.30pm bedtime

Hey, don't knock it. It's called acting.

Or is it? Is that what this life is? For many, Mark's schedule is the equivalent of letting daylight in on tragic. Once the inspiration for *Entourage* – indeed, that comfortingly silly series and his Calvin Klein adverts are Mark's sole serious contributions to the culture of the past three decades – our hero now exists in a permanent state of physical readiness for creative challenges unspecified.

Instead of an actor, then, perhaps it makes better sense to think of Mark as the machine on which a small community of people depend for their livelihoods. Think of him as an ancient loom or an 18th-century plough. The contraption must be maintained at almost all costs, or the economic ecosystem collapses. Or perhaps you prefer to picture Mark as a corporation, with his abs expected to post quarterly results. And by quarterly, I mean per quarter of each day.

He's hardly alone. These days, Gwyneth Paltrow has almost stopped acting entirely and reversed her business model into the business of what being an actor apparently entails. Which is to say, an extreme form of highly monetised physical self-obsession. There is a point where you have so many accessory muscles to target and so many crystals to place in your orifices that you literally don't have time to look into a camera 27 times and say: 'Will that be all, Mr Stark?'

Looking at the physiques of a good seven of the top 10 highest-grossing Hollywood stars, including the aforementioned Mr Stark, it feels as if an actor's tradecraft long ago shifted on its axis. The bit where you pretend to be someone else as part of an artistic project is really such a small percentage of the life that it occupies far less of the schedule than juicing. And infinitely less of the schedule than talking about juicing.

It's a real cross to bear. Almost literally in the case of Tom Cruise, whose insistence on sacrificing his corporeal self in the cause of the *Mission Impossible* franchise is increasingly messianic.

Then there's Daniel Craig, whose James Bond role bafflingly has yet to draw the attentions of the Victoria Cross committee. 'I work myself to death,' he explained during the promotional tour for *Spectre*. 'It's getting harder. But such is life.' Keen not to miss out on this scintillating discussion, the movie's actual producer gave interviews about Craig's thighs. 'He went into a six-month physical thing that really transformed his body. I've never seen anything like it. He must have added, I don't know, 10 inches to his thighs and the whole chest. He actually transformed himself. And he kept at it. And he eats this scientifically controlled diet all the time, and he goes to bed at nine o'clock at night when he's making the movies. He's like a monk.'

Yes. I think I'd rather Bond's evil master villains got all of our hard drives and secret whatnots than have to listen to very much more of this. But there *was* more. As is increasingly common, the star's trainer got several outings on the interview circuit himself. 'As an ex-military man,' explained this chap, 'I think I was uniquely placed to understand the discipline, mental strength and stamina required in order to train to become the ultimate cinema super-spy, James Bond.' Thank God dear Roger Moore got out before this nonsense started. Can you imagine? What is really required to become the ultimate cinema superspy, James Bond, is the ability to turn to a snake and say, 'Hiss offf' (*Octopussy*, 1983, dir. John Glen) – and you simply can't bicep-curl your way to that.

Not that bulking up is new, of course. When Jimmy Stewart wanted to enlist in the US army after the bombing of Pearl Harbor, he found himself below the military's required weight, and consequently embarked on a beefing-up regime with MGM's in-house personal trainer. Clark Gable had the opposite problem, and embarked on a Dexedrine regime. It's unclear whether the cause for which they were doing all this was more important than Wahlberg's movie about a man who finds himself in over his head when he and his wife adopt three kids is. But at least they didn't bang on about their routines.

The mistake today's stars make is to imagine that any of this passes for conversation. It is perfectly acceptable to have a nutrition or exercise regime, and in many cases necessary. However, discussion of either is the last refuge of the most ocean-going of 21st-century bores. Should you find yourself discussing them at any length whatsoever in company, you should wake up the next morning beset by the sort of shame levels that might follow an evening of hideous drunkenness. 'Why did I say that? What nonsense was I blathering? Why am I such a complete idiot?'

If you are updating your etiquette books, then, please be advised that the old rule that you should never discuss religion or politics in polite company has dated. Both subjects are now back on the table. Their conversational-pariah status should instead be applied to diet and exercise. If someone asks you what you 'do' about either, you should cock your head in a manner that implies that even the question has been a faux pas; then outline your answer as absolutely briefly as possible, and ideally in fewer than 20 words; then move on to topics of greater interest. Furthermore, please never refer to any form of exercise or any exclusionary method of eating as 'a philosophy'. Existentialism is a philosophy. Raw food is food that has not been heated above 40 degrees. Let that clear up any persistent muddling of the two.

No community needs to grasp this more urgently than celebrities. In the name of entertainment, please never speak about eating steamed fish and vegetables for dinner and drinking three litres of water each day. Please work off the principle that you are paid a lot of money, and your obligation in interviews such as this is to at least attempt, at some level, to be interesting or amusing. Remind yourself: your diet is not interesting. Your diet is – in the words of Jerry Maguire – an up-at-dawn, pride-swallowing siege that you will never fully tell us about.

Unless, of course, it is as brilliantly ridiculous as Mark Wahlberg's. Then you must tell the entire world about it, to add to the gaiety of all the nations. I mean, honestly . . . even when you think of all the ghastly things the Hollywood studios have hushed up down the years, Mark's day-in-the life could hold its own with 90% of them. More please, Mark, whenever you next get a spare 15 minutes.

Gwyneth's Ark: sailing towards wellness but never quite getting there

30 April 2021

The Goop cruise is essentially a floating church freighted with expensive non-solutions. Yet there's no shortage of believers

'If you want to get rich, you start a religion.' This was the reported opinion of Scientology founder L. Ron Hubbard, who in 1967 bought the first in what was to become a fleet of cruise ships. According to various whistleblower accounts, long-time devotees were finally initiated into the innermost secrets of Scientology on board one of these vessels, having spent years passing through various confected levels and parting with incremental payments totalling hundreds of thousands of dollars. This was where you found out about Xenu, among more weapons-grade lunacy – the galactic tyrant who 75bn years ago exiled multiple individuals to Earth in special craft that weirdly looked exactly like DC-8s, then imprisoned them in mountains, before blowing them up with hydrogen bombs and brainwashing them with a huge 3D film. My theory has always been that they told you this stuff at sea to reinforce the notion that you were now in too deep to get off the boat, both literally and metaphorically.

So, yes, it's no real surprise to learn this week that turbocapitalist fanny-egg pedlar Gwyneth Paltrow has got into the cruise business. Face it, there's never been a better time, with the possible exception of 13 minutes after the end of the Black Death.

As it turns out, Gwyneth had announced a cruise as part of her Goop brand over a year ago but was forced to hit pause with the advent of The Great Unpleasantness. But there was obviously no way a deadly pandemic was going to sink Gwyneth's latest big idea for long. Indeed, you wouldn't even fancy an iceberg's chances against a Goop cruise.

Anyway, madam has partnered with Celebrity Cruises and will become the brand's new 'wellbeing adviser'. 'I'll be behind the scenes, working on some special projects,' explained Gwyneth, with the air of someone who would rather die than mingle front-of-house with whichever dreary civilians actually go on these things. 'My team @goop is curating programming and fitness kits to add to Celebrity's wellness the [*sic*] experience.'

Ah, there it is: wellness. 'Wellness' is part of a class of words unified by the fact that only the most dreadful bores on Earth know what they mean. See also 'neoliberalism'. Celebrity Cruises itself adds that the fitness kits will enhance 'self-care and collective wellbeing', with Gwyneth's role expected to focus on 'wellness programming' and something called the 'Women in Wellness initiative'.

Along with Goop's £1,000-a-day health summits, it all marks a move towards more organised forms of wellness religion by Gwyneth. 'She's not necessarily discovering new things,' Goop's former content director once breathed reverentially, 'but she's bringing ancient things into the mainstream.' Mainstream life expectancy in ancient times was about 32 – but whatever floats your cruise ship, of course.

Certainly, Paltrow has often described setting up Goop as 'a calling'. Without wishing to come off as Joan of Snark, though, I have to wonder what sort of company much of her activity places her in, however much she might hate to admit it. A few years ago, the business publication *Quartz* produced a fascinating article revealing how large numbers of the exact same products were sold on both Gwyneth Paltrow's Goop and Alex Jones's Infowars outlet, only with different packaging. (To refresh your memory chakra, Jones is the far-right wingnut and conspiracy theorist who believes the Sandy Hook school shooting was a hoax, among myriad other grotesqueries.) A supplement called Bacopa is marketed on Goop as part of a pack branded Why Am I So Effing Tired and promises to 'rebalance an over-taxed system'. Over on Infowars, Bacopa features in Jones's signature Brain Force pills, pushed on the premise that 'Top scientists and researchers agree: we are being hit by toxic weapons in the food and water supply that are making us fat, sick, and stupid.'

Not quite the words Gwyneth would ever use – and yet, how they lurk beneath the surface of a $250m-plus empire that unavoidably implies the path to happiness is via intense consumerism. It's also very much an iterated journey – you buy the vagina egg for one problem, which gives you back pain, so you buy the FasciaBlaster, which gives you bruising, so you buy the homeopathic arnica montana. And so on and so on, forever course-correcting towards wellness but never quite attaining its shores. It's possible to see your life in this church as a cascade of highly priced non-solutions, each purchase flowing from the problems caused by the previous one. How does it end? I guess by then you're an old lady and you swallow a horse. And end up dead, of course.

It goes without saying that Paltrow is not short of believers. Whether Gwyneth's pushing post-Covid quackery or recommending something called 'whole body vibration' as a treatment for multiple sclerosis, there is something powerfully religious about the brand she has created in her own image.

I guess you could call this type of arguably exploitative luxury retail the sale of indulgences, though I'm hearing the Catholic Church trademarked that one early in the Middle Ages. Even so, it is increasingly clear that Paltrow is quite happy to accept the occasional bit of reformation by mandate of the Federal Drug Administration, as it has never yet affected the bottom line. You get the feeling the one unpardonable sin for an employee would be to turn whistleblower and suggest that any part of it was an obvious load of bollocks. I certainly wouldn't try it at sea. On the blasphemy laws front, Goop trails well behind Somalia and is ranked only just above Iran.

Like a phone dropped in the North Sea, Vardy v. Rooney is full of absolute gold

13 May 2022

The lost mobile that could have explained it all, the jaw-dropping quotes, the battle of the outfits . . . the only ones benefiting from this libel case are the rubberneckers

There are battles. There are libel battles. And then there is . . . Wagnarok. Yesterday afternoon, several hours into her cross-examination in the high court, Rebekah Vardy returned from an emotional break in proceedings to observe from the witness box: 'It's been a very long few days.' Yeah, well. Chat shit get banged.

It was Rebekah's husband, Jamie Vardy, who first uttered that deathless adage, back in 2011, when he was playing non-league football, though weirdly he wasn't actually making a heavily ironic comment on Britain's libel laws. Spool forward to the present day, though, and we have to ask: which shit-chatter is getting banged in the high court? Is it defendant Coleen Rooney, against whom Rebekah chose – actually chose! – to bring this action, with Vardy's pre-trial legal costs alone estimated at £1m? Or is the shit-chatter in fact the sender of messages including '[I] would love to leak those stories' and 'I want paying for this'? Or, to put it much more iconically, is the shit-chatter . . . Rebekah Vardy's account?

Whatever happens during both Coleen's cross-examination and the final judgment, the sheer volume of Vardy's dirty laundry that has been aired this week suggests the gavel has already come down in the court of public opinion. I have yet to see a non-sarcastic #TeamVardy hashtag out there in the wild. This trial is now by far the worst thing Rebekah has ever bought (including the yellow latex dress for the 2018 *TV Choice* Awards).

Admittedly, proceedings have added several hilarious entries to the annals of quotable quotes. The court heard how Vardy declared in 2019: 'Arguing with Coleen is like arguing with a pigeon. You can tell it that you are right and it is wrong, but it's still going to shit in your hair.' So at one end of London's Strand we have Nelson's Column in Trafalgar Square, and at the other end we have Rebekah Vardy in the high court. Both are covered in pigeon shit. Who wore it better?

Speaking of outfits, Coleen turned out for day two of the trial in a £32.99 Zara dress, arguably nailing the 'mum-of-four-who-literally-hasn't-got-time-for-this-bollocks' look. Rebekah, meanwhile, was in something vastly more expensive, having seemingly fallen for a stylist spiel along the lines of: 'I'm thinking Jackie O, with top notes of Amal Clooney.' It must be said that Rebekah has not been fantastically advised by a number of people around her in recent times, from anyone who failed to discourage her from issuing proceedings to the agent and close friend who somehow dropped the phone she had been ordered to retain into the North Sea during a boating excursion.

You know, the North Sea. Classic Wag holiday destination. This detail – merely one aspect of the Vardy team's full-spectrum data loss – yielded another quote of the trial, with Rooney's barrister, David Sherborne, observing deliberately obscurely that the phone 'is now in Davy Jones's locker'. Rebekah to the judge: 'I'm sorry, I don't know who Davy Jones is.' Oof. That horrendous-whitey moment when you think some guy called Davy Jones has somehow recovered the handset and cached it. Fortunately, perhaps, the phone remains somewhere beneath the waves, and is easily the most valuable North Sea resource since Brent crude.

So where did it all go wrong? If she leaked those stories, Rebekah's key social miscalculation was to fail to realise that ever since Coleen was thrust into the limelight as an innocent school-girl – and promptly derided as Queen of the Chavs, and voted

Britain's Worst-Dressed Woman of 2004 by some snooty tabloid – she has always prized loyalty above almost anything else. And, as you might expect from a proud Liverpool girl, she is not particularly crazy about the *Sun*. Anyone who cares to read the things Coleen has said down the decades would be left in absolutely no doubt as to her intense loyalty to family and friends, most of whom she goes back to childhood with. She likes fashion, yes – but she likes her mates and her family immeasurably more. (Total mensch, if we're honest.)

All this is the background to her now-legendary detective investigation – an attempt to prove that Vardy had betrayed a code that profoundly mattered. And there WAS a sisterly code among the Wags, back in the peak days of the 2006 World Cup. Contrary to the way a lot of the papers portrayed it, there wasn't catfighting and one-upmanship among the wives and girlfriends of the England team back in those era-defining Baden-Baden days. As Coleen noted furiously soon after: 'It makes a better story to say there were divisions in the camp.'

The Wags were monstered back then, of course, in another preposterous outbreak of tabloid snootiness. And the unwitting irony inherent in much of their monstering of Rebekah this week is that she is exactly what the papers want: the sort of person who might flog them unpleasant stories. If only there were literally decades of evidence that that would turn out to be a devil's bargain.

As for the lessons to be drawn from this epic rubberneckers' ball . . . if memory serves, I've written before about the wisdom or otherwise of talking to the press. Forgive the disloyalty to my profession, but my cast-iron advice to any friend who asks is always: don't. The experience is utterly asymmetric. It will be an infinitely bigger deal to you than it will be to them, and more often than not turns out in unfortunate ways you didn't predict.

What I haven't said is that this advice was really inspired by some that was given to me once by a very good lawyer and very good friend. And that advice was: never litigate. Never, never litigate, unless it is absolutely unavoidable. Unless we're talking about some serious crime, which is obviously different, then just don't go to court. Do anything to avoid it. It is totally consuming, and it weighs on you in a way it never could for all the lawyers making money off it (and off you). In the months and even years while you wait for your case to be heard, it'll be the first thing you think about when you wake up, and the last thing on your mind when you go to bed at night. In 99 out of 100 instances, the best advice is to leave it and get on with living your life.

Anyway, I merely pass it on. As Rebekah Vardy is perhaps now discovering, more than two and a half years after Coleen's fabled Instagram post, very few things in this life are more horrifyingly overrated than 'having your day in court'.

2017: STRONG AND STABLE

After an itchy finger sees her trigger Article 50 – the mechanism via which the UK will leave the EU – Theresa May goes full Dave Stewart. The Eurythmics star famously once opted to have his appendix taken out for no reason, later claiming he was suffering from something called Paradise Syndrome. May does something similar by calling a general election when there is no acute need, offering voters the choice between her and Jeremy Corbyn (aka the Argentina–West Germany final no one wants to see). Instead of getting away with it, like Stewart, May loses her majority and is effectively left on life support for the rest of her premiership. (Boris Johnson spends a lot of time hanging around the plug socket looking shifty.) Britain's divisions continue to be exploited by rightwing populists, who are at their most grimly opportunistic in the wake of two terror attacks. The first, in March, takes place in Westminster; the second at an Ariana Grande concert at the Manchester Arena in May. A total of 29 people die, including the attackers, while many hundreds sustain injuries.

Look out, America! Here comes Katie Hopkins with her London-loathing hate speech

23 March 2017

The country-living controversialist has long had it in for cities, but now the Westminster attack has given her the opportunity to hawk her views to a whole new audience on Fox News

Is there any animal, vegetable or mineral less London than Katie Hopkins? There are bits of the Outer Hebrides that have more of the capital to them than Katie, with her dull, self-satirising snobberies and clear sense that the city – perhaps all cities – are a joke in which no one cares to include her.

Needless to say, madam has rushed straight from the traps to put her stamp on the Westminster terror attack, with a gazillion-word *Daily Mail* thunk-piece on London. Or, as Katie has it: 'An entire city of monkeys: see no evil, hear no evil, speak no evil. Blind. Deaf. And dumb.' Mmm. It's like that bit in *Mean Girls* where the girl makes a histrionic speech in front of the whole school and the guy at the back says: 'She doesn't even go here!?'

'Liberals in London', Katie also declared, 'actually think multiculturalism means we all die together.' Um, you don't even go here!? YOU LIVE IN DEVON, MATE. I'm not going to say where, because it's not fair to cause a house price crash (and her exact location may be covered by some sort of Shitness Protection Programme).

Still, even as the police urge caution on the Westminster attack, Katie's intemperate intervention serves as a reminder that where some people see tragedy, others see tragitunity. 'No anger for me this time,' wrote Katie. 'No rage like I've felt before. No desperate urge to get out there and scream at the idiots who refused to see this coming.'

There was, however, a desperate urge to get booked on Fox News. And since this is a showbusiness column, may I congratulate Katie and her publicist in pulling the gig off this time. Katie seems marginally more frantic to break America than even Robbie Williams once was. The problem is that Over There hardly lacks for its own supply of reactionary wingnuts. And with a protectionist president openly demanding a return to American-made goods and services, a foreign purveyor of discord will rarely be first choice. Katie knows there will only be a few times a news producer is going to call her instead of Ann Coulter. The Westminster attack is one of them.

Consequently, we are in what Katie and her agent may well regard as a golden window. These are the hours and days you need to make count. She wants that phone ringing off the hook. She wants to graduate from Tucker Carlson to helping Sean Hannity talk about anything but Trump and the FBI. Deep down, she wants a *Vanity Fair* cover saying 'The Alt-Right Brits Are Coming', in which she and Nigel Farage are in bed like Patsy Kensit and Liam Gallagher were.

To read Katie Hopkins is to know that she would have disagreed with the Enlightenment if she thought there was a *Loose Women* appearance in it. She writes like a not-very-bright sixth-former trying to ape the prose style of Tony Parsons – no argument, just a portentous moodboard. Her Westminster article reads like a series of Google Calendar reminders to herself. 'Shots fired. An Asian man rushed to hospital. And I grew colder. And more tiny.'

Here she is on the rest of the country's relationship with London: 'We are taken under the cold water by this heavy right foot in the south, a city of lead . . .' Oof. Prose of lead. The concrete shoe of no verbs. Too many. Staccato sentences. Passing for gravitas. In fact, having performed a highly scientific linguistic analysis, I can confirm Katie uses fewer active verbs than even Tony Blair or John Keats. Presumably, it's because she really doesn't have anywhere to go, philosophically. Still, were Katie on hand now, I expect she would retort that what we say is more important than how we say it. In fact, I know she would, because it wasn't long ago that she said the diametric opposite. 'The thing that would hurt me', she told an interviewer, 'is if people suggested that I was bad at writing.'

For now, it falls to her to explain London to the Americans. 'Londoners can't even be honest about these attacks,' she told Fox News. 'Because it would mean everything they believed in was false.'

Ah, the false idols of the decadent metropolis! Had Katie spent more than 10 minutes in the World History aisle of Wikipedia, she would know there have always been people who hated cities for what they stood for. The metropolis has at many times served as shorthand for a kind of moral decay and wicked permissiveness that requires (usually forcible) regression.

'This place where monsters lurk and steal lives away in an instant,' thunders Katie of the capital's wickedness. 'For nothing.' Dear, dear – it does all seem rather terminal. I wonder what Katie would do with the failed, corruptive experiment that is London? The Khmer Rouge decided that the only solution was to empty the cities and send their suspiciously educated denizens to the country-side. Come Katie's revolution, perhaps Londoners will be forcibly migrated too.

Yes, in a sledgehammer irony that will nonetheless have escaped her, Abu Hopkins detests the liberalism of the city. A serial preacher of hate, she speaks of humans as cockroaches, and of non-military matters in terms of struggle and war. 'We stand divided,' she tweeted at Sadiq Khan, 'cowed by your religion.' She now seeks to demonise London among her faithful, calling for an end to its degenerate values in the most apocalyptic terms she can muster.

Fortunately – and I hardly need to state this – she will get about as far with such smallness as she will with breaking America. Devon's loss remains the capital's gain. For all the tragedies and assaults enfolded into its history, London is a city that will never be so defeated as to have the time to explain itself to Katie Hopkins.

Heroic humour or Katie Hopkins? This was a week to choose British values

26 May 2017

In its brave stewardship of his memory, the tribute offered by his brother to Martyn Hett, one of the Manchester victims, gives us all something to aspire to

From all I have read about the luminous-sounding Martyn Hett since he was murdered at the Manchester Arena on Monday night, he sounds like he would have relished his brother's jaw-droppingly brave stewardship of his memory in the days since. When Martyn's name began trending on Twitter, Dan Hett's response was a masterclass in sombre seemliness: 'He would, I think it's safe to say, be fucking loving this.'

The next day Mariah Carey posted a picture of Martyn in a Mariah Carey T-shirt, accompanied by a devastated quote about the death of a member of her fandom. His brother's response was one of those jokes that makes you gasp and laugh at the same time: 'I was a little dubious about Martyn's recent bold social media move,' he deadpanned. 'But it worked.'

God, the sheer balls of that. How on earth can he manage to be properly funny at such an unimaginably awful time? Properly, involuntary-laugh-inducingly, heartbreakingly, inspiringly, tragically hilarious? Their mother, Figen Murray – previously the beneficiary of one of Martyn's genuine social media moves, when he managed to sell out her under-appreciated knitting craft stall – clearly raised some extraordinarily spirited children. 'Martyn's life was not wasted,' she said in the most noble and dignified of interviews, as she held a clutch of knitted teddies.

I must say, I kept thinking of them as our old friend Abu Hopkins continued to preach hate on Twitter all week. Occasionally, there are cultural moments when it seems right to pick a direction – to turn towards those who offer an ideal of who we as people might wish to be, and turn away from those who offer nothing, and do even that artlessly. The horror of Manchester is one of those moments.

Whatever our idealised 'British values' are – and codifying them would obviously be appallingly against British values – they feel to me better embodied in the heroically black humour of Dan Hett in the days after his brother's murder than in anything Katie Hopkins has said or written, ever. In fact, were television's Vernon Kay to host an episode of the ITV show *Family Fortunes* in which 100 people were asked to name British values, humour would probably rank at number two, after democracy and before regarding 40 minutes of unpleasantries about the weather as our birthright. Without wishing to get too lost in speculation, any *Family Fortunes* contestant who answered, 'Calling for a final solution?' would probably earn their place in the quiz-show hall of shame. And yet, this was what Hopkins did call for, the very morning after the bombing. As she put it: 'We need a final solution.'

The bigger the horror, the smaller Katie has always seemed, and this week she appeared vanishingly so. Indeed, one of her employers – LBC radio – has decided this is the moment to vanish her entirely. This morning it was announced that madam was to leave the station by the exit marked 'mutual consent'.

No doubt, no doubt. Either way, there is no need to offer a syllable of congratulation to LBC, which went ahead and hired Hopkins even after she'd written a column describing migrants as cockroaches. Although I suppose it's possible that they're experiencing the last five years on a time lag, and are only up to 2013. They'll be really kicking themselves when they finally get up to speed.

Clearly, Katie's departure from the airwaves is hard lines for those who trade in fake Churchill quotes and the like, who have just discovered that free speech is the right to say what you like within the law, and not the right to have a boringly repetitive radio show. Who knew? For those catching up on this incredibly subtle distinction, and there do seem to be a few, Katie can still say whatever she likes on social media – and in the *Daily Mail*, for as long as Paul Dacre will retain her services.

But LBC seems to have decided, to adapt the senior officer in *Top Gun*, that Katie's ego was writing cheques her body couldn't cash. Then again, it is reported she has cost the *Mail* group at least £474,000 in libel damages and costs thus far, while she was found personally liable for £131,000 of the same after losing a case to the writer Jack Monroe. So it is possible that – how to put this? – Katie's hand may soon be writing cheques her bank account can't cash.

Still, this latest unemployment development is all exactly as predicted in *The Book of Hopkins*. As she explained portentously last year: 'One day I will say something that takes it so far over the line I will have to go and I accept that too. I think that is part of the condition of living your life on the line.' Living your life on the line ... I do like how Katie makes 'being a twat on the radio' sound like fighting in 'Nam.

Even so, I'm afraid our contestant doesn't get to take a lot home with her. We must relieve her of her favourite poses, with this week's 'suffer the children to come to me' a case in point. Never forget that Katie Hopkins gives so much of a toss about the children affected by an extremist murder that she has pursued a relentless online vendetta against Brendan Cox, who has the temerity to have been widowed by a rightwing extremist last year.

Similarly, you never heard her say anything about the horrific murder of schoolchildren at Sandy Hook, or any of the other school shootings in the United States. Being furious about that isn't going to get her booked on Fox News, and consequently it wouldn't get a run-out in one of her 3,000-word, five-verb columns.

Perhaps the only thing Katie does get to take home is her antipathy to laughter. But then, the defining characteristic of self-styled 'voices of the people' is their total and utter humourlessness, which has its roots in a terror of being undermined.

Katie's spiritual analogue is Roderick Spode, P. G. Wodehouse's piss-take of Oswald Mosley, and a chap to whom Bertie Wooster is moved to remark: 'The trouble with you, Spode, is that just because you have succeeded in inducing a handful of half-wits to disfigure the London scene by going about in black shorts, you think you're someone. You hear them shouting "Heil, Spode!" and you imagine it is the Voice of the People. That is where you make your bloomer. What the Voice of the People is saying is: "Look at that frightful ass Spode swanking about in footer bags! Did you ever in your puff see such a perfect perisher?"'

Well, did you? Certainly, Katie has her followers. They always have their followers: horrendous, needy bores who, had they had different starts in life, might have found themselves drawn into the orbit of alternative preachers of hate. But their cause is not – to borrow an insult they can understand – true Britishness. It is a perverted form of Britishness, because it has *no jokes*. Ever. At all. If I may be so presumptuously bold, Martyn Hett's brother contains more Britishness in his typing thumb than Ms Hopkins contains in her entire output. His spirit will remain something to which we can truly aspire, long after hers has gone the way of all Spodes.

Boris: guaranteed to bring the house down and not get buried in the rubble

6 June 2017

When this general election was called, the foreign secretary was briefed against as a liability. Now he's being called up as a charismatic safe-hands figure

Tell you which police haven't been cut: ones outside Boris Johnson's campaign events. Not only were there plenty to begin with outside the County Durham venue where the foreign secretary made a short speech on Tuesday in front of about 40 party supporters, but the presence of a similar number of Labour activists chanting outside apparently warranted a call for backup. Further officers duly arrived at the back door, while Johnson remained secure inside the building.

'We were on a training day but we've been redeployed,' one officer said. 'It must be bad because we've been called in.' Bad? Well, there were a couple of double buggies, a man in a wheelchair and some rather unmannerly shouts at local Tories departing in their X-Types and so on. But we're not talking the Iranian embassy siege. Easily the most disturbing aspect of it was the enthusiastic chant of 'Backdoor Boris! Backdoor Boris! Backdoor Boris!' File that one under Movie Titles You Can Now Never Unsee.

Inside, things had been only marginally more seemly. 'We've spent £31bn on Trident,' Boris enthused, in one attack on Jeremy Corbyn's nuclear beliefs. 'What is the point of sending it to sea with no missiles on board, so the whole country's literally firing blanks!' Damn straight. That's how we need to see Britain – as the sort of virile, charismatically rogueish country who can knock up a woman just by looking at her. (Probably easier all round if she doesn't keep it, though.)

The speech was nominally about Britain's decision to break up with the EU, with the warm-up music being Adele's 'Someone Like You', a song about moving on – or otherwise – after the end of a relationship. We wish nothing but the best for Brussels, I'm sure. But as Boris explained: 'It is time to lift our eyes to a wider horizon! . . . We have so much to look forward to!'

Mmm. And sometimes it hurts instead. Perhaps keen to remember the good times, Boris was still trumpeting a McKinsey report that said Britain would be the largest economy in Europe by 2030 – a report that came out in 2015, the year before the Brexit vote. Still, on with the show. 'Just imagine the scene in Brussels if Jeremy Corbyn was to mosey in.' Team Corbyn negotiating would be 'a family of herbivores at a watering hole for lions'. The EU was 'a great glutinous conglomerate of privileged interests' (a line which would probably work better as his Twitter biography).

Boris's rhetorical style is a matter of taste. The level of self-congratulation with which he produces a phrase like 'tricephalous monster' marks him out as the classic stupid-person's-idea-of-a-clever-person, but among the faithful it is undeniable that some of his most recycled lines still bring the house down. And the lovely thing is, he's never buried in the rubble.

What about the reports that the Italian intelligence agencies had warned their UK counterparts about the man named as the third London Bridge attacker? 'I'm not familiar with the details of the investigation that you've just announced.' Look, he isn't going to talk about something he hasn't got a clue about – he's not Diane Abbott.

Back when the election was called, Boris was briefed against as a liability who would be firmly sidelined throughout. Now – in seemingly less stable times – he's been called up as a charismatic safe-hands figure. (A Bruce Grobbelaar, certainly.) Was it panic measures? Of course not, Boris insisted, almost able to keep the relish out of his voice. Theresa May and her team had done wonderfully. She had a plan. She had just made an excellent speech.

To which the only realistic response is: do me a favour. Even if the Conservatives win extremely well, many Tories believe that May has been found out by the campaign. There is – how to put this? – something of the shite about her. In fact, in terms of what it has exposed about May, calling the election has been the equivalent of the prime minister swimming a mile out into the Atlantic and cutting off her arm. To adapt Peter Benchley's famous opening line: the Tory big fishes are now moving silently through the night water.

For many people, Boris making another leadership comeback would be a plotline as preposterous and unwelcome as that of *Jaws: The Revenge* (the one where a disgruntled pal of the original shark follows Chief Brody's widow to the Bahamas. Caine stars). On the other hand, it's the classic Bullingdon move: smash the place up by pulling off the Brexit vote, leave boring little Theresa to clean up that ghastly mess, then swan back in to take charge in 2019 on the slogan 'Uncork the wine, Fallon, there's a good chap.'

Whether Boris's #massivelegend appeal would break up on contact with the Watford Gap is, of course, something that has never properly been tested. And as long as he keeps hiding in community centres, we will remain tantalisingly in the dark on that point.

The PM is like a deadbeat dad who's gambled away the housekeeping

9 June 2017

And then solemnly explains to the kids that only he can deliver the strength and stability they need

It's important to remember that the worst thing Theresa May had ever done before this election result was to run through some wheat fields. So while she may have been on the Tory authorities' radar at some point, there was nothing in her record to suggest she posed this level of security risk. Despite helming a campaign with more suspiciously unforced errors than the first round of a tennis grand slam, though, Prime Minister May has no intention of resigning. Is this a bit like when she had no intention of calling an election? Either way, I hope the BBC is already cutting a farewell montage of her best bits to Sting's 'Fields of Gold'. 'We'll remember her, when the West Wing blows, upon the fields of barley . . .' Or however it goes.

Jeremy Corbyn, meanwhile, has got 'Eye of the Tiger'. 'Went the distance, now he's back on his feet – just a man and his will to survive.' And he didn't even trade his passion for glory. Or, as the Labour leader put it: 'I think it's pretty clear who won this election.' Is it? I assume someone broke the news to him off camera. Could have been awkward outside Buckingham Palace otherwise – I hear the doorman's a bit of a jobsworth.

Elsewhere, and before the day is out, most of the political class are to be forcibly tattooed – choice of our foreheads or the arses we talk out of – with William Goldman's famous dictum about Hollywood: Nobody knows anything. I mean, really. Really. With a few notable exceptions, there are uncontacted Amazon tribes with more of a clue – certainly ones that are less prone to collective failures of imagination. In fact, if you'd flown a plane over north-west Brazil last week, you might have spotted some rocks and pottery or whatnot arranged into a giant message reading 'You're all going to drop a complete bollock with this youth turnout stuff'.

That said, it wasn't the biggest one dropped. Last year, David Cameron gambled and lost. Now, May has gambled and lost. Guys, when the fun stops, stop.

And it was hard lines too for the Tories' Aussie strategist Lynton Crosby, the so-called 'Wizard of Oz', who has now reached his pay-no-attention-to-the-man-behind-the-curtain moment. Received wisdom was that the Tory election machine was a crack special forces unit. So thanks for the laugh, Delta Farce! Crosby has masterminded a campaign akin to one of those *Funniest Home Videos*, where someone attempts to light their own farts and ends up in hospital. They're still the government, but they'll never use the bathroom in the same way again.

They wouldn't be the government, of course, without having made a pact with those cuddly cuties of the Democratic Unionist party (DUP). Quite how long Tory high command will continue to tolerate May remains to be seen. Her return to Downing Street came against a backdrop of menacing silences from the likes of Boris Johnson, while ministers lost no time in briefing the *Telegraph* that she would face a leadership challenge should she water down Brexit. So it turns out May *has* revived a traditional bloodsport – just not the one she mentioned in her manifesto.

Look, I know a lot of bleeding hearts are always appalled by the sight of the Conservative party in pursuit as a wounded leader desperately tries to get back to its foxhole. But I'm afraid those hand-wringers simply don't understand the traditions involved or the wonderful community bonds that are forged over the activity. Well done to May for supporting its return.

Many Tories will be hoping the hounds are offered an hors d'oeuvre in the form of May's two special advisers, Nick Timothy and Fiona Hill, who were about as popular as syphilis before the campaign even kicked off, and are now at Ebola levels. If so, they would be joined on the general election 2017 obituary reel by any hope of a second Scottish independence referendum, as well as the now-resigned Ukip leader Paul Nuttall. Owing to some auto-parodic failure to be registered to vote where he was standing, Nuttall didn't even manage to vote for himself.

Nigel Farage, meanwhile, is furious, so is welcome to stand for parliament again and do something meaningful about it. Eighth time's a charm. Until then, the only TV shows he should be booked on are *I'm a Celebrity* or Danny Dyer's *Most Washed-Up Men*.

The other death in the family is May's 'stronger hand' shtick. This was the notion, shat on by several game theorists over the age of seven, that the size of May's victory would strengthen her negotiating position in Brussels. She has revealed herself to be a poker player with skills and cunning roughly analogous to those of Homer Simpson, who is dealt four jacks and cocks it all up by dancing round the room.

Yet May remains painfully unable to pivot. Having destabilised everything with an election she called unnecessarily – and having done so on a 'stability' platform – her genuine verdict was that 'the country needs a period of stability'. You what, madam? This is like some deadbeat dad coming home after having lost all the house-keeping money on the nags and explaining solemnly to his kids that only he can deliver the stability they need. Though not the food.

As for those against whom she sought the 'stronger hand', the Europeans with whom we begin Brexit negotiations in 10 – yes, 10! – days, they are the soul of discretion. According to the EU's chief negotiator, Michel Barnier: 'Brexit negotiations should start when the UK is ready.' And I think we know that 'when the UK is ready' is diplomatic-speak for 'when the UK is at least house-broken'. It's all very well history repeating itself as farce, but when farce is repeating itself as farce, any comment feels like intruding on private grief. Or as the Germans preferred to put it, they wouldn't be commenting on the results 'out of respect and politeness'.

Whichever way you slice it, then, this latest shitshow must finally bury the cherished delusion that British politics is somehow like *Game of Thrones*, as opposed to what it actually is: a gif of Norman Wisdom and a banana skin. And a political class that keeps forgetting what happens next.

Still, you have to laugh. Don't you? For those of us who like political merriment – and, frankly, you might as well get into it – another boggling summer stretches ahead, with the odds on another election later this year currently set at 11–10. So come on – lean into the lunacy, buy shares in distilleries now, and let us continue to add to the gaiety of other nations.

May's breakup speech made Brexit sound magical . . . if you're drinking Bacardi

22 September 2017

The prime minister's set-piece in Florence was as platitudinous as ever. Only in a parallel universe does it spell the start of a beautiful new partnership

I increasingly picture Brexit as one of those criminally underwhelming Christmas theme parks in which the UK specialises. You know the ones: visitors are sold expensive tickets to a magical wonderland, and turn up expectantly to find a muddy car park with brawling elves, a grotto that turns out to be two strings of fairy lights inside a Portaloo, and a chained, motionless husky which, you tell your kids, is 'probably just sleeping'. There are at least a couple of these festive horror shows annually. As one of the elves at the infamous Lapland New Forest informed customers a few years back: 'Santa's gone home. Santa's fucking dead.' The two men who sold tickets to that one on a false prospectus ended up being sentenced to 13 months each.

I see Boris Johnson is still redrafting his own Brexit prospectus, most recently in a *Daily Telegraph* article that spent much of the week threatening to derail Theresa May's major speech, if not to presage his own resignation. Why? Because that's just the shit the Tories pull these days. There is nothing so perilously unstable they couldn't somehow contrive to destabilise it further. Nothing gets them hotter than the clock ticking or the possibility of running each other out. Instead of taking back control they find new ways to be incontinent. You can tell the people who got us into this mess were former journalists, because despite having just the 50 years to work out what type of deal they wanted, the cabinet is doing it right on deadline.

And so to May's speech, heralded by some as a big reset that would clarify a UK approach that might hitherto have been euphemised as cryptic. It took place in front of a backdrop reading 'Shared history. Shared challenges. Shared future', which is Italian for 'Is it too late if we stop being delusional? It is, isn't it?' The Florentine location suggested that the government has now spent easily as much time laying the ground for multi-layered Renaissance metaphors as they have wondering vaguely what's going to happen to the automotive industry in 18 months' time.

That said, the odd thing does seem to have become clearer. May has now asked for a two-year transition deal, which would give the UK unfettered access to the single market in return for us accepting both free movement and the fact that Nigel Farage is going to completely wet his pants.

The optics in Florence were slightly better for May than they were at her speech at the UN earlier this week, which pictures showed was as sparsely attended as a one-woman Edinburgh fringe show about self-harm. Delivery-wise, though, there were no surprises. The prime minister came across as the most humourless and uptight Brit in Florence since Maggie Smith threw open her casement at the start of *A Room with a View* and discovered the prospect of a brick wall. 'I thought we were going to see the Arno,' says Helena Bonham-Carter, in the tone of voice one might otherwise reserve for the observation 'I thought there was going to be a grotto,' or 'I thought we were going to have an extra £350m a week for the NHS.'

For the past few months, May's messaging strategy has been predicated on the fact that the EU doesn't have the internet. Thus, you can spend a year being as rude and dismissive about them as you like for the benefit of the media back home, then fly to Europe and smilingly urge them to 'be creative', and everyone will take kindly to it.

To call the speech optimistic doesn't really cover it. Many of the lines had the flavour of something you'd say if you were leaving your wife of 40 years for a Babestation presenter who'd once read out one of your texts. This period could be remembered 'not for a relationship that ended, but a new partnership that began'. Well, I mean . . . it COULD be. *If* you're drinking Bacardi. (Incidentally, my favourite story of the week suggested that civil servants in David Davis's department are so concerned about the lack of preparation for a no-deal scenario that they have begun writing emails stating the perils, to cover their backs in preparation for the inevitable Chilcot-style inquiry when it all goes tits-up.)

This was a breakup speech that again reminded Europe that it was not us; it was them. But the fact remains that if you had killer information that you had to protect at all costs, the text of a Theresa May speech would be the place to conceal it. So instantly forgettable is anything she says that it is highly possible she has been fitted with a perception filter.

Thanks to advance briefings, we already knew that Britain would fork out at least £20bn by way of an exit bill, which Boris

Johnson has repeatedly suggested we shouldn't pay. At least when the Bullingdon Club smashed things up they left a cheque at the end. Then again, in later life Boris has been – how to put this delicately because of the others involved? – less *present* to deal with the consequences of his actions. I suppose on the scale of things one can just walk away from in life, the EU isn't the most unforgivable.

As for Boris's own manoeuvres, his allies seem to think he has done enough this week to be able to resign later and say he told them so. What a man of principle he remains. I am reminded of a passage I shrieked with laughter at in his book about Churchill (a work that obviously turned out to be a thinly veiled fantasy portrait of himself). 'To some extent all politicians are gamblers with events,' this ran. 'They try to anticipate what will happen, to put themselves on the right side of history.'

Remarkably, Boris characterised Churchill's 1930s opposition to Hitler as just this type of self-motivated punt. Churchill 'put his shirt on a horse called anti-Nazism . . . and his bet came off in spectacular fashion'. Dear, dear. If only we had Churchill's other column – the one where he argued the case for a fascist dictatorship, *Lebensraum* and the elimination of Jews from Germany. Still, as Johnson went on to note of Churchill, these kinds of reputation-stakings 'gave him the chance to test his egocentric thesis that he was special'.

At least the focus returning to May on Friday afternoon offered a brief opportunity to forget Brexit's Special One. But, for the prime minister's part, her speech showed her to have once again identified the wrong sort of deficit in her Brexit approach. The problem is not that she hasn't been positively, repetitively platitudinous enough; it is that she has never begun to outline the specific negatives to those expecting a cakewalk. She may never acquire the courage to admit it – and her less washed-up colleagues are still too treacherously ambitious to do so – but Santa's gone home. Santa's dead.

From Boris the Lion King to Theresa May's P45 – my malarial week at the Tory conference

4 October 2017

A bogglingly unsuccessful few days in Manchester showed that the Conservatives are less the natural party of government than cowboy builders who really ought to stop trying to 'fix' things

By the end of the Conservative party conference, Theresa May had suffered so many painful betrayals and humiliations that she should have ditched her speech and dropped a 60-minute visual album on Tidal instead. A lot of people wouldn't have begrudged her the chance to stalk along the street in a yellow dress, baseball-batting a few cars.

That, clearly, would have been a show of strength a million miles beyond the prime minister – currently third among equals, dropping down the rankings fast and agonisingly handed a P45 by a bottom-tier comedian during her own coughed-out conference speech. Even bits of the set were trying to escape. She had already spent four days in Manchester having to suck up all manner of indignities, while Boris Johnson's address concluded: 'Let the lion roar!' Thanks, Uncle Scar! But you probably want to wipe Mufasa's blood off your chin before you get the party faithful to sing along to 'The Circle of Life'.

I lost count of the number of things that were obviously being said for a dare. 'We were pleased with the way it went,' judged May's spokesman of her speech. 'I witnessed a great speech from a prime minister at the top of her game,' declared Michael Gove. 'That is their cosmic role in life,' explained James Cleverly about Labour, 'to screw things up, so we can come and fix them.' Has he not been paying attention for the past two years? The Tories are like something out of *Cowboy Builders*: they tell you that you need a new boiler, and by the time they're done, you've got no roof, a sinkhole and euro parity. For the love of God, guys, please stop fixing things.

May herself was asked if she would change tack and do the leaders' television debates during the next general election. I mean, really . . . you might as well ask her if she's going to take four strikers to the Qatar World Cup. 'Weak leadership', she said later, 'is having a cabinet full of yes-men.' A reminder of how lucky we are to live in the time of this inspiring *Team of Rivals* reboot. With the Brexiteers, it was mostly excruciatingly easy to see what they were playing at. 'We are the country of William Shakespeare and Jane Austen,' announced David Davis, 'of Alexander Fleming and James Dyson.' Assuming anyone can join in this game: we are the country of John Milton and George Eliot, of Isaac Newton and that guy who owns Wetherspoons.

But before we go on: the science bit. Last year, the Tories were bedding in for a good 15 years of uninterrupted rule; this year they were coming to terms with the fact that the bed had been shat. 'We had an election that nobody expected to take place,' said party chairman Patrick McLoughlin. The snap election had caught the Tories off guard, May explained to *The House* magazine, recalling that moment a highly emotional Withnail accosts a farmer and explains: 'We've gone on holiday by mistake!' The Tories seemed to have called an election by mistake.

This conference was a bogglingly unsuccessful attempt to contain the fallout, which repeatedly threatened to spill over into open recrimination. Everywhere you went, you could hear party members muttering furiously about wanting big ideas, a big vision. Yet the main vision they were offered by main-stage speakers was the dystopian one of Jeremy Corbyn being in No. 10. Thus, by the time of May's almost unwatchable speech announcing a council-house building programme, it felt logical to ask: if he's so appalling, why are your only memorable policies ones you've nicked off him (or, in the case of the energy cap, off Ed Miliband)? Forgive me, that's unfair. May had raised the curtain on the conference with a promise of a 'revolution in tuition fees', which turned out to be keeping them at the same level. Chris Grayling announced 'a revolution in rail ticketing', which turned out to be the chance to get your season ticket on your smartphone. The key revolution seemed to be in the definition of the word 'revolution'.

Other unhinged moments? No one could fail to salute whichever Tory brain judged that this already toxic conference would benefit from issuing a guest pass to Katie Hopkins. It's akin to surveying survivors of the *Lusitania* and thinking: 'You know what would really lift the spirits round here? A visit from Typhoid Mary.' For reasons I briefly considered researching before deciding not to bother, Katie had got herself up in a full wedding dress for her turn at a fringe event. All that effort and still only the second-most irksome and publicity-crazed blond at the conference.

And so, without delay, to wantaway foreign secretary Boris Johnson, the blond black hole, whose gravitational pull is such that nothing here could resist it. He's not so much a cabinet minister as an event horizon. Almost entirely because of Boris, the Tories now resemble a franchise of the reality TV show *Real Housewives*: a cast of behaviourally incontinent people with zero idea of how to act when people are looking at them, with the most ambitious star seemingly having decided that conflict is winsome. Boris's May-undermining *Sun* interview on the eve of conference was the intellectual equivalent of pouring a whisky sour over the head of someone called Cristee, yet was analysed as though it were one of Talleyrand's more complex gambits. According to what one cabinet minister told the *Financial Times*: 'Boris's own psychology is a matter of infinite fascination.' Only to Boris, surely. For the rest of us, a one-word diagnosis always suffices. Having said that, two-word analyses were not in short supply. According to various ministerial briefings, these ran the full gamut from 'vain tit' to 'fat fucker'.

The general consensus was that Boris actively wanted to be sacked: a political version of suicide-by-cop. It's a little flattering to him, but after this week we must finally accept that Johnson is the Tories' Raoul Moat. Like Moat's story, Boris's will eventually end the way it was always going to end; it's just a question of how many people/economic regions/diplomatic relationships he takes down with him on the way.

Over the course of the conference, I heard several former loyalists advancing the theory that their former darling had finally gone too far. And by the time Boris was answering a *Newsnight* query as to where the 'red lines' row had come from with a 'Search me, guv!', it was hard not to be reminded of Sharon Stone down the cop shop in *Basic Instinct*. As that earlier exhibitionist reasons: 'I'd have to be pretty stupid to write a book about killing and then kill someone the way I described it in my book.' Yup, well. SPOILERS.

Even so, the foreign secretary's confidence did seem to have been slightly dampened by the time he got to his speech, which leaned less heavily than usual on a rhetorical style best summarised as: 'Let me impregnate you with my word-seed.' Consider its rather wan conclusion: 'We are not the lion. We do not claim to be the lion. That role is played by the people of this country. But it is up to us now – in the traditional non-threatening, genial and self-deprecating way of the British – to let that lion roar.' As Steven Seagal is forced to inquire in *Under Siege*: 'What kind of babbling bullshit is this?'

The only possible satisfaction to be gleaned was in imagining Johnson's reaction to being eclipsed on the fringe by Jacob Rees-Mogg – that bumptious squit from F block, in the parlance of their school. Moggmania is clearly a midsummer night's *Downton* wank from which the party should have awoken by now, but it was all the rage in Manchester. To see the queues outside the North East Somerset MP's events and the party members running after him in the street for selfies was to picture Boris somewhere across town, smashing his magic mirror and preparing a poisoned apple.

For his part, Rees-Mogg turned in various scenery-chewing performances at no fewer than nine fringe meetings. He is now at that stage in an overexposed starlet's career when they've got four independent films in pre-production and have just made the gatefold cover of *Vanity Fair*'s 'Young Hollywood' issue. To couch this in terms Rees-Mogg would instinctively understand: let's hope it doesn't all go Mischa Barton from here. As far as that other rising star goes, Scottish Tory leader Ruth Davidson mostly stayed well out of it, bar her speech on opening day, possibly concerned that too much fraternisation with colleagues from south of the border might result in her catching total inadequacy.

Was there any light relief at the conference centre? Well, there was a massage tent in the shape of a cloud, sponsored 'lounges', and a retail area known as 'the maker's market'. This amounted to various opportunities to buy pashminas, terrible art and plenty of scented candles.

Unfortunately, there was nothing on sale to mask the stench of 'natural wastage', which seems to be the Tories' euphemism of choice for the fact that the average age of their members is around the 70 mark. 'The truth is we've all been caught rather blindsided by this,' confessed George Freeman, chairman of the PM's policy board. And yet, looking back, perhaps there was the odd clue that this sort of reckoning was in the post. The endless giveaways to baby boomers. The pollsters who used to cheerfully explain that the only demographic one needed to pay less attention to than young people was dead people. The sense among the constituency associations that Iain Duncan Smith was a nice young man.

Either way, the party does now seem to have become aware that it has a couple of problems with young voters. The first problem is that it doesn't have any, and the second is that the definition of young stretches to anything under 48. This made the thrice-hourly cautionary reminders of the 1970s from the likes of Philip Hammond seem rather misguided. At this rate, the Tories might have to accept the inconvenient affront that even some people who can remember the Winter of Discontent prefer Jeremy Corbyn to them.

And yet . . . it must be must be said that for all their wanton ineptitude, and at times grotesque dysfunction, the Tories are still polling around 40%. Meanwhile, in the last count by YouGov – the firm that called the election most accurately – Theresa May led Jeremy Corbyn by eight points on who would make the best prime minister.

Each party – even given their occasionally radioactive levels of self-regard – must be privately gripped by one question: how the hell are we not thrashing this lot? Behind closed doors, both sides must surely be experiencing something of the sensation that has memorably attended various England football internationals down the years. Namely: 'How is it possible we're 1–0 down/only 1–0 up to a ski resort/country with the population of Bristol?'

At moments such as these, most England fans know all too well what that says about their side. Yet neither the Tories nor Labour – both of which can't wait to tell you how historically useless the other lot are – seem even dimly aware of what their failure to put themselves comfortably ahead against that kind of adversary says about them.

Consider how each has characterised the other. Do the Tories wonder in private: 'How is it possible we're not 6–0 up against Venezuela's commie king-over-the-water? What does that say about us?' Do Labour wonder in private: 'How is it possible we're not 6–0 up against this empty-of-ideas, toddler's *telenovela* of a government after seven long years of austerity? What does that say about us?'

The numbers suggest that at present Labour and the Conservatives are not far from evenly matched, while each side openly professes themselves the natural party of government. Yet we might hesitate to characterise them as what is known in fiction as 'worthy foes'.

You know the sort of thing: they're such class acts that when they meet in battle, one adversary might break off momentarily to compliment the other's swordsmanship and say what a shame it is that they're going to have to kill them.

No, as conference season draws to a close, it feels a stretch to imagine we are watching two equally formidable adversaries grappling at the Reichenbach Falls. Two drunks fighting in a puddle feels more like it. We might get a clear victor, we might not. But let's not be deluded as to the quality of the spectacle.

Oh yes, May's 'sticking it' to Brussels. Like a zebra sticking it to a lion pack

20 October 2017

The prime minister's pleas to EU leaders haven't fully paid off, it seems. Her captors' response is that the torture bit isn't over yet

Theresa May is now contractually obliged to appear only in footage that can be soundtracked by Coldplay whining about how easy it isn't. Watching her in scenes from the European Council summit in Brussels, it sometimes seems she's already biting her lip and turning away in slow motion, sparing the *News at Ten* the task of editing it for the montage.

Still, at least the EU has now agreed to start internal discussions on how it will approach the second phase of talks on trade with the UK. This offer has all the bonhomie and promise of a captor telling his victim that while the torture bit is not yet over, they can start the desperate bargaining phase in parallel. The problem, we keep hearing, is that we have a lame duck negotiating for us. Who do lame ducks negotiate with? Acas-trained foxes? Farmers-of-few-words bearing down on them with a ligature and a sack?

As she repeatedly stated, May called the snap election because 'other parties' were trying to frustrate the Brexit process, and because a bigger majority would give her a 'stronger hand' in negotiations with the EU. Anyhow . . . here we are now. Don't sprain your eyeballs rolling them, but the greatest enemy to the Brexit process is the wingnuts in her own party, while No. 10 briefings are suggesting her weakness is our ace in the hole.

According to *The Times*, government sources told them the prime minister had made a series of weekend phone calls in which she 'stuck it' to EU leaders about the reality of her political predicament. Please don't question this use of the term 'stuck it'. If you've ever watched one of those wildlife documentaries where a zebra 'sticks it' to a lion pack, you'll know what a powerful line of attack that can be.

Even so, given the reliance on poker analogies that has sustained the government for over a year now, one has to ask: in what poker games do you see people using begging and weakness as a strategy? That's right: games in which some stupid deadbeat has just lost the money for his kids' food and is imploring the guys to go easy on him or his wife will sling him out.

What an adorable irony it is that the Brexiteers went into the referendum effectively casting the UK as 007 at the peak of his game. We are now literally begging Le Chiffre for our car keys back, while he cries bloody tears of laughter over our predicament. Yes, the *Casino Royale* villain's lachrymal tic was the worst poker tell in the history of the game – until the UK premiered 'Please help me: I am being propped up by the DUP and am holding a 2–7 offsuit.'

Even after the Conservative party conference and that astonishingly brutal spectacle in the Coughosseum, it seems May's torments are going to become only more exquisite. Not only is time causing her negotiating position to decay faster than a corpse in a hothouse, but she is condemned to do it all with the least helpful noises-off possible.

In Westminster, Tory MPs are reaching their constituents the best way they know how without using hand sanitiser: by slagging off the EU27's behaviour on the airwaves and in the papers. This approach is either reliant on the assumption that no one in the EU has the internet or that the White Cliffs of Dover serve as a perception filter that prevents the Continent from seeing what they're up to.

Over in Kensington, meanwhile, single-issue newspaper editor George Osborne continues to roll exactly the same undermining front page out of his *Bagpuss* chocolate biscuit mill each day. (Brave of the *Evening Standard* editor to go so relentlessly after May on competence, when he is surely due some competence questions of his own by now. Four months on, where is even the start of his landmark, agenda-setting investigation into Grenfell Tower, the biggest story of his editorship? Or is he just going to keep splashing with his one joke about the person who sacked him? Something to keep a raised eyebrow on.)

Meanwhile, 38,000 feet over the Atlantic, May's arrival in Brussels was overshadowed by Goldman Sachs's boss, Lloyd Blankfein, tweeting: 'Just left Frankfurt. Great meetings, great weather, really enjoyed it. Good, because I'll be spending a lot more time there. #Brexit.' Every cloud, and all that. Except not really. Unfortunately, Blankfein is a guy who knows the only thing more apocalyptically monstrous than him is the reality that we actually need him for sustenance. For the UK, accepting this is like accepting that a tragic but essential co-dependency has sprung up between you and the alien protruding from your chest cavity.

Having said that, perhaps we're underestimating the potential no-deal solution that is transport secretary Chris Grayling's brainwave for UK farmers to just grow more food. If you missed this plan, which I like to think of as the Great Leap Backward, it was outlined last Sunday by the minister with arguably the strongest claim to be the Westminster village idiot. Let's simply cut to the reviews. 'I was just horrified,' said the chair of British Summer Fruits. 'Our farmers are unable to find labour this year, let alone after Brexit.' 'This is not about ploughing the verges to grow more food,' judged the deputy president of the National Farmers' Union. 'It's about the absence of any food policy. We haven't had a food policy for 43 years.'

Oh. Perhaps we now do? Perhaps we should have realised that when Boris Johnson promised 'sunlit uplands' after Brexit, he meant that we were all going to be forcibly tilling said uplands, probably with Grayling as our gangmaster.

Elsewhere in subtweets of the prime minister, it certainly doesn't look as though we should be pinning hopes on cutting all sorts of exciting deals with Donald Trump's America. On Friday the US president released his latest evidence-free tweet-mugging-off of Britain, declaring: 'Just out report: "United Kingdom crime rises 13% annually amid spread of Radical Islamic terror." Not good, we must keep America safe!' Oh dear. I know that if you're a citizen of the world, you're a citizen of nowhere. But the big no-deal question is: if you're a trader with the world, could you end up being a trader with nowhere? (Asking for Liam Fox.)

Something for May to be 'very clear about' as her torment drags on, anyway. In the meantime, no one in Britain could be said to be doing very well out of the past few months. With the exception of Coldplay, obviously, whose residuals may soon become as economically indispensable to the exchequer as the remaining staff at Goldman Sachs.

Coming next, a Brexit divorce: the kind that involves the police

8 December 2017

Forget Gwyneth Paltrow's idea of a conscious uncoupling. On the evidence so far, this will be anger, rancour and tears

To Brussels, where, according to football's Michael Gove: 'The final whistle has blown and the prime minister has won.' The manager's safe for another week, then. Unfortunately, Arlene Foster has been brought in as director of football. Still, this is probably my favourite Gove reaction shot since he said of Theresa May's coughed-out conference speech horror show: 'I thought it was a fantastic conference speech from a prime minister at the top of her game.'

Luckily, Gove doesn't have a reputation for self-deluding treachery, or the prime minister would be watching her back right about now. Also paying May a compliment she couldn't refuse was Boris Johnson, who on Friday morning congratulated her and looked forward to 'remaining true to the referendum result – taking back control of our laws, money and borders for the whole of the UK.' Yup. There's still everything to slay for.

The upshot, for now, seems to be that the magical thinking on the Irish border is going to be allowed to continue for a bit longer. Even so, the tone of the European commission president, Jean-Claude Juncker, in his joint press conferences with May is always akin to the one José Mourinho might adopt towards the manager of a League One side that his reserves have just knocked out in the FA Cup fourth round. She's a tough opponent, she doesn't make it easy for them . . .

Friday morning's post-match interview was stagily gracious to someone who clearly hasn't troubled the EU's defences for so

112

much as 30 seconds. For her part, May's claim that the process 'hasn't been easy for either side' was confirmation that at any stage it would have been perfectly safe for the EU keeper to have popped round the back of the net to have a fag and do a sudoku.

Obviously, not everyone is pretending to be happy. Pantwetter-in-chief is Nigel Farage, Britain's biggest comeback-seeker, who persists in seeing himself as a Terminator figure when he's actually just Norma Desmond. Much as he must be enjoying graveyard appearances on Fox News and endorsing alleged paedophiles for Steve Bannon, Farage is comically desperate to get back into politics. 'A deal in Brussels is good news for Mrs May,' he spat, 'as we can now move on to the next phase of humiliation.' I love the idea that a man who conceded then unconceded defeat *twice* at his own referendum-night party would have the nerve, let alone the brain, to do any better.

Even so, Farage's underlying point is instructive because it's one that's becoming more widespread among hardline Brexiteers. Namely: Brexit would be amazing, except it's being done wrong. Advocates of this view remind me of those people who think the primary problem with communism is just that it wasn't done right by the Soviets. Over the years, I have spoken to various individuals who will tell you that Stalin obviously went too far – 25 million's rather a lot, isn't it? – but who fairly blithely concede that a certain number of deaths was inevitable; call it a round 10 (million). That these same people regard the Iraq war as the greater stain on the conscience of the left always seemed to me quite the curiosity, albeit one that should be examined only when wearing rubber gloves.

There are already several variants of this afoot, as far as Brexit is concerned. There's Farage, obviously. There's the provisional wing of the leave campaign saying the problem with Brexit is that it's being delivered by the establishment. There's the Vote Leave director, Dominic Cummings, saying it would have been great, if only we had rebooted the civil service entirely.

There's something rather Stalinist about Brexit's wreakers of so-called creative destruction. In his *Memoirs of a Revolutionary*, Victor Serge quotes the Romanian writer Panait Istrati, when the latter visited the 1930s USSR of purges and show trials. 'All right, I can see the broken eggs,' he said. 'Where is this omelette of yours?'

Maybe the omelette's coming with phase two of the talks, on to which we now move. If you've spent the past eight months thinking, 'What this shitshow needs is to hear more from Liam Fox,' then this is the phase for you. The trade secretary is a former GP who still uses his title 25 years after the fact – unlike various irrelevances such as retired rear admirals and so on, whose professional achievements presumably amount to rather less than writing antibiotic prescriptions in Beaconsfield in the 1980s. Anyway, *that* guy is pretty sure that striking a deal with the EU will be 'the easiest in human history'.

Happily, hearing more from Fox doesn't mean we will be hearing less from David Davis, whose antics over his Brexit impact assessments are most kindly summarised as Bring Your Anxiety Dream to Work Week. Simon Hoggart used to have a great line about Davis having been in the territorial SAS – 'strangling the Queen's enemies with piano wire, but only at weekends'. After this week's semi-detached performance, I can't help feeling Davis is just the territorial DExEU secretary: he does do detail, but only every third weekend.

As for his phoned-in impact assessments, MPs and peers are now allowed to read the documents, though they have to do it with an official chaperone. The entire shtick recalls the moment on Scientology's pathway when believers are finally let into the innermost secrets of Hubbard's religion. It was always estimated to cost at least $360,000 to reach this point, so we can only imagine the sense of serious WTF-ery that stole over the average Operating Thetan as they started reading about Xenu, the intergalactic tyrant who sent his forces to Earth 75m years ago in craft that, strangely, looked exactly like DC-8s. The Scientologists used to reveal this information on a ship far out to sea, presumably so that by the time they dropped you dejectedly back on shore, you'd had time to stop screaming about being completely had.

For now, Britain feels equally adrift. And phase one was supposed to be the easy bit. As European Council president Donald Tusk said: 'Breaking up is hard. Building a new relationship is harder.' How successfully will the UK consciously uncouple from the EU? Well, without wishing to introduce a note of caution on such a triumphant day, there is a nagging sense that Britain is going to fall short of the Gwyneth Paltrow model. Perhaps the UK will transition to taking the divorce well. But on the basis of the past eight months, it will instead transition to a lengthy period of driving round to its ex's house at night and sitting in the car outside with a bottle of vodka, texting a cocktail of pure venom and pleas to get back together, until the police are called.

SPORT: FROM HEROIC WINNERS TO ABSOLUTE LOSERS

'Overpaid' and 'pampered' athletes prove to be the usual punch-bag for politicians and some pundits, even as one Premier League player singlehandedly forces a government U-turn on free school meals. Twice. No wonder they just want them to shut up and play. English athletes remain incapable of cheating, which is nice, while some men observe the rise in popularity of women's sport and absolutely refuse to be a good sport about it. Sporting governance? Don't talk to me about sporting governance – arguably the only thing still done worse than actual governance.

Using footballers' wages as an example of excess is patronising and lazy

18 January 2017

Top-flight football is one of the few engines of social mobility that still works, and those who play to the gallery are too lazy or dim to formulate a proper argument

In one sense, it is not the most enormous shock to find footballers' pay is something on which Jeremy Corbyn disagrees with himself. A subject on which the Labour leader cannot hold two diametrically opposed opinions on the same day is increasingly a rarity. The problem with the new strategy of letting Jeremy be Jeremy is that – a bit like various football sides of cliché – you never know which one is going to turn up.

Last week, Corbyn declared that there should be a cap on 'grotesque' salaries. And whaddayaknow – the very first example of such salaries upon which he alighted was in football. 'Certainly, the salaries that are paid to some footballers are simply ridiculous,' he stated, adding: 'Some of the salaries paid to very high-earning top executives of companies are utterly ridiculous.'

Then, at the weekend, Corbyn seemed to have changed tack. His idea of a salary cap would not be extended to footballers, he told Andrew Marr, because they weren't bosses. As he put it this time: 'Footballers, while they are paid ludicrous sums of money which I suppose we all pay for through our tickets, in reality they're employees for quite a short time with those clubs.' Mmm. You'll note the quality of Jeremy's mercy is strained.

At the time of going to press, it was difficult to speculate which way the pendulum inside Jeremy's noggin was swinging or, indeed, where it would be 48 hours hence. What can be said with certainty is that in all arguments about pay and equality – whoever is making them this week or any week – football should be right down anyone sensible's list of give-a-tosses.

It is always telling when people who are supposed to have big ideas fall back on tipping all over the Premier League. I hate to break it to them, but whingeing about footballers is not a big idea. They should have other fish to fry. Aside from anything else, top-flight football is one of the few engines of social mobility that still works in this country. Albeit for only a talented few, but hey – that already makes it more effective in this regard than almost every other profession. Yet it is footballer remuneration that is mentioned most frequently and most disparagingly by people in public life seeking to get attention.

What is it that they so detest about top-flight football, with its remorseless habit of creating working-class millionaires? And so many black working-class millionaires at that. I mean, really – of all the possible professions to pick, football would be one of my last ones, not least because it entertains so many people (however much they moan about it). It's odd how you never hear politicians banging on about movie actors getting paid too much. Perhaps it's because the working-class actor is a more endangered species than it was even decades ago, so that branch of entertainment is not regarded as such a pressingly uppity problem.

And so it is that you frequently hear a footballer's contract discussed in terms of how many NHS nurses it would fund, but weirdly never hear how many Mesut Özils a banking bailout or cocked-up Royal Mail flotation could have provided instead. That certainly says something about the way our society is structured – but not the thing that the anti-Premier League crowd think it says.

For my money, there is no clearer indication of a policy's essential weakness than to find it illustrated primarily via recourse to the Premier League. Using footballers as an example for anything is the lamest sort of playing to the gallery, always indulged in by people too lazy or dim to formulate a proper argument. Furthermore, it always has the whiff of something patronisingly packaged to appeal to 'ordinary people' in the sort of language 'they' understand.

Indeed, instead of going along with it, I wish Corbyn had firmly resisted Marr's reliance on that old footballing insult, 'We pay your wages.' 'We pay your wages' is such a loathsome sentiment. Some might think it more refined to say it on a TV show sofa, as opposed to screaming it behind the goal, but it made me shudder even harder.

Those who think it's OK to direct that comment at footballers should probably ask whether they'd toss it in the direction of serving staff in a restaurant they were eating in or a station cleaner who looked like they'd missed a bit. If they would, then at least they're consistently unpleasant. If they wouldn't, they need to dispense with the idea that the sums of money involved make it justifiable in one instance and not another. There are a few obvious exceptions to this rule – discovering your elected member of parliament has abused your trust and claimed moat-cleaning expenses and so on – but as a general principle, 'We pay your wages' is a cringeworthy thing to say.

As a man who gets paid an extra £62,440 from the public purse, supposedly for the task of leading Her Majesty's opposition, it's probably not one Corbyn ought wisely to get into.

Fifa lets Qatar 2022 sail on, its moral lines in the sand still on the horizon

28 June 2017

War fears, deaths, slavery . . . the main lesson of the Garcia report appears to be that there is no conceivable dealbreaker that could derail Qatar's World Cup

Thanks to the long-overdue publication of the Garcia report into the bidding process for the 2018 and 2022 World Cups, we now know that England's efforts to secure the 2018 tournament amounted to 'a form of bribery'. Obviously, the only thing less surprising than the fact that England break the rules is how bad they are at it. If an England bid team ever gets within 30 sniffs of actually winning a World Cup bid again, no effort should be spared in investigating how they do business. They are, in the words of pursed-lips grandmas, no better than they should be.

For now, however, England remain as likely to win a World Cup bid as they do to win a World Cup, and we must turn our thoughts to more pressing questions raised by the report by Fifa's then chief ethics investigator. Namely – and I don't mean any disrespect to the emir and his accidentally vagina-shaped stadium – is the Qatar World Cup a thought experiment? It is, after all, to be set in a region where imagineers build ski resorts in the desert and raise hotel citadels from the ocean and whatnot. Given the sheer volume and variety of red flags now raised over Qatar 2022, surely we should at least entertain the possibility that the entire event and its buildup are a highly sophisticated real-time simulation that is specifically designed to tease out the moral boundaries of any number of authorities, from Fifa to our own Football Association.

And, you know . . . I don't think we're passing, here. I don't think we've answered a lot of the questions in a manner pleasing to our notional moral philosophy professor.

The more we learn about the Qatar World Cup, the more we have to ask: what would it actually take? What would it actually take for Fifa and its president, Gianni Infantino, to say: 'It is just possible we've dropped a bollock here. It is juuuuuust possible that the worst thing about a notional Qatar World Cup isn't the fact that the country is frequently more than 50 degrees in the summer and has as much genuine interest in football as your average Conservative sports minister.' What would it take?

More than we've seen so far, is the rough answer. I mean, we've had the slave deaths. It was OK with the slave deaths. Despite the evidence, Fifa never demanded the end of the *kafala* system, wherein the rights of the migrant labourers working on Qatar's infrastructure projects were abused, denied and the subject of intensely critical reports from the likes of Amnesty and Human Rights Watch. This appears to have been a price Fifa was willing to pay. Not pay itself, obviously – they have some faceless, indentured help from the Philippines or Nepal or wherever to pay it for them. And we don't know how many have paid that ultimate price in the construction of the stadiums and the concomitant infrastructure because of Qatar's secrecy about the actual figures or studied indifference to even cataloguing them. But, clearly, the tournament's still on. The deaths were not a dealbreaker.

Given that, it's no surprise to find the conditions in the migrant labourer camps weren't either. Another straw that failed to break the camel's back is this small, recent matter of the Saudi Arabia-led economic and diplomatic blockade of Qatar. Several weeks in, this dispute is deepening. Indeed, there are some sporting bodies that would read reports containing phrases such as 'stockpiling food', 'licensed funding of terrorism' and 'looming prospect of destabilising regional conflict' and wonder whether those weren't vague warning signs as to the wisdom of locating your football contest there. But these people simply don't have what it takes to work at Fifa.

There has been no meaningful comment on the gathering storm by Fifa – which is, I forgot to mention, sponsored by Qatar Airways (because no aspect of the modern sporting–industrial complex is considered a proper joke unless you're really slapped round the head with it). What Fifa has done, instead of issue a statement saying it is seriously reviewing the location of its tournament, is issue a statement assuring people that construction is progressing rapidly on Qatar 2022 stadiums. Swings and roundabouts, isn't it? Sure, there are rumblings of Middle Eastern war. On the plus side, though, the fanny stadium's food court is on schedule.

So, as indicated, these minor issues are not going to upset the 2022 apple cart, much less the gravy train. And now we've finally seen the confidential Garcia report, three years after it was publicly 'summarised' so controversially by Fifa's ethics judge, Joachim Eckert, that it prompted Garcia's resignation.

We have learned that a former ExCo member congratulated members of the Qatari federation, thanking them for their 'support' immediately after Qatar was awarded the 2022 tournament. A month later €300,000 found its way into his bank account. Other lowlights? The $2m paid by an adviser to the Qatari bid into the savings account of a then Fifa ExCo member's 10-year-old daughter. The three voting ExCo members private-jetted by the Qatari federation to a party in Rio. Money from the Aspire sports academy in Qatar being used to 'curry favour' with voting Fifa members. On it goes. Garcia judged the Aspire actions 'served to undermine the integrity of the bidding process'. Yet Eckert summarised that they 'were not suited to compromise the integrity of the Fifa World Cup 2018 and 2022 bidding process'. To which the most deferential response I can offer is: HAHAHAHAHAHAHAHAHA. Compromise the what, sorry? The only bidding process with less integrity than any Fifa bidding process is the one between rival cartels for ownership of a rookie Mexican police officer.

And yet Qatar 2022 sails on regardless. What could possibly be Fifa's line in the sand? Where does the useless Infantino draw the line? Pestilence? Actual war? You'd hope we might be close to finding out – but on the form book, you shouldn't hold your breath.

Britain is fine booing Justin Gatlin, but what about closer to home?

9 August 2017

The opprobrium directed at the new 100m world champion has hardly been a surprise, but British fans should be wary of a holier-than-thou attitude

Before we begin in semi-earnest, a word on 'serving one's time' in the athletics-ban sense of the term. I am all for doing one's time and that being an end to it, but it does seem worth acknowledging what this means in any other place of work.

Say you worked at a building society and were eventually discovered to have been cheating it out of funds, not to mention stealing from your colleagues' wallets too. You're out, you're disgraced, you 'do your time', whatever form that may take. And at that point your debt to society is paid and you should of course be allowed to get on with life. However, no one seriously expects the building society to have to welcome you back to your old job. And if it were somehow obligated to do so, not too many of us would begrudge the other employees – or the customers – their pursed lips. Or, indeed, their boos.

And so to Justin Gatlin, whose victory in the 100m at the London Stadium on Saturday has inevitably been marked by various people who watch athletics once every two years explaining that you can actually learn a lot from poor old Justin. Perhaps, but why would you want to? I mean, I'm trying to watch some athletics here. I've written before about the modern mania for all sport to be a learning experience, as opposed to something to be enjoyed in purely sporting terms. Call me old-fashioned, but I don't really want to 'learn' anything when I'm watching the 100m final. I'd far rather see amazing athletics I can actually believe in and leave the prodigal-son cobblers for religious education class. (Which I am pleased to no longer have to take.) 'Learning' from Justin Gatlin, or whoever it is next time, is sport for people who don't actually like sport. I can't help feeling that if they had their way, we'd eventually find phone-lines flashed up on the screen during competitions: 'Have you been affected by any of the issues raised in this 100m final?'

Still, to hear the boos ring out around the London Stadium as Gatlin won was to be reminded of how lucky we are that British athletes don't cheat. Historically, this sceptred isle has been a place where athletes can get really good as they approach their mid-30s – a place where even people suffering from asthma or other performance unenhancing ailments can, with the right medication, realise their potential as champions.

Sure, much of the rest of the world bafflingly declines to accept this exceptionalism without a raised eyebrow – but the rest of the world would, wouldn't it? The questions that have dogged two of our most recently knighted sports stars – Sir Bradley Wiggins and Sir Mo Farah – have been discounted by many of the most ardent home fans of the sports they represent. And we must hope this fundamental belief in our own probity is permitted to continue, because you have to wonder if Britain could take the alternative, at this most delicate stage in its post-imperial journey.

Increasingly, though, I find myself gripped by a perhaps irrational yet powerful suspicion that a big revelation is indeed in the post. Unlike various other countries, Britain has hitherto managed to escape the trauma of one of its most nationally treasured household names being revealed as a cheat. Linford Christie's second failed test came two years after his retirement, and Dwain Chambers wasn't big enough.

That was then. The fall of any idol would be felt far more acutely now, at a time when so many of the stories Britain has enjoyed telling itself seem to be hanging by a thread. Discovering one of our major sporting heroes wasn't what we thought they were would feel, well, a bit . . . Brexitty, perhaps.

For those who believe that Britain is suddenly about to be found out on all sorts of fronts, there would be a certain narrative cohesion to athletic virtue being yet another one of those. Across the board, a nation that has been getting away with it for a long time may be about to rub up against a reckoning. I suspect sporting rectitude may be a part of all that – so perhaps one-eyed fans should enjoy their booing while they still can.

Tiger Woods's Masters win was no tale of redemption – it was revenge

17 April 2019

His stunning return to golf's major highs thrills as much for him sticking it to the old guard as it did for pure sporting spectacle

As someone who cried at Tiger Woods's spectacular Masters victory on Sunday – having spent years waiting for it and much of the weekend shouting quite unprintable forms of encouragement at the TV – I urge hard-headedness about some of the reaction.

Although I have limited myself to reading just the 587-odd articles about it all, it's hard not to spot certain common themes. By far the most dominant is the idea that this is a story of redemption

– that Tiger Woods has, in some not-entirely-explained way, become a morally better man than he was, and that that is a big part of why he is winning again.

Oh dear. I do hope not. In fact, I'd much prefer Tiger to be secretly worse than ever, and still winning again. You can have one without the other, whatever the High Sparrows insist. In fact, Woods did for years. Those who seek to turn the madness and majesty of sport into trite little fables are always to be resisted, especially when those fables are just convenient morality tales. Woods the man has always been a matter for his family – no one else ever had any business feeling 'let down' by him. Part of the amusing, exasperating, exhilarating nature of sport is that awful people can be wonderful at it.

Inevitably, the fabulists have been working overtime since Sunday to take ownership of Woods's return journey. By far and away the most prevalent term to be bandied around in the wake of Tiger's stunning comeback is 'redemption' – a word which connotes a quasi-religious passage from sin to salvation. This sounds like just the sort of story that small-state, multimillionaire evangelicals might like to tell themselves about Tiger Woods. And given what a grip these hypocritical moralisers already have over the upper echelons of this particular sport, perhaps we should avoid assisting them in the matter.

In some ways, obviously, the need for a simple fairy story is understandable. Narrative templates are the way we make sense of the much more formless tide of experience. But Woods's journey back both from the implosion of his personal life and from serious injury and surgery is sufficiently complicated and nuanced to defy any reading of it as the 'right' one. Can't we pick an alternative to 'redemption' out of the air? Can't we make it a revenge narrative instead?

How about Woods's comeback being one in the eye for all those horrendous golfing conservatives – I use the term euphemistically

– who were only too pleased to write him off once his Hooters habit was discovered? As a matter of personal taste, I would have preferred it if he had been greeted off the 18th on Sunday by a couple of cocktail waitresses. But you can't have it all. Furthermore, I can only celebrate anything that Woods has ever done to 'betray' what the Augusta National Club represents. His first Masters victory, in 1997, came just seven years after the club had admitted a black member, and may consequently be judged to have been a terrible upset for much of its old guard.

Even now, there is no more skin-crawling sight in golf than the green jacket presentation in the wretched interior of Augusta's Butler Cabin, a place of staggering charmlessness and aesthetic death. Here, competitors who have achieved sporting triumph have to sit obediently on twee dining chairs while some dreadful commercial real-estate lawyer (the chairman) informs them at remorseless length that they have been a 'worthy' champion over the past year, or that the club is pleased to confer upon them something they literally just won. (Incidentally, no Masters TV viewer can imagine giving a millionth of a toss what 'the club' feels about anything – because the club certainly couldn't give one about them. Augusta detests ordinary golf fans so much it can barely stand to give them a glimpse of its tournament. The sheer amount of time Masters TV viewers are expected to spend watching a shrub or listening to birdsong, until they deign to show you some scores or even some actual golf, is the most naked illustration of elite contempt in all of world sport.)

One of the great frustrations with Woods in his pomp, for some, was his refusal to come over all Muhammad Ali and use his victories to make pronouncements about racial inequality in America. He was simply the greatest golfer in the world, but he wasn't a spokesman for anything other than extremely high-paying commercial brands. The only time Woods did afflict the comfortable, then, was when his non-apple-pie personal life was discovered, and the golf–industrial complex duly forced him into a series of quite extraordinary actions. There were months of in-patient sex addiction therapy, which forced the game's most impenetrable mind to 'open up'. And then there was Tiger's formal televised apology for his infidelities, easily the maddest golf-related moment of the past decade (unless you count the Trump presidency). Should you have forgotten the detail, this took place at the PGA Tour headquarters, no less, at a podium and in front of exactly the same sort of blue curtain they use for White House press conferences. There was an audience of spectators – including Woods's disapproving mother in the front row.

It was shortly after this mind-boggling horror show that Woods told his old coach he was, from now on, going to play golf 'only for myself'. Quite right too. But the idea that he had to be 'a different man' to win again on Sunday is cobblers, and exactly the sort that would appeal to the hardline PGA Republicans who are baptised in Disney World swimming pools. I do hope Tiger Woods keeps beating them, until they can no longer praise him even through gritted teeth.

Pity the poor man who's had the Women's World Cup shoved down his throat

12 June 2019

From Mr Inferior Product to Mr I Prefer Parks, the tournament has caused a cosmic imbalance that we must redress

Once again I am hugely grateful to the community that will not allow us to forget the great under-reported story of this Women's World Cup: men. Most specifically, the men who are not watching it. We hear so much about the tournament itself. Too much, it is argued – and at the expense of one of the four great civil rights questions of our era: (1) When are we getting a White History Month? (2) When is International Men's Day? (3) Isn't it time we had Straight Pride? And (4) can you imagine how sexist people would say it was if we had a men's World Cup?

I could not agree more with the gentlemen who dare to ask these questions – and not just so that I can buy time while I frantically locate the exit. Indeed, as part of this column's tireless commitment to celebrating the underdogs, this week let's redress the dangerous cosmic imbalance caused by the Women's World Cup. Here follows a celebration of all the different guys who currently need to explain to you – at length – why they aren't watching it. As always, you don't have to be a woman to have met some of these men over the past week. But it certainly helps!

Mr Stop Shoving It Down My Throat
Listen, this guy is absolutely fine with this tournament existing, being alive, whatever. He's open-minded – it's not the dark ages any more. Nothing against it. What he objects to – and he'd like you to know that you'll find a lot of other perfectly decent people like him – is it being 'shoved down his throat'. Yes, it's the shoving. Down the throat. It's like: fine, I'm happy for you to do your football in the privacy of your own wherever, but please, have some sensitivity and realise that not all people are like you. So basically just don't do it in front of him or involve him. Seriously: don't involve him. Also, don't do it near his kids, especially the girl. For reference, ways that it can be shoved down his throat include 'being on TV' and 'being on a website he normally looks at' – for instance, that of the British Broadcasting Corporation, which, by covering a sport that averaged 4.6 million viewers on Sunday night for England's game against Scotland, is pursuing a right-on agenda. Actually, let's be real for a minute: no one wants to see this. Put it away.

Mr I'm Being Branded Sexist

This guy is fairly sure he's being 'branded sexist' for not watching the Women's World Cup. I think if you need to ask, 'By who, specifically?' then in a very strong but also abstract sense you're part of the problem. He is definitely getting this definite feeling that he is being made to feel sexist. It's all part of an agenda. No, he'd rather not continue this conversation. He can't win, because you just can't say anything these days.

Mr Inferior Product

Nothing but respect for the guy who declares 'the game's gone' about every tiny piece of commercialisation in men's football but falls over himself to describe the women's game as 'an inferior product'. I mean, on the one hand, a reminder: if you refer to football as either 'product' or 'content' – ever – you are an endless wanker. No exceptions. But on the other: I'm sure it felt like an interesting point when you made it. Your points are not inferior products: keep producing them to surplus.

Mr I Prefer Parks

No one more than me wants to help the guy whose chief point about the 2019 World Cup is: 'I would so much rather watch parks football on a Sunday morning.' I would also rather he did this.

Mr Stop Telling Me It's Massive When It's Really Not

Totally. But, dude: read that one over and then probably just delete it. I know you'd hate for anyone to take it out of context. And that's what they do: they take things out of context and then they twist what you say.

Mr I Always Support England

Always supports England, no matter what. No one loves his country more than him. But this isn't 'England' by any reasonable yardstick. Which bit of England do they represent then? Not a bit he recognises.

Mr Have Fifa Got a Point?

I love this guy, who has spent years – decades – scoffing that Fifa are a bunch of incompetent chisellers who leech money out of the game and do less than the bare minimum to grow it while lining their own pockets. Unbelievable that they don't pay local taxes and have a cash surplus of $2.7bn, when they should be a force for good. But this chap looks at the fact that the men's World Cup prize fund is $400m, that the women's is $30m. He knows he can't fall back on viewing figure ratios, given that the men's gets four times the viewers of the women's but 13 times the prize money. And he knows the gap between the men's and women's prize fund has actually risen over the past four years. Even so, and for reasons he can't quite put his finger on: haven't Fifa got a point in just this one case? Oh, just to be clear, that's a rhetorical question. Which means you don't get to answer it.

Mr I'm Just Not Watching

Short of hearing what other people dreamed about last night, hearing which things other people aren't watching on television is even better. Have you never seen an episode of *Game of Thrones*? Do you dislike *Love Island*? Are you not watching the Women's World Cup? If so, this is massive. Make sure to tell as many people as possible today.

Geoffrey Boycott was convicted of domestic assault, so why has May knighted him?

11 September 2019

Glacial opener, failed captain, convicted assaulter – no wonder the former PM has idolised him since childhood

Geoffrey Boycott has always represented Theresa May's idealised version of herself, and in that sense it is no surprise that the former prime minister has given him a knighthood in her resignation honours. She can see the hero where others can't, and if only people could look past the social awkwardness, and the thinly disguised selfishness, and the various nasty businesses, then they would surely realise what heroic qualities truly are.

Indeed, perhaps this knighthood foreshadows how someone who has herself exhibited these characteristics in her own career could go on to a highly successful second act in the political commentary box or on the board of one of the better arms firms. Perhaps in retirement, that someone too will become the effervescent opposite of her playing self. Or perhaps she will grind out the rest of her remorseless innings pointing at potholes for the local constituency paper, as Mrs May was doing this week.

Anyway, a recap of the facts: in 1998 Boycott was convicted by a French court of assaulting his then girlfriend, a verdict off which he continues to smash soundbites with outrageous abandon. Those who regard no morning as complete if they haven't lost their shit with Radio 4's *Today* programme were certainly given what they wanted on Tuesday, as Boycott was interviewed on the news of his knighthood. 'I don't give a toss about her, love,' was his retort to Martha Kearney's mention that the chief executive of Women's Aid had called his knighthood 'extremely disappointing'.

Nor is there any shortage of 'colourful background' on Boycott's position on the honours system. Boycott felt his earlier gong, an OBE, had been devalued by those given to the 2005 Ashes-winning side, who went on to suffer a 5–0 series whitewash in Australia two years later. 'People like me played 100 Test matches to get one, and [scored] 8,000 [runs],' he fretted at the time. 'I didn't play five Test matches and get one. I feel so bad about mine I'm going to tie it round my cat. It doesn't mean anything any more. It's a joke.' Yet Boycott felt the prospect of upgrading his cat jewellery was slim. A couple of years ago, he claimed further honours for him had been 'turned down twice', adding that 'I'd better black my face'. West Indians, he thought, received them 'like confetti'.

So, as every reader of the sports pages already knows, this is what you're dealing with. You always were. Apart from Boycott's forthcoming acquisition of an honour that ghastly businessmen mostly pay for, nothing – to coin a phrase – has changed. Those who don't trouble themselves with sport seem to be waking up not just to the news that Boycott has received a knighthood, but that he works for the BBC. Even so, it is not 2005 again.

His domestic violence conviction is a longstanding matter of record, and is frequently written about by many of us. I see I most recently mentioned it at the end of June. But he didn't honour himself. Of much more immediate concern, then, must be the person who decided to do so, despite the above. We know all about Geoffrey Boycott. What does this knighthood tell us about Theresa May?

We certainly know May continued to adore her childhood cricketing hero, even after his conviction, as did many who found themselves disappointed by, say, the plodding commentary of Ian Botham. But even accounting for this, to knight him is something different.

Plenty of people couldn't believe the domestic violence of Boycs. Was Theresa May one of those? She wouldn't have been alone. Sports writer Ian Wooldridge described Boycott's assault charge as 'a hiccup in his personal life', adding that he would 'be happy to appear as a character witness on his behalf in a court case still hanging over his head in France'. It is at least difficult to imagine a column like that being written nowadays (even if the current parliamentary sketchwriter of *The Times* does appear to think his job is to be character witness for the prime minister). Yet if May didn't accept the conviction, it is remarkable. She was not otherwise famously soft on law and order, nor given to believing the best of people. Or did May believe it but not mind? Again, this would not be of a piece with the May worldview, where redemption and second chances were not in ready supply. Perhaps the most realistic verdict is that she preferred not to think about it, just as she seems to have preferred not to think about the impact of her own egregious acts.

Many of us turn a blind eye to certain aspects of our heroes; May's ability to overlook such a monumental one as far as Boycott is concerned suggests a deep personal need to do so. Here is a man regarded as socially inept, never mixing with his teammates during his playing years or his commentary box colleagues thereafter. Here is a man whose guiding principle was a uniquely selfish form of caution allied to a warped yet clearly intense idea of public service. Here is a man who for many was completely unwatchable, and who for all his glaring character flaws never appeared capable of reflection. Here is a man whose brief England captaincy ended in failure and humiliation. Ring any bells?

Yet here is a man who, despite enduring the slings and arrows of opponents and teammates alike, will nonetheless be regarded as an all-time great, and who will – especially now – regard himself as having won. Looked at like that, the question is not 'How could Theresa May knight Geoffrey Boycott?' but 'How could she not?'

Sport loves athletes with mental health issues – if they just shut up and play

1 June 2021

The grand slams say Naomi Osaka's decisions about doing press conferences are 'injurious' to tennis. Perhaps they should look closer to home

Amazing, really, that the most appalling people in tennis are not the ones who applaud piously when the Wimbledon umpire tells the crowd to ensure their mobile phones are switched to silent, nor even the ones who are far more hysterically enchanted by the appearance of a pigeon on Centre Court than they ever could be by an otherworldly Roger Federer forehand.

Much more ghastly are those simply unable to deal with world No. 2 Naomi Osaka announcing last week that she didn't feel mentally up to doing press conferences at the French Open. This drew frothing anger from all the usual suspects, including the only highly paid news anchor in history so fragile that he recently stormed off air on his own show. The French Open fined Osaka for missing her first-round press conferences, and the official Roland Garros Twitter account posted (then later deleted) a collage of players doing press conferences, with the leadenly pointed caption: 'They understood the assignment.' On Monday Osaka announced that she would be pulling out of the entire tournament, revealing she had had long bouts of depression since winning the US Open in 2018 and had often struggled to cope.

You do have to admire tennis's position on health. The women's No. 2 has been pushed into withdrawing from a grand slam for having the temerity to take a small step to protect her own mental equilibrium, while the men's No. 1 has spent the past 14 months continually honking out anti-Covid-vaccine messages. Novak

Djokovic has not been officially censured for that, nor for the ridiculous super-spreader tournament he hosted across the Balkans last summer against all advice, which saw several players (including him) catch Covid. As for the hierarchy of the sport's sins, how predictable that it should be 'doing press conferences' that united all four slams in a joint condemnatory press release, while they remain utterly silent on world No. 6 Alexander Zverev, many months after he was accused in great detail of domestic violence and mental abuse by his ex-girlfriend. Zverev issued a denial; and denial in any case remains tennis's comfort zone. For a major sport it is fundamentally incurious. According to a 2016 investigation, it tests for performance-enhancing drugs at the same levels as kayaking or handball.

Anyway, back to Osaka. If you're not familiar with the French Open, it's a tournament in which the best tennis players in the world are split by means of a draw and have to outperform each other at a series of press conferences. I mean, I think? Otherwise, how much can it honestly matter if a 23-year-old does or doesn't turn up to them and go through the banalities? This is TENNIS. Watch the match, listen to the commentary, read the analysis, and if there's still something you didn't understand, then honestly just naff off and read a children's book instead.

Alas, it seems that 'scrutiny' is a cornerstone of both liberal democracy and clay-court singles. And yet, it does seem quite mad that we even use the same word for asking a tennis player what went wrong with their serve as we do for asking a health minister if he lied about discharging untested vulnerable people into care homes.

We don't know quite why the frothers are so angry about Osaka, because they're currently too angry to precisely explain. So I'm only speculating, but I imagine one woman's decision not to do press conferences at the French Open is regarded as that most all-purpose of bogeymen: the thin end of the wedge. The thin end of the wedge is the street name of the slippery slope. One minute you're allowing a 23-year-old not to say whether she feels the third-set tie-break could have gone better; the next no one is answering any questions about third-set tie-breaks, fans are only able to find out how players feel from their multiple daily social media updates, and sponsors are paying stars less because no one's sitting in front of their logos to take questions any more. In which case . . . so what? Never mind? Big wows? Fred Perry never had to take this many questions, and maybe the players of the future won't either. I know we have to pretend there's a continuum between this and actual totalitarianism, but let's not and say we did.

The weird thing is that we DO want athletes to have mental health issues – very much so, in fact – but we only want them to reveal them at a time and a place that suits us. Namely: after they've retired, and in a book. Then we can profess ourselves fascinated to have learned that an athlete walked out for this or that fixture absolutely broken inside. The key thing is that you couldn't tell from the outside – that's the bit we love. The hidden pain, the belated literary reveal. If they won the fixture, we like to learn from the book that they didn't mean whatever elated thing they said to the journalists at the press conference afterwards – they were just going through the motions because they were broken inside. If they lost, we like to learn from the book that it wasn't for whatever reasons they gave the journalists at the press conference afterwards – they were just going through the motions because they were broken inside.

It's almost as if the common denominator here is the fact that the press conference is mostly a place where one goes through the motions and just says some shit to shut them up. Any athlete lauded for their honesty about mental health – 'demons', in sporting parlance – is only lauded if it's long after the event. The same people who raved about Tony Cascarino's brilliant autobiography *Full Time* would have lost their minds if the footballer had dared voice any of his turmoil while he was actually playing.

Tennis was quick to tell us Osaka had been fined for behaviour judged 'detrimental or injurious to the grand slam tournaments'.

This reminds me of the Football Association's charge of 'bringing the game into disrepute', which it likes to level at players who've done a bad tweet, when no one has done as much to bring the game into disrepute quite so serially as the FA itself. It's the same with tennis. Do remember that the minute she came back off a drugs ban, Maria Sharapova was given a wildcard into the main draw of the US Open and other players bumped off the Arthur Ashe court for all her primetime matches. In many and various ways down the years, no one has acted in a way more injurious to grand slams than the grand slams themselves. You'll never see them do a press conference about that, though, so let's not wet our pants when the mere players don't feel able to either.

Footballers can say it, but for England's politicians, 'sorry' really is the hardest word

13 July 2021

The emotional maturity of the Euro 2020 players is in stark contrast to that of the prime minister and government

These days, English people expect more from our football team than our government. Which is a funny old switcheroo, when you think about it. My apologies to the other home nations for making the 'we' of this particular article the English – but All This is very much an English problem, and there's no point kidding ourselves about that.

England Expects That Every Footballer Will Do His Duty. For the players, faultless competence is that duty, and – if it is not delivered – public apologies and contrition are in order from those who failed. And very promptly indeed. It's not like we kick it down the road to a public inquiry that reports in two tournaments' time.

Since England lost the final on Sunday night – and despite many being deluged by racist abuse – we have seen players break cover to apologise for their mistakes, for letting fans down, for not being quite enough in the moment.

It is, of course, a fundamental tenet of sporting greatness that reckoning with failure makes you stronger, that the mistake or the falling-short is not the defining moment. Rather, it is how you respond to it: first by owning up to it, then by learning from it and folding it back into your story so you come back stronger. Gareth Southgate knows that journey of old; he was beginning it again in the immediate aftermath of the final, fronting up to the nation to insist that failure 'totally rests with me'.

These are the lessons you might want to teach your children. That having been brave in the first place is ultimately more important than having failed in the moment, even if it doesn't feel that way at the time. That facing up to things is hard, but right and helpful for the future. And maybe that saying sorry even when it really isn't necessary can be a decent and humble gesture.

Children hear these messages so often from people who want the best for them that many of them already know they are the right things to say. After his own letter to fans, Marcus Rashford posted some of those he has received from children since Sunday's defeat, and they themselves make for extraordinarily humbling and emotional reading.

Where is any of this in our politics, I wonder? There is something completely antithetical to modern political culture in it all. It is, on every level, absurd that it should feel socially necessary for footballers barely out of their teens to pen missives to the nation apologising for missing a penalty, but not for a government to even acknowledge vast and lethal mistakes, much less say sorry for them.

For much of the past 16 months the government has seemed so hell-bent on learning nothing that the same terrible errors are repeated twice and more, by exactly the same people. These mistakes

– these 'misses', if you will – have led to thousands upon thousands of avoidable deaths. They have led to far longer lockdowns than would otherwise have been necessary, to the far longer removal of people's basic freedoms, and to all the attendant mental and financial misery that comes with that, to say nothing of the pressures placed on the NHS, now dealing with mindblowing backlogs in treatment and surgeries.

Is yet another avoidable foul-up in the offing, even as the government enlivened the football hangover by confirming it was fully opening up for its 'freedom day', with its own ministers briefing that they were 'flying blind'. You certainly wouldn't bet against it. Yet at no point in any of this has Boris Johnson offered a single apology, much less a sincere one in which specific failures are faced up to and responsibility 'totally rests with me'. Perhaps that's why the government doesn't 'grow' as a set of players, much less feel like the type of people we would hold up as role models to children.

As you're supposed to learn from early childhood, it is a mark of weakness never to apologise or own up. Even when she was found to have bullied her staff, Priti Patel couldn't say a proper sorry. So it's no surprise to find her refusing to reconsider her statement that people had a right to boo players taking the knee – despite, as Tyrone Mings has now so arrestingly put it to her, 'the very thing we are campaigning against' is happening to the players in the wake of defeat. If only Patel or Johnson were a strong enough character to say, 'You know what, I got that wrong. I'm sorry, my eye was off the ball at the time, but I think given what's happened since, we can all see what these players face.' It's really not that hard. Everyone can make mistakes – even politicians.

Yet in his serial refusal to take responsibility for his past statements – or even concede he ever really made them – Johnson seems to have rather more in common with the sort of guy who claims their social media account has been hacked. (Amazing what hackers get up to these days. The big prize seems to be gaining control of some random guy's Twitter for a single hour after a football game, or hacking a male public figure's account to send a single picture of his penis.)

England Expects . . . what, honestly? England expects no one to take responsibility. England expects less than what it deserves. As long as we're ruled by people who regard self-examination and the odd sorry as a sign of weakness as opposed to one of strength, we will continue to be let down and short-changed by what they deliver. Taking responsibility should be for politicians as well as footballers – otherwise the country can expect plenty more years of hurt.

2018: MAY, YOU LIVE IN INTERESTING TIMES

Much in the manner of Arnold Schwarzenegger's T-800 unit at the end of *Terminator 2*, Theresa May cannot self-terminate. Nor can she get close to a deal with the EU that will satisfy even half the people it needs to. The Tories can always go from nought to regicide in six seconds; by the end of the year they exist in open mutiny. Even as the moral stain of the *Windrush* scandal is revealed, both parties punch down at minority communities. Labour fails to tackle its antisemitism problem, while Conservative Islamophobia is stoked by low-profile figures such as Boris Johnson. A great year for screaming into a pillow. Still, best to keep it in perspective – 2019 will end up being even worse.

Corbyn and Blair: are they really so very different?

30 March 2018

Both believe in their own moral infallibility. In the movies, this type of guy redeems himself. In real life, it's not quite so simple

'Are we so different, you and I?' the emperor wonders of Maximus in *Gladiator*. 'You and I are very much alike,' Belloq tells Indiana Jones in *Raiders of the Lost Ark*. 'I am but a shadowy reflection of you.' 'You and me . . . you and me, we not so different,' a rather poorly drawn Mexican tells Vin Diesel in *Fast & Furious 4*.

Even when the characters don't say it, we know it. Pacino and De Niro in the restaurant in *Heat*. The bit where Keanu Reeves has a clear shot at Patrick Swayze in *Point Break* and he can't do it because he's in too deep and he just has to howl and empty the chamber into the sky (later parodied hilariously in *Hot Fuzz*). Luke cutting Vader's hand off in *Return of the Jedi*.

It's usually the villain who points it out to the hero, but sometimes things are deliberately muddy. 'We're not so different as you might think,' Truman tells his murderous doppelgänger in *Capote*. 'We are not so different, you and I,' George Smiley says ruefully to Karla in *Tinker Tailor Soldier Spy*.

'You and I . . . we are not so very different.' There's a reason a version of this line has appeared in so many movies down the decades. It tells a psychological truth about our uncomfortable similarities with the very people we prefer to define ourselves against.

Having meandered through that, I must now ask you as a matter of urgency to imagine Jeremy Corbyn in the grubby vest of Vincent Diesel, staring down the barrel of a gun at Mr Tony Blair, who is taunting him: 'You and me . . . we not so deefferent.' Or, if you are the other way inclined, do imagine Blair in the heroic vest and Corbs as the villainous Mexican.

As defining characteristics of politicians go, an unshakeable belief in one's own moral purity is surprisingly rare. For whatever reason, it is not believed to occur naturally in the Conservative party. Our dear leaders have many and varied strains of self-belief, of course, which are frequently quite virulent. But that specific and rather terrifying conviction that something MUST be morally good because it is they who are doing it – or that something they have done CANNOT be morally bad because it was done by them – is really a class of two for me, in my lifetime.

The first is Jeremy Corbyn, whose fundamental belief that he couldn't possibly have encouraged antisemitism because of the very person he is was on show this week. And the second – can you guess who it is yet? – was a chap named Tony Blair.

You don't hear much about that guy any more, so I am pleased to offer a refresher course for anyone who became obsessively inter- ested in politics in the past few years and may care to buff up on their heritage. Blair was a guy who believed he was a pretty straight sort of guy. Indeed, those were the very words he used when responding to the media (he detested what we now call the main- stream media) about a bad situation he brought on himself shortly before he took office.

He flatly refused to accept that the thing looking awful might actually be awful. He was actually 'hurt and upset' by what the media had written about him. A lot of his supporters thought it was disgusting, what they were doing to Tony – total agenda. Some of this may sound vaguely familiar.

For those of us who already thought Blair was suspect at this early stage, this was just a worrying sign of stuff to come. The faintly messianic act, the belief that media interrogation of what he was doing was evidence of an 'agenda', the bullying dismissals by his henchmen and outriders of legitimate inquiries – these, those of us who were not Blairistas believed, were things that could end up really mattering.

Not that many Labour supporters wanted to hear it at the time. Indeed, some may now be asking: OK, so what? The guy just thought he was morally right about everything – what's the worst that could have happened? What's so dangerous about that?

Well . . . I don't want to spoil it for those catching up with the Blair years box set. But mistakes were made.

Indeed, this particular form of self-belief became the *sine qua non* of Blair for me, the thing from which all the mistakes flowed. They were expressions of the trait. It feels vanishingly unlikely that Corbyn would make the same mistakes because of his similar conviction of purity. But he would make other mistakes, potentially grave in different ways. People who believe they are morally infallible always do. To govern is to have your personality relentlessly and unsparingly exposed by events.

That sort of exposure has befallen Corbyn over the past week, while he is still in opposition. Some of his defenders are even the same people who shored up Blair's worst bits. Chris Mullin, once one of Blair's best little helpers as a Foreign Office minister between 2003 and 2005, was this week tweeting: 'Sorry to see Jewish leaders ganging up on Corbyn.'

Oh dear, Chris (again). I guess enablers gonna enable. Corbyn still cannot accept the reality that antisemitism has flourished under his leadership, often encouraged by his actions, and certainly by his inactions. He can't accept it because of the things he thinks he is. This is a failure of the imagination, just as Blair's inability to countenance faults was a failure of his.

As the much-praised Avenue Q song goes: 'Everyone's a little bit racist.' It doesn't go: 'Everyone's a little bit racist except Jeremy Corbyn.' All of us – to varying degrees obviously – make judgments based on inherent prejudices, frequently without realising.

Realising that it's possible we don't realise – that's important, especially in someone regarded as a moral leader, never mind someone who styles himself as one.

None of us should kid ourselves that we're immune from making mistakes in this department, perhaps terrible ones. Given the history of the 20th century alone, none of us should imagine that we couldn't fall prey to dark currents, dog whistles, lazy thinking that over time calcifies into dangerous thinking. In Primo Levi's arrestingly simple words: 'It happened, therefore it can happen again.'

As far as the fatal flaw Blair and Corbyn share goes, it's hard to imagine things not ending badly for anyone in its grip. We know neither man can stand the other. But him and him, they are not so very different. In films, the moment that line is said is ideally the moment the hero pulls back from the edge and starts to redeem themselves. With Blair still unable to accept his mistakes, and Corbyn still convinced of his moral infallibility, escaping the cycle feels difficult. It would certainly be nice. But maybe it's the sort of thing that only happens in the movies.

Tory ministers milking the system are the real shirkers

20 April 2018

Lose one form and you lose cancer treatment and your liberty; lose a generation's forms and you're the effing PM

If I were editing a tabloid newspaper this week – and I'm always open to guest stints – I would have had advertising vans out since Monday. They would have been crawling v-e-r-y slowly back and forth past the houses of Theresa May, Amber Rudd, Nick Timothy and David Cameron – and those just for starters. Instead of the repulsive 'GO HOME' message that adorned the infamous vans May's Home Office sent out, which resulted in the eventual deportation of precisely 11 migrants, I would have something along the lines of 'STAY HOME'. Stay home, permanently.

Whether they would get the message is uncertain. Collectively, Britain did its very best to provide a hostile environment for May with the election result. The message was very clear: take a hike. Not one of your hiking holidays, but the full hike.

Yet the import does not seem to have got through to the prime minister or the various arse-coverers around her. It's fair to say we are dealing with a very specific class of unworthy here. There are few groups who take less responsibility for their actions, as this week in the *Windrush* scandal has laid starkly bare. Some of the most senior political figures in the land are – in the purest sense of one of their favourite terms – shirkers. They are feckless. They act like these things are happening to them, as opposed to because of them. Given the judgments they like to visit on the weaker members of society for comparatively minuscule transgressions, this makes them the most raging hypocrites too.

In the Home Office, Amber Rudd can't even commit to a personal pronoun. 'I am concerned that the Home Office has become too concerned with policy and strategy, and sometimes loses sight of the individual,' was the verdict of the specific individual who is the actual home secretary, and who was clearly very much wishing people would lose sight of her. Complete tools always blame their workmen, and the civil servants' union chief has now come out to imply this failing in Rudd.

In No. 10, Rudd's Home Office predecessor still, bogglingly, resists any personal blame. In one of his newspaper columns, May's former chief of staff, Nick Timothy, claims – wrongly – that May was against the vans and was on holiday or something, while referring to the 'so-called hostile environment policy', when it was literally called so by him and his boss. Meanwhile, David Cameron – in pursuit of whose ludicrous back-of-a-napkin immigration targets all this was done – disembarked from the gravy train momentarily this week to ignore the subject entirely in a CNN interview.

And on they all go. If the government is in any doubt as to why so many millions think it's one rule for them and another for the little people, then this week couldn't be a better primer. You lose one form and you lose your job, your cancer treatment, your benefits, your liberty; you lose a generation's forms and you're the effing prime minister. Those condemned to battle the systems that ministers design know what happens if they make tiny errors. Furthermore, they know that if they messed up a tenth as badly in their jobs, they'd be sacked. But in the arse-over-tit world of government, you're safe because your sacking would make the big boss – May – look weak. Just like your HR department, right? Except on LSD.

I don't want to fall back on a series of politicians' best-loved clichés, but this level of irresponsibility is just scrounging with a red box. They play for high stakes – but never their own. It's the sort of system-milking demonised in a benefits office in Grimsby but regarded as career progression in Westminster. It makes it appear there's no glass ceiling in modern political life, just a reinforced lead floor. Once you're in, you basically have to die to stop earning rewards. Take Timothy, who we can't describe as back on his bullshit, because he's never been off it. I've had yoghurts in my fridge longer than he was in the political wilderness. Or Cameron, whose CNN interview saw him still regurgitating his catchphrase 'It was the right thing to do.' I do hope his forthcoming book embraces the absurdity and is called *All the Right Things to Do That I Did*.

Perhaps the most staggering part – for those of us not being imprisoned or barred from our mother's funerals, I should stress – is how little self-awareness our leaders have about their failures and their own part in them. May still reckons the worst thing she ever did was run through a cereal crop.

In his 1997 Edinburgh show, the brilliant and subversive comedian Simon Munnery had this thing called the Self-Knowledge Impregnator. If an audience member transgressed by heckling, the imperious Nietzschean character he was playing would shout: 'Activate the Self-Knowledge Impregnator!' Six people would then wheel an 8ft black box on stage, which contained a very powerful flash behind a piece of wood with a single word cut out of it. The lights would go out. And then . . . well, over to Simon. The box 'would be placed directly in front of the heckler. And I would go: "Are you aware of what you are?" And they'd go: "No." And then we'd go [*FLASH!*] and it would burn the word "cunt" on to their retina.'

I saw this show several times. Even if you weren't the Self-Knowledge Impregnator's target, you could still see the word every time you shut your eyes for ages afterwards. Don't tell me we don't invent beautiful machines in this country any more.

Or at least we did. That was 21 years ago. Where is the Self-Knowledge Impregnator now? Has the hour of need ever been greater? Can't it be strapped to the back of an advertising van and driven at top speed to the next cabinet meeting, in the name of human decency?

Keep calm – the Top Guns of Brexit have got our backs

8 June 2018

Here's hoping the EU negotiations can be fixed with a little psychopathic machismo. Because the Tories are awash with it

Barely two weeks after Russian phone pranksters taped him being indiscreet, I see Boris Johnson's been the victim of another leaked recording. Speaking at a private dinner for Conservative Way Forward, the foreign secretary asked his audience not to panic during the coming Brexit 'meltdown', warned we may not get the Brexit we want and implied the UK needed more 'guts' in EU talks.

Secret recordings are the Westminster equivalent of sex tapes. A violation and a betrayal and all that jazz – but if you play your cards right, you can clean up on the royalties and parlay the notoriety into serious power. Witness the Kardashians. In five years' time, everyone could be *Keeping Up with the Johnsons*. I'm gutted for the foreign secretary that someone took a moment that should have been so intimate and personal and gave it to Buzzfeed. I'm sure it feels very violating. But as a tenuously devastated Tommy Lee reflected after his sex tape with then wife Pamela Anderson went viral: now everyone knew he had the biggest dick in rock.

So, yes, I suspect the foreign secretary will somehow get over this invasion of privacy, which is, after all, only his latest attempt to distance himself from a collapsing building of which he was one of the leading architects.

There is something mesmerically psychopathic about the way Boris talks about Brexit betrayal when he is the holder of a great office of state in the government that is – right now – delivering it. His laments recall one of those police TV appeals where the weeping boyfriend of a missing woman looks straight into the camera and pleads for any information as to her whereabouts. I shan't insult your intelligence by stating who the cops eventually pick up for the crime.

Boris also revealed he was warming strongly to Donald Trump, who'd be great at negotiating Brexit because 'he'd go in bloody hard'. There's always a slight frisson among the self-styled alphas, isn't there – the momentary whiff of the beach volleyball scene in *Top Gun*. Brexit just needs a Kenny Loggins soundtrack, and Trump could be its wingman anytime.

Still, tell you who else goes in bloody hard: David Davis. Don't take my word for it – take Nadine Dorries's, even if she hasn't been playing with a full set of patio furniture since the MPs' expenses scandal. 'David Davis is ex-SAS,' thundered the member for Mid Bedfordshire this week. 'He's trained to survive. He's also trained to take people out.' Actually, don't take Nadine's word for it, take David's himself. Here's the DExEU secretary on the joker who ambushed Theresa May during her conference speech last September: 'He's lucky I didn't hit him. He'd have been down for a long time.' Ooh. Diet Coke break, girls!

Reading this faintly excruciating comment at the time, I went back to the footage from the conference hall and could see that the main reason why David Davis doesn't take down the potential security threat to the prime minister is that David Davis stays sitting in his chair the whole time. So all we're really left with is his time-worn yen for self-dramatisation. When Colombian criminals kidnapped a British defence attaché in Bogotá in 1995, Davis was the Foreign Office duty minister, and inspired a Cobra meeting with the declaration: 'Failure is not an option.' Personally, I think it's fine to quote *Apollo 13*, which was in cinemas at the time – but it is poor form not to attribute.

He was back on the theatrics on Wednesday over this backstop business. Are you on top of the 'backstop', which the EU has predictably rejected? It feels apt that the UK has chosen to invoke the not-even-a-sport of rounders. There's a reason why rounders is what people play on their office awaydays – it's because you don't have to be any good at it, or know the rules, or even know what's going on. Unfortunately, these are not the criteria for handling complex negotiations with the EU. For them, the UK twatting around with backstops is just not cricket. They don't really deal in backstops. What they really need to hear is that the UK is going to have four slips and a gully, and a forward short leg. Or, given our increasingly defensive needs, everyone on the boundary, including a third man and a deep fine leg.

Instead, we're trying to play rounders. And David Davis spent much of Wednesday hinting he was going to take his bat home. He was on the brink, then he was stepping back from it, then he was back on it, and so on. Davis has threatened more farewells than Barbra Streisand. Do they give VCs for being a diva in the Territorials?

Incidentally, when I was writing this newspaper's Diary column – sometime in the early Cretaceous period – I solicited reminiscences of Davis's time in the SAS (Territorial). A couple of his former brothers-in-arms got in touch with memories of TA 21 SAS (V). I had two favourite anecdotes. The first was when Davis was required to coordinate an ambush and opted to position his men on either side of the road, so that – had the exercise been real – the soldiers would have opened fire on each other. The Sun Tzu of DExEU, there. The second story saw Davis charged with managing an 'escape and evasion' mission. 'It was supposed to last five days,' recalled one of his men. 'But he accidentally led us through a choke point – a kind of bottleneck where trackers always wait – and got us captured inside 36 hours. So we were put in a truck, blindfolded, driven around, and dropped at night on an undisclosed remote hill to start all over again.' I mean . . . the jokes are too easy, aren't they?

As for Brexit's other hardmen, don't forget those who, in the arse-about-tit world of Westminster, have reinvented themselves as players whose rhetorical currency is 'passion' and 'hardball'. The likes of Jacob Rees-Mogg – a sort of monocled Sergio Ramos who's going to do this thing by any means necessary.

All in all, I haven't felt this sarcastically aroused by Brexit virility since that week when one of Ukip's MEPs lamped one of its other MEPs, causing him to collapse at the European parliament. We were then treated to the spectacle of Ukip's Neil Hamilton – a man who dresses as his wife's ventriloquist's dummy – swaggering on to the news like he was Jason Statham and growling that the punched one had 'picked a fight and come off worse'. Defending his own decision to punch his business partner, Brexit financier Arron Banks then told a Twitter user: 'You wouldn't understand. It's called a competitive spirit. It's why some people are winners.' Damn straight. Shirts versus skins. Go big or go home. Loggins on the boombox. Or, as Nigel Farage whined last week: 'I never said it would be a beneficial thing to leave and everyone would be better off.'

Ukip's sojourn in Brussels always felt like a two-decade stag weekend. But if you ever doubt how fully the Conservative party has imported their hold-my-beer culture, just look at how leading Tory Brexiteers keep acting now. I know we're all men of the world, but honestly – how much more Brexit machismo can we handle before the swooning becomes a coma?

Antisemitism, Islamophobia – and this is just the Brexit phoney war

10 August 2018

Boris Johnson's swipe at Muslim women has left both major parties in conflict with minorities. It all feels a bit ominous

Never less than up-to-the-minute, I have just read Boris Johnson's 2004 novel *Seventy-Two Virgins*. If you're wondering if that title doubles as a description of its readership, you're on the wrong track. It sold well, and the reader is duly lured in by the cover quote promising that 'Johnson scores in his comic handling of these sensitive issues.'

Mm. For some of us, Boris's reputation as a dazzling writer is very emperor's new prose. But he is certainly better suited to fictions than facts. The most majestic thing I read this week was a review of Johnson's Churchill biography by the eminent historian

Richard Evans, which contains such affectless drive-bys as 'The Germans did not capture Stalingrad, though this book claims they did.' Body bag for Mr Johnson, please.

That said, a lot of psychology does fall into place when you discover that in *Seventy-Two Virgins*, Boris's hot 23-year-old female character is (a) called Cameron and (b) regards a certain type of posturing verbosity as the ultimate knee-trembler. Or, as the author puts it: 'Cameron had a deep and sexist reverence for men who really knew stuff. It amazed her how little appearances really mattered.' I bet it did. Still want more? Tough, because you're getting it. 'If that man's disquisition had enough interest, fluency and authority, it would speak directly to her groin.'

Ooh, Boris, can you quote Thucydides while opening a kiddie daycare centre again? Can you do the speech about selling tea to China and French knickers to France for the 900th time? Can you say 'mugwump' like it's the Manchurian trigger word for activating the most abandoned form of female sexuality? Come on, don't stop now, we're all ALMOST THERE.

Well, sorry, sex hounds – but not today. The recovering foreign secretary needs to laugh at women in niqabs in order to stiffen up his new base. Don't worry – the product all comes in discreet packaging.

As you will doubtless be aware, Boris used his *Telegraph* column this week to joke that women who wear the burqa – he meant the niqab, but whatevs – look like 'letterboxes' and 'bank robbers'. These gags have now been described as 'pretty good' by *Johnny English* star Rowan Atkinson, though I think I'll wait for late-era John Cleese to praise them before I make my mind up.

Either way, I am amused (though not surprised) to discover that the hijab-wearing Remona Aly once wrote a satirical *Guardian* column suggesting different uses for the burqa. But I am even more amused at the suggestion that this is precisely the same as a senior politician making fun of women who wear the garment in order to advance his leadership ambitions. It is, as Spinal Tap's David St Hubbins once remarked, such a fine line between stupid and clever.

That said, the furore has inspired various valuable public services. A 2013 clip from *Question Time* was resurrected, in which Emily Thornberry explains she wouldn't want her child looked after by someone wearing a burqa. A reminder that, while it may currently suit some people to forget Thornberry's essential snootiness about all manner of things, they're not going to be able to ignore it for ever.

As for Atkinson, who has previously made many valuable points about free speech, I'm sorry he can't see that punching up at Islam is fine, while punching down at the tiny number of women who wear the niqab and are already disproportionately likely to suffer street abuse is something else. It's the equivalent of that classic footage of Boris flattening the 10-year-old Japanese kid while playing rugby on a trip to Tokyo. You show him, big guy!

Of course, absolutely none of this is really a freedom-of-speech issue. It is one of the cast-iron rules of modern political discourse that if someone tells you that you can't say a certain thing any more, you will use your next breath to say that very thing. Every time. 'You can't say this any more, but Muslim women make me feel uncomfortable'; 'I know you're not allowed to say this any more, but these are Jewish mind games.' I mean . . . you patently can effing say it, can't you, because you literally just have.

Still, it's instructive to see who rides to whose defence. One of the other great rules of the modern era for a certain stripe of populist is that you don't punch right. (Or, in the case of Jeremy Corbyn, you don't punch left.) You need those guys. So Donald Trump tells Infowars wingnut Alex Jones that his show's 'amazing'. Similarly, that hammy old fraud Jacob Rees-Mogg isn't about to ask for a bit more civility from Johnson.

Instead, the North East Somerset MP declared Boris 'completely entitled to say it'. To which the only response can be: is this the same Rees-Mogg who is against even raped girls committing the 'second wrong' of abortion – but who snowflakily accused the BBC of 'straying into religious bigotry' for asking about views such as this? Like I say, it's such a fine line between stupid and clever. (A friend who had to sit through many of Rees-Mogg's debating society performances at Eton memorably described him to me as 'like a posh Karl Pilkington'.)

So here we are, with the Tories and Labour still pretty much neck-and-neck in the polls, just as they were a year ago, each unable to pull ahead against what they've decided are the worst bunch in modern history. It is easy, in the clichéd Punch-and-Judy world of Westminster, to sigh knowingly at the pendulum swing. Last week, we were on Labour's latest grim paroxysm of antisemitism; this week, it's the Tories and Islamophobia.

And yet, if we take a step back, doesn't the picture resolve into something that should be much more worrying? It turns out we are now a country where both major parties are locked in sustained, self-started fights with minority communities. That feels ominous. We are still only in the phoney war of Brexit, after all – the period where the questions are all about who benefits. Who benefited from what even some Brexit voters such as Danny Dyer have decided is turning pear-shaped? Was it Arron Banks? Is it Johnson? Will it be Gove?

If much of history is any guide, we might reasonably fear that once the realities kick in, another phase will follow the period of asking who benefits. And that will be the period where people decide who gets blamed. Who is at the sharp end when things don't turn out how they were promised? Who is turned against? Who gets it in the neck? It certainly isn't well-off and socially insulated politicians, however much of a metaphorical pasting they might imagine they take for things that are, after all, their own fault. The weak will suffer. In this context, it is more than a grim symmetry to find significant factions in both major political parties pitting themselves against minority communities. It is an alarm bell.

Karen Bradley routs her rival imbeciles with Ladybird guide to Northern Ireland

7 September 2018

The Northern Ireland secretary's ignorance of the most sensitive region of the UK takes the cabinet beyond shame

Pay attention, entrails-pickers: this dead government has yielded up a new sign. She is Karen Bradley, actual secretary of state for actual Northern Ireland, and she has granted an interview to Parliament's *The House* magazine. 'I freely admit,' Karen freely admitted, 'that when I started this job, I didn't understand some of the deep-seated and deep-rooted issues that there are in Northern Ireland. I didn't understand things like when elections are fought, for example, in Northern Ireland – people who are nationalists don't vote for unionist parties and vice versa.'

For me, I think that quote may be the equivalent of the death blow in *Kill Bill*. Do you know the one? You get hit just with fingertips, 'and then he lets you walk away. But once you've taken five steps, your heart explodes in your body, and you fall to the floor, dead.' So it is with the Northern Ireland secretary's hot take on Northern Ireland. My mechanism might be shot for good after reading it. I may well be typing my last five steps here.

Clearly, it is not simply the initial imbecility of having no clue about the central facts of Northern Irish politics and history, even though you were 28 (TWENTY-EIGHT) when the Good Friday agreement was signed. It is also the second imbecility of thinking you should ever mention that in public, much less as delightedly as Karen did. 'It's when you realise that,' burbled the secretary of state, 'that you can then start to understand some of the things that the politicians say and some of the rhetoric.'

I mean ... ideally, you would start understanding these things some decades before you were the cabinet minister with operational responsibility for arguably the most highly sensitive region of the United Kingdom. Instead, Karen's breezy 'My Learning Curve' speech casts high office as a remedial scheme for the unreachable outliers of *Family Fortunes* survey respondents. 'We asked 100 people what they imagined were the Ladybird-level facts about Northern Ireland...'

Karen's answer is the type of WTF-ery that allows even Vernon Kay (VERNON KAY) to mug to camera with the practised eyebrow-raise that says: 'Where do they find these quarterwits?' It was previously thought that any challenge to Andrea Leadsom's position as stupidest cabinet minister would have to hail from the mineral or at least vegetable kingdoms. Or be Chris Grayling. But this is quite sensational from Karen, who places herself in the IDS class at a stroke. Theresa May's decision to appoint her to this government of all the talentless underscores exactly where we are. If you hadn't already swallowed the red pill, you may safely consider Karen's interview as your dose. No going back now. The answer to the question 'How low is the bar?' is: the bar is in another hemisphere. The bar is orbiting Jupiter. There is no bar.

Any bright spots this week? Well, I see Arron Banks has once again had his bid to sign for the Conservatives knocked back. At this rate, he's going to notch up more failed medicals than John Hartson.

But darker portents attend Karen's predecessor as the cabinet minister most wantonly and insouciantly unsuited to their job. It's been a mixed few days for Boris Johnson. On the downside for us, Boris has been explicitly backed for the leadership by cruelly miscast kingmaker Jacob Rees-Mogg. On the upside, Johnson's statement announcing his divorce from his wife tees up a series of excruciating *Love Actually* plotlines for when he later – or sooner – gets the keys to No. 10. (And if you're still doubting the heart-exploding inevitability of that scenario, you must have been watching the global upsets of the past two years on tape delay. Everything that can go wrong does. Buy shares in distilleries today.)

As for the coveted endorsement from someone Boris would unquestionably have pitied mercilessly at school (he and Mogg missed being Eton contemporaries by a year), it came in an LBC interview. 'Two years ago, in the Conservative party leadership campaign, I supported Boris Johnson, because I thought he would deliver Brexit extraordinarily well,' Rees-Mogg intoned, suggesting he has inherited all his father's gifts of prophecy. 'I haven't seen anything that would cause me to change my mind on that.' Not anything?! Should have gone to MonocleSavers.

Yet Boris is undeniably back. He has never been more back. Perhaps the most striking feature of the immediate period is how people decisively written off as wrong-'uns in the very recent past are emerging again as comparatively attractive prospects. Two years ago, Michael Gove had been deservedly downgraded to a mere backstabber; now he's apparently a leadership contender once more. Outside Westminster, what a pleasure to see Mervyn King given so much airtime this week to sniff about Brexit 'chaos'. Is this the same Mervyn King who, as governor of the Bank of England, presided over the first run on a British bank since the 1860s?

Perhaps the preposterous inadequates of the past do all seem like elder statespeople now. Others appear so inspired by their accelerated rehabilitation that they are trying to pull off something similar instantly. Take David Davis, who announced this week that he would attend a Leave Means Leave rally in Bolton 'as a matter of principle, to ensure Brexit is delivered'.

What can you say? Until about 10 minutes ago, David had spent two years as the cabinet minister literally in charge of delivering it. This is like setting fire to a building, running away, then standing outside telling the emergency services how you'd be handling the rescue differently.

Expect plenty more auditions for the role of Captain Hindsight in the weeks and months ahead. First the government and its renegades were post-truth; now they are post-shame. And that just about wraps up this week's round-up. Try not to choke on it.

It's Theresa May v. Boris Johnson at the Tories' Groundhog conference

3 October 2018

The story of this year's event was one of a government unable to fill the main hall for its cabinet speakers, while activists queued round the block for fringe events

When David Cameron held his referendum to 'settle the issue of Europe for a generation', I wonder if he envisaged a Conservative party conference like this one taking place more than two years after the fact. It is the third conference since the EU referendum, and the second since Article 50 was triggered. The Tories are still fighting their forever war; we all just have to live in it.

MPs who should, years ago, have been relegated to the status of taxidermal curiosities still stalk these lands. 'I see some people are here who were part of the original Maastricht referendum campaign,' bellowed Bill Cash at some deranged fringe event. 'Give them a clap!' Give them the clap, more like.

'Last week was the 30th anniversary of Margaret Thatcher's Bruges speech,' ran another rallying cry. Somewhere at this gathering in Birmingham it was always turn-of-the-1990s o'clock. It's as if there's some tear in the Tory-bastardry continuum. Who's going to fix it? Theresa May, who mostly resembles a Quentin Blake drawing of an unravelling postmistress? Boris Johnson, the Cabbage Patch Draco Malfoy, who turned up for about an hour and bottled his big fight? Or perhaps you prefer some of the other prospects. Jeremy Hunt? Sajid Javid? Liz Truss?!

Still, take up your tiki torches and join me at the Tory survivors' tribal council, which felt as though it lasted at least 17 days. The conference slogan – 'OPPORTUNITY' – was not so much phoned in as faxed in. That is it in its entirety. 'OPPORTUNITY'. As in, we had an opportunity to choose something that didn't sound as if it was thought up by a small-portfolio buy-to-let landlord whose wife was calling up the stairs: 'Can you hurry, Les – Kwikprint shuts at six?' The slogan called to mind that line in *The Thick of It* when the night editor says: 'Just tell me what the fucking news is and I'll stick it on the front page. It's not like we're the *Independent*, I can't just stick a headline saying "CRUELTY" and then stick a picture of a dolphin or a whale underneath it.'

As it turned out, 'OPPORTUNITY' was a slogan that mainly had some floundering secretary of state stuck underneath it. The story of this conference was one of a government unable to remotely fill the main hall for its cabinet speakers, while activists queued round the block for fringe events protesting against its central policy. Javid, highly fancied for the Tory leadership, spoke to a half-empty room.

Three individuals, and what they represented, dominated these four days: May herself, Johnson (99% absent) and Jacob Rees-Mogg. We shall come to these dramatis personae shortly. As for the big policy announcements, there is a pop art comic strip where a sobbing woman is saying: 'I can't believe it. I forgot to have children.' This, but for policies. The Tories had forgotten to have any policies. If your answer to 'What is going to win us back Canterbury?' is 'Action on middle-class cocaine users,' you must actually be on cocaine. May's ludicrous 'festival of national renewal' idea was immediately dubbed the festival of Brexit Britain. You've heard of straight-to-DVD; May's policy agenda is now straight-to-meme.

The only retail offer here was literal retail. As always, there was a wide range of shopping opportunities for activists. I saw several men being measured for a suit, as you do at a party conference. I saw a huge amount of felted goods and ceramic jewellery. I saw lots of Conservative baby bibs. (Interesting to market your logo as something that specifically is going to get thrown up on.)

But on with the main event. It was difficult not to conclude that the Tory party has been gamified in a way that rewards aggressive imbecility. The signal that you wish to be taken seriously as leadership material is to say something incredibly stupid. For Jeremy Hunt, that meant declaring, pointedly: 'The EU was set up to protect freedom. It was the Soviet Union that stopped people leaving.' Yes. Last year, the EU was Hitler; this year, it is Stalin. Like almost every minister who has insulted the other side in this negotiation since Article 50 was triggered, Hunt predicated his trash talk on the idea that the EU doesn't have the internet, and that this sort of WTF-ery is somehow firewalled by the English Channel. It isn't, as furious condemnation from the people we want a deal off has since confirmed.

Furthermore, if you ever wonder what has happened to our political discourse in recent times, consider that 10 years ago this level of analysis was the preserve of imaginatively limited internet commenters. 'EUSSR' took its place below the line, alongside such exquisitely crafted points as 'Tony Bliar' or 'ZANU Liarbore'. EUSSR is now the sort of thing the actual foreign secretary says on an actual conference stage.

The best thing you could say about Hunt's speech was that it wasn't being made by Philip Hammond, who still delivers lines with all the rhetorical flourish of a reversing Securicor vehicle. If you wanted to hide pictures of Johnson blowing rails with Donald Trump, inside a Hammond speech would be the perfect place. Indeed, the chancellor did stash some fairly outré material in his dirge, such as the statement 'the Conservative party is sceptical of ideologues'.

Even less appealing was Gavin Williamson, who continues to look as though he took the rejection letter from Starfleet Academy pretty hard. Still, the defence secretary is going to start his own force of 'cyber cadets'. Alas, to watch him make repeated pauses for laughter that never came was to watch a man finding out in real time that he isn't going to captain this particular starship.

Other lowlights? That old reverse Midas, Chris Grayling, being late for his own speech, which turned out to be the replacement bus service of oratory. And then there was Dominic Raab. Soap operas that have seriously lost their way often deploy an 'evil twin' device. I can only assume that this is what has happened to the Tory *telenovela*. Raab is playing both roles simultaneously. He devoted much of his speech to lambasting Cassandra-like warnings about a no-deal Brexit. 'This time [they'll] claim that no deal means patients won't get their medicines, mobile phone roaming charges will go through the roof and –' Dominic? DOMINIC??? Sorry to cut you off, but those were the impact assessments put out by your own department, of which you are the secretary of state. 'Honestly,' Raab continued ironicidally, 'it would be pathetic if it wasn't so dangerous.'

And with that, we can avoid him no longer. Boris Johnson had almost full-spectrum dominance of this conference. Talked about feverishly by attendees, his moves endlessly speculated upon, the effect is to make the entire event seem like a lavish party missing only its host. Think of Boris as the Great Twatsby. The effect of much of his manoeuvring this week was to remind us that he is someone so far away from having a clue that he constantly suggests building a bridge to it. Does Johnson even have a psychoanalyst? Like several of the worst men of the age, he appears to deem high office the place to explore issues that really should be worked out via his dream journal.

Still, here comes the Unaboris with his 4,600-word manifesto, ready to commit another act of political terrorism. His fringe speech on Tuesday chastised a government for which he was collectively responsible for two whole years; his *Sunday Telegraph* manifesto was a document in which not a whole lot of detail was manifest. The former foreign secretary's reputation as a rousing prose stylist remains baffling. Johnson writes like someone who has failed to enable the find-my-point function on his phone. Even so, the word-dump ensured the prime minister couldn't even get pre-title billing for her own conference.

Three full days into this psychodrama, May was asked on the *Today* programme what she would say to Johnson. Chat shit get banged, surely? Unfortunately, she went with: 'What I would say is, "I'm concentrating on what is important, which is getting a good deal for the UK."'

Thus, it was left to others to do the banging of the shit-chatter. There was a strong sense among MPs here that they are so very, very tired of Johnson that they can't even be bothered to be artful about it. 'As far as I'm concerned,' Henley MP John Howell reflected, 'Boris can just fuck off.' The Scottish Tories have launched a campaign to stop him becoming party leader, under the name Operation Arse. As one put it: 'We called it that so we'd be clear who we were talking about.' Asked what the big challenge for the Tories was, the former minister Lord O'Neill judged: 'I guess key people in this party have to stop being dickheads, really.'

So quite a lot was hinging on Johnson's speech. Unfortunately, Johnson has a psychological tell, where he likes to see Britain as the sort of country that is so sexually potent it could impregnate the rest of the world just by looking at it. In last year's election, I saw him rage that sending Trident to sea with no missiles on board would mean 'the whole country's literally firing blanks'. In Tuesday's Birmingham speech, he announced that he had come to 'put some lead in the collective pencil'. Again, one for his psychoanalyst from the Tories' Freudian candidate.

As he knows, Johnson hasn't anywhere near the numbers among MPs yet to get his name on the members' ballot in any leadership contest. So Tuesday's speech, however rapturously received till that point, concluded thus: 'I urge our friends in government to deliver what the people voted for, to back Theresa May in the best way possible, by softly, quietly and sensibly backing her original plan.' Thank you, Cuck Norris.

Until Johnson finally turned up in Birmingham, his place in the activists' affections was occupied by that appalling bacillus Rees-Mogg. Hey – if you can't have the lead singer, you'll settle for the roadie. I enjoyed him most on how the Tories can win the youth vote. Rees-Mogg, who spent his youth being 73, seems to think that all the youths he speaks to want to take back control of their laws, their money and their borders. It is to be assumed the data sample was the 12 members of Durham University Conservative Society he met when he blew into town to debate some motion like 'This House Would Nationalise Daytime TV'.

Never ones to be rushed, the Tories seem to have finally realised that people want houses, and were consequently free to move on to arguing their way to deadlock on what sort of houses they should build. Rees-Mogg is against the plan to build the sort of houses that people don't want, and instead wants 'Georgian pastiche houses'. Also, he wants a bridge (who doesn't?). He said he wanted the Bath bypass to be 'a Georgian pastiche bridge with little pavilions at both ends'.

The problem with Rees-Mogg saying 'pastiche' every 15 seconds is that it reminds you he is one. Still, they absolutely lap it up here. He pointed out to one pant-wettingly amused audience that he wore his conference security pass on a buttonhole chain. 'It's the one thing I learned from Michael Heseltine.' This particular event had required Rees-Mogg to enter via a staircase, and he is almost at the stage of dancing down it at that sideways angle of the light-entertainment host. A barrage of cameras attends his every affectation. 'Oh, poor Jacob,' cooed a woman in front of me. 'He's just trying to sit quietly in the front row until he's called to speak.'

Madam, I regret to inform you that this is a defective take. You are as entitled to your fantasy of a knee-trembler in the scullery as the next forelock-tugger, but the camera at which Rees-Mogg does not wish to affect lengthy surprise has yet to be found.

Meanwhile, he never fails to give them what they want. 'As you would expect,' began a typical piece of self-reference, 'I'm going to give you a historic analogy.' Explaining that he was happy with a 'supercalifragilisticexpialidocious Canada' Brexit model, Rees-Mogg noted: 'That is a word developed by a nanny, and nannies are jolly good things.'

Time and again this week, the likes of Rees-Mogg, Priti Patel and Andrea Jenkyns suggested that no deal was much the preferred outcome, as then we wouldn't have to pay the EU '£40bn of your money'. 'Why aren't we doing that anyway?' they kept saying, to loud applause. But please don't imagine they haven't thought it all through in remorseless analytical detail. 'Brexit will be a success', explained Rees-Mogg, 'because it is a Conservative thing to be doing.'

As for the prime minister, her own speech was entitled 'Campaign 2022', a prospect radically more depressing than even 'Qatar 2022'. Thanks to last year's calamity, any speech in which she doesn't cough up a lung is a positive. But her wide-ranging, Abba-dancing turn as the unity candidate was strongly applauded in the conference hall, seemingly as something other than self-satire.

So here is where we are at the end of this conference. Theresa May is still prime minister. Boris Johnson still wants to be prime minister. And somewhere in a £25,000 shepherd's hut, David Cameron is sleeping easily, tweeting his pedicures and continually popping his memoirs back a few months in the hope that his mess will have been cleaned up by publication date.

Yet if Labour are comforted by this shitshow, they must consider its implications as far as their own performance markers go. Imagine not having a 10-point poll lead over this lot. 'Don't know' (39%)

still outpolls both May (36%) and Jeremy Corbyn (23%) as to who would make the best prime minister. This is Groundhog Year. For all their big talk, and their dick-waving, and their self-started fights with minority communities, both parties are exactly where they were a year ago in the poll tracker, even as various doomsday clocks have ticked closer to midnight.

Whether or not they can admit it to themselves, both parties (though Labour more so, being the opposition) are effectively waiting for a crisis to shift the numbers in their favour. No deal, a recession, a welfare system failure – the best hope for moving the polls is one disaster or another befalling the people whom their different forms of ineptitude have already shamefully failed. That is the most likely gamechanger – and a reminder that however atrocious the current state of politics feels, it is still not the darkest timeline. There are much darker ones, and we could easily cross into several of them.

Finally, some good news: the ERG has been aggressively made love to by an ass

13 December 2018

After the failed ERG coup, Theresa lives to die another day. Now can the mad bastards of her party come out of their 'kill zones' for a Christmas truce?

Of all the mad bastards out there, there are none madder than the Conservative party. The Tories' self-indulgent bastardry is now at such thermonuclear levels that it could surely cause a rip in the very fabric of time and space itself, opening a portal into another dimension from which the dark lord Cthulhu may emerge to lead them. But can Cthulhu get a bold, creative and bespoke deal that takes back control of our borders, our money and our . . . I'm sorry, I can't any more. Maybe tomorrow. The one thing I would say about the dark lord is that he'd probably realise taking back control of the Conservative party would be an effing start.

And so to where we stand after a ludicrous 24 hours – a midwinter night's dream after which nothing has changed as far as the Brexit deadlock in parliament goes. But at least the ERG have been aggressively made love to by an ass.

Theresa May has lived to die another day, after a Wednesday of almost mundane grotesquery. In some ways, you get so desensitised to watching Tories get their mark of Cain badge that distaste gives way to ennui. At other times, it surges back. In order that they might vote for May, the Tory whip was restored to alleged inappropriate toucher and bully Charlie Elphicke, alleged bully and prolific extreme sexter Andrew Griffiths, and Cyrus the Virus from *Con Air*. Labour? Don't ask me about Labour. I believe they're having a meaningful-Brexit-position reveal party in late January.

Anyway, before we go on, a word about the ERG. This was the second failed attempt to unseat May in three weeks, by a bunch of guys who'd be picked last for paintball and are led by rejected *Paddington* villain Jacob Rees-Mogg. According to some reports, the ERG nicknamed the room in which they coordinated Wednesday's mission to terminate the prime minister 'The Kill Zone'. Course they did. They're hardmen. Zero Dark Have-We-Got-to-Thirty. Seal Team Six, only with actual seals, honking their fishy bullshit across the airwaves, apparently for all eternity.

Tell you what, when you finally apply for your totemic blue passport and the form asks for your country of residence, just put 'the Stygian Banterlands'. That is the place where we live now, shackled to the same lunatics in the Conservative party we've been tied to for three decades. Why couldn't we get the pushing-the-boulder-up-the-hill punishment instead? Or the sword-hanging-above-our-head one? I'd take any of them all day long over having to clap eyes ever again on Andrew Bridgen, who should be playing Captain Hook's dog in a Leicester panto, where small children could throw sweets at him every time he came on stage, wagging his vestigial tail.

I know the ERG aren't details men, but just for the record: in tactical military vocabulary, 'the kill zone' defines a space within which killing occurs, being comprehensively covered by firepower, rather than one from which killing is masterminded. And now in Westminster vocabulary too, as nanny has to set her face and change the sheets for the second time in a month.

As for the young masters of the ERG, they were furious about 1922 committee chairman Graham Brady's decision to hold the confidence vote within 24 hours of the letters threshold being reached. 'It is an absolute outrage,' one told the *Telegraph* in a typical category mistake. 'Whether we end up with a change of leader, we will end up with a change of '22 chairman.' Waa waa waa, we need a new leader. Waa waa waa, we need a new chairman. Waa waa waa, we need new voters. Buck up, boys. I'm sure wildly miscast Aslan metaphor Boris Johnson will rise from the dead and save you in due course.

Needless to say, those weren't the only tears. According to various sources, even some ministers were crying during Theresa May's pitch to the 1922 committee, when she told them she wouldn't lead the Conservative party into the next election. She might as well have added 'or lead the England side on to the pitch at the 2022 World Cup'. Still, it won't have escaped your attention that at least one general election is likely to be already in the post, and due to arrive a lot sooner than that. May has only ruled herself out of 2022, although she apparently told the room that 'in my heart' she wanted to exorcise the 2017 demons and win then. A bit like when Stuart Pearce scored the 1990-exorcising penalty in the quarter-finals of Euro '96 – except with a robotic round of heavily controlled factory visits that somehow ends up getting Theresa May a landslide. The point is: she can CHANGE.

In this, as in so many other things, the alleged party of government continues to misunderstand itself. How else to explain the fact that, after the week we've just had, Theresa May stood in Downing Street on Wednesday morning and literally said the words: 'A bright future for our country has not wavered, and it is now within our grasp.' For the rest of the day, members of the government kept popping up in the TV field hospital that's been erected outside parliament and saying things like how the confidence vote 'risks dividing the Tory party'. Babes, we passed dividing-the-Tory-party three towns ago. We're now at the city limits of trial-by-combat. Sorry for the spoilers.

As for where we go from here, many of us may find ourselves reaching the burn-it-all-down stage of a character's journey. Perhaps both sides of the Conservative party could declare a Christmas truce and emerge from their kill zones and trenches to play a football match on the big day? Before, obviously, returning to attempt the senseless slaughter of each other the next.

DONALD TRUMP: REALITY TV, UNREALITY POLITICS

Having explained in January 2016 that he could stand in the middle of Fifth Avenue, shoot somebody and still not lose any voters, Donald Trump proceeds to win the US presidency and make a fool of anyone who claimed his inner statesman would soon emerge. His ascent recalls that line in *The Picture of Dorian Gray* – 'You are the type of what the age is searching for, and what it is afraid it has found.' The Trump presidency begins with lies about his inauguration crowds and concludes with a mob of his supporters storming the Capitol building in a day of violence that leaves five people dead. His tenure in the White House comes with a steady deluge of grotesque lies, conspiracism, Covid denialism, corruption, sexual assault allegations, 37,000 rounds of golf and any number of 5am tweetstorms from his toilet. It ends with an outright assault on democracy itself that is still ongoing. It's difficult to summarise the enormity of it all in any one way, other than to observe that it is just possible the American Century is officially over.

Guys, there is one Donald Trump, there is one speech

20 January 2017

Hopes that a new Trump might step up to the inauguration podium were quickly crushed under the fist of 'America first'

As a man mesmerised by his own television persona, Donald Trump couldn't stop himself staring directly down the lens of the camera poised to capture him just before he emerged on to the steps of the Capitol to be sworn in as the 45th president of the United States. 'Hello,' breathed the star of *Mr Smith Goes to Watchimself*. Thus begins reality TV's stunningly unsettling reboot of the fish-out-of-water genre.

The president's inaugural address sounded like it had been assembled by an automated Donald Trump content generator. Bridges, tunnels, 'a historic movement the likes of which the world has never known'. It was as out-of-focus as his hair – until it suddenly, chillingly wasn't. 'We are issuing a new decree,' the new leader of the free world yelled. 'From this day forward, it's going to be ONLY America first, America first . . . America will start winning again – winning like never before! . . . This American carnage stops right here, and stops RIGHT NOW!'

Twenty minutes of that, and Barack Obama's airborne departure had shades of the last helicopter out of Saigon. Washington had fallen, the new president very much wanted America to know, as he stood right in the heart of it and denounced its every effort. As he assured the crowds, strikingly diminished in comparison with Obama's: 'Now arrives the hour of action.' It arrives for the media too, especially those who marked time in the buildup by asking:

'Will we see a new Donald Trump out there today?' Guys, there is one Donald Trump, there is one speech. There is no fault with your TV. President Trump's demeanour was so openly populist and bullish that it seemed primarily designed to provide portentous establishing footage for future documentaries with titles like *Dark Star Rising* or *The Gathering Storm*.

So unboundaried has the president been in his years-long campaign to lower the tone that it was difficult for any of the speeches, prayers and readings given by anyone else not to sound like a veiled lecture to him. 'Pray for wisdom.' 'God blesses those who are humble.' May he grant you the ability to resist 4am tweetstorms. Some of the requests were so dementedly hopeful they could only have been included as a dare. 'We ask that you give him the meekness of Christ.' But at this point we'd settle for the meekness of Kanye West.

It was a day to be glad of the displacement rituals of protocol, especially if you were the Obamas. You come up the stairs. We shake hands. You stand there. Now we wave. I think you take the farther car door. You see – you just made it through five minutes without giving in to the impulse to mention my birth certificate or the unprecedented size of your hands. Only three years, 364 days, 23 hours and 55 minutes to go. A clearly inspired Trump manfully got through the swearing-in oath, even though he must have regarded the whole hand-on-the-Bible aspect as a conspiracy to focus global attention on his little paws. In the event, it was far more dignified than Mike Pence's oath, which was punctuated by someone in the crowd screaming, 'LOCK HER UP!'

And so to Hillary Clinton, forced to participate in the world's longest loser's reaction shot. At the Oscars, you only have to grit your teeth and grin for a minute when Liz Hurley's name comes out of the envelope instead of yours. On inauguration day, you have to keep that going for hours. The camera trained on Clinton as she waited inside the Capitol, ready to be formally introduced to the crowds by the announcer, caught her taking in a huge breath and setting her jaw.

Comic interludes? Trump failing to understand his chair-based dad-dancing was bad at the Lincoln Memorial rock concert on Thursday night, but more excruciating still when swaying and nodding along to the Mormon Tabernacle Choir. Then there was the detail that portable toilets for the crowds were provided by the same local firm which traditionally does it, only this time organisers were so antsy that they covered up the company name on the doors: Don's Johns. Pretty sure that's not the urination association they have to worry about.

There were also oddly touching moments – like George W. Bush being unable to keep the pleasure off his face when Michelle Obama picked him out and turned the full warmth of her spotlight greeting on him. Certainly, it was the first time I've seen that smirk look endearing. And it was hard not to feel sympathy for Melania Trump, who still looks like she's wearing a First Lady costume and radiated anxiety about not putting a foot wrong.

In the end, for those on board the Trump train, the aggressive display marked the day the slogan could start becoming a reality. But for much of the watching world, it will seem as if the lamps are going out all over America. It's unclear when we shall see them lit again.

Putting the nuke into nuclear family:
it's Trump and Kim Jong-un

11 August 2017

Severe daddy issues, atomic weapons . . . The volatile leaders of the
United States and North Korea now have a scary amount in common

There's something almost too psychiatrically candid about nuclear scientists always being called 'the father' of the bomb or 'the father' of their country's atomic programmes. I mean, you don't need Sigmund Freud to get to the bottom of that one, do you? Even Matthew Freud could probably explain it to you.

The daddy of them all was 'father of the atomic bomb' Robert Oppenheimer, but search the terms 'father of' and 'nuclear programme' and you'll find plenty more of his professional descendants – a whole host of chaps who don't really look like they're the kind of dad who'll take the bomb to the park, fix its bike, and not be a prick about putting on a washing load or giving it a cuddle. They are, of course, Brilliant Men, which traditionally gives them a free pass for being a parental grotesque, both in terms of their atomic offspring and, usually, their flesh-and-blood variety.

That their laboratory creations are now in the hands of two of the world's leading untreated daddy-issue sufferers – Kim Jong-un and Donald Trump – feels decidedly apt. Is 'apt' going to see you through a nuclear winter? Is 'apt' the antidote to radiation poisoning? 'Fraid not. Still, it'll be something to muse urbanely over as the ashes fall.

The Trumps and the Kims are both nuclear families, in the Chernobyl sense of the term. It would take one of the vast machines at Los Alamos to compute the sheer number of radioactively dysfunctional angles in both domestic set-ups, though most would agree the horror is passed via the paternal line. The entire premise of both families is obviously entirely oxymoronic. The Trumps are the anti-elite Manhattan billionaires; the Kims are a communist dynasty. One advantage the Trumps have over the Kims is that their succession issues have thus far been less brutal. Donald Sr's only brother didn't want to go into the family real-estate business and died at 42. The quote Trump gave to the *New York Times* when his father died concerned the latter's commercial decision not to develop property in Manhattan. 'It was good for me,' ran this well-adjusted eulogy. 'You know, being the son of somebody, it could have been competition to me. This way, I got Manhattan all to myself.'

As far as the next generation goes, there was clearly some kind of unspeakable trial by combat in the nursery via which Ivanka prevailed over her brothers Donald Jr and Eric, settling her into the Oedipal first-daughter role she now enjoys, at least until Barron gets dragons. (Tiffany? Nobody worries about Tiffany.) But the question of filial supremacy with the Kims was settled far later. So limited is the information that much of what is known comes from the account of Kim Jong-il's former sushi chef, who foretold Kim Jong-un's succession, explaining that one brother was considered too effeminate, while the elder son, Kim Jong-nam, was out of his father's favour after his famously brief attempt to visit Tokyo Disneyland. Last year, Kim Jong-nam was poisoned in Kuala Lumpur airport, which must have felt bittersweet for Kim Jong-un. Yes, he'll have exorcised his insane jealously that his brother had got within 10 miles of the Pirates of the Caribbean ride and he hadn't. But that will have mingled with a profound sense of sadness that he never got to bound puppyishly in to his late father and deposit his poisoned brother's corpse at his feet with the inquiry: 'Have I pleased you, Papa?'

Indeed, now his daddy's gone, is Kim Jong-un doing that classic thing of looking for a proxy? Of his defence spending, he has said:

'I have to let them know I have missiles because this is the only way the US will talk to me.' Perhaps touched, Trump said of Kim back in April: 'He's 27 years old. His father dies, took over a regime. So say what you want, but that is not easy, especially at that age.'

Empathy is Trump's phantom limb, so we have to marvel at the way he is able to look at the vast misery of North Korea and find the one thing that twitches his pity to be Kim Jong-un himself. It feels only slightly less bonkers than that great *Austin Powers* scene where Dr Evil attends father–son group therapy with his recently discovered son and begins opening up about his own father issues and his occasionally filicidal megalomania.

As the US–North Korea war of words threatens to escalate into a war of actual war, then, it's hard not to feel like the potential collateral damage in two family psychodramas. What funny, insignificant little ants the rest of us are, trying to nurture family relationships, work through family problems or, in the last resort, just survive them. That is the perverse order of things: hundreds of millions of people making immense, daily, heart-driven personal efforts to deal with their psychological shit, all of whom could be eradicated in seconds by a pair of complete dad-cases who wouldn't dream of doing the same.

Or suffer the same consequences. One of the many deathless ironies about nuclear weapons is that those who give the order to use them would be among the vanishingly few to be protected from their effects. Still, perhaps there would be a Sartrean sort of poetic justice to that. Do just imagine the hell of the Trumps and the Kims locked in their shelters, with nothing but their own toxic interpersonal relationships for company, and all the time in the end of the world to explore them.

Donald Trump and Stormy Daniels: brief encounters of the 'textbook generic' kind

18 January 2018

The dignity of the presidential office has plummeted to a new improbable low with the revelations from the adult film star. Obviously, this column is clearing its diary to hear the whole story

Even for a messy president who lives for the drama, it must have hurt that Donald Trump's inaugural Fake News Awards were so completely overshadowed by a kiss-and-tell trailer containing the phrase: 'She talks about what he's like down there.'

I mean . . . no offence, Mr President, but your critique of the 14-month-old Paul Krugman column you're trying to get my attention with now desperately needs to contain speculation about bottoming-out that is unrelated to post-election markets. Does Krugman make some fanciful claim about how you guys met, and how he had to tolerate some horrendous, although mercifully very brief, discussion about economics with you, in which you maintained one position throughout and were 'textbook generic'? Does he claim you got him to sign a copy of his Nobel Prize citation? Because, otherwise, I need you to pipe down while I listen some more to Miss Stormy Daniels.

By now you should be aware of Stormy's work – if, indeed, you were not already. I confess myself a philistine as far as her *oeuvre* goes, but have since taken the time to sample *Three Wishes*, which is the film that Trump is said to have got her to sign his DVD copy of after one of their encounters. Initial impressions? Mainly that the guy in it has made the absolute basic error: he didn't make his first wish a wish for unlimited wishes. Went for something involving two ladies and a jacuzzi instead. Perfectly reasonable ambition, but surely not something you can build your entire future on. The lack of economic planning in some of these films is really very disappointing. Were I working in the adult entertainment industry, I would immediately consider offering Paul Krugman a consulting role.

Anyhow, if you do need a recap of where we are on this story, this is how we got here: adult-film star Stormy Daniels (real name Stephanie Clifford) claims to have had a series of encounters with Donald Trump over the course of about a year, beginning in 2006. Shortly before the 2016 election, it is alleged that Trump finally paid a $130,000 (£94,000) legal settlement to Daniels in exchange for her silence. Trump's lawyer, Michael Cohen, declines to address the matter of the settlement, but denies that any sexual relationship between the president and Stormy took place. Back in 2011, however, Daniels had conducted a lengthy interview (and polygraph test) about the affair with *In Touch*, and the magazine has been publishing teaser excerpts from it this week. According to an anonymous source – who talks like someone we'd probably all enjoy a riotous cocktail with – the full account that *In Touch* will publish on Friday is '5,500 words of cray'.

For her part, Miss Daniels has gone to ground since the story broke. Still, she seems to have left quite enough material for the annals of quotable quotes to be getting along with. Her ability to really put you inside the action is there from the first hookup with Trump, when she emerges from the bathroom to find him sitting on the bed and inviting him to join her. '"Ugh, here we go," thought Daniels. She described the sex as "textbook generic".'

Oof. I don't know anything about opera, but I do know this would really benefit from an ironic Puccini soundtrack. When the full 5,500 words of cray drop, I'm going to read them all listening to that Kiri Te Kanawa one from *A Room with a View*. 'It was one position,' Stormy continues, 'what you would expect someone his age to do.'

'He told me once that I was someone to be reckoned with,' she mentions later, 'beautiful, smart, just like his daughter.' *O mio bab-bino caro* . . .

Primarily, though, the extracts published thus far reveal a majestic hey-ho quality to Miss Daniels's engagements with the man who would one day become president. Her hilariously affectless candour is a study in that ancient sexual philosophy known as let's-just-get-this-over-with. As for the act itself, we can't know whether Stormy took the opportunity to make a mental grocery shopping list or remind herself that she must get her grandpa's boiler fixed, but it's fair to say she never surrenders entirely to the erotic moment. 'I actually don't even know why I did it,' she muses at one point, 'but I do remember while we were having sex I was like: "Please don't try to pay me."' LET THE PUCCINI BLOW YOUR SPEAKERS.

For all the diversionary detail, though, it should be said that this business could have significant implications. After all, if Donald Trump was willing to pay a six-figure sum to someone he says he didn't have sex with, just imagine what he'd do to keep something quiet if he WAS compromised.

Furthermore, it serves as a reminder that each day you get up and think the bad-taste barrel of this presidency has been finally scraped is a day you lie to yourself. Guys, we're not even close! I think you can already see that even this episode won't really end until Stormy is called to testify on Capitol Hill. Picture it – she'll turn up in an immaculately tailored black suit, probably accessorised with a mantilla. Thereafter, everyone will be glued to a testimony that will include, among a hundred lowlights, some ambitious Democrat leaning towards his microphone with the words: 'And if I can just direct you to the section of the *In Touch* interview which begins, quote: "Oh my God, down there he was just . . . "'

Yes, the entire nation will stop work to watch their TV screens, except for the people who are so grand they'll just read about national productivity plummeting in a Paul Krugman column the next day. It's a noble sacrifice on their part, but an entirely wasted one. I'm afraid the streams of sex and economics have now been irreversibly crossed, and we're powerless to do anything but let it all play out across the stormiest of skies.

Donald Trump, the one person more of a political basket case than Britain

6 June 2019

Over three endless days of state visit to the UK, the US president was welcomed as grist to our dark satanic content mills

It is finally over, then, the state visit during which US President Donald Trump treated Britain like a Moscow hotel mattress. God, we deserved it. The event served most tellingly as a vicious satire on British public life, with every fevered reaction to it recalling Sybil Fawlty's assessment of her husband Basil's way with guests: 'You never get it right, do you? You're either crawling all over them, licking their boots, or spitting poison at them like some Benzedrined puff adder.'

And so with the entire political class, who spent three days either fawning over this Nascar royal wedding or shriekingly defining themselves against it to boost their personal brands. Much better to have treated Trump with the exquisitely polite disinterest of a competent hotelier – perhaps the only language he understands. Instead, he was welcomed as grist to our dark satanic content mills. Rolling news offered the 24-hour spectacle of Britain being borne back ceaselessly into its past, while our best hope for the future is apparently to beg for a few scraps of chlorinated chicken in exchange for a go on the NHS.

In some ways, Trump ended up as a plot device, his subservience to proceedings underlining the curious indignity of any visiting world leader. All superpower guests have to go along with the place settings and the artefact-cooing and the floor-length reminders that the British were the best at things once, until they weren't. If you'd taken a drink every time someone said 'pomp' or 'pageantry', you'd have been dead before Trump got out of the airport.

Smart call. All the 4,876 most boring things to be said in the UK this year were said during these three days, usually over footage of Trump inspecting troops and D-Day veterans with the imperious nod of a five-time draft dodger who described avoiding STDs in 1980s Manhattan as 'my personal Vietnam'.

Much as a toddler intimidated by a new present will play with the box instead, Trump dealt with the aspects of the visit that were beyond his skillset by returning to areas firmly within it. In Westminster Abbey, he was shown a white marble slab commemorating the Romantic poet Lord Byron and took the opportunity to ask what stone the flooring was made from. Doubtless it will make a lovely splashback when they refit the executive bathroom at Mar-a-Lago.

'Oh, to be a fly on that wall at that meeting!' anchors kept saying, underscoring the comical lack of access as Trump met with Nigel Farage or whoever, while they went on about how long it took to lay the dinner table. Some meetings were more intriguing than others. Fair play to third-string Tories Owen Paterson and Iain Duncan Smith for driving into the US ambassador's residence like a couple of wedding crashers, having somehow managed to convince Trump they were relevant.

There was the usual obsession with hardware. 'In a sense,' mused one pundit, 'I'm out of my depth as to how motorcades work.' Some cars follow each other. Next? 'These guns saw action in the first world war.' Well, that is now only the second-most senseless waste in which they've been involved. Who could give one tenth of a toss about 'The Beast', the most annoyingly anthropomorphised vehicle since Duchess Fergie wrote her Budgie the helicopter series?

The coverage was screamingly dull, for three days straight. I lost count of how many attempts to avoid a million cubic miles of dead air were prefaced by the lie: 'What's going to be so interesting is . . .' You could imagine that all correspondents had compiled one sheet of mildly tolerable factoids for when Trump was out of eyeshot, a second sheet of lesser trivia, a third sheet for absolute desperation, and a fourth in case nuclear apocalypse required the station to keep on broadcasting so that viewers could hear at least the sound of another human voice as they succumbed to radiation. We were always on page four. As Marine One landed behind the US ambassador's residence, someone talked at length about 'the reaction of the wind of the propellers on the grass . . .'

Countless moments would have been best served by silence. Sarah Huckabee Sanders scowling out of an upper window of Buckingham Palace like Mrs Danvers. A close-up of Trump's comically ill-fitting attire for the state banquet, a far more disrespectful act of tailoring than even the time the late Alexander McQueen sewed the words 'I am a cunt' inside the lining of a suit for Prince Charles. Any footage of Melania Trump, whose miserable countenance seems living testament to the old adage that when you marry for money, you earn every penny.

Any laughs? I enjoyed someone who used to work in the US embassy describing Melania as 'a great diplomat', as well as the talking heads who felt they had to be a bit American. On one atrocity of a Sky News panel, rightwing commentator James Delingpole kept saying 'Hello?!', apparently under the impression that the occasion required him to come as a 1990s Valley Girl. Meanwhile, the shadow foreign secretary, Emily Thornberry, whose grandeur far outstrips the Queen's, spent Tuesday morning explaining why she wasn't at the state dinner: 'I had to write to the palace saying please don't invite me on this occasion, as I would embarrass everybody by having to say no.' So good of you to spare their universal blushes. Would you accept a posy as a token of admiration?

As far as the real royals go, Camilla's possible wink at the cameras was greeted by some as 'epic trolling'. Incorrect. The Tea Act of 1773 was epic trolling. Or, to put it another way: in the Profit column I've got 'a £40m state visit', and in the Loss column I've got 'a wink'. Wake up. That said, I did miss our former best player. You spend a lifetime cringing at Prince Philip insulting people, and the one time you want him to, he's retired.

Still, we shan't miss people remarking archly that 'Donald Trump is getting what he wanted out of it'. As are you, dear! In fact, we might go so far as to say that everyone from the Trumps to Corbyn to Farage to half the Tory leadership field 'got what they wanted out of it'. The whole political class were on the grift just as much as Trump. The only people to not 'get what they wanted out of it' – and really, it's such a tiny constituency – were people who think that Britain's mad nostalgia and political self-harm is at an advanced clinical stage, and that just because we've found the one person who's more of a basket case than us, it doesn't mean we're winning.

Trump joked while people suffered with Covid. Well, is now the time to stop?

2 October 2020

Maybe the real victims of the president's diagnosis are his Maga disciples who don't believe the virus even exists

Well, it's definitely a plot twist. Like a lot of people who sat through Tuesday's presidential debate, I'm amazed the week has ended with Donald Trump ingesting bleach, and not me.

As you may vaguely have heard, the US president and his wife, Melania, have tested positive for the novel coronavirus – which feels untimely, given that, mere hours earlier, Trump had been declaring: 'The end of the pandemic is in sight.' Perhaps this is a one-last-job movie. Alternatively, picture a Wuhan bat staring pensively into the fireplace as its butler suggests not thinking too hard about Trump's motivations. Some poorly facepainted men just want to watch the world burn.

Still, let's stay on track. God knows, it's excruciatingly hard to chirp 'Get well soon!' to this particular patient, but . . . get well soonish. Those of us who want to escape the cesspool Trump has helped drag the world into will wish him a better time with the virus than the one to which he blithely condemned so many of those he was elected to serve. Each to their own, but I'm against all forms of the death penalty, karmic or otherwise.

Jokes, though? Oh, jokes are very much permitted at this stage. I consider myself deeply pro-joke, for moral reasons. I appreciate that the Old Testament isn't exactly a gagfest, but I believe in a joke for a joke, you know? And no one – NO ONE – has told more jokes about the coronavirus than Donald Trump. He's the Covid Joker, if you'll permit another Gotham callback. He would surely want us to follow his lead.

The very last thing Trump would wish to imply is that his life is worth any more than the lives of all those people who were dying when he was joking about masks, joking about Joe Biden and masks, joking about Biden being practically dead . . . to say nothing of all those times past when he joked about Hillary Clinton's pneumonia, or had his proxies joke speculatively that she had suffered a stroke, or was afflicted by dysphasia, or had secretly suffered serious brain trauma . . . I'm sorry, I'm running very low on space here. The point is, this is what he'd WANT – because he loves the lulz. Please honour him thusly.

Anyway, as Trump pointed out last week, the virus 'affects virtually nobody' and has currently only affected 200,000 American nobodies to death. Arguably the real victims here are the president's

Maga disciples, who are devoted to him but also don't believe the virus even exists. Trump being officially diagnosed with it is category 5 cognitive dissonance – a logical contradiction so intense it could crash their circuitry, causing them to immediately lay down their assault rifles and open a chain of abortion clinics.

And so to the political implications of Trump's Covid diagnosis, which I couldn't predict less accurately if I were picking through some sacrificed goat entrails. Joe Biden is already under pressure to suspend his campaign, just as Trump totally would if the boot were on the other foot. Then again, who knows – maybe the boot is on both feet?

On Tuesday, the world watched the ancient esoteric ritual whereby leadership of the tribal land of America is decided by two septuagenarian males spending 90 minutes spraying spittle at each other, apparently after drinking ayahuasca. A somewhat primitive society, all told, though supposedly it's culturally insensitive to point that sort of thing out these days.

Perhaps there's a certain neatness to the conclusion that virtually all reality TV elimination formats now look more sophisticated than the US election. It could really elevate the contest only if Trump and Biden were forced to battle out the rest of the campaign in isolation in a multi-camera McMansion, or on a specially adapted tropical island, or atop an abandoned karaoke soundstage. Unfortunately, the entire planet has to keep watching the show for the age-old reason. Namely: that when America shits the bed, the rest of the world has to lie in it. (That's not actually one of Henry Kissinger's famous adages, trivia buffs, though I'm happy for it to be included in *The Little Book of Realpolitik*.)

On a personal level, meanwhile, it's not clear how President Trump will cope with the standard Covid isolation lifestyle – holing up in front of endless hours of TV and communicating only via social media. He famously cheats so wantonly at golf that it's reasonable to imagine him continuing to notch up record-breaking scorecards at his various courses while never leaving the White House. And while Melania says he's not feeling below par, this isn't the same as saying he has no symptoms. We know, for instance, the virus can affect one's taste, suggesting Trump could order all his properties to be stripped of all animal print and reproduction gilt.

Alas, the news has brought the first serious snowflake fall of the autumn, as Republicans intensely relaxed about very young children being separated from their parents and held in cages at the border now wet their pants over a few aperçus about a man whose own wife says he is 'feeling good'. According to the White House physician's statement, 'The president and first lady are both well at this time.' (Having said that, according to a 2018 White House physician's statement, the president was 6ft 3in and weighed 239 pounds, placing him in the same category of physique as a number of 30-year-old pro athletes.) It's quite a spectacle, anyway, watching people who only a couple of months ago were threatening revolution over their constitutional right to get a haircut or something, but who are now calling for the smelling salts over mere discussion of the president's health.

Then again, it was only a couple of weeks ago that Trump was asked whether he was worried about Covid spreading at his indoor rallies, eliciting the deathless reply: 'I'm on a stage and it's very far away.' Nobody – nobody! – cares about people more than him. This morning it emerged that the White House had been aware of his aide Hope Hicks's symptoms when Trump flew to a New Jersey fundraiser, where he was in much closer contact with his own supporters at a roundtable. No doubt it would have been an honour to be infected by him, and all that.

As for the 4D chess grandmasters suggesting the whole 'diagnosis' is a fake-news hoax by Trump designed to buy him two weeks of fairly uncritical coverage during the crucial final month of the election campaign . . . well, it's one conspiracy theory. There are a lot of conspiracy theories doing the rounds today – always the sign of an unhealthy democracy. (Trust us Brits on that front, because it takes one to know one.)

Whichever way you slice it, though, all news media will now spend a good 23 hours a day talking about Trump and Covid – a considerable part of which is likely to zone in on his handling thereof. So . . . the most audacious ruse of his entire presidency to own the libs – or a simple case of severe acute respiratory syndrome? And will we ever make it out of the rabbit hole where these questions are routinely asked?

After Donald Trump's deranged balcony address, we're all gasping together

6 October 2020

The president tells us he beat coronavirus like a man – the kind who takes all the best drugs and leaves everyone else exposed

A rare moment of unity in the US election, as Donald Trump marked his return to the White House by gasping along with his detractors. On Monday night the president puffed up the front staircase of his residence, his face coated in several more gallons of paint than the front elevation of the building. 'Don't let it dominate your lives,' he panted of the virus, a bad case of which tends to dominate your death.

Yet there he was, this hideous kink in the arc of history, giving the most dangerous balcony performance since Michael Jackson had his baby crowdsurf off one. The American people are all Blanket now.

As for the optics, 'deranged balcony address' is certainly a look – but not one that tends to end well. How might this version turn out? Unfortunately, it's not a question Trump's attention span equips him to answer. His reference points for the form are the occasional three minutes of historical documentary he's forced to watch while searching his stomach-folds for the TV remote. It feels like he switches over to Fox News before discovering how a whole series of 20th-century balcony stories ended.

Still, don't call him Wussolini. He beat this illness – which he still very much has – like a man. One of the really manly ones, who takes all the best drugs and leaves everyone else exposed and misled and unprotected. Even so, early reactions to the gasping spectacle suggest the move could only have backfired more if Trump had ascended the front steps of the White House via a hastily installed stairlift and carrying a pack of adult diapers.

Once he'd wheezed through the unpleasantries, all that remained was to remove his mask and set about infecting any remaining staff yet to be exposed to his droplets. Think of Trump as Covid's 82nd Airborne, parachuting his deadly particles deep into butlers' respiratory systems. He won't give you a Purple Heart, but he might give you purple lungs.

Alas, it's disappointing to find potential victims failing to feel grateful for the opportunity. One current secret service agent assigned to the first family's detail expressed frustration, telling CNN: 'We're not disposable.' Two housekeeping staff have already tested positive for the virus. As the events of the past week show, the president's respect for human life is so low that he is willing to send an entire army of servants into 14-day isolation or worse in order to keep up a steady stream of trans-fats being fed to him. Dying in the line of duty used to mean taking a bullet for the president; it could now involve taking him a Diet Coke. Thank you for your drinks service.

As for how Trump spent the rest of his evening, I assume it was straight on to the monstrous leaders' WhatsApp to josh with the other bros about how they kill their underlings. RocketmanKim loves a firing squad, Vlad69's a huge chemicals guy, but Trump just clears his throat while being brought his fourth burger of the day. Boom! 'I cough on them like a bitch! When you're famous you can do that.'

Face it, he's absolutely bossing the likes of Kim and Xi and MBS in the fantasy evildoer leagues. It's not that the other guys don't have lethal motorcades and abysmal interiors taste and balcony addresses and death cults and doctors who mislead the world. But doing them in a democracy – well, that makes it triple points.

Speaking of physicians who really need to heal themselves, what a striking misinformation campaign it's been from presidential medic Sean Conley, who has been continually obfuscating about Trump's condition since calling his symptoms 'mild', only for even the White House to contradict him. For me, that's the new low. Of course, we now expect the president of the United States to lie as default – to tell us black is white or up is down, or to claim he never said something he's on camera saying. But for a professional and senior doctor to mislead apparently without remorse shows how necrotic the body politic has become, from the very top down. The reality-denying is not a one-off case – it's the other epidemic.

In fact, it's kind of amazing that conspiracy theorists have lined up so supportively behind Trump, when he's really the most convincing proof yet of all their worst fears. The Man really is lying to them, he really is wicked, and he really does want to kill them. The damning evidence is right there in front of everyone. Only instead of begging Oliver Stone to make a film about it, they want to give Trump a second term.

Like me, you probably hate to see a conspiracist wimp out of their beliefs just when it's coming up roses for them. It's as if the moon-landing hoaxers were signing over their life savings to Nasa, or the flat-Earthers booking a round-the-world ticket. So come on, guys – back yourselves! After all, if not now, then when?

What to do when your president has a temper tantrum

6 November 2020

For parents of small children, Donald Trump's post-election meltdown is extremely, totally, instantly recognisable

There are several reasons presidents cry. Anyone who has ever had one and been up half the night with it – or all the night with it, night after night – can tell you this. Sometimes presidents cry because they're tired, sometimes they cry because they need their nappy changed, sometimes they cry because they don't want you to leave them, sometimes they cry because they have a gnawing pain in their tummy, and sometimes they cry because they're just being impossible that day and you should probably go to bed and leave them to it but somehow you just can't.

To anyone going through it currently: this phase will pass. Of course, a crying president demands incredible amounts of attention, and while you're in the thick of it, consumed by this, it may feel like it will never stop, or at least that you won't make it out. There are many moments in the small hours when you stare at this crying thing and think wryly: 'Wow, what happened to my life?' I think I vaguely remember when it wasn't like this.

The television news – I like to think of it as the president monitor, lighting up each time he needs attention – has been on what feels like pretty much constantly in our house since 2016, the year that Donald Trump won (and the UK began its own extended period of toddler meltdown). A child's formative years are so precious, and I'm sure our children will benefit enormously from all the times I've said, 'Shhhh, I'm watching the president,' or occasionally even been forced to momentarily stop watching the president to deliver a behavioural verdict: 'I know why you're acting up – it's to get my attention away from the president acting up. Well, it won't work.'

Everyone has their parenting gurus; as a realist, I follow the Philip Larkin model. And it is typical of the parenting in our house that we, hugely belatedly, started thinking not that we should switch the president monitor off – don't be ridiculous! – but more along the lines of: should we . . . maybe say something?

Anyway, after a while we did. We said stuff to the children like, 'We should probably mention that this isn't normal – at least, it didn't used to be. I mean, I know it's pretty much all the news you've ever known in your short and possibly already terminally disillusioned lives. But seriously, in the not-all-that-olden times, you could go DAYS without particularly thinking about politics. Longer!' Eventually, we wondered if saying 'This isn't normal' was even accurate. All our children are under 10. Technically, it was kind of normal.

Even in this golden age of TV it was the biggest show on air, and frequently inspired us to seek out other family content. Really, it was impossible to watch the president's rosebud anus mouth puckering up and screaming at some rally and not ask one another: 'I wonder if the children would enjoy *Rosemary's Baby*? Go on one of those parenting websites and see whether it honestly merits its 18 certificate. Come on, it was made in the late 1960s – these days, even the news is scarier! Which reminds me: can you just put on the news? He's about to have one of his moments in the Rose Garden, and we should watch the full horror show as a family.'

As time wore even further on, we would remark mildly to the children: 'Sorry about [*expansively vague gesture*] all THIS. As with all the worst stuff in the world, I'm afraid adults did this. Will it get fixed? Hopefully! If adults don't fix it pretty quick, they'll fairly soon be moving on to the phase where they bend down and pat your head and say: "Hey guys, we need your generation to grow up and fix all this!" That is really the worst, and you SHOULD in fact be outraged that people like that somehow have the power to say to you, "Go to bed," or "Right, I'm taking away the iPad."'

But now, this. After four years we have FINALLY moved on to much, much safer cautionary-tale territory – because now the president is really just crying. For parents of small children, and also for anyone who has ever seen a small child behave badly in the supermarket or the street, the thing we are watching on TV now is extremely, totally, instantly recognisable even to the very young. The big orange guy is angry because it is not his turn any more. He is being a Bad Loser. Look at him! Someone should stop him. Yes, I agree with you he needs a punishment for this behaviour. Yes, no iPad would be a start.

I remember the huge excitement of being got out of bed as a child for major news events, on the basis that 'This is history.' Yet watching Trump have his meltdown on Thursday night, I didn't exactly feel inspired to get the children out of bed for it. They could watch the giant baby in the morning. We are finally, just about, near the point where it isn't history. It is just histrionics.

2019: OVEN-READY PRIME MINISTER

In January, nearly two agonising years after triggering Article 50, Theresa May is pleased to present her Brexit deal to the House of Commons. The House of Commons is pleased to vote it down in the heaviest parliamentary defeat of the entire democratic era. Incredibly, this does not turn out to be rock bottom for May. Meaningful votes become meaningless votes, and by the end of May Theresa and the Conservatives have decided there is nothing for it but to switch the UK off then on again. The age demands a titanic figure; the age gets Boris Johnson. At the December general election, the country has the choice of him or Jeremy Corbyn, which feels like being given the option of smallpox or bubonic plague. (Sidenote: deadly infectious disease metaphors are about to go waaaaay out of fashion.)

Welcome to the Westminster apocalypse.
Have you thought about theocracy instead?

16 January 2019

After May's Brexit deal flame-out, Tories are claiming this all-systems clusterfuck is an 'opportunity' – just like the second world war

The world's most densely betwatted space at the best of times, Westminster became even more wantonly apocalyptic in the days and hours leading up to the historic defeat of Theresa May's Brexit deal. Behold, a bell-tolling, haute remainer, yellow-vested, journalist-infested, shitbird-MP-crawling, flashmobbed perform-ance art piece entitled 'HAVE YOU THOUGHT ABOUT THEOCRACY INSTEAD?'

If not, don't rule it out. An awful lot of things are apparently back on the table after May's flame-out, including – but not limited to – default no deal, extending Article 50, a Norway-style arrange-ment, second referendum, and return to absolute monarchy, under either the Queen or David Attenborough.

The scale of the task of unbreaking Britain is jointly summed up by the vote result and by each of the polar-opposite factions of pro-testers outside parliament being convinced they'd won. Everyone celebrated maniacally. As far as the UK's lo-viz yellow-vest move-ment goes, Westminster pavements are now a great place to get hooked up with the right militia for you in the event of no deal. As for the more provisional wing of the People's Vote, we no longer need to computer-model the answer to the question: what would happen if you gave everyone on Henman Hill crystal meth?

At the heart of this scene, a physically crumbling parliament building, half propped up by scaffolding. Unfolding inside on

Tuesday night, a parliamentary procedural with quite staggering plotholes and continuity errors. Welcome to the Blunderdome.

After Stanley Baldwin, then prime minister, had made the abdication announcement in the house in 1936, the MP Harold Nicolson bumped into him in a corridor outside the chamber. The moment was obviously one of electrifying historic drama, yet Nicolson's diary entry archly conveys Baldwin's self-centric take on it: 'I detected in [Baldwin] that intoxication which comes to a man, even a tired man, after a triumphant success . . . "I had a success, my dear Nicolson, at the moment I most needed it . . ." No man has dominated the House as Baldwin did tonight,' Nicolson concluded, 'and he knows it.'

The same could not be said of Theresa May, who rose to the occasion like an anglepoise lamp. Basic shambles model. Indeed, speaking of the abdication, it's grimly amusing to consider that May's big intervention in the 2015 general election campaign was to warn that 'if we saw a Labour government propped up by the SNP, it could be the biggest constitutional crisis since the abdication'. As it turned out, madam would have something rather bigger up her own sleeve.

So what now? Well, there's a motion of no confidence to while away today, and 72 days left on the Brexit clock. May's serial dishonesty throughout this entire process saw jeers greet her post-vote claims of a new 'constructive spirit' in which 'the government will work harder at taking parliament with us'. The jeers were well founded, given it took barely hours for it to become clear that this wouldn't extend to even speaking to Jeremy Corbyn. Which might well suit Labour's leader, the High Triangulator, who is reportedly going to keep calling no-confidence motions until one produces the answer he likes. An irony that will doubtless be appreciated by those of his supporters angling in vain for a second referendum.

As for May, her clinical standoffishness is entirely of a piece with the way she has behaved for the best part of the two and a half years since the vote, and certainly since the 2017 election. One of the most remarkable, and indeed excruciating, things about May has been her insistence on governing like she's got a landslide majority. Why has no one told her? She's the Florence Foster Jenkins of politics, insulated from the realities of her situation by weird or venal enablers. Never has the intervention of a candid best mate been more needed. At some point in July 2017 surely Amber Rudd or whoever should have gone round and given May 'The Talk'. Along the lines of: 'Babe, true friends tell you the truth, amirite? Because if no one else is going to say this, then I will: the referendum vote was problematically close anyway, and then you totally spunked your majority. Like, you literally have no majority. So . . . you need to stop acting like Mariah Carey, OK? On the plus side, you look great in that trouser suit and I've brought round two bottles of cava. Let's get pissed and watch *Working Girl* again.' Alas, at no point since the election does this essential public service appear to have been performed.

Somehow even less appealing than May's performance, though, was the spectacle of politicians rushing to the telly cameras in its wake. Here comes Chris Grayling, the least appealing ferryman since Charon, who's going to rule out a customs union right off the bat.

Here comes voluminously overcoated Jacob Rees-Mogg, which made him look like an 11-year-old Jacob Rees-Mogg sitting on his concealed Nanny's shoulders for a nursery game called Disaster Capitalist's Bluff.

Here come a lot of Tories claiming this all-systems clusterfuck is an 'opportunity' to 'go back to the EU'. And say what? 'Look, if you'll just give me three cosmetic concessions, then I feel sure I can get those elusive last 230 Infinity Stones.'

And here comes the affectedly shambling figure of Boris Johnson – not so much a statesman as an Oxfam donation bag torn open by a fox – who could conceivably still end up prime minister of no-deal Britain. May needed to go to the EU again 'with a high heart, fortified by the massive rejection of the House of Commons', judged Johnson, speaking as always like a Taiwanese news animation of Winston Churchill. In the meantime, 'we should be actively preparing for no deal with ever more enthusiasm'.

As for Dominic Raab . . . dear, dear. Show me someone who is trying harder than Dominic to make himself happen. OK, you've shown me The Saj and Gavin Williamson, and even cub health secretary Matt Hancock. One of the things you really have to admire about the Tory males is the time they make for self-care. Even at moments of really cataclysmically pressing national business, they insist on carving out the sort of me-time that is, say, a thinly disguised leadership speech at the Centre for Policy Studies. Yes, let the historical records show that on the eve of the vote, Dominic Raab was trying to look like tomorrow's man in an address that, among other things, floated the idea of 'Asbos for business'. Not now, mate, yeah? We're a bit busy. Yet Dominic did a second lectern event in the hours before the vote, this time teaming up with David Davis and Arlene Foster, who still has all the warmth of the matriarch of a remote farm who retains the passports of her labourers.

As for Davis, we'll play out with an interview the former Brexit secretary gave a German magazine last weekend, in which he handpicked two mind-boggling examples of situations in which Britain was Definitely Not Wrong. 'Oh, I'm certain that Brexit will be a success,' Davis breezed. 'Remember, every single major issue in our history is one where you might be right or wrong. Appeasement before the second world war, we might be right or wrong. Suez, we might be right or wrong.' Well. I for one can't wait to see what's going to happen next.

Brexit Britain is now the only argument on Earth for rising sea levels

1 February 2019

The rest of the world will look at what happened this week in parliament and want to put the UK out of its misery

So many people have been branded traitors in the past year of Brexit that many of us now have traitor fatigue. But everyone should salute Ukip leader Gerard Batten for totally revitalising the genre this week by calling the Queen a traitor. Gerard, a sort of radicalised Just for Men box, wrote to Her Majesty to ask her to prorogue parliament to save Brexit. He also took the opportunity to inform Queen Elizabeth II that she had committed treason when she signed the Maastricht treaty.

'To presume to convey rights on or to impose duties on Your Majesty was, and remains, unlawful and treasonous under the bill of rights and the coronation oath,' wrote the Ukip leader, whose treatment for low-budget legal drama *Better Call Gerard* is thought not to have tempted the networks. 'Your Majesty's ministers were gravely in error and wrongly advised you.'

Don't try to follow this reasoning; just let it coat you like three really hard sprays of Brut Musk. I think it's fair to say that it wasn't drafted for Gerard by his new spad, Tommy Robinson, given it relies on legal expertise outside the area of mortgage fraud. But even with help from a lawyer, it still reads like the sort of letter Raoul Moat might have written in the storm drain.

Then again, this level of up-against-it madness is increasingly widespread. Did you watch Tuesday's Brexit amendments shitshow live from parliament? The vast majority didn't, yet MPs do seem to think their ratings are somewhere north of *Bodyguard*'s. These days, they are forever standing up to inquire rhetorically how they might look 'to those watching at home'.

Outside, on Westminster's College Green, a tented media village-cum-field-hospital provides pundits with 24-hour opportunities to be sassily wrong. Looked at in the round, Brexit is easily the most expensive show on television, watched only by people who detest it. For that money, I really expect CGI dragons, sentient sex robots or the ever-present possibility that Jeremy Clarkson might implode in a high-velocity fireball. Instead, Wednesday offered the trade secretary, Liam Fox, in an anorak, explaining that how parliament acts now is important 'for future referendums'. FUTURE REFERENDUMS? I mean, no one more than me is looking forward to the *Sharknado 6* version of this franchise, but I wonder if in some ways we'd just be chasing this first high.

And so to the performance of our entire political class. The UK is now the only argument on Earth in favour of rising sea levels. If our economy does go tits-up after Brexit, we could recoup some money in the form of sponsorship by Exxon or the plastics industry. We could become the first country to be propped up by petrochemicals lobbyists as an argument for everyone to use MORE of their product. Accelerate freely to put Britain out of its misery.

Speaking of Mother Earth, meanwhile, it does feel time to accept that, like Los Angeles, the Conservative party is built on a fault line. LA has San Andreas; the Tories have Europe. (Calculating 20 years ago that LA had been destroyed 138 times in novels and films, the writer Mike Davis described it as 'a Book of the Apocalypse theme park' – a description I would also apply to the annual Conservative party conference.) Over the past few decades extraordinary amounts of energy and ingenuity have been expended to keep the Tory party together, despite these seismically challenged foundations. Quite how long the fragile ecology can hold before the big one hits is unclear.

But if you had to condense the past couple of years into a movie trailer, you'd surely get something that starts out suggesting a romantic comedy, before the voiceover kicks into a much pacier and more urgent register, and swiftly descends into the demented disaster movie genre. 'How far would YOU go to keep the Conservative party from splitting?' it would begin breezily. 'Would you offer people a choice one crazy summer? Would you call half your country citizens of nowhere? Would you deport people with British children who have lived here for 24 years? Would you start saying things like "There will be adequate food"?

'Would you declare it was worth running the car industry down because "these things happen"? Would you demand Ireland leave the EU because you've shat the bed? Would you watch people being warned of essential medicine shortages? Would you tell schools that they'll have to be flexible over food standards? Would you refuse to rule out deaths from drug shortages? Would you write some insane column wanking over rationing cookbooks for a war you were born after? Would you stockpile trauma packs out of concerns over risk to life? Would you –'

STOP. Christ . . . what are we even watching? Is The Rock in this one? He'd better be, because any minute now the freeway's going to collapse and the only way out is him slinging us over his shoulder and physically carrying us to safety. We have reached the stage in our national journey where we must rely on the kindness of strangers in torn tank tops.

Theresa May, meanwhile, has reached the stage in her journey of realising she needs Labour. I liked that she and Jeremy Corbyn prefaced their talks on Wednesday by trading leaden insults during prime minister's questions, allowing us to manage our expectations and realise the meeting itself would be an acting-regional-manager version of an epic duel. It's an encouraging prospect: talks between Siri's 2009 beta version and a man whose USP is not having changed his mind since the mid-Mesolithic period. Unfortunately, there were no flies on the wall at the meeting, as they all took the decision to plough suicidally into the lightbulbs.

It's hard not to be inspired by a Labour leader whose Brexit approach is 'How much will I, personally, be blamed for this?' Pretty sure everyone is now clear that Brexit belongs to the Tories, but Corbyn's level of uninterest in the results of that does arguably tarnish the halo. Perhaps the 30-year papers will reveal May used their pow-wow to quote *Mean Girls* at him. 'God, at least me and Regina George know we're mean! You try to act like you're so innocent!'

As when they found the billion pounds for the DUP, the government hasn't got money for fripperies such as alleviating rampant homelessness, but they've always got a little something squirrelled away when it matters. Or, as Labour members being offered investment in their constituencies might put it: don't piss on my back and tell me it's a rainy day. Until now, the government has preferred to operate on that old proverb: give a man a food bank, and you feed him for a day; force him to build his own food banks, and you feed resentment for a lifetime. May's appealing new tactic is to buy off Labour by promising money for former coalmining areas. No rush, no rush.

No rush on any of it, really. Parliament is allowing prearranged half-term holidays to go ahead, which is good news for ski-booked MPs who regard Europe as something you might slide down on the way to a long lunch. Any senior Brexiteers remaining can continue their practice of telling TV cameras that they expect the EU to cave at the last minute. Keep saying your plan out loud, brainiacs – what's the worst that could happen?

With Theresa's 'turd' deal flushed away, pray for an EU invasion

13 March 2019

We need competency, and quick. Not this bunch of MPs, who are finding out in real time the consequences of their actions

'It . . . sends a message . . . to the whole world,' croaked Theresa May to the Commons before her latest meaningful vote on Tuesday night, 'about the sort of country . . . the United Kingdom will be . . . in the years and decades ahead.'

Fairly sure the world has got the message by now. They are 'up to speed' and 'across the detail' of the sort of country the UK is. The question of whether Brexit represented a midlife crisis or the descent into senility appears to have been answered. The land that likes to picture itself as a David Niven world war two movie is in fact a look-away episode of *The Jeremy Kyle Show*. On close inspection, the 'beacon of democracy' turns out to be a bin fire.

By now you will be aware that the prime minister failed to end her meaningful vote hoodoo, with this sequel to her last attempt – 2Meaningful 2Vote – knocked down by a margin of 149. Amusingly, some are suggesting that Meaningful Vote: Tokyo Drift could yet happen. A free vote on no deal takes place tonight, with potential amendments piling up. May herself ploughs on. It's as if someone has popped a grey wig on Munch's *The Scream*, then cast it in an ITV drama about the female governor of a category-A prison.

Quote of the debate – arguably quote of the entire Brexit – went to a Conservative backbencher by the name of Steve Double. 'This is a turd of a deal', he intoned to the House of Commons, 'which has now been taken away and polished, and is now a polished turd. But it might be the best turd that we've got.'

For many, the now-reflexive action when they hear this kind of stuff is to inquire: 'Why didn't u put that on the side of ur bus m8???' And yet, was Steve's interjection in the actual chamber the moment that well-worn joke format ascended to its purest – which is to say, its most grotesque – form? Putting turd all over the side of a bus, having half the country vote for it, and then driving this dirty-protest-mobile past every single warning sign of the past two and a half years has brought us to this particular precipice. Tuesday night's Commons spectacle reminded me of one of Jonathan Swift's last poems, about the Irish parliament – specifically this bit:

> Let them, when they once get in,
> Sell the nation for a pin;
> While they sit a-picking straws,
> Let them rave at making laws;
> While they never hold their tongue,
> Let them dabble in their dung . . .
> We may, while they strain their throats
> Wipe our arses with their votes.

So yup, pretty much all covered by Dean Swift there back in the 1730s, right down to Theresa May's strained throat. However unique this moment might feel, I suppose we must remember that politicians have been letting down their people for centuries and centuries.

Even so, the abysmal calibre of those in whose hands we're in can feel remarkable. Nigel Dodds! Have you beheld Nigel? If you didn't know he was the deputy leader of the DUP, you'd say he has the face of a head of geography who has been suspended pending an investigation into accusations he struck a pupil. Or perhaps you prefer Boris Johnson, who stood up to urge parliament to 'behave as a great country'. Says the guy who's been behaving like a complete country since prep school. According to that guy, no deal is 'the only safe path to self-respect'. Boris Johnson showing you the only safe path to self-respect is like Paul Burrell showing you the only safe path to dignity, or Hannibal Lecter showing you the only safe path home. With his elite-busting reference to 'Carthaginian terms', Boris is entirely of a piece with Jacob Rees-Mogg, who on Tuesday tweeted simply: *'Dies irae, dies illa.'* To read fan replies humbly begging, 'Give us a clue Jacob!' – in vain – is to observe a mass tugging of the forelocks.

Fans of sledgehammer imagery, meanwhile, may care to note that disgraced former Conservative politician Jeffrey Archer was sitting in the public gallery on Tuesday night, while disgraced former Labour member Fiona Onasanya became the first MP to vote while wearing an electronic tag. Four decades of gathering uselessness and mendacity had brought us to this occasion, to which we might as well picture Archer and Onasanya as bookends.

If it feels unfair to lump most of the House of Commons in together, please don't let it. It must not be forgotten that MPs voted 498 to 114 to trigger Article 50 two years ago, apparently without a clue about what the predictable implications of negotiating against the clock with a much stronger opponent were. Most of those 498 MPs are a reminder than no one in this country should ever suffer from impostor syndrome again. I really do hope to see as many of them as possible at the eventual public inquiry.

The story of Brexit since the referendum has in large part been the story of politicians finding out in real time what the thing they had already done actually meant, then deferring the admission or even acceptance of it. We hear a lot about low-information voters, but low-information politicians are the bigger problem. Even this week, Tory Brexiteers Esther McVey and Daniel Kawczynski were spreading arrant lies about enforced joining of the euro. It is traditional at these moments to ask if the politicians in question are stupid or liars; in the case of Esther and Daniel, the question is moot as they are both.

Westminster has become so unmoored from reality that half of its denizens can't even remember which lie they told. In the wake of her defeat, Tory deputy chairman James Cleverly informed the BBC that May had 'inherited this job', like it was some loss-making family business she had sportingly tried to make a go of, as opposed to the position of prime minister, which she'd remorselessly pursued, to the point of having been too self-interested even to fight for her side in the referendum.

On the other side of the house, meanwhile, sat Jeremy Corbyn, who famously wanted to trigger Article 50 before anyone else, on the very day after the referendum. Yet on Tuesday he was wittering at the prime minister: 'The clock has been run out on her!' Corbyn now seems to be back to pushing his phantom Brexit deal, as opposed to the second referendum he briefly suggested was Labour policy. I know rebelling against the leadership is Corbyn's comfort zone, but it does make you look a historic tit when you are the leadership.

As for what happens next, one Tory MP judged: 'Fuck knows.' Welcome to Fuckknowsville. Population: us. In Westminster, an MP leaving the ERG meeting had called the mood 'realistic', before adding: 'But the question is, what is reality?' No. The question is, what is this complete bollocks? Morpheus, but if he was the member for Wycombe? In the north, Nigel Farage's Leave Means Leave army girds itself to march south from Sunderland to London. And in Brussels, one EU diplomat warned ominously that 'behind the scenes people are increasingly saying it is better to call it quits', which is diplomatic speak for 'so completely done with the UK's shit'.

We might as well play out with former Brexit secretary David Davis, whose appearance before the eventual inquiry will, I fantasise, be lengthy and sensationally uncomfortable. 'If we walk away,' David breezed breezily on Tuesday, shortly before U-turning and voting for a deal he had spent months pissing all over, 'what can they do? They cannot invade you, can they?' More's the pity. If only there was an option for 'invasion by competent people'. They don't have to be FROM the continent, but they do have to BE continent.

Apocalypse it is, then. Not now, but probably next week

21 March 2019

Fresh from turning on MPs, May spent today not convincing foreign leaders that Meaningful Vote 3 will save the franchise

Forced to summarise Theresa May's Downing Street address to the nation last night, I'd go with: Prime Minister Kurtz . . . she mad. 'They told me you had gone totally insane,' Martin Sheen says to Marlon Brando's rogue colonel in *Apocalypse Now*, 'that your methods were unsound.' 'Are my methods unsound?' pants Colonel Kurtz. A pause. 'I don't see any method at all, sir.'

Or, as one minister put it of May: 'No fucking plan, nothing.' 'One day there will be a public inquiry,' another member of the government observed, 'and she will be judged to have been unfit for office.' Meanwhile, in the most ambitious crossover event since *Avengers: Infinity War*, both the CBI and the TUC have put out a joint plea for Theresa May to return to at least the same postcode as her senses.

Instead, madam arrived in Brussels on Thursday afternoon, seeking just a short Article 50 extension from EU leaders. Alas, Emmanuel Macron is merely one of those believed to have had enough of *le* absolute bollocks. The EU says it'll only grant one if parliament passes her deal next week in Meaningful Vote 3: This Time It's Meaningful. If May loses that, there are some suggestions that she is coming round to no deal, in a bid to keep her beloved

Conservative party together. I realise you don't care about spoilers at this stage, so let me confirm: that bid ends up failing anyway.

Still, back to the PM's speech, which she really ought to have delivered in a yellow vest. If you're keeping track of the various lunacies, please note that parliamentary sovereignty is no longer the glorious destination of Brexit but its evil enemy. It has long been a quirk of this uniquely artless prime minister that her sole memorable lines are ones that can only be said with sarcastic air quotes. 'Brexit means Brexit.' 'Strong and stable.' 'Nothing has changed.' But Wednesday night's scripted attempt to turn the people on parliament may turn out to be one for the history books: 'I am on your side.' To which the only possible response, given her run of form, is: more's the pity. May is the sort of player you want to sell to your bitterest rivals.

Yet her national address suggested that for all her well-established limitations, her thermonuclear dullness and her firmly suppressed ability to tell interviewers whether she mildly prefers *Sherlock* or *Midsomer Murders*, Theresa May is in fact an extremely dangerous individual whose priorities are now so far out of whack she shouldn't be anywhere near the controls of this particular automobile.

It was so ghastly that it contrived to unite entrenched enemies Mark Francois and Phillip Lee, who appeared this morning on Sky News. 'You don't persuade people by insulting them,' observed Francois, the ERG vice chair. A little late for Mark to learn this lesson about negotiation, but he is merely a verruca on the footnote to this moment in history. Remain supporter Lee went further: 'Whoever wrote the PM's speech needs to have a long, hard look at themselves.'

Quite. It is not simply the prime minister behaving in this historically irresponsible way, but her advisers too. The whole of the inner station is rotten. The only person who could have saluted it is aspiring memoirist David Cameron, who now has an excellent chance of being considered only the second-worst prime minister since one or other of the great 18th-century inbreds (probably Lord North).

Not that you'd theoretically rule out both records being smashed by Jeremy Corbyn, whose Brexit strategy, even at the hour of peril, amounts to looking present but not involved. The Labour leader's decision to leave a cross-party crisis meeting because Chuka Umunna was there confirmed him as a small and peevish man who wouldn't have what it takes if the chips were down. On an administrative note, though, anyone wanting to keep Corbyn in a meeting room next week should have an emotional support terrorist on standby to help him through the process.

As for May, the received wisdom about her little lectern speeches is that they tell us nothing, but for my money this one told us everything. You could suddenly see it all, and at once. Back to mad Kurtz, in fact – though this time in the Joseph Conrad novel that inspired *Apocalypse Now*. 'Oh, I wasn't touched,' recalls Marlow, the narrator of *Heart of Darkness*. 'I was fascinated. It was as though a veil had been rent. I saw on that ivory face the expression of sombre pride, of ruthless power, of craven terror – of an intense and hopeless despair.'

Mmm. Same. It was all there, from the contempt for parliamentary democracy to the mob-inciting tropes to her willingness to take terrible decisions out of self-interest or profoundly misguided factionalism. If May sees through what she implied, then all the hideously unwarranted insults thrown at others over the past two years – traitor, saboteur, enemy of the people – should legitimately be levelled at her.

As we head into the crunchiest of all crunch weeks, then, it must be said that only in a political class so bereft of heroes could people be hailing John Bercow as one. Bercow has been the subject of multiple accusations of bullying by people who have worked for him, and his apotheosis by some haute remainers is a reminder that Brexit has driven people on both sides crazy, or at the very least into behaviours of which they would, in their right mind, feel somewhat ashamed. I certainly don't exclude myself from this analysis. After two and a half years of this shitshow, grasping at Bercow or an online petition or even no deal as the latest saviour is a form of rock bottom. We are all Renton from *Trainspotting* now, diving down the worst bog in Scotland in search of the suppository.

Is there a single blue-rinse Tory who doesn't fancy a knee-trembler with Boris Johnson?

17 May 2019

The leadership candidate is said to connect with people emotionally. But his only genuine emotion is self-love

'I wouldn't kiss you if you were the last man on Earth!' It's one of the great clichés of romance novels that any woman saying this will, in due course, be doing just that. Maybe it'll be a hate-kiss in the hayloft above the stables; maybe it'll be a momentary lapse just after he's rescued her from a predatory ranch hand. But you can absolutely bet on it: she's going to be 'sharing herself' with this man within 100 pages. The Tory parliamentary party's relationship with Boris Johnson is the hardcore porn version of this.

For so long, you couldn't move for Conservative MPs saying they'd leave the party if Johnson ever became leader, that they wouldn't vote for him in a million years, that he didn't have a chance of getting anywhere near their special place. One hundred pages deeper into the shitshow, where are we on these holdouts?

Well, weirdo Fleet Street convention demands I describe this as a family newspaper. So I can't even begin to detail the stuff the Conservative party are probably going to do for Johnson – and, indeed, the stuff they're going to let him do to them. But I can tell you that while he's doing it, they will not be protesting, but instead moaning: 'DO ME UP THE WTO! PERVERT ME LIKE THE FACTS IN YOUR CHURCHILL BIOGRAPHY! IMPREGNATE ME WITH YOUR O-LEVEL LATIN!' The clear message you should be getting from 'the party of business' is: buy shares in lube today.

Is he even possibly going to be our next prime minster, then? Boris Johnson? This *Queer Eye* 'before' photo, this off-brand Flashheart, this radioactive haystack, this Frankenstein assemblage of all the rejected personality disorders of the minor Greek gods? Oh, wait – this overpromoted journalist whose style philosophy is 'sleeping in my car for a domestic misdemeanour'? According to what one experienced hand at the heart of government told *The Spectator*'s James Forsyth this week: 'The only person who can stop Boris is Boris.' Right – just like how Mike Tyson said his hardest opponent was always himself. In a way.

If Johnson's is one of the two names that makes it past the parliamentary ballot, he is surely nailed on. Among the Tory party's madly reactionary members, who lag about 30 years behind the rest of the country in every attitudinal survey, there is barely a blue-rinse out there who doesn't secretly fancy a knee-trembler with this winsomely naughty boy, 54. Sure, there will be a few Tory MPs who keep their word and decline to stick around in the event of Johnson winning – your Dominic Grieves (who's already lost one confidence motion in his constituency), and perhaps your Nicholas Soameses. And we'll come to how heartbreakingly brief that could render BoJo's premiership in another column.

But, in general, you should give as much credence to Tory MPs' earlier expressions of principle as far as Johnson is concerned as you should have done to all the celebrities who said they would emigrate if Labour got into power in 1997, and to all the US stars who said they'd move to Canada if Donald Trump won the US presidency.

As for what has caused this great assuming of the position in the Conservative party: it is, of course, the twin threats of Nigel Farage and Jeremy Corbyn. Yup, this is real Clash of the Tapeworms stuff.

Every now and then, it pays to take a step back and consider the stature of the dramatis personae of this era. Towering figures these are not – in fact, their slightness is truly remarkable. Perhaps the best way of characterising the horror of our age is to note that Nigel Farage is the most successful politician of it. Growing sections of an existentially panicked Conservative party believe that Johnson is the man with the momentum – the Bomentum, if you will – to counter not just Farage but Corbyn, a man who lavished deserved decades in obscurity on frotting the IRA while bizarrely dressed in the brightly coloured jackets of a daytime gameshow host.

But that was then. Nobody cares about things like the IRA, or lying, or how many mistresses you've knocked up and left, or any of that shit any more. They don't care who funds Farage, or how. Read all the wanky articles: they care about emotion, and the stories you tell them. Johnson is judged supremely able to connect with people emotionally – amusingly, given he is personally incapable of any non-ironic emotion other than self-love. The most authentic slogan he could run under would be: 'Not a serious person for not a serious country.'

Corbyn's much-vaunted USP is that he has been fighting the hard right, in all its forms, for his entire political career. So how come he's so openly unwilling to do so as far as Farage is concerned?

Arguably, the only person who could throw all these three men into sympathetic relief is Theresa May. In terms of political gifts, or horrifying lack thereof, May recalls the bit at the start of *Edward Scissorhands* where Edward's inventor dies before he's been able to fit his creation with hands. The kindest way to put it is to say that May has spent the past three years coming off as unfinished. Her attempts to reach out have been calamitous. To watch her at work for any length of time is to end up screaming, 'Oh my God, PLEASE – please! – just STOP TOUCHING THINGS.'

Still, you will note that May has been resigned again this week. Over the past few months I've lost count of how many times I've seen her pictured in the classic back-of-the-car shot that's supposed to indicate 'taxi for the prime minister'. May feels like the only person to have resigned more than Farage – and yet she's still there. We're all still here, more's the pity. The UK remains in toxic stasis, presided over by a necrotic government, but now with a gathering sense that much worse could be in the post.

Opium-pipers, bluffers and no-dealers impress in this Tory battle of nonentities

31 May 2019

The Conservative party leadership race is already providing rich entertainment at the whole country's expense

The official tagline for the Tory leadership contest is 'EXPERIENCE MAGIC THIS SUMMER'. Its key value divide is between candidates who would smoke opium at an Iranian wedding and candidates who would order a drone strike on one. We haven't even begun to hear from frontrunner Boris Johnson, that fly-tipped sofa, who will probably be endorsed next week by visiting indignitary Donald Trump.

Still, plenty to be getting on with. Esther McVey would order you a drone strike, no problem. The only issue is whether she'd be able to get all the gays in one place. This week, Esther waded into the grimly regressive row about LGBT teaching, suggesting that parents should have the right to deny their children educational access to reality (I'm paraphrasing). As she put it: 'I believe parents know best for their children.' Yes, babe! That's why measles is back. That's why you personally defend the refusal to pay a mother benefits for her third child, unless she can prove she was raped.

McVey joins every other Tory candidate in promising to 'deliver Brexit', even though it's a parcel 30 times bigger than Britain's letterbox. Esther's full no-deal, naturally, while Sajid Javid . . . well, The Saj has bravely refused to reveal any spoilers about his thinking on Brexit.

Or perhaps you prefer the look of Dominic Raab? For reference, that look is 'white-collar guy who's never done anything wrong in his life before this. You have to believe him, he was just trying to keep her quiet – OH MY GOD OH MY GOD THERE'S SO MUCH BLOOD – OK, keep calm, keep calm. Panic's how they're going to get you. There's that bit of copse past the golf club . . .' And so on. Dan Stevens stars.

As for Jeremy Hunt, I do enjoy the way Jeremy talks about his previous business running an educational courses database as though it were the East India Company or something. 'Doing deals is my bread and butter,' he Andrew Carnegie-d this week. 'I've taken risks, I've employed people. You have to do deals the whole time.' Deals Jeremy has struck with the taxpayer include claiming 27p for a 900-metre car journey and repaying £9,500 for second-home expenses. You win some, you lose some. Still, I'm looking forward to the bit in early July, if the field is whittled down as expected, where I find myself whispering, 'Maybe . . . maybe Hunt's not the worst?' at my reflection in a bathroom mirror, which I will then punch into a thousand pieces. Michael Gove . . .? I can't. I just can't. Maybe next week.

Across all candidates there is an absolute refusal to admit Brexit is a mass Tory sex game that's gone badly wrong. See modernity's Matt Hancock, who this week attempted to attack Boris Johnson with the words: 'To the people who say "fuck business", I say fuck fuck business.' Gut response to this is: life, no parole. But for those who believe Matt's crime should be in some way understood, this grammatical construction is known as the 'double fuckative'. Contrary to assumption, there are policy positions beyond it – for instance, 'fuck the fucker of fuck business' and 'fuck fucking the fucker of fuck business'. Don't ask what they mean – just surrender to them and let them do their business on you.

Meanwhile, this is an election where shooting a selfie video makes you some Tomorrow Man who's just landed in a whirly-bird from the future. In my particular filter bubble, this tactic has helped make Rory Stewart everyone's favourite outsider. He is certainly to be commended for an absolute refusal to admit that the target voter in this particular election is a 73-year-old woman from Beaconsfield who wants to bring back hanging and describes Aids as 'nature's way'.

That said, the Tory membership are easily sophisticated enough to get that there are two kinds of class A drugs: the ones you take out of politeness 14 years before being appointed prisons minister, and the ones that get you sent to prison, where they're just as easy to get hold of, unlike any sort of a job once you get out. Make sure you take the right kind, kids! Also, please don't expect us to have a grown-up drugs policy ever. That's one of the many, many things we're leaving to your generation to sort out, while we wank on about sovereignty and the Blitz.

Meanwhile, on with the show, with viewers asked to accept increasingly ridiculous plot developments. On Thursday this was a person called 'Mark Harper' claiming to have been chief whip under David Cameron. I mean, maybe??? Mark joins a slew of candidates who might as well have been living in solitary confinement, who are now suggesting their anonymity makes them the perfect cleanskin to get us out of this mess.

In similar vein, The Malthouse Ultimatum has also entered the fray. Leadership pitch: 'You may know me from the compromise I named after myself.' Or, as Kit prefers it of his momentarily-coalesced-around fantasy that had already been unequivocally pre-rejected by the EU: 'Many commentators said it was the first time in 45 years that the Conservative party had been so united on Europe.' Remind us: how's that looking now?

Ultimately, the intractable problems of Brexit mean anyone claiming to be 'untainted' will be tainted by actual reality within minutes of acceding to the job. A 'new face' is going to solve the Tory party's underlying problems about as much as a 'new face' used to solve Michael Jackson's underlying problems.

Still, there will apparently be TV debates for this election you can't vote in, which will at least facilitate a drinking game. The rules of this particular one are: as soon as you see the opening credits, drink. Then keep doing it until the mid-2030s.

Boris Johnson is the Howard Hughes of this Tory leadership race

14 June 2019

Courtiers are keeping Johnson from his subjects like a porphyric king they daren't parade in public

Journalist, novelist, Churchill biographer, politician, urban planner, diplomat. At this stage in Boris Johnson's storied career we have to ask: is there anything he CAN do? Have a crack-eroo at being prime minister as Britain faces its greatest challenge in peacetime seems to be the obvious answer after this radioactively dispiriting week in the Conservative leadership contest. Or 'the good old days', as we will be thinking of it in around six months.

One pantingly auto-parodic article in the Boris fanzine, the *Daily Telegraph*, decided the runaway favourite looked like 'a prime minister in waiting'. So close, but not quite. Johnson looks like

Chucky if he'd borrowed a suit for a court appearance, or a Yewtree version of Worzel Gummidge, or what would happen if you started making Margaret Rutherford out of papier mâché but got bored halfway through. This week amounted to watching the detonation of that time-worn cliché that the Conservative parliamentary party is 'the most sophisticated electorate in the world'. Do me a favour. They've just slathered 114 first-round votes all over a subclinical narcissist whose chief qualification for the gig is knowing the ancient Greek for 'raghead'.

Still, other options were available. At a series of intimate Westminster gigs, prime ministerial hopefuls partied like it was 2016 and – with the exception of Rory Stewart – absolutely refused to tell the truth about the state we're in and our options for getting out of it. I lost count of the times candidates began sentences with a lofty 'I represent . . .' Babe, I don't know if you've noticed, but we're incredibly up against it here? NO ONE GIVES A TOSS ABOUT YOUR SPIRIT ANIMAL. At his launch, Matt Hancock was asked how he planned to deal with the serious threats posed by Silicon Valley. His reply? 'I offer an emotionally charged platform to improve lives that is rooted, rooted in objective fact.'

I can't believe that even as I was typing that paragraph, Hancock withdrew from the race. As for who else we've lost, it's farewell to dishonesty's Esther McVey, whose televised mugging-off by Lorraine Kelly serves as a reminder that late-1990s GMTV was such a legendary snakepit that it is still destroying ambitions two decades later. Brexit's Oxo mum, Andrea Leadsom, also failed to make the cut, as did unintriguing stranger 'Mark Harper', who claimed to have been chief whip under David Cameron, but has blown back out of town as mysteriously as he blew in, having failed to sell us his version of the monorail.

It was a week to make one begin seriously wondering about the political philosophy of General Sir Nick Carter, Britain's chief of defence staff. Would a military coup really be so bad? Gotta wonder, when even the remaining candidates are openly touting alternative solutions to parliamentary democracy as we know it.

Johnson, Britain's id, has refused to rule out proroguing parliament to push through no deal. Shortly after the result of the first ballot, a defiant Stewart declared that if Johnson did take that path, then 'we will hold our own session of parliament across the road in Methodist Central Hall and we will bring him down'.

Another absolutely normal day in our normal country. Perhaps it helps to see Stewart as a Charles de Gaulle figure, who – on the basis of not much more than a borrowed office in Carlton Gardens and a pretty high opinion of himself – spent a good chunk of the second world war acting as the equal, if not superior, of Churchill, Roosevelt and Stalin. As Julian Jackson remarks in his brilliant biography of the general: 'Behaving like a great power was de Gaulle's way of becoming one.'

If Stewart has a certain idea of Britain, it was exceedingly clear from his own campaign launch that Johnson does not. Or even any ideas. Despite starting at 11am, the event served breakfast, which feels about right as far as Johnson's reputation for hard work goes. Short of putting the 'rogue' in 'prorogue', his Brexit strategy seems to be to barge back to Brussels, unwisely essaying machismo. More on that game plan shortly.

Other launches? Michael Gove's was just a mobile number you had to ring an hour before it started, before making your way to a field, where he plied you with base speed, illegal repetitive beats and ideas from middlebrow public intellectuals.

Meanwhile, many will still be confused by Sajid Javid. By day, he's the charmless rich guy who enacts borderline racist Home Office policies and stands on the docks declaring national emergencies on the basis of the seaborne arrival of about 12 desperate migrants. By night, he's the champion of underdogs who publicly laments not being asked to Donald Trump's state banquet and strongly suggests this might be on the grounds of discrimination. I mean, what even is this character? A sort of equalities Bruce Wayne?

Either way, he is vastly more appealing than the thinly disguised men's rights activist Dominic Raab, whose standout launch anecdote found him down his local boxing gym – where else? – where he'd met a 'young lad' who'd turned his life . . . well, you know how all boxing gym stories go. The Raab story you aren't going to find out about is the bullying accusation covered by a non-disclosure agreement, with Raab this week insisting: 'The right time for the confidentiality obligations to be lifted on both sides for a fair and balanced airing of the dispute was before the court back in 2012.' Totally. THAT was the right time. The time when he is running to be actual prime minister is absolutely not the time, and I'm kind of disappointed people are asking.

Ultimately, though, all elections are psychosexual events for the Tories. Even mild-mannered Jeremy Hunt was looking at things in a way that might intrigue his analyst. Here's the foreign secretary's tweet on the day of the first ballot: 'Woke up this morning and felt a bit like the morning of my wedding. Something big is going to change but don't quite know how it will unfold.'

Ah. In retrospect, inviting Johnson to this metaphorical wedding was always going to end up one way. Honestly, you turn your back for one minute to pay the photographer, and your wife's . . . well, I hope you can both patch it up. I expect everyone had had a lot to drink.

As for Johnson, to listen to what passes for his plan is to be struck by a very profound sense that he is going to somehow shag our way out of this. Hand on heart, I do think pretending that politicians are credible sex objects should most swiftly disqualify you from voting. But to the likes of the 'chemistry'-obsessed *Telegraph*, Johnson is the country's romantic lead. They insist you see him as the Tory party's Mr Darcy, emerging shirtless from a lake of shit to concede to having knocked up at least three of the Bennet sisters. (Of those, only silly Kitty went and kept it, of course, though Darcy doesn't feature in its life, having reluctantly parted with a small part of his ten thousand pounds a year to make the matter go away.)

And so to Johnson's MP backers. Voting for him in craven desperation to keep your seat doesn't make you a beta; it makes you an omega. It is about as likely to be successful as the way England used to play football. Hoof it up to the big man. See if he can get something on it. In a crowded field of depressing statements this week, we might still single out the former international development secretary Andrew Mitchell's justification for Johnson swerving the forthcoming TV debates: 'There's no reason for him to debate with everybody, I would have thought.'

I can think of a reason. But if you lacked reminders that the public at large is a mere plot device in the bigger story of Johnson's careerism, then that 'no reason' is one. The idea of public service has been so totally inverted by Johnson that it is the public doing the serving. Even people previously thought to be relatively sensible and intelligent Conservatives, such as Mitchell, see no reason to treat the populace with anything approaching respect.

So this is where we are at as we head into week two. Johnson's courtiers are keeping him from his subjects like some porphyric king whom they daren't parade in public in case he speaks his mind or mounts the help. In his later years, Howard Hughes was guarded by a 'Mormon mafia' who protected him from the public gaze and catered to his every whim. Occasionally, their overlord would desire to move on from whichever curtained hotel penthouse he'd been holed up in, and the logistics were quite something. Over the next month, then, let us imagine Johnson's own political guards moving him covertly around London, down service stairwells and through back doors, his fingernails three inches long, his hair even more unkempt than usual. Only instead of dying at the end, as Hughes did, he becomes prime minister.

Cummings, the new Rasputin, is outshining Johnson as antihero-in-chief

9 August 2019

After laying down the law on 7.55am meetings, Cummings is planning a perfect Brexit on 1 November, valid for one day only

How did you enjoy Thursday night's Downing Street address by Prime Minister Smirky McSmirkface? Boris Johnson began by describing his morning: 'I was at the nuclear fusion labs in Culham.' Please say a freak accident befell you there, causing you to emerge, if not with superpowers, then at least as tenuously adequate.

Alas, not. Johnson's tight-framed, air-jabbing, fist-banging, weirdly emphasised delivery is still like that of a Bloomberg pundit trying to make the currency markets sound scandalously interesting. (Soon, he won't have to.) But it was the climax of his speech that caught the attention, as the PM stared right down the lens and declared: 'I want this country to be . . . the greatest place to bring up your kids.' The greatest place to do what, sorry? 'The greatest place to bring up your kids.' OK, babe – but you have to do it too.

I mean . . . I keep reading about the galaxy brains Johnson's surrounded himself with – and we'll come to the galaxiest of them all in due course. But can it honestly be that not one of them thought to cross out this particular line, on the basis that not only will the prime minister not say how many kids he has, but he isn't even bringing at least one of them up?

Alastair Campbell famously protected Tony Blair from himself by interrupting an interviewer's question about faith with the words: 'We don't do God.' In Johnson's inner circle, you would think that there might be someone who could take a look at his speeches before they're read out and go: 'Yeah, we don't do kids, because it draws attention to the prime minister's serial inability to either wear a condom or take full responsibility for not wearing a condom.'

And so to the man whose job title is apparently assistant to the prime minister, but who is currently getting pre-title billing. Poor Johnson. Imagine waiting your whole life for it, and then not even being the antihero of your own administration, let alone the person in it people thought was the cleverest. Whatever happened to Baby Boris? He used to be such a thing.

Still, the spotlight is fickle. This week, it was mostly shining on Dominic Cummings, a sort of skinny Cartman who really wants you to know he's got the highest score on *Call of Duty: SW1*. Every photo of Cummings going into Downing Street sees him shiftily meeting the camera's gaze with the same defensive sneer you'd see on the proprietor of a holiday caravan park who has just been released on police bail after a fatal gas explosion thought to have been caused by poor maintenance. Britain really is the land of crap Rasputins, each one dragging us one step further back towards the primordial soup, like some grim Descent of Man. Hilton, Timothy, Cummings . . . What's the next term in this sequence? Milne? Chuckle? Sutcliffe? It could go one of several ways.

Naturally, Dominic regards himself as rather better than that. To get some idea of the level of pretension we're dealing with, his former Twitter handle (for the account he admitted to) was @OdysseanProject. His bio? 'Physicist Gell-Mann said we need an Odyssean education.'

Cummings still has his blog, where he posts 20,000-word . . . essays, is it? His is a writing style I call Briar Rose, on account of the requirement to take your sword and hack your way through the densest thicket of impenetrable prose this side of a Jordan Peterson integrated theory of his mother. A few thousand words into one of Dominic's blogs, it is very easy to become disheartened. You find yourself asking: is there an incredibly hot princess of meaning lying asleep in the middle of all these branches of history, or am I basically just doing some lazy castle-owner's gardening for free?

Yet his attempts to cast himself as Whitehall's Minotaur have been bizarrely successful. Cummings appears to have been specifically engineered to appeal to that particular media demographic which reckons British politics is just like Westeros. Guys, just because you ejaculate during the title sequence of both *Game of Thrones* and *Politics Live* doesn't mean they're the same.

This week, a lot of people went nuts over a brief clip of Cummings smirkingly getting into a car saying things like: 'I don't think I'm arrogant. I don't know much.' Pretty sure we've heard that one before, albeit in a thick Portuguese accent. 'Please don't call me arrogant, because what I'm saying is true. I think I am a Special One.'

Maybe that's why Dominic is putting Boris in the shade. People always used to say José Mourinho was such a genius for protecting his star players by acting like a maniac himself. I can't remember whether we were still supposed to think it by the time Mourinho was gouging a rival coach's eye, or whether by that stage it was OK to conclude that Mourinho was simply a complete . . . But no. It's too simple. It must be 'mind games'.

Thus, Cummings is not a rejected 1990s David Mamet character, but a master strategist who schedules 7.55am meetings. This feels like an even more extreme version of the bit in *The Prime of Miss Jean Brodie* where Maggie Smith's teacher is summoned to the headmistress's office at 4.15 and sniffs: 'Not four, not 4.30, but 4.15. Hm. She thinks to intimidate me by use of quarter-hours?' No doubt Cummings would say that the no-five-minutes-spared look is an important part of his messaging. And the message many of us are getting is: he's a prick. Physicist Gell-Mann said they needed a supercomputer down at Los Alamos that was capable of calculating how much of a prick he is, but they couldn't even build one, because something something systems and red teams, something something Darpa and the Santa Fe Institute.

In what would surely be a historic instance of bathos, then, it seems all this high-blown theory might be leading to a general election on 1 November, hours after we have left the EU automatically, but hours before the chaos of no deal would properly have kicked in. Michael Gove has even floated the idea of 1 November being a bank holiday. You can't have turmoil on the financial markets if the banks are shut, amirite?

So, yes, let's be hugely encouraged that Johnson's team is treating the general election, at the most critical moment in the UK's post-war history, like a bank heist, where the window of opportunity to steal this thing will be incredibly small. Instead of having to work in the two minutes when the security cameras are pointing the other way and the security guards are changing over or passing that one blind spot on ground level, the masterminds need to pull off this job just after Britain has left the EU, but just before the collective meltdown has begun.

The main thing is to picture Cummings as the T-shirted Danny Ocean of the left-behind, telling his crew: 'I don't need a sensible Brexit, or a safe Brexit, or even a medicines-first Brexit. I just need 15 perfect hours on polling day. After that, who cares?'

Dazed and confused, Johnson stumbles into the twilight zone with a police escort

6 September 2019

A discombobulated appearance at a police academy in Wakefield sparks concern for the prime ministerial franchise

Why do people still call it a Tory 'split' on Europe? It's not a split; it's an episiotomy. The Tory episiotomy on Europe went septic this week as Boris Johnson expelled 21 MPs, including two former chancellors and his hero Winston Churchill's grandson; lost his own brother in a tale we'll call 'Cain and Far More Able'; and gave a speech so hallucinatorily bad it whiteyed a policewoman. At the current rate, even Robert Caro will only need a week to write this Johnson biography.

Then again, Johnson might get a majority, and we'll look back on these as the good old days. More on the prospect of that banter-apocalypse later.

For now, it feels remarkable to think that barely five weeks ago, the vast majority of Tory MPs were telling us Boris Johnson was the only possible answer to various questions. It turns out those questions were: 'How would Dudley Dursley and Draco Malfoy's baby look and behave?', 'What if you shaved the Honey Monster and put him in a suit for a court appearance?' and 'Does anyone know the ancient Greek for shitting the bed?'

Despite practising since boyhood, Johnson's entire demeanour is that of a man who has won a competition to lead the country for a day. He is Mike Bassett: England Prime Minister, yet wheels out jokes he's done 437 times before as though he's Frank Sinatra and reckons the crowd can't wait to see him do 'My Way' again. Johnson must be the only performer whose audience spends his gigs screaming: 'PLEASE, DO YOUR NEW STUFF.'

Physically, he seems in a remarkable state. Apart from looking like he cuts his hair with the bacon scissors, the PM's shtick is bizarre and juddering, as though some of his innards are trying to escape. Perhaps they have found the tension between the bodily functions they are required to provide and the national interest unresolvable.

Oratorically, his PMQs debut merits a mere five-word review: 'Welcome to the Commons, bitch.' As a dispatch box artiste, Johnson has all the accomplishment of one of those pisshead chancers who go house to house at 10pm in December and 'carol-sing' for pub money. His delivery was that of a man finding out in real time that material which slayed at the accountancy corporate he did in 2007 is less well received by those who haven't drunk themselves to within an hour of renal failure. That is as much as 30% of the House of Commons. I'd give it a fortnight before Theresa May is waving an ironic 'WENGER IN' banner behind him.

As for his turns away from Westminster, Thursday afternoon found him at a Yorkshire police academy, where he appeared deeply confused. He resembled a political Elvis – twilight years – who'd had to be slapped awake on the tour bus by his manager, given some of his special medicine and shoved on to greet the LA crowd with the words: 'Hello, Philadelphia!' This, but in Wakefield.

Having very belatedly taken the stage, Johnson proceeded to die on his arse in front of rows of police officers. Does this technically count as a death in custody? Certainly, it bore all the hallmarks of such an event, of which there have been 1,102 since 1990, with not a single conviction for murder or manslaughter. Which is to say: it was brutal and disturbing, it happened right in front of multiple police pretending not to notice, and the victim was officially concluded to have done it to himself. (Thank you in advance to the Police Federation for their forthcoming letters on this paragraph. I'll make time to read them when I retire at 50, after three years on the sick.)

There is much discussion about what really 'cut through' this week, with Johnson's greatest shits collection set against such viral delights as a factual yet simultaneously car-crash delineation of Labour's Brexit policy by Emily Thornberry on *Question Time*. It is quite something to be got the better of by fellow panellist Richard Tice, a sort of radicalised Damart catalogue model, but the shadow foreign secretary managed it.

As for Jacob Rees-Mogg, the leader of the House of Commons, his insolent frontbench loll-about is still lighting up Facebook. I'm not going to go full ad hominem on Nanny, who was probably only following orders, but I do think the time has come when we all have to ask: has anyone EVER done a worse job and stayed in post longer? She's still there! Jesus Christ, Nanny: YOU HAD ONE JOB. Teach him some manners, yes? Jacob Rees-Mogg is 50 (FIFTY). Is he even housebroken?

Then again, why expect more from a guy who believes that even incestuously raped minors should be forced to give birth, at the same time as his investment fund profits from the sale of abortion pills? Asked about this hypocrisy once, Rees-Mogg declared airily: 'The world is not always what you want it to be.' You're telling me, mate. Very much ditto. With the world as it is, we have to tolerate the spectacle of the chancellor of the Duchy of Gilead spreading his loins all over the frontbench and comparing an NHS doctor who co-wrote official no-deal contingency plans to disgraced anti-vaxxer Andrew Wakefield. This last piece of utter yobbery saw Jacob humiliatingly ordered to apologise, presumably by Dominic Cummings (a man widely believed not to have completed the Norland Nanny training course).

Perhaps it was terror of Cummings, then, that prevented Johnson from giving in to either basic human or political instincts and assisting the fainting policewoman in Wakefield. The PM chose instead to gibber out the last of his prepared lines, and the bulletins duly led with his claim that he'd 'rather be dead in a ditch' than delay Brexit.

As for who would find his remains, it increasingly feels like a case for Brad Pitt and Morgan Freeman, the pair of cops in *Se7en*, a movie in which various people are ritually deadly-sinned to death. A man of many uncontrollable appetites, Boris Johnson has embodied each of the sins at points in his life, and this week it almost felt as if he was being strapped in like the glutton and forced to prime minister himself to death. Had enough prime-ministering yet, dear? I think you can fit just a bit more prime ministering in, and a bit more, and a bit more, and . . . [*Cut to shot of Pitt and Freeman battering down the door of No. 10 and choking into their handkerchiefs.*]

Anyway, you get the idea with that one. I guess the major philosophical question facing some of us this week was: would it all be worth it? Would you take three years of political paralysis, a toxic public realm, bitter family rows and no prospect of even medium-term national healing just to watch this one absolute monster reap his own whirlwind, live on telly, in a horrifyingly hilarious cautionary tale about getting everything you always wanted? The answer, of course, is no. Not even close. And he still might get a majority.

Having said all that . . . you've got to get your kicks somehow in these dark times, and if you can't enjoy a good bin fire, what's really left? So chuck some more furniture on the flames, take your warmth where you can, and try to get some rest before he takes a crack at next week.

Jennifer Arcuri came late to the party. But the Johnson show is unthinkable without her now

4 October 2019

The prime minister's former technological educator is hilariously good value, even in a supermarket car park

Kick back and pour yourself a tech-o-tini, because there's a new political star in town – and she is finally talking. She's talking in a Los Angeles supermarket car park for now, laughing merrily while holding a large carton of almond milk. But if her lawyer gets his way, she'll be talking in a high-paying British newspaper this weekend. She is, of course, Jennifer Arcuri – model, infosec entrepreneur, and the businesswoman responsible for the technological education of Boris Johnson.

On Thursday a US attorney was fielding multiple calls attempting to broker a deal for her story. Asked if that would include her confirming a romantic relationship with Johnson, he replied: 'It depends on your definition of romantic.' Wow. Go on. 'I've known Jennifer for 14 years. There's a lot of scrutiny of Mr Johnson. Get in the queue – if you want her services, you have to pay for it.' Ought he to be making his client sound like Lol Flanders? It's not for us to judge.

For now, by way of a taster, we have Jennifer's car-park chat with the *Daily Mirror*. I can't play favourites with the sheer volume of brilliant quotes. But how about: 'Men just trip over themselves in front of me. They fall in love with me in about 10 minutes . . . because I know what to say. I make men trip over their dicks. That's what happens. They go insane around me. They've been doing it for years. It's just what happens.' And very much fair play to her. I suppose that, literally speaking, Boris Johnson remains my prime minister. But, spiritually, Jennifer Arcuri has now taken the role.

Maybe you prefer the following gem, perhaps prompted by a question about the stripper's pole she had in the technology-lessons apartment: 'I had the best fucking flat in east London. The reason why Boris would stop over was because of the clusterfuck of emails. And he was like, "Jen, what the fuck's a Google hangout? Where are you at three o'clock, I can, you know, stop over."'

'You know.' And, yes, you may feel like you DO know. At first glance, Arcuri would seem to be a throwback to the golden era of kiss-and-tells, epitomised for me by Bienvenida Buck (then Lady Buck), who did a primetime TV advert for the *News of the World* in which she purred: 'Tomorrow I reveal how your chief of defence staff was a Torrrrrnado in my bed.'

That said, it must be stressed that Arcuri claims there is no kissing to tell of. 'Complete bullshit,' is her verdict. 'If I was banging the dude,' she opines mildly of the prime minister, 'and there was some kind of, like trail or sex tape, but there's nothing. There is a human side of my very complex relationship.' And if you've seen the picture of her biting the head off one of three fondant-icing

Boris Johnsons on a London mayor-themed cake, you'd be mad to argue with that claim of complexity.

However unlikely this possibility may seem, I now hope against hope that she didn't actually have sex with the prime minister. The image of Boris Johnson turning up in the expectation of it and having to listen to Silicon Valley blather while not actually getting any is my new idealised version of this story. Just picture him, asking leading questions about the stripper's pole, while she shows him how to do a PowerPoint. If there is a hell, this is what Johnson's would be like.

Either way, thank God for this incredible new character. Jennifer has rocked up now, at a relatively late stage in the story, but already you couldn't imagine the franchise without her. Like Yoda, who doesn't appear until the second *Star Wars* movie. Ditto both Inspector Dreyfus and Cato, who only show up in the *Pink Panther* sequel. Indeed, in many ways Jennifer combines different traits from all those three characters – a kind of pseudo-gnomic wisdom, allied to an incipient craziness. And a very real sense that she could judo-chop the shit out of you as soon as you got through the front door.

Here she is on why she was being promoted by the UK embassy in the US: 'I was extremely proactive. They didn't stop and go, "Wait a minute, did you fuck Boris Johnson?"' At this point, the British ambassador inquiring, 'Did you fuck Boris Johnson?' is about the only thing that could make the story better.

And that is all credit to our picaresque heroine. I'll admit I didn't get it at first. But Jennifer is, by the sound of things, hilariously good value. Even under pressure in a supermarket car park, she is miles more amusing than Johnson, whose hollowed-out narcissism has left him as little more than a repository for the same seven knackered jokes and a series of second-class classics allusions. Jennifer, on the other hand, sounds like a card. I suspect she might grow a little rich for the blood in the second hour of dinner *à deux*, but she'd be a complete hoot to have along at a party. Party, trade mission, whatever.

Alas, having posted one of her top quotes online, I was disappointed to find gentlemen replying to sniff of Jennifer: 'Who talks like that?' I don't know, guys. Whoever wants to? Maybe not to a reporter in a supermarket car park, I'll concede . . . but in the end, so what? I salute Arcuri for being able to laugh swashbucklingly about her cray-cray situation, even in the eye of the media storm. I am not remotely interested in those who are now going to question Johnson's judgment for ever going near her. She doesn't even make the cut of the top 1,000 people he should never have gone near – several of whom are in the cabinet or bankrolled his leadership bid.

Yes, Jennifer Arcuri can talk how she likes and do what she likes. And while I'd selfishly like that to be 'talk to a Sunday newspaper and offer much more of the same', it really is up to her. For now, she's a breath of Californian air in the increasingly rancid pea-souper of our politics, and I await her next move as a decided fan.

Pity our Conservative MPs, forced to go on strike to protect their way of life

25 October 2019

Boris Johnson's latest threat paints his government as a victim. At least the party long ago outlawed sympathy action

It was the worst of times, it was the worst of times. On the one hand, inflatable reservist Mark Francois MP has previously promised that we will leave the EU on 31 October, or 'this country will explode'. On the other, Devon-based extremist Katie Hopkins has previously tweeted that we will leave the EU on 31 October, or

'I will drink a pot of tea naked in the *Apprentice* losers cafe with Farage's face on each nipple.'

We will not be leaving the EU on 31 October.

According to some reports, Brexit coins minted with the 31 October date 'could be worth up to £800'. So could €1 coins, soon enough. Still, the cabinet hoarding the misprinted Brexit coins to pay for their skiing holidays would be an irony we could all get behind.

If you're keeping track of the accounts, Boris Johnson has just blown £100m on an ad campaign insisting the UK was leaving on 31 October, even though the chances of this were always so slim they amounted to Conservative party election positioning. Given that seven months ago the prime minister was describing the £60m spent on the historical sex abuse inquiry as money 'spaffed up a wall', it's important that you get his Brexit ads in perspective. They were complete bollocks, and at the same time almost twice as valued as investigating mass institutionalised child rape. It's a very exciting branding space for the Tories to be in.

Strange to think that, in another timeline, we would all currently be pooling our corned beef and lightbulbs in anticipation of Theresa May's planned Festival of Brexit. Instead, we're waiting to see whether the French will give us an election. Yesterday, Boris Johnson told MPs in the Commons tea room that he had asked the French to block the Brexit extension request. In a documentary filmed when he was foreign secretary, Johnson told the cameras that the French were 'turds'. So it will be interesting to see which version of our friends and partners turns up. What's the French for 'You want picking up in the morning, pal?'

The prime minister wants a Christmas election, but at present that old Scrooge Jeremy Corbyn won't give him one. Despite having a deal that parliament merely wished to properly scrutinise, we are told that no-deal plans are being stepped up by Michael Gove (who frequently appears to have been visited by three large spirits).

'We are triggering Operation Yellowhammer,' he announced on Sunday. You're triggering us all, dear.

And what if they can't get an election? Then, like a lot of other comedy shows, the Conservative government will have a strike episode. *South Park* did one once, where the nation of Canada goes on strike because it feels disrespected by the world. As for how the Tory version will play out, instinct suggests you should put your money on 'for mirthless laughs'. We'll have no choice but to watch Conservative ministers presenting themselves as victims of The Man, which is a bit like Peter Sutcliffe presenting himself as a victim of the Yorkshire Ripper. Consequently, they'll be forced to band together and take industrial action to protect their way of life. Listen, they just want their dignity. They know that when these jobs go there'll be nothing else, bar retraining as an arms lobbyist or non-executive director of Goldman Sachs.

Sadly, we know from bitter experience the privations of a winter strike for those involved. The Conservatives wisely outlawed sympathy actions in the past, so they won't face having to go through it without essential auxiliary services such as unwanted child collection and Ocado. But do begin putting aside your spare pennies to buy the young Rees-Moggs footwear, while their da makes soaring speeches behind an SW1 brazier. 'My father went down the money pit, I went down the money pit, and, so help me, my son will have a money pit to go down.'

Except not. This week, Jacob could be found in the House of Commons, explaining why the withdrawal agreement bill that the government actually had a majority for was suddenly nowhere to be seen by adapting the famous poem from *The Scarlet Pimpernel*. 'The answer lies with Sir Percy Blakeney,' he honked of that novel's hero. 'They seek it here, they seek it there, those parliamentarians seek it everywhere. Is it in heaven, or is it in hell? That damned elusive Brexit bill!' Oh dear. Of course, much to the chagrin of their silly 50-year-old boy, the hugely bourgeois Rees-Moggs would have been entirely safe during the French Revolution. The voluminously suited Jacob's chief exposure to Sir Percy Blakeney would have run along the lines of the latter's remark to the ghastly government official Chauvelin: 'Sink me! Your tailors have betrayed you. T'would serve you better to send *them* to Madame Guillotine.' I suppose it's nice to see Jacob disporting himself with the confidence of a man yet to realise Dominic Cummings is building an oubliette for him to spend any election in.

And so to that gilet-clad Loki. This week, we've had so many definitive and yet contradictory anonymous No. 10 rants about what fiendish stratagem is next. Yet here we are, in the same place. The October Surprise is that there is no surprise. There are mayflies that survive longer than Cummings's briefings, which now have a four-hour lifespan, yet somehow always achieve their destiny. They are an essential component of a media ecosystem that kind of knows that not signing a mandated letter means jack shit in legal terms, but will write it anyway because their news editor is Mr Right Now and needs the appearance of fresh meat. Hey – it's all retail. Isn't it?

With both main party leaders taken up with hourly contradiction, their extravagantly gifted junior troops have been on hand to desecrate the airwaves. Informed by Kay Burley that the polls said Labour wouldn't win, shadow lord chancellor Richard Burgon retorted: 'The polls said we wouldn't win last time.' Burley: 'You didn't.'

Reposting this exchange, Tory minister Johnny Mercer failed to appreciate his precise comic status as the Tory Burgon. 'I sometimes get teased for being thick because I spurned university to join up and serve when I was 19,' Mercer sensationally revealed. 'Then I see what a Cambridge degree and career in politics does for this guy and so many others of my colleagues, and think I got it about right.' If you say so yourself. I do enjoy Johnny's tireless attempts to disguise his raging self-regard as affable humility. His entire output reads like one of those guys who replies to the pictures porn stars tweet: 'Mornin darlin! All the better for seeing u! Think u posted that one just for me!!!!!'

All in all, another vintage week in the national journey. We remain in the wandering hands of a government that doesn't want 16- and 17-year-olds to vote because they aren't mature enough, but will go on strike if it can't get its election exactly when it wants it. Meanwhile, 16- and 17- year olds are having to bunk off their childhoods to draw the attention of infantilised adults to the looming risk of ecological and social collapse.

One month ago, members of Boris Johnson's government were lining up to tell teenagers that missing one day of school was unacceptable and wrong. Presumably, we'll now hear from those same ministers about how missing weeks of your six-figure-salary job running the country is right and heroic. What a time to be existing, when the best escape route might be giving Xboxes to politicians and waiting for the nation's children to grow up.

In this climate, how does Boris Johnson not melt with shame?

29 November 2019

The prime minister's reputation sank to new lows this week, despite – or because of – his dad's attempts to help

Boris Johnson's big contribution to reducing plastic consumption is not wearing condoms. Or, as Gavin Williamson put it this morning: 'Boris Johnson has done more for the environment than any other politician.' Quite. We don't need a joined-up strategy with the largest and most successful trading bloc the world has ever seen to prevent climate catastrophe, because Johnson's going to bareback our way to the higher ground, while we serve as galley slaves on his privatised sex ark.

Maybe I'm being a shade unfair. So let me say that this election marks a change of behaviour for the prime minister, who has finally started withdrawing. Unfortunately, he's pulling out of climate debates and BBC interviews, as opposed to single mothers. Still, baby steps. And he's certainly missed a few of those.

So that's the icebreakers out of the way. And, indeed, the ice sculptures. Thursday night saw Boris Johnson refuse to turn up to Channel 4's climate debate, along with Barboured harbinger Nigel Farage. The broadcaster replaced the pair with ice sculptures that melted while the rest of the UK's party leaders discussed an impending planetary catastrophe which, according to the BBC's news headline rankings, couldn't be more important unless it was a letter of complaint from No. 10 to Ofcom. Given the debate's subject matter, this stunt served as a reminder that the most important skill for an irreversibly overheated world will be being a psychopathic shit. Today's Downing Street lackeys are tomorrow's militia chiefs, and you should expect either to be killing for them or being killed by them in due course.

And so to the morning after the night before, when a Channel 4 floor manager is still applying Kleenex to the prime ministerial puddle, and hopefully making his refusal to mop up Nigel Farage a union matter. Where are our dramatis personae? On LBC a single mother has read Johnson's recently unearthed 1995 *Spectator* column, in which he tips all over single mothers. What a quaint period piece, from a time when all you ever heard about was single mothers, and not the deadbeat dads that left them to it. The single mother's voice is wobbling while she asks how he can talk about her family like that when he won't even talk about his own. Presenter Nick Ferrari asks Johnson how many children he has and whether he plays a full and proper role in all their lives. The prime minister twice refuses to answer.

Meanwhile, whither Stanley Johnson, the father that public life really needs to be abandoned by? By Friday morning this desperate ligger had already bagged several media appearances out of his son's C4 no-show. But I imagine Stanley will now have been spirited to the dungeon in which Jacob Rees-Mogg is being kept, after his appearance on Victoria Derbyshire's BBC programme. Here, Johnson Sr's reaction to being told that one viewer had called his son Pinocchio was: 'That requires a degree of literacy which I think the great British public doesn't necessarily have. They couldn't spell Pinocchio if they tried.' A line somehow redolent of that deathless Donald Trump quote: 'I love the poorly educated.'

This triumph of a media round started with Stanley opting to be in the Channel 4 spin room, despite his son wimping out. Having your dad in the spin room is the most embarrassing thing I've seen since what feels like for ever, which is the new way of saying 'yesterday'. It is even worse than Trump's regular deployment of his large adult sons, Don Jr and Eric. Or, as a friend calls them, Uday and Schmuday. Stanley Johnson is arguably the most talentless political relative of all, miles outstripping fabled duds like Billy Carter or Terry Major-Ball or Cherie Blair's sister Lauren Booth, and making Jeremy Corbyn's climate-denialist brother Piers look like someone you would prefer to have a pint with. Possibly. The pushiest of all parents, living through the child he helped to damage – just think of Stanley Johnson as the Joe Jackson of British politics.

Friday morning brought a press conference featuring Boris Johnson and Michael Gove, which unfortunately turned out not to concern the imminent arrival of an asteroid. I can't think of anyone who could motivate the living to embrace the kindness of death more gladly than these two, whose images should be plastered over the walls of abattoirs. Instead, Johnson and Gove – enabled by former Labour MP Gisela Stuart – lied about getting Brexit done in days, with the advance briefing floating the theme as 'Remember how you felt that morning?' (a reference to 24 June

2016). I certainly remember how Gove and Johnson looked that morning. Like a pair of absolute journalists, at least one of whom had already tucked away a couple of bottles of rosé, but who'd both just got a massive legal on a story they'd thought would fly under the radar. Three years on, things have only got worse. Can't believe that letting newspaper journalists run the country has come to this. If only the state of the newspaper industry had offered some clue as to how it would play out.

Indeed, somewhat ironicidally, Michael Gove seems to be pivoting to video. The actual cabinet minister turned up to Channel 4 with his own three-person crew to film what he lied was his 'no-platforming' – a reminder that Gove's frequently waved reusable coffee cup is no offset against his vast output of toxic emissions.

The chilling thing is that even a month ago, this stunt would have felt far-fetched. What will the next 12 days bring, other than things we might place in the file marked 'MUCH WORSE'? It's difficult to be sure about anything, other than the realisation that there are highly unstable radioactive isotopes deteriorating less quickly than our standards of public debate.

Fridge-hiding, the final frontier in election WTF-ery

11 December 2019

The prime minister now has something in common with honey, potatoes and avocados

We begin with a fact-check. This general election campaign has officially been going on since around the mid-Mesozoic period. Its final day saw an update to the list of things you actually shouldn't keep in the fridge, with the likes of honey, potatoes and avocados now joined by 'the UK prime minister'. All the party leaders embarked on a frantic cross-country campaigning dash on Wednesday, but only one of them ... no, I'm sorry. I can't face it yet. Give it a minute.

At dawn Boris Johnson embarked on a sort of softcore *Confessions of a Prime Minister* tour, which by 10am had already seen him dress up as a milkman, then pop something in someone's oven. What next? Pool boy? Cable guy? At this rate of innuendo it seemed reasonable to assume Johnson would simply be barebacking grateful activists live on the lunchtime news. Of course, his version of all this does subvert the classic porn trope. Traditionally, it's a blue-collar guy coming to the suburban professional's house while he's out at work. In this case, it's an old Etonian milkman knocking on the door of working-class homes. Someone's certainly going to get screwed, but not in a sexual way.

Unfortunately, things would take a wrong turn for Johnson back at the dairy – a sentence I might once have found mildly unusual, before I realised that Johnson's workwear adviser for this election was probably going to get a CBE in the new year honours. This week alone, Johnson has dressed up as a fisherman, a digger driver, a milkman, a builder and a baker. How old is his election strategist? I assume they say 'basgetti' instead of 'spaghetti' and still wear pull-up nappies at night. Yet despite the relish with which Johnson embraces cosplaying as a working man, he always seems oversized and grotesquely out of place in these scenes, as though a vast unlicensed buttock implant has just been cast in *Camberwick Green*.

Anyway: the fridge. Back at the Modern Milkman HQ, a producer for *Good Morning Britain*, filming live, asked whether the programme could get a chat with the prime minister. 'For fuck's sake!' said a senior Conservative source called Rob Oxley, still live on air. At which point the prime minister scuttled into a large fridge.

Time for a historical perspective, perhaps: despite having an underground bedroom as part of the war rooms complex, Boris

Johnson's hero Winston Churchill declined to sleep in it any more than four or five times in the entire second world war, including during the Blitz, when London was under sustained nightly bombardment. Hand on heart, it is difficult to imagine Churchill fleeing a lone Pathé news camera to conceal himself inside a refrigerator. Johnson's move forces an urgent reordering of the top three most embarrassing places British politicians have hidden because they couldn't handle the consequences of their actions. This now goes:

3 Edinburgh pub – Nigel Farage
2 Disabled loo – Ken Livingstone
1 Fridge – Boris Johnson

Because the smallness of the man could not be conceded, Tory campaign staff attempted to insist the interview request and the prime minister's presence in a fridge were correlated but not causal. According to the *Guardian*'s deadpan report on the matter, Conservative sources – I don't know which ones, but 'for fuck's sake' let's have a guess – claimed that Johnson was 'categorically not hiding' in the fridge, from which he later emerged carrying a crate of milk bottles. Instead, they fucksaked, his aides were taking a moment to prep the PM for a separate, pre-agreed interview.

Spellbinding. They honestly would have been better off going with something along the lines of: 'As you could see from the fact he'd rather steal a phone than empathise with the picture of a sick child, the prime minister is an extremely cold man. We had word from the dairy manager that one of the units was nudging over four degrees and the whole batch would have to be scrapped, so we whisked the prime minister in there to lower the temperature. Hey presto – milk lollies for all. The guy's like Elsa or something. Let's get Brexit done and sign an ambitious trade deal with Arendelle.'

For their part, on this final day Jeremy Corbyn's Labour wanted to talk about the NHS crisis. Not sure what the costume is for that

– perhaps a grim reaper's cowl, although that would make Corbyn look like he was playing Ben Kenobi in a panto version of *Star Wars*. Inevitably, though, the Labour leader couldn't help talking about the fridge. 'I've not come here to deliver milk,' Corbyn informed a rally in Middlesbrough, 'or to hide in a fridge.'

Yet hilariously – and indeed hallucinatorily – the Labour party then issued a formal statement featuring the following sentence about Boris Johnson: 'He is hiding in fridges to dodge interviews precisely because his fake Brexit slogans can't stand up to scrutiny.' Oh, man. Who knows whether in retrospect this will look like the moment Labour were finally defeated by Johnson's WTF-ery? But I can't help but notice that Her Majesty's opposition have just immediately normalised the idea of hiding in fridges as a political act, suggesting that it's something logical a prime minister might do 'precisely because' of something else, as opposed to what it is: a prime minister, of an actual country, hiding in a fridge. Guys, you can't fit this into the old attack templates. You're fighting a war against a fridge-hider. There aren't any established conventions. We're in the cold storage Wild West here.

And what of Britain's next prime minister, Jo Swinson? Alas, even she was unable to dodge the fridge-iverse. I kept seeing her supporters say versions of 'You know what? She's turned up to every TV interview and debate. She's never hidden in a fridge.' So let the record show there's a new benchmark. Here we are. This, then, is us. On the eve of polling day for the general election of 2019, the fridge is now the black hole of UK politics. None of us can escape its event horizon, so I can't say, 'See you on the other side.' In totally scientific terms, there is no other side to see you on.

This was a stunning victory for the bullshit–industrial complex

13 December 2019

Boris Johnson is world king now. Where there is discord, let him sow his wild oats

Well. A new dawn has shat, has it not? Shortly after 7am Boris Johnson slipped into the costume Dominic Cummings has been sewing for him out of the skins of missing statesmen. 'I am humbled that you have put your trust in me,' announced the nation's foremost liar in front of a backdrop reading 'The people's government', as though this ideally axiomatic concept was an innovation.

With the emphasis on 'a sacred trust', this government's senior personnel are immediately keen to stress it will be a servant of the people. I assume the specific servant it's modelled on is Paul Burrell. They've already dragged the Queen into it, and will soon begin amassing the nation's property in their attic 'for safekeeping'. Brexit will be done for Christmas, with Johnson scoring a stunning victory for the bullshit–industrial complex. From the outset, the Tories decided it was more effective to pretend you're listening to people who have doubts about you than to invite them to fuck off and join the Labour party. But hey – everyone's a strategist after the event.

In financial news, the pound pounded exuberantly to its money shot, and I imagine there were big moves on the US chlorine markets. Back in Westminster, the UK's prime minister took to the podium like a gelatinous Sith, introduced by Michael Gove as part of the Conservative scheme to rehabilitate former knife-wielders. Three and a half years ago, Michael was telling the world that Boris Johnson was unfit for leadership; now he was giving a community theatre performance worthy of the League of Gentlemen's troupe Legz Akimbo. Solemnly, Gove announced that Britain's Jews 'should never have to live in fear again'. Britain's Muslims, not so much, given the prime minister's multiple racisms on that and other fronts, and a grotesque TV riff merely hours earlier on burqa-wearing fighter pilots from world's worst stage dad Stanley Johnson.

Still, where there is discord, let Boris sow his wild oats. And then leave you to raise them. The point is: Johnson is world king now. And so to what happens next.

The Tory programme for government was not so much a mani-festo as a Mumsnet 'Am I being unreasonable?' thread. It also stopped after the first year, with the only clue for Act 2 being plans for voter suppression, and the so-called page 48 material, paving the way for the government to dismantle judicial and even parlia-mentary constraints on itself. As for the 2019 Tory intake, you may find yourself gripped by a hunch that the party has spent about 15 minutes vetting half the newbies, whose moral eccentricities will gradually reveal themselves to us like so many exquisite lotus blossoms.

Johnson announced his intention to bring the country back together, presumably by walling us in and forcing us to farm his sunlit uplands. Speaking of which, Ashfield was won by a Tory named Lee Anderson, who put out a video during the campaign stating that 'nuisance' council tenants should be made to live in tents in the middle of a field, where they would be woken at 6am and forced to pick vegetables until the end of the day, when they'd get a cold shower, then 'back in the tent'. Labour came third – THIRD – here.

A historic triumph for the Tories, then. Less so for the others – bar, of course, the SNP. Even hopes that Dominic Raab would soon be spending more time with the contents of his lock-up were misplaced. For their part, Labour line-takers were keen to con-centrate on the differences between the 2017 and 2019 elections, but would arguably benefit more from accepting the similarities. Which are that they lost both times. This one was the real bed-shitter, though. Jeremy Corbyn has announced he will not fight the next election but will stay in post to preside over the process of dealing with its fallout. This feels a bit like BP pitching for the contract to clean up the Gulf of Mexico after the Deepwater Horizon spill. Unfortunately, Corbyn's promise of a 'period of reflection' did not seem to be politician-speak for looking at himself in the mirror. Instead, a period of reflection led by a man who hasn't changed his mind since 1970 seems an inevitable act of political Dadaism.

In reality, though, the timing doesn't much matter, with the scale of this victory likely to take a decade to turn around. Corbynism has turned out to be for the very, very few. Which is to say, nobody at all. Yet. There was some talk this morning of it being a 30-year project, suggesting the plan will come to glorious fruition just in time for the moment when we're living, *Children of Men*-style, in Britain's catacombs. At that point, Corbynism will sweep to power with an ambitious programme of nationalising the urine distilleries via which we obtain our drinking water. If you totally agree they shouldn't be in the hands of the private militias, make a calendar note to get very excited about this bold and transformative vision in 2045.

Today? Well, according to a range of senior Labour figures, 'the real fight starts now'. Now?! No rush, of course – though it would be nice to get a heads-up on whether they think it'll be a fight for medicines or fuel. On the other hand, some people are just about beginning to tire of Labour fights starting after the knockout, when someone else has won the belt and the party's woken up in the head trauma unit.

BIG GUYS: FROM STREET HARASSERS TO SUPREME COURT JUSTICES

The perennial suggestion that feminism has 'gone too far the other way now' meets a number of Waterloos, from the #MeToo movement to the spectacle of yet another man ascending to the Supreme Court despite detailed allegations of sexual assault being made against him in public at his confirmation hearings. (Two out of nine now. Good times!) In the UK, the 2020 rape and murder of Sarah Everard by a serving Metropolitan police officer draws a wave of public fury and revulsion, yet men's rights activists continue to focus on the true victims. Themselves.

Harvey Weinstein's rehab – just your basic $2,000-a-night sex offender programme

12 October 2017

The radioactive movie mogul is hoping for a second chance, once he has completed a stint in his very own boutique, indie criminal justice system

'A villain is just a victim whose story hasn't been told yet,' wrote Chris Colfer in *The Land of Stories*, which I am pleased to see will be made into a movie by someone other than the Weinstein Company. Even so, you may find yourself declining to submit to reports about Harvey Weinstein's pending stint in rehab, where professionals will help him get to the bottom of his terrible condition. He has basically punished himself by checking in to a place where wandering round in bathrobes is almost mandatory.

As the radioactive movie mogul put it himself to reporters on Wednesday night: 'I'm hanging in, I'm trying my best. I'm not doing OK but I'm trying. I gotta get help, guys. You know what, we all make mistakes . . . Second chance, I hope.' Second chance? There seems to be some kind of accounting error here. The second chance is estimated to have been used up some time in the very early 1990s. If not before. Either way, that's certainly the most boggling statement from Weinstein since his first attempt to hand-wave away his mushrooming sexual harassment scandal by describing himself as 'an old dinosaur learning new ways'. I guess you can't libel the dead, which insulates Harvey from a class-action suit brought on behalf of every stegosaurus that hasn't reportedly wanked into a restaurant plant pot.

Still, let's focus on the help he gotta get. There are varying reports of Weinstein's clinical plan, but many suggest he has now begun several weeks of in-patient treatment at an Arizona head spa, before journeying for the final stages to a second facility in Europe. Some kind of happy-finishing school, presumably.

Here's hoping it's just your basic $2,000-a-night sex offender programme. Wherever Weinstein ends up, I picture the place as a sort of alt-justice simulator which lovingly recreates the atmosphere of the classic nonce wing, right down to the Michelin-starred salad bar and fluffy bathrobes. Or maybe they're trying to wean Harvey off bathrobes, I don't know. The key point is: it operates outside standard correctional procedures. In many ways it's like the indie criminal justice system. As well as the boutique feel, there's a freshness you don't get with the big studio prisons.

According to multiple reports, Weinstein is to be treated for sex addiction, which seems . . . inappropriate. You might as well treat him for anorexia, or diphtheria, or some other illness he hasn't got. Harvey Weinstein isn't addicted to sex in any accepted definition of that condition. Weinstein's alleged behaviour is abusive, coercive and non-consensual. Is he an 'abuse addict'? Is that a thing now? Has this twirled conveniently into the rarefied realms of a mental health issue, and out of the vulgar dimension of criminal offence?

So it seems. If you are still resisting this narrative direction, please don't. Just relax. Stop making a scene. You're embarrassing him. Come on. Five minutes. Please. As one of his representatives said in a statement to *The New Yorker*: 'Mr Weinstein has begun counselling, has listened to the community and is pursuing a better path. Mr Weinstein is hoping that, if he makes enough progress, he will be given a second chance.' Let's assume the progress will be measured in days clean of allegedly carrying out sexual harassment, or perhaps in a 50% reduction in alleged sexual harassment incidents, with a view to eliminating them completely around the same time the US pays off its national debt.

As for the wider implications of the scandal for Hollywood, it would be easy to get carried away. In one sense, the record-breaking

G-force fall of Weinstein leaves a huge gap in the industry. Purely in terms of business temperament, Weinstein was almost wistfully considered the town's Last Great Monster, especially since Michael Ovitz handed in his badge and nunchucks (circa 1995). On the other hand, you certainly wouldn't rule him out of making some sort of return in due course. I still recall fondly the scoffing correspondence I received after suggesting that Mel Gibson would in fact be back after that business with the Jews and the sugar-titted traffic cop. My favourites were obviously the people pointing out that Hollywood is all run by the Jews, so he would never be resurrected. As you may know, Mel is a much-respected moviemaker again these days, able to draw big stars, and was nominated for a best director Oscar only this year.

For now, though, the focus on the Weinstein story makes one strongly suspect that Harvey is taking one for the team. If everything can be telescoped on to him, that would be better all round. In fact, I can't decide who wants this story to go away quicker – the 'similar operators' to Weinstein in Hollywood or the 'similar operators' to Weinstein in the news media. Various parties' desperation to treat it as a political football serves as a reminder that this is never about women's rights for them. Consider Fox News village idiot Tucker Carlson, who on Tuesday called for a justice department investigation into 'Hollywood's culture of systemic sexual abuse', lamenting that 'people in charge have covered it up and made excuses for it, in each case protecting the powerful from the powerless and the abused'. Strong words, and all the more resonant coming from one of the few Fox figures yet to be exposed as someone who regards the sound of them masturbating as suitable hold music during calls with their PA.

For those wondering when things will die down, I spoke to a made-up Hollywood scientist who calculated that that moment will come at the precise second that anti-Weinstein coverage stops grossing more than Weinstein movies. Meanwhile, you will have noted that the coverage has already metastasised again. Second stage was Glynn from your accounts department snorting that 'the whole town knew for years', in the manner of someone who'd like you to assume he spent the early 1990s round at Carrie Fisher and Bryan Lourd's house but never brags about that whole scene. We're now at the third stage, which is guys explaining that having daughters made them re-evaluate their views on sexual assault. (As a woman, I'm always grateful for these takes, which are the equivalent of the authors publicly branding their own foreheads with the words: 'TOTAL SEX CASE'.)

But I suppose we'll have to play out by finding some kind of bright side. So let's just say it's not all bad news for the lady actors of Hollywood. Frankly, there has never been a better three-week window to get cast for a role. That may be an overestimation of the period for which the town's grossest powerful men will be on their best behaviour – but I think if you manage to nail down your next two roles in the next two weeks, you pretty much guarantee a hiring process free from the threat of reflexively inappropriate behaviour or peremptory sexual assault. After that you'll be too old to work anyway, at least for the couple of decades until you start qualifying for Madeleine Albright biopics or films about a latter-years companionship between Elizabeth I and a Moorish servant or whatever. So happy hiatus, gals! God knows you've earned it.

A hug's life: Pixar's John Lasseter leads the way in Hollywood's golden age of euphemism

23 November 2017

'Unwanted hugs', 'missteps', 'pursuing shared feelings' and 'uncomfortable situation' – the entertainment world is offering a masterclass in rebranding sexual impropriety

What a golden age of euphemism we are living through. Each night brings a snowfall of fresh allegations against powerful men; each morning a flurry of exquisitely sorrowful statements in which those same powerful men can't bring themselves to say precisely what they are sorry about.

Is anyone collating all these in a really expensive coffee-table book yet, perhaps to offset any downturn in studio profits incurred by having to axe people and projects now tainted by Unpleasantness? There should definitely be a special font for these quasi-apologies. Comic Sans Underwear. Comic Sans Career. Comic Sans a Clue How They Sound.

Venerated talkshow host Charlie Rose thought he was 'pursuing shared feelings', but now has 'a profound new respect for women and their lives'. That, right there, is beautiful. I mean, it's not up to me to tell our apology-book publishers how to lay out their lavish product, but I really hope they illustrate this one with a reconstruction photo of a 75-year-old man answering his dressing-room door, to some underling five decades his junior, with his dick out. Several other fallen angels have gone with the circumlocution 'uncomfortable situation', which is a place they are sorry if they've put any women. And all, but all, absolutely 'respect women'.

And yet . . . there is something so screamingly absurd about chaps who appear to have spent the best part of two decades issuing orders from open bathrobes suddenly being overcome by such fits of euphemistic primness. Their apologies come with inbuilt lace hankies as standard, masterclasses in not causing even linguistic offence by doing anything so coarse as to hint even remotely at what it is they've done.

The standout this week comes from *Toy Story* creator and Pixar founder John Lasseter, who announced he was taking a six-month leave of absence from Disney in a statement whose length-to-meaningful-content ratio even rivals some of my worst columns. I'm subbing this down from a gazillion words, but according to John, he has taken this course of action after some 'painful conversations' about 'unwanted hugs'.

Well, now. I think we need a little more detail on John's 'hugs' before we classify them along with the sort of family-movie embraces you might see between Lightning McQueen and one of his service vehicles. Even if she has got a great little spoiler on the back of her. (Need to watch *Cars* again – in light of new information it could be more covertly warped than even David Cronenberg's *Crash*.)

Then again, according to John's statement, it is not just 'hugs' that have forced the leave of absence – it is also 'missteps'. What are 'missteps'? Given the current climate, we have to ask: are they accidentally sexual pratfalls? They sound like something out of a Ray Cooney farce, where the lead character – Roy Looney, a film producer – has to juggle a suspicious wife and his tendency to trip over and land face down in the cleavages of junior animators. *Mind My Missteps!* Now booking till June.

So on it all goes, with no sense of where or when it will end. Still, we must be thankful for perspectives such as that of one CNN reporter, whose later-deleted hot take was to lament the 'talent drain', this unprecedented exodus of genius from the industry. I know! How will Hollywood cope? Who's going to make *Whichever Superheroes 9* now? It's unclear, but clearly the working title has to be *Avengers: Age of Consent.*

Speaking of family movies, though, it's a relief to know there are some good guys left, who seem to have a game plan for how we can move past everything. Enter Mel Gibson, star of . . . hang on, let me get my reading glasses . . . *Daddy's Home 2*, a Christmas movie also featuring Will Ferrell, Mark Wahlberg and John Lithgow. Promoting this, recent best director nominee Mel intoned of the current state of affairs in Hollywood: 'Things got shaken up a little bit, and there is a lot of light being thrown into places where there were shadows and that is kind of healthy. It's painful, but I think pain is a precursor to change.'

Yup, you'll have heard the expression 'be the change you want to see'. Mel IS the change he wants to see. Specifically, he knows he said some bad stuff on the hard shoulder of the Pacific Coast Highway to the Jewish traffic cop and the sugar-titted traffic cop. But after that, he changed. Except for that one time a few years later, when it was reported that a tape existed of him screaming racist abuse and threats of violence at his girlfriend and mother of his child. That, he later said, he 'felt regret' about, adding that he was 'betrayed'.

Anyhoo . . . *Daddy's Home 2*. Hard to pick a favourite critical notice thus far, though I did enjoy the one-star *Empire* review that stated: 'Gibson is even more of a one-dimensional toxic manchild than Wahlberg.' And which wondered, vaguely, why the *Daddy's Home 2* producers thought Mel Gibson was the man to make 'jokes about dead hookers, non-consensual kissing or doling out a "big slap on the caboose"'.

Well. I think the answer to that question is: if not Mel, then who? Who else is left to make these jokes? That he should be styling himself as some kind of elder statesman really brings home the scale of this: so many powerful guys have had to be shuffled down to the bottom of the deck that MEL GIBSON is back on top. That's right: Mel Gibson is dispensing Hollywood's moral lessons. He's the noble Morgan Freeman voiceover to the post-Weinstein era, and the sooner we all make our peace with that, the better. It's just like the title says: Daddy's home.

'My name is Brett Kavanaugh and this is my testimony . . .'

28 September 2018

The furious Senate hearing performance of Donald Trump's nominee for the US supreme court is reimagined by our columnist

Good afternoon, Mr Chairman, ranking member Feinstein and members of the committee. My name is Brett Kavanaugh, and this is an even madder job interview than the one for *The Apprentice*. Same boss, though. To the Republicans among you, I would say: I know you believe my accuser, but I thank our mutual God you don't care. To the Democrats, I would say: Don't ask me if I've ever blacked out from drinking. HAVE YOU?

[Sniff] If the classic job interview question is 'What are your weaknesses?' I guess mine are that I'm occasionally coherent. Otherwise what you see is what you get. If this angry, aggressively maudlin guy accused of multiple sexual assaults can't just adjudicate everything for ever, then what was even the point of the last 27 years? Who are we? Where is the justice? What was . . . How can . . . When is America?

I LIKE BEER. I STILL LIKE BEER. DO YOU LIKE BEER?

[Sobbing] You get a lot of sex cases on the supreme court. At least two, if I'm approved. Dear God, I can't wait till this nonsense – NONSENSE! – is over with and I can get a keg with Clarence and start impacting women's lives in multiples of millions, as opposed to having to do each one individually. Did I say that out loud? Can

you imagine my inner monologue when this is what I'm willing to televise? Do you like how I ramble? *[Sniff]* Do you like how I'm not even in the same zip code as my point? I don't even . . . what is detail? What is restraint? *[Screaming]* What is a hippocampus? It sounds like something my dentist shot in the country of Africa.

[Sobbing] I LOVE ALL MY FRIENDS! No matter that crying and howling 'I LOVE ALL MY FRIENDS' is the textbook behaviour of an insanely drunk person. I want you to realise that this display today is the precise level of hot mess that still won't be taken as self-sabotage. I could walk into this room, vomit neat tequila on the desk, and still get confirmed to a position in which I plan to have more impact on your kids' lives than you, OK?

I WAS A VARSITY ATHLETE! I HAD A LETTER JACKET!

You've heard of bestman.com – I got a lot of this material off supremecourtjock.com. So, yes, this session is going to be the sexual assault testimony version of *The Producers*. The more grotesquely absurd I act, the more intemperate I am, the more I cry in a way that you've only seen George on *Peppa Pig* cry, the bigger hit I have on my hands. Seriously. I can act like an improv comic who's just been given a card reading 'Safeguarding issue' and I'll probably still be approved.

I am on a HAIR TRIGGER HERE! I coach little league! Yes! Maybe you've seen guys like me round your kids' sports games. On the sidelines, right? Maybe you've seen me screaming my unique blend of judicial calm about disputed calls at second base. And if you have, you will have thought: 'I really want that guy to be in charge of my uterus.'

Yes. Don't interrupt me, woman senator conducting this delirious job interview – because I am the Gipper of your womb. You hear me: I AM THE GIPPER OF YOUR WOMB.

[Sobbing. Sniffing] I LOVE ALL MY FRIENDS. Laurie. Maura. Clair. Blair. LaToya. Shania. Alanis. Thane . . . Se . . .

Seniquis . . . Seniquista. All names. All real names. Of my friends. I have a weak stomach.

I cannot stress how absolutely irrelevant things that happened in high school are. They are irrelevant and meaningless. Do you know how much I worked out at Tobin's house during high school? Do you know what I could bench-press in high school? I could bench-press you, Senator Feinstein. And I have spent days demanding a hearing to explain what I could bench-press in high school and I was DENIED. DENIED!

OK, I accept the wheels of justice turn slowly. Unless I'm driving the car, when it's just a road-rage incident waiting to happen. But did I mention my workouts with Tobin? God, he was such a great quarterback.

[A primal scream is heard] Thank you. Thank you for that, Senator Graham – especially considering that a rape of your certainties has been attempted today. AN ATTEMPTED RAPE OF YOUR CERTAINTIES. But by the Lord, you held strong. After today you can call yourself a survivor, sir. Also, thank you for making sure I wasn't even the worst guy at my own sexual assault hearing. Did you ever see *The Accused*? Day one on the court, I plan to repeal that movie.

OK, I need a five-minute bathroom break. Yes, I'm drinking a lot of water. Hey – at least I'm housebroken. I'm HOUSEBROKEN. WHAT MORE DO YOU WANT FROM A SUPREME COURT JUSTICE?

[Hearing resumes] I am an optimistic guy. I always try to be on the sunrise side of the mountain. *[Hearing adjourns for another 15 minutes]*

Like me, you will be incredibly moved by my own tears and great honking sniffs. I haven't seen a display of emotion like it since Oscar Pistorius had a bucket placed beside him in court so he could throw up at the evidence of his own crime. Yet people demonised him. Women! Women demonised him. I know, I'm rambling again.

But, you know, the single psychology report I've ever believed came from the one they found for that case, which said Pistorius had a warped fight-or-flight reflex because a guy with his challenges didn't have the option of flight. What? I DON'T CARE IF HE CAN RUN THE 100M IN 11 SECONDS. God, I wish I could reach out to him now.

[Sobbing] Why can't the supreme court have jurisdiction over South African appeals? WHY? We are the international gold standard of how justice is served. Look at this. Look at what has happened in this room this afternoon and tell me we aren't the shining city on the hill, and that the entire world isn't sitting slack-jawed at what we're capable of.

You know, the other night my daughter said we should pray for someone I'm simply going to call The Woman. Such wisdom from a 10-year-old. What? No, she's not available to sit on the supreme court instead of me. Like I told her: the president would nominate a dead Democrat chimpanzee to this job before he'd nominate a female over your daddy.

To conclude, I am under a lot of stress here, which is why I am screaming. Dr Ford can't be under any stress because she didn't lose her shit at all. Indeed, flicking through my Rolodex of ways to dismiss women – I keep all my Rolodexes, like my father did before me – I alight on a card reading 'Not emotionally screamy enough'. I have other cards. In fact, it's right along from 'Too emotionally screamy'. But this is the card I am playing today. And I have NOTHING further to add.

Kavanaugh, Ronaldo . . . how many more male victims must there be?

5 October 2018

Amid the tumult of all these sexual assault allegations, thank goodness we have the men's rights movement to fight back

I had never even heard of the term 'incel' back in April, when some guy drove a van into pedestrians in Toronto, killing 10 and injuring 13. Yet nine days later I was reading a column about 'the redistribution of sex' on the op-ed pages of the *New York Times*, which took what we'll call the killer's 'ideas' about involuntary celibacy and really tried to understand them in a slightly more theoretical way than doing something that gets you charged with 10 counts of premeditated murder.

Nine days! I love how fast the men's rights movement gets stuff done, when women spend for ever fannying about getting nowhere with theories such as 'Honestly, it's *my* uterus' and 'Sexually assaulting us is bad'. It totally makes you wonder what dizzying victories the men's rights movement could achieve if they put their minds to it. They definitely top my Ones to Watch list for 2019.

Needless to say, a lot of women take these big and weighty ideas the wrong way, citing various things. 'The telly show with the women in the red gowns', for instance, or 'the sweep of human history'. Maybe when women read men talking about 'the redistribution of sex', they have this weird, instinctive notion of what that might actually mean for them. But I for one appreciate that men have opened up this unbounded space for us to talk freely about such complex matters. In fact, in that same spirit, I often wonder if the best short- to medium-term solution to this apparent 'supply problem' would be for the guys sympathetic to incels to wank them off themselves? Just until women understand the theory a bit better. I can write up that suggestion a bit more Keynesianally, if preferred.

In the meantime, I increasingly think about the incel thing every time I hear about the privations of Brett Kavanaugh's youth. Like many people, the guy who will probably become a supreme court justice seems to have spent a huge amount of his younger years trying to get women to redistribute sex to him. This week, the *New York Times* published a letter from Brett to his friends about the ideal guestlist for an expensive beachside property they were renting for a vacation in 1983. As he put it: 'I think we are unanimous that any girls we can beg to stay there are welcomed with open ...' (that's Brett's ellipsis, there).

What marks Kavanaugh out today is how angry and resentful he seems to remain about the market's failure. As one of his classmates sufficiently repulsed by his performance at last week's hearing put it: 'Brett wanted to be the guy who got the girls, and he wasn't the guy who got the girls.' Does it ever leave you? It certainly should. But the fact that it clearly doesn't will probably get some theorist to remind us that it is simply economic sense to redistribute sex to guys like the young Brett, in order that they reach their full potential, instead of being limited to positions like supreme court justice.

I hope I have that right. As I say, I am still feeling my way in terms of seeing super-toxic, often allegedly criminal behaviour as a failing economy. Part of where I'm struggling is how this kind of theory applies to the president of the United States, who is also accused of various assaults that have arguably served as a career glass ceiling. From what we read, Donald Trump could always get girls, and still can. Yet even at the age of nearly 60 he was recorded explaining how he just liked to 'grab them by the pussy'. Is this what Adam Smith meant by 'the invisible hand'? Is there some market economist who could explain to me why this might be? I don't want to fall into the trap of thinking that sexual assault is a question of power and violence, as opposed to being a matter of supply and demand.

While this economist is on the line, maybe they could clear up a related confusion – which is the idea that even hot, rich, powerful guys in peak physical condition are not above getting women to 'redistribute sex' to them. Most likely, your first reaction to the news that Cristiano Ronaldo has been accused of rape is, 'I don't understand; this makes no economic sense. I can't find anything in Friedman or Hayek about why this would happen at all.' But let's recap what we know. According to a lengthy investigation by *Der Spiegel*, Kathryn Mayorga claims she was assaulted by the footballer in Las Vegas in 2009, and that he paid her $375,000. One version of Ronaldo's testimony to his own lawyers reportedly states: 'She said no and stop several times.' He denies all the allegations.

According to an official statement by his new club, Juventus: 'Cristiano Ronaldo has shown in recent months his great professionalism and dedication, which is appreciated by everyone at Juventus. The events allegedly dating back to almost 10 years ago do not change this opinion, which is shared by anyone who has come into contact with this great champion.' If you run this news release through Google Translate, it reads simply: 'When u spend 340m euros in transfer fees, salary and taxes on someone.'

So where are we? As Trump noted of one famous Democrat donor when he got in a spot of bother: 'I've known Harvey Weinstein a long time. I'm not at all surprised to see it.' I'm afraid I felt about as encouraged by this as I do about the show of credence given to Ronaldo's accuser by internet handles like Barcafan4eva and Torinissimo. They have most in common with the people who stood behind Trump at his rally this week and cheered as he mocked Christine Blasey Ford. They make believing sexual assault allegations seem like just another partisan activity in our hideously polarised public sphere.

Until sexual assault becomes something that someone's base – be it Juve fans, be it Republicans – believes their own side capable of, we really haven't inched meaningfully along this road at all. Not through want of trying, you understand. But until people stop placing team loyalty over everything, sexual assault will continue to be treated about as seriously as diving in the penalty box. Which is to say, only a big deal when your opponents do it.

Pity Jordan Peterson. Can a giant lobster analogy ever replace a sense of humour?

1 November 2018

The leading member of the self-styled intellectual dark web likes to think he is 'locked out' of the mainstream media. Which makes his interview in this month's GQ *all the more revealing*

The nights have drawn in, the rains have come, and it is time to start unveiling some of the lines in the Lost in Showbiz Winter Collection. Let me say right now that one of our absolute key pieces will be Jordan Peterson.

Quite how it's taken this column so long to alight lovingly on the winningest public intellectual of our age is unclear, but please now consider me officially very into him. This week, I read Jordan's most famous book, *12 Simple Rules for Dating My Teenage Daughter*, and found it an absolute scream. Forgive me – the opus is actually called *12 Rules for Life*, but it certainly forced me to tear down every other thought-leader poster peeling off my bedroom wall. I am highly excited to get around to Jordan's only other published book, some kind of vast theory of everything which took him 12 years to write. Oscar Wilde wrote *The Picture of Dorian Gray* in about a fortnight, so imagine how much better

Jordan B. Peterson's *Maps of Meaning: The Architecture of Belief* is going to be.

But we race ahead. Are you even familiar with Peterson? A University of Toronto psychology professor, his raging stage show involuntarily reminds me of that incredibly moving speech from the *South Park* movie: 'This is aboot dignity. This is aboot respect. [*Laughter*] This is aboot – [*More laughter*] What's so goddammed funny?' Anyway, you may simply know Jordan as 'the lobster guy', after his most famous proposition/abstraction: the idea that lobsters and their serotonin levels explain why human hierarchies exist and are good. But were better in the 1950s. Put simply, you're really doing this wrong if your first thought on seeing a lobster is: 'I'd like to eat this thing, not surrender my abortion rights to it.'

Owing to his sell-out speaking tours, huge YouTube following and multimillion book sales, Peterson is frequently described as a 'Pied Piper' of angry and disaffected men – though my understanding of the original Pied Piper was that he took all his followers away to some kind of mountain from which they never returned. Yes please! Except, how come Peterson's followers continue to wander around our metaphorical Hamelin, explaining stuff like there is no patriarchy because of crustaceans? Can we try DynoPest instead?

Anyway, Peterson is also a leading member of the arseoisie, or the 'intellectual dark web', as they prefer it. Again, are you familiar with the 'intellectual dark web'? I do hope not. It's a self-styling by a loose group of *soi-disant* intellectuals you'd cross continents to avoid having a pint with (although they didn't go with that tagline in the end). There isn't space for a full passenger manifest, but they include Peterson, talkshow host Dave Rubin, *Newsweek* columnist and perma-pundit Ben Shapiro and a bunch of other people bizarrely obsessed with what students do, even though we've known since time immemorial that students often act like idiots, and mostly grow out of it unless they're Hamlet or whatever. Think of the intellectual dark web as a very whiny superhero team.

Marvel's A-Whingers. Guardians of the Galaxy Brains. The League of Extraordinarily Fragile Gentlemen.

Like the rest of the gang, Peterson apparently imagines himself 'locked out' of the mainstream media, despite having sold 2m books and being interviewed every 10 minutes by actual international media outlets. I can't help feeling that Jordan is 'locked out' of the mainstream media in the same way that Justin Bieber is 'locked out' of pop music.

As I am given to understand it, all these chaps ply their trade in the 'marketplace of ideas', which largely seems to be grown men shrieking, 'Not the face! Not the face!' at their detractors. Truly, to watch their online arguments is to enter a scale intellectual model of the Athenian agora.

I'm not even being sarcastic. A lot of those guys who hung around the ancient Athens debating society (while helpmeets of one sort or another took care of their day-to-day shit for them) were quite clearly insufferable edgelords. Come on – Diogenes lived in a large urn and would absolutely have been into bitcoin. In some accounts, the Oracle told him to deface the currency, which seems not entirely Delphic of her, though he found a way to make it so and decided she meant he should deface the currency of prevalent ideas. Arguably, then, Diogenes is the Jordan Peterson analogue, as he was the agora's leading NoFapper. Hang on, that's wrong – he was the agora's leading scourge of pleasure-seeking. But I'm pretty sure he'd have been one of the senior thinkers in today's anti-masturbation movement.

If you need a further Peterson catch-up, can I recommend a video posted by *GQ* magazine this week, in which Jordan is interviewed by the *New Statesman*'s Helen Lewis. It's hard to pick my favourite moment from the nearly two-hour-long encounter, but I very much enjoyed the bit where Lewis reasons: 'Lobsters don't get depressed. I think you're anthropomorphising to a ridiculous degree. These are creatures that urinate out of their faces.'

Then again, it must be said that Peterson spends most of the interview looking like he's about to urinate out of his face. In the entire exchange, he smiles about once, at some perceived irony in something wistfully arch that he himself has just said. One's primary takeout is not 'Here is a man who can laugh at himself.' Which is such a missed opportunity. I am reminded of the time when Jeffrey Archer told Dame Edna Everage that 'the most important thing is to be able to laugh at yourself'. 'You'd have to do that,' came the deathlessly sympathetic reply, 'otherwise you'd be missing the joke of the century.'

Other takeouts from the *GQ* interview? Peterson dresses and looks like the third Gruber brother from the *Die Hard* franchise. As all world cinema fans will know, the first brother to lose to Bruce Willis's grubby-vested cop was played by the late, great Alan Rickman in *Die Hard*, while the second was played by Jeremy Irons (himself blue-vested) in *Die Hard with a Vengeance*. Peterson very much presents as the third sibling that Mother Gruber kept at home because he was 'chesty' – though without the self-knowledge to accept he is a character actor rather than a leading man.

Perhaps it might be kinder if his agent or publicist helped him to come to terms with this? As things stand, each of the several times Peterson intoned 'life is suffering', all I could think about was how very much hotter it was in *The Princess Bride*, when Cary Elwes's character Westley goes to Robin Wright: 'Life is pain, highness. Anyone who says differently is selling something.' I mean . . . I'll take that sort of line off Westley all day long. But this guy? This 56-year-old adult in the steampunk-lite outfit who cries on stage at his own rightness? I am – how to put this tactfully? – not feeling it in quite the same way.

What happened to me was nothing – the nothing women know all too well

12 March 2021

At 4.56pm on a spring afternoon, countless women in the UK were being harassed on the street. It turns out I was one of them

I don't know why I'm writing about this really, because nothing happened. Compared to what happens, nothing really happened. And in the five minutes it took to not happen – between 4.55pm and 5pm yesterday – he was never closer to me than three feet. What a respectful distance from which to be called a 'dirty cunt', my ha-di-ha-ha brain is saying. I was merely verbally aggressed by a stranger in a socially distanced way.

Plus it all feels a bit convenient for a columnist, right? And I agree – being followed and simultaneously screamed at by some guy I'd never clapped eyes on before yesterday afternoon was nothing if not convenient. Look, I'm writing a column about it today. But before this outbreak of convenience, this column honestly was going to be a fictional imagining of the royal family attending implicit bias training. I don't want you to conclude I didn't have other wares for this space if it hadn't been for the convenient nothing that happened.

I'm absolutely and completely fine, I said to my editor, when I told him what I'd write about instead. Really, it's just – [don't say 'part of life', don't say 'part of life'] – it's just part of life! I told him the truth: that I genuinely forget about these things soon after they happen. Except I'm writing this stupid record of this one now. Should have just tied a weight round it and sent it to sleep with the fishes, with all the other ones. The healthy option. But please, I said to him, please tell me if it comes out wrong. I never say that with any other column, but of course we ladies worry about telling our own stories wrongly or unsuccessfully.

Anyway, I'm walking to collect one of my children after school yesterday, down the street I always take. It's never lovelier than now, when all the magnolias are coming out. He stares hard, passes. Stops.

Behind me: 'What are you looking at?'

Honestly? The end of the street. How is it that the end of this empty London street, where there's a busier road and then a square, has suddenly stretched to a point somewhere just beyond Moscow? What happens to time and space when these nothings happen? This whole nothing is going to take five minutes, yet feel so long it's like I could have learned Mandarin or written a novel. You absorb every incidental detail. Just in case! And in every split second you're somehow able to consider multiple possible theories as to what is, or isn't, happening.

'I'm talking to you. Fucking turn round.'

Really? Today? When it starts not happening, I'm just thinking: Oh, but this is such a COINCIDENCE! I mean, I've spent all day reading women's stories of nowhere near all the things that have happened to them just walking down streets. Maybe this is happening because I didn't offer up my own stories. Maybe I've angered the social media gods.

'Dirty cunt.'

Man, this guy is really ruining the magnolias for me. I'm walking so fast now I'm not even looking at the magnolias. Still, this is SUCH a coincidence. Actually, let's be statistically rational. It's just an incidence. Whenever these nothings happen, you understand very powerfully that they are singling you out to tell you *you're not special*. You, a 46-year-old woman in a double bobble hat that makes you look like Mickey Mouse, which is why you chose it, are not special. Right now, at 4.56pm on a spring afternoon, countless women are being harassed in the street. I wonder what a UK heat map of incidence would look like. Hot, I guess.

He's walking alongside me now. 'Hello? HELLO?'

Quick, do the triage. How seriously do I take him? He hasn't grabbed me, so my sense is that he's one of the good street harassers. That would be great news for this fucking whore currently being asked who the fuck she thinks she is. Hang on, he's got a shopping bag. New data points, need to establish what's in it. Oh. A really big box of chocolates. I wonder if he's saying sorry to someone. Or maybe I love you. 'I love you. Also, you'll never guess what I did on the way home.'

He seems to be wearing A Distinctive Jacket, which is point-less, since I'm not going to be troubling the police with this. You can't, can you? Where would you start? Where would you stop? Hopefully he'll stop. On the back of the jacket – thank God, I'm seeing the back of his jacket now, which means he's passed me by again – it says 'The Wonderers'. They sound nice. I wonder what he's wondering about. Why I'm some fucking lesbian whore, is what he's saying. But I wonder what he's really wondering about. If this is the bit he's saying out loud, I wonder about the inner monologue.

Oh dear. Now I'm seeing the front of his jacket again, and he's coming back towards me. Can't he see there are now people around, because I've reached the square? But he's one of the ones that doesn't mind an audience. What do people who can now see us think is happening? I wonder crossly. Crossly enough to find my voice and say: 'Stay away from me.' I say it loudly and clearly, so the two guys working on the road about 15 metres away will hear. They look up, and I look right at them, quickly because I daren't take my eyes off The Wonderer. But then they carry on with their work. Come on, guys – don't you read the internet? Hashtag be an ally!

Given I'm still learning what a fucking bitch I am, and at quite some volume, I say it again. 'STAY AWAY FROM ME.' I can see I'm holding my hand out in a stop sign. Who am I – the street harassment Gandalf? My hand seems a little shaky. Let's be real. If he wants to, this street harasser shall pass.

He hangs around even as I pick up my son, so we get a great send-off as we hurry away. I used to think holding the hands of children, tightly, would exempt you from the consideration of street abusers, but I've long noticed that for some guys it simply makes it more special. 'Why was he doing it if you didn't say anything to him?' wonders my son. I know! It does seem very irrational, doesn't it. What a silly man. 'He's like The Angry Man,' notes my son, which is what my children called some other guy who followed us down our own road screaming about something to do with their bikes. 'Exactly,' I say.

'Why are they so angry?' Oh wow . . . I don't know. I mean, there are . . . a lot of theories. Anyway, how was school? 'Fine. Why are we going home this way?' Because this is the way we go now. We're probably going to go a few different ways for a bit. So this is one of the ways we go now. Let's just get home. I mean, nothing really happened.

Still, good question, all things considered. Why are they so angry? It does feel like way, way, way past time we found out.

Women killed: 118. Statues 'killed': 1. So guess which is the national priority?

16 March 2021

The government wants tougher sentences for attacks on statues than for those on women. Its culture war gets ever more absurd

Such a strong look for the government's police, crime, sentencing and courts bill to allow for longer sentences for attacking statues than are handed down for attacking women. What if the victim of crime is one of those living statues who busk in public spaces – a Queen Victoria, say, or a Statue of Liberty? Do you prosecute the defendant as though he's merely harmed a woman, or do you go for the fullest force of the law and treat him as if he has defaced an inanimate object?

Doesn't have to be a female living statue, of course. There's sometimes a living statue of Winston Churchill outside Covent Garden tube station. If a load of drunks set upon him – and living statues are constantly set upon, by their own accounts – do you close the investigation within about six hours owing to lack of resources? Or do you act as though someone has scrawled 'is a racist' on a pedestal beneath 12 foot of insensate bronze and push for 10 years in jail for a crime so supposedly emotive the perpetrator will be begging to be transferred to solitary after he's endured three days of HMP Frankland's welcoming party?

Either way, given how very far we have to go in dealing with violence against women and girls, it seems insulting in the extreme that the government is lavishing so much as three seconds of legislative time on statues. When Labour MP Jess Phillips stood up in parliament on International Women's Day last week and named all the women who have been killed in Britain in the past year where a man has been charged or convicted, it took her over four minutes. There were 118 women, and there will have been more since.

In the same time frame, there has been precisely one – ONE – statue 'killed', which feels incredible given the absolute bedwetting about it all for months now. Four people in Bristol have already appeared in court charged with causing criminal damage to the long-contentious monument to slaver Edward Colston (1636–1721), and will face trial in December. But to repeat: one statue. Face it, if that's the casualty count in the so-called 'woke war on statues', all we've learned is that snowflakes are utterly useless at war. (Except in Russia, admittedly. As one of the tsars once remarked: 'January and February are my best generals.')

Anyway, those who appear to care more about statues than women are surely not the sort of company the government ought to keep. This is the domain of someone like Tommy Robinson, who along with the rest of the far right sees 'defending statues' as his new hot-button issue, having exhausted the money-spinning possibilities of pretending to give a shit about women and girls.

I say 'pretending', because when Tommy isn't trying to collapse grooming-gang rape trials – which would clearly force victims through the anguish of a second trial and having to testify twice – he's got form for wholly inappropriate contact with them. 'You're pretty fit for a Muslim,' ran his opening gambit in one Twitter exchange a few years ago. 'I'm 15,' replied the girl, 'and you got the cheek to call Muslims paedos.' Robinson's reply: 'Hows it feel to be nearly twice the age Aisha was when your prophet raped her . . . Now stop flirting with me.'

Robinson has now shifted this moral gaze to statues, with his clarion calls on the subject in recent months pulling in the donations and encouraging troops of volunteers to 'defend' statues they regard as under threat. Though, like all superfans of *Middlemarch*, I very much enjoyed the comic spectacle of five would-be hardnuts lined up in a defensive cluster around the statue of George Eliot in Nuneaton.

Naturally, it's not just Tommy Robinson stoking this culture war. The UK is unfortunately rich in the sort of narcissistic idiots who should serve as cautionary tales to the government to steer well clear of turning this into a bigger deal than they've already made it. Take Laurence Fox – please – whose big idea for his campaign to be London mayor is to erect 'even MORE statues'. The former actor is pledging that not a single statue would ever be pulled down on his watch, because 'parents should be able to educate their children about those who came before, both good and bad'.

If that's the case, where was Laurence in 2012, when a statue of Jimmy Savile was being removed from Glasgow's Scotstoun leisure centre? Sorry, I've just looked it up and can see he was playing the future George VI in some mad historical drama directed by Madonna. But keeping that question rhetorical: where was Laurence when the Savile statue was removed from the leisure centre? Hang on: I can see he also banged out a few episodes of *Lewis* that year too.

But returning to the rhetorical: where was Lozza when Savile was toppled in a Glasgow leisure centre? By rights he should have been fighting 'woke' Glaswegians in the foyer of Scotstoun, pointing out that Savile had been deeply woven into the fabric of a period of national life and was consequently covered by Laurence's decree that 'parents should be able to educate their children about those who came before, both good and bad'. As he keeps explaining, we must 'celebrate our shared national history'. Doesn't matter if that's slaving or paedoing – you HAVE to celebrate ALL history.

This level of dazzling absurdity is obvious to anyone who contemplates these issues for two minutes or more. It may be cheap for now, needlessly fanning the flames of culture wars instead of coming up with actual ideas to make people's lives better. But, wow, you really end up paying further down the line, where the government's preference for posturing over policy will turn out to have been the real insult to 'British values'.

All women know they are prey – and that no one with any authority seems to care

1 October 2021

Despite the horrifying levels of violence against women, there is no strategy to end it. Just promises to 'learn lessons'

Cressida Dick must be the last woman in the country who thinks there may be 'lessons' to be learned from Wayne Couzens's rape and murder of Sarah Everard. At least 80 women in the UK have been killed by men since Everard. Only 1.6% of rapes in England and Wales reported to police even result in a charge. Fifty-two per cent of police found guilty of sexual misconduct kept their jobs. Women already know all the lessons. Women live with the all-pervasive understanding that they are prey.

The women who love you have to communicate the fear to you when you're still a girl, knowing that one day you too will have to communicate it to the girls you love. They pass you down their strategies – their defences – like your birthright. And when you're big enough to be out in the world on your own, those same women spend their time hoping till it hurts that this fear, which they had to gift you out of love, will somehow save you. 'In the evenings,' said Sarah Everard's mother in her unforgettable victim impact statement, 'at the time she was abducted, I let out a silent scream: "Don't get in the car, Sarah. Don't believe him. Run!"'

Where do you even start? When will it ever stop? On the very same morning that Couzens was being sentenced in one Old Bailey courtroom, another Old Bailey courtroom was being used to charge the man accused of the murder of the primary school teacher Sabina Nessa, brutally killed two weeks ago on her way to meet a friend near her home in south-east London. The prosecution alleged it was a predatory and premeditated attack on a lone woman not known to him.

To all those who could be found pointing out that 'we' have to remember these are extreme cases: thanks for dialling in. They are extreme, yes – but they are part of a continuum of male harassment and the fear of it that women experience every day of their lives. Women are constantly, constantly performing risk assessment. Dare I pass down this street at this time? Is this the routine sleazy comment that turns into something worse? Is he going to keep walking or will he turn around? To make a troubled peace with it, we have to euphemise this lifestyle as 'being sensible' or 'taking care', but it's really just a statistically justified fear as part of daily life. Every woman has experienced various things along that continuum.

But wait! Because, excitingly, it turns out there are now even more things for ladies to add to their list of Shit I'm Advised to Do to Stay Safe Because It Saves Anyone Else Having to Do Anything. Today the Met advised people approached by a lone plainclothes officer to ask very searching questions, such as 'Where have you come from?' and 'Exactly why are you stopping or talking to me?' Probably best not to try these while being black. If they fear for their safety, women are advised to run into a house or 'wave down a bus'.

To which, I am afraid, the only acceptable reaction is: NO. No to this bollocks, no to thoughts-and-prayers, and no to accepting this standard of policing – though that's clearly what everyone from the prime minister to the leader of the opposition to the mayor of London does, if they're happy for Cressida Dick to have just been given another two years on her contract after this many huge mistakes. Who looks at that record and thinks: 'You know what? I think we need the same old broom.'

But, of course, we have a cross-party political culture where the women and equalities brief is still bundled with some other job as a kind of weird afterthought/poisoned chalice. In government, Liz Truss is foreign secretary – AND women and equalities minister. For Labour, Anneliese Dodds is both chair of a party trying to reverse its calamitous electoral fortunes AND shadow women and equalities minister. What are these bizarre ministerial biathlons other than confirmation that the women and equalities position is something you tack on to a real job just so you can say that some overworked woman is 'dealing with all that stuff'.

The message from women this week is loud and clear: no more learning. Our consciousness about male violence and how far it reaches is well and truly raised, and so is that of a vast number of men. That thing about having to devote 10,000 hours to something to be an expert in it? You really don't have to be very old as a woman to have already spent way more than 10,000 hours thinking about your safety and, by extension, the safety of women in general. So if anyone – ANYONE – in a position of authority would like to offer something more concrete than the equivalent of thoughts and prayers for how to tackle an epidemic of male violence and harassment, then let women reassure you: you don't need to roll the pitch any more. Take it from us.

Alas, authority figures have not had a great week on this stuff. Or, indeed, a great few decades. When the Yorkshire Ripper's killing pattern changed, a senior investigating officer made that infamous statement: 'He has made it clear that he hates prostitutes. Many people do. We, as a police force, will continue to arrest prostitutes.' (And to use them.) 'But', he went on, 'the Ripper is now killing innocent girls.' That comment rightly became notorious. And yet, I was sorry to see that even the judge who yesterday handed down a whole-life tariff to Wayne Couzens spoke of Sarah Everard being 'a wholly blameless victim', a way of putting it that implies that there are other victims of rape and murder who have to shoulder some of the blame. Would police have made an arrest so quickly had Couzens's victim been one of the sex workers he is alleged to have been in the habit of using?

If only the unfortunate echoes ended there. Peter Sutcliffe was nicknamed the Ripper as 'a joke' by some of his colleagues at a trucking firm; Wayne Couzens was nicknamed 'the rapist' by some of his earlier colleagues *in the police service*, also 'as a joke'. I mean . . . I want to think there's been some progress, but that particular detail suggests otherwise.

Certainly, there remains no major or even minor strategy to deal with this culture. We see Priti Patel down at Dover in a HOME SECRETARY coat, announcing action on asylum-seekers arriving by boat. We hear Boris Johnson talking about a knife-crime strategy or a chain-gang strategy or an antisocial-behaviour strategy.

Could they please put their puffer jackets on to announce and follow through on a serious male-violence strategy? Can we have a joined-up plan to tackle male violence that starts in primary education and takes an ambitiously holistic approach to a problem that riddles our society with poisons, from child abuse to terrorism?

If not, maybe all the people who fall back on the 'one bad apple' defence can have the balls to stop omitting the second half of the saying. One bad apple spoils the barrel. And as any number of women can attest, this barrel is long past putrid.

2020: PLAGUE, AND HOW TO SEND IT PACKING IN 12 WEEKS

It's 31 January 2020, and Brexit is done! In a way! Time for actor Laurence Fox to emerge as a political thinker, while Boris Johnson kicks back and spends time on the important things in life. Namely: getting divorced, telling an unspecified number of his children that he's engaged again, and working on his book about William Shakespeare. Slightly rum news from China about some virus thingummy, but nothing worth turning up to Cobra meetings for, especially after health secretary Matt Hancock assures the British public that the risk to them is 'low'. By May, the prime minister has notched up the highest Covid death toll in Europe, months of lockdown and his own near-death experience, while his most powerful adviser, Dominic Cummings, has forever changed the way we think about optometry.

Want to know what racism feels like?
Ask Laurence Fox

23 January 2020

Question Time's latest breakout star may not have learned much history at his minor public school, but the left-behind luvvie knows it's wrong to cast a Sikh in a first world war film

Cold open: an Oxford police station. Maybe a guy with a long scarf bicycles past with a pile of books and an oar on each shoulder. Inside, we find a black woman attempting to report a crime to a police inspector, who is theatrically banging his head on the desk and shouting: 'Bo-ring!' Could she just tell him about how – No, she couldn't, he says, because this is a lovely country, so her experience simply hasn't happened. He wants us to come together. Why doesn't she? She needs to stop being the – what's the expression? Fly in the ointment? Skeleton in the closet? It's on the tip of his tongue. In fact, if anything, says the inspector, he has been the victim of a crime. Warming to his theme, he rules that the real criminal is her for raising it.

Cue opening titles of ITV's big new Sunday-night detective drama: *HATHAWAY*.

In any sane world – I know, right? – this show would already be in production, because that's the way it has always been, meaning it's the RIGHT way. First, there was *Inspector Morse*, starring Inspector Morse, and he was deferentially assisted by Sergeant Lewis. Then, when Morse went to the great whodunnit in the sky, Sergeant Lewis was made inspector and, in due course, got his own show: *Lewis*. Inspector Lewis was in turn deferentially assisted by Sergeant Hathaway, whom I assumed was real, but was apparently played by the actor, musician and thought leader Laurence Fox. In due course, Inspector Lewis himself bowed out, by which point Hathaway had been promoted to inspector.

And yet: no eponymous Sunday-night show of his own. No deferential sergeant of his own. It's a scandal. This was the way things were – but now they are not. Similarly, just as there had always been iconic roles for James Fox back in the day, so there would surely always be the same for his son Laurence.

But now, evidently, there aren't. So I want you to forget everything you think you know about what happened since Laurence went on *Question Time* last week and told a mixed-race audience member she was being racist to him by making boring charges of racism. Tempting as it might be to misdiagnose, this is not just the sort of midlife crisis you would expect from one of the lesser telly chefs. No, THIS is the reality: Laurence's story is a tale from acting's rust belt, about the hollowing out of the theatrical heartlands, where the job and dignity your father could count on have been stolen. By whom? I don't know. Sikhs maybe? We'll get on to that later. For now, it is increasingly clear that the old certainties have evaporated. And there are some people who are going to feel very, very left behind. We should listen to these actors.

Indeed, this is why Laurence could be found on Julia Hartley-Brewer's TalkRadio show by Monday morning, expanding on his *QT* rant, going: 'We lay all our troubles on the working man. And the working man has had enough of it.'

Damn straight. I've always felt Laurence has huge second-toughest-at-Rada energy to him. And just like him, I'm sick of these elites who have never done a tough day down t'acting pit. The hardscrabble truth is that the theatrical economy no longer works in the way it did for your daddy or his daddy before him. Or, to put it more specifically re. Laurence's situation: how come HE'S not admiring Hitler in *Remains of the Day* like his pa once did, while Tony Hopkins has to miss his own dad's death because he's got the dinner to serve? Instead, Laurence feels as if his only choice is going on James Delingpole's podcast to lose his shit that there's a Sikh in Sam Mendes's movie *1917*. I mean, I guess it's zeitgeisty. But set against his dad's zeitgeisty stuff, it's not exactly sharing some acid and a French chick with Mick Jagger in *Performance*, is it?

And, of course, when hope moves out, Trump moves in. I think this is why Laurence recently announced that he put on a Maga hat and walked round wherever he lives in south London. He says one woman told him he was crazy. A bit like that scene in *Die Hard 3* where Bruce Willis has to stand in Harlem wearing a racist sign or else everyone's going to get blown up by villain Jeremy Irons. (Sidenote: a contempo version of that is exactly the sort of part Laurence should have had. But Hollywood producers have skipped him and gone straight for Tom Hiddleston, haven't they? The shits.)

As for what attracted Fox to Trump, maybe it was the president's deathless comment: 'I love the poorly educated.' And putting my own public-school heritage to incredibly non-sarcastic use, I want to attain the levels of empathy Laurence rose to on *Question Time*. So I'll just inform him definitively that a huge amount of his bitterness springs from the fact he went to a minor public school. (Harrow. I will not be taking letters on this classification; thank you.)

Certainly, his outsider shtick is my favourite since Jacob Rees-Mogg (who didn't go to a minor public school) told last year's Conservative party conference: 'But as I grew up in the British establishment, I know how awful it is. I see its faults perhaps more clearly than most do, and its determination, its anti-democratic wish to cling to its power come what may.' Then again, I think we all have to make a lot of time for the latest effusion from Lily Allen (Bedales), who reacted to Laurence's nonsense by announcing she was 'sick to death of luvvies forcing their opinions on everybody else' and advising him to 'stick to acting'. Say what you like about this story, but it really has brought all the preposterous pricks to the yard – and, yes, I certainly count myself in that.

As for where Laurence could have gone after *QT*, I suppose he could have donned the Black Poloneck of Poorly Essayed Contrition. I refer, of course, to the night that Dapper Laughs opted to become Dapper Tears and appeared on *Newsnight* to apologise for 'pushing the boundaries'. Instead, Fox decided to double down, telling Delingpole of the 'oddness' of casting a Sikh in *1917*. 'It is kind of racist,' he honked. 'If you talk about institutional racism, which is what everyone loves to go on about, which I'm not a believer in, there is something institutionally racist about forcing diversity on people in that way.'

When the contribution of Sikh soldiers to the first world war was later mentioned to him, he replied: 'I'm not a historian.' But, luv: you don't NEED to be a historian. You honestly just need access to the website google.com. Because if you search the words 'Sikhs' and 'first world war', every single result from the very first one down will tell you how Sikh soldiers arrived on the Western Front from 1914, how they were instrumental at Ypres, and so on for miles and miles. It literally couldn't be easier to find out about. But, you see, basic investigations aren't the Hathaway MO. The Hathaway MO is to be profoundly incurious, to not ask any questions at all, or attempt to learn anything, or to think that people with different experiences may have a different point to make from yours. You just accuse the Sikh of ruining the movie.

As for where people of colour go after their latest tedious schooling, perhaps they could take #inspo from Laurence himself. After all, this is a man who has repeatedly hawked his divorce experiences round the TV interview sofas, in return for the show plugging his band or whatever – yet who begrudges people of colour having the temerity to have their own problems.

Yet again, I think the conclusion is that people of colour need to be EVEN more creative in the way they talk about their experiences to snowflakes like Laurence. Just spitballing here, but would it help if they got caught up in a celebrity divorce, then had a crap album to promote? Because I feel like then it might finally be permissible for them to speak. Until then, his message is clear: you're still doing it wrong, guys! Pipe down.

That was Brexit: the mad energy of *A Midsummer Night's Dream*, but lasting three and a half years

31 January 2020

It unearthed some of the worst people in the country – on both sides. And the worst of all were the politicians

Tonight's Parliament Square party to mark Brexit was hit by a ban on booze, live music and fireworks – the first three in a presumably infinite series of things that we now won't be able to blame on boring Brussels bureaucrats. Right about now, you're probably starting to think: 'Oh my God . . . what if . . . what if we were the bastards all along?' Crazy as it may seem on this day of national emancipation, it's just possible that one day we might yearn to be plugged back into the matrix where it was all someone else's fault.

Still, to the victor go the spoils. Brexit is done, except for the many big bits that aren't. All UK humans must absorb the sledgehammer implication of the fact that a man with the mind and moral stature of Nigel Farage is far and away the most successful politician of his generation. Like Farage said last week: 'Unless this government drops the ball, and I don't think it will, you will never, ever see me again.' And like he said this week: 'I look forward to a new role with *Newsweek*, where I shall be commenting on the battles ahead.'

Either way, there are indications that the curtain between reality and metaphor has finally been rent. Consider the fact that on

Brexit eve, Farage really did stand in what appeared to be a London restaurant's attic and unveil a hideous portrait of himself. Instead of being accompanied by a brilliant Wildean dandy, he was introduced by occasional Dubai émigré Jim Davidson, who made a joke about France that I can't lavish a keystroke on. Trivia completists may care to know that the title of Nigel's portrait was *Mr Brexit*, and not *55?!?!?! – Fuck Me, He Had a Hard Paper Round*.

To mark the occasion, the government has newly minted, or rather reminted, a special Brexit 50p coin. If you get one, hang on to it – it might be worth something one day. Something like 20 euro cents. Or 1/600th of a threadworm tablet under the new US-friendly drug pricing. When coming up with their big Brexit marker, it's interesting that the Tory right decided to go with pieces of silver, a concept closely associated with historic betrayal. Perhaps they're trying to reclaim it for themselves, along with Calais and the idea it's fine to say the N-word because rappers do it.

They're certainly using the moment as a fundraising opportunity, and have spent much of the week acting as a sort of off-brand Franklin Mint. Tuesday's big push alerted buyers to their range of Brexit 'merch', which is exactly how the target market for this stuff talks. A second drive offered people the chance to 'own Brexit', in the form of a copy of the withdrawal agreement signed by Boris Johnson. Tickets for the draw are £5. It's a lovely idea – and is it scalable? Even now, perhaps one of the oddballs hired by Dominic Cummings is working out whether you could technically fund a new hospital by selling copies of the statement 'I will build a new hospital' signed by Boris Johnson. Soon enough, the dominant form of intranational trade in the UK will be the exchange of items signed by Boris Johnson. Johnson has long been aware of the value of his signature, which is why he has avoided flooding the market by withholding it from a number of birth certificates.

In terms of economic prospects, meanwhile, it's a huge psychological boost for Brexit that most of Britain's newspapers are in favour of it. Remember: always take business advice from journalists, the runaway market leaders in the poorly-managed-decline sector. Brexit could be the UK pivoting to video. To get a visual feel for what the *Daily Express* calls 'the glorious future', go on the paper's website and try loading a *Daily Express* story inside of five minutes. People call Brexit a project of false nostalgia, which here feels right: Renaissance masterpieces were actually downloaded on to canvas quicker than an article headlined 'DI TOLD ME BREXIT WON'T AFFECT MY HOUSE PRICE'.

But here we all are. That was the Brexit that was. And what was it? It had the mad energy of *A Midsummer Night's Dream*, but went on for three and a half years. The sheer litany of WTF-ery that occurred would take precisely three and a half years to recount. At one point Michael Howard threatened war with Spain. It was the golden age of television drama, but people instead found themselves watching BBC Parliament in the evenings, initially capable of making wan comparisons with *Game of Thrones* but eventually lacking the energy to do anything but wish a dragonfire apocalypse on everyone involved.

It certainly unearthed some of the worst people in the country. On both sides, let's be honest. By the time we were a few months in, most of the haute remainers could make you turn hard Brexit whenever they appeared on the news. Just as Donald Trump would be richer if he'd simply invested his inheritance in a tracker fund and done nothing, it feels likely that the leading forces of remain would have been in better shape three years into the horror show if they'd taken a vow of silence on 24 June 2016 and stopped trying to 'help'.

For my money the Brexiteers were even worse, but others will argue we're comparing Aids with syphilis. The second I saw Pimlico Plumbers boss Charlie Mullins (remain) park for one Brexit high court challenge by mounting his personalised-plated Bentley on the pavement, I immediately channelled arms and strategic intelligence to pro-Brexit contras.

To each remainer their Brexit analogue. Charlie's was Wetherspoons boss Tim Martin, a man who looks like a cautionary tale about his own pubs. Or take Brexiteer James Dyson (actually, I think Singapore already has). Dyson, as we never stopped hearing, is an inventor – a term that apparently allows him to walk through the same door as the creators of the steam engine and radio. Naturally, I yield to no one in my admiration for minor hand-dryer improvements. But Dyson basically does things that blow or suck, doesn't he? Maybe that's why he was drawn to Brexit.

Needless to say, the absolute worst people of all were the politicians, from the sensationally limited Theresa May to supply cult leader Jeremy Corbyn, via committed anti-elitist Jacob Rees-Mogg, reservist idiot Mark Francois and so on via a gazillion Tory wingnuts to the ghastly John Bercow – accused of multiple instances of bullying – whose lionised impunity served as a useful 'How radicalised are you?' test for remainers.

The ultimate victor, pyrrhic or not, was Boris Johnson. On the day of withdrawal, then, I guess the key philosophical question is: how can something whose own internal logic made Boris Johnson prime minister be wrong?

From his days as the *Telegraph*'s Brussels fabulist, Brexit has been an end-to-end service by Johnson, who you'd think ought to look happier about it. But as tonight's broadcast will unwittingly show, emotion is his phantom limb – which he feels the twitch of occasionally, but primarily experiences as a sort of yawning absence assuageable only by the usual temporary fixes.

He does not appear to be a man who enjoys a short leash, which is perhaps why he has set the clock on himself for the trade negotiations, to introduce some of the jeopardy he has historically sought out in other pursuits. But no longer. Boris Johnson must now play the Henry V to his own Falstaff, which is his tragedy. We all have to watch, which is ours.

When Johnson says we'll turn the tide in 12 weeks, it's just another line for the side of a bus

20 March 2020

There's something unsettling in seeing the prime minister repurpose his Brexit media strategy for a deadly contagion

Britain. A nation of shopfighters, presided over at a time of mortal peril by a newspaper columnist who has for three decades moonlighted as his generation's leading liar. Still, as the words clawed into the side of the plague pit probably once read, 'We are where we are.'

But where, currently, is that? It is a place where, at a daily 5pm press conference, the disease-threatened populace is expected to take prophylactic advice from Boris Johnson. From Monday, most British parents will be home-schooling their children. Not Johnson, of course – I imagine he doesn't want to break his own pledge on class sizes. The prime minister keeps saying that the forthcoming test to determine whether you have coronavirus will be 'as simple as a pregnancy test', spaffing his sole area of expertise rather early in what is likely to be a long campaign.

Actually, that's unfair. His other area of expertise is disguising rather basic points with needlessly obscure language. Once this made him merely an overrated writer; now it could make him an accomplice to the death of your relatives and friends. 'The key message,' Johnson key-messaged on Tuesday, is that people follow the advice 'sedulously'. Ah, *sedulously*. Sedulously. The signal for 10 million hardworking families to draw down the leather-bound thesaurus from their shelves and browse synonyms for the word 'twat'.

The government's crisis communications strategy could not be going worse if it was being led by the last speaker of a dead language, with Typhoid Mary on bass. People are still clearly extremely confused by what the advice is. Never have bullet points been more called for, and you'd think someone as obsessed with the second world war as Johnson is would know that an effective Ministry of Information was inextricably linked to the success of the war effort. Unfortunately, as indicated, Johnson is basically just a columnist. I don't want to spaff what we might euphemise as my own area of expertise too early, but trust me on this: he is hardwired to spin that shit out for 1,150 words. How to put this in terms that even a wildly overeducated prime minister can understand? JUST TELL US THE INFORMATION. It's a public safety briefing, not a fricking ring quest.

The government's inability to clearly define essential terms means we are in a situation where 'self-isolating' demonstrably means a range of things to different people. Same with 'social distancing'. These urgently need simple and precise definition and a comms blitz everywhere from social media to news bulletins to short TV ads.

Instead, Johnson prefers to chuck new soundbites on the pile. The current one is the pledge that 'we can turn the tide within the next 12 weeks'. If you missed this clip, don't worry. My suspicion is that you'll be seeing it hundreds of times more this year. It has a strong 'over by Christmas' vibe to it and is the sort of thing you could imagine on the side of a bus.

There is something deeply unsettling to watching Johnson and Dominic Cummings's Brexit media strategy being lightly repurposed for a deadly contagion. The prime minister is already crossing the streams, declaring repeatedly on Thursday: 'I'm very confident we'll get this thing done.' Mate . . . that's your slogan for the other one? We're about three days off him telling us we can take back control.

Yet control is once again looking somewhat tenuous. Huge amounts of government spin this week have been dedicated to gaslighting the nation that, last week, no one in a position of power said 'herd immunity' out loud. And yet, they did. Meanwhile,

Cummings, high priest of the 20,000-word blog, can tell you everything about what the Manhattan Project taught us, but he seemingly can't work out that if you let a 'London will be imminently locked down' story go viral for 18 hours before you deny it, then people WILL physically fight over bog roll. Nurses coming off 48-hour shifts WILL cry in videos because they can't buy anything in the shops. I guess Cummings is interested in behavioural science in the way I'm interested in Olympic figure skating. Which is to say, I like it, but I'm unbelievably, lethally shit at it.

Physically, meanwhile, Johnson is ageing slightly quicker than the guy in *Indiana Jones and the Last Crusade* who drinks from the wrong grail and goes from middle-aged to ancient to exploding skeleton in around six seconds. There seems to be some unholy symbiosis between him and Rishi Sunak, who appears to be growing younger with every appearance. Perhaps for every year that the prime minister gains, the chancellor loses one. In a fortnight Sunak will require home-schooling, while Johnson will be over 70 and consequently allowed to self-shield from having to do his job.

Of course, we are not the only nation to be conducting an interesting social experiment to determine what happens if you elect a clinical narcissist to run a country which later turns out to be facing grave danger. At this stage, the US's experiment appears to be going rather worse, and you certainly wouldn't rule out Donald Trump judging November's elections to be something that had better be suspended under the circumstances.

Even so, it has been quite something to watch Johnson's boredom and terminal ironist's smirk kick back in, live on air, as the week has progressed, even while people are asking him about the soon-to-break ventilator crisis in intensive care. 'Operation Last Gasp', as Johnson reportedly called the need to address the equipment deficit in a conference call to manufacturers this week.

What can you say? If there were any kind of movie justice, the key component for the coronavirus vaccine would occur naturally only in Johnson's brain stem. Alas, even in that eventuality, he'd decline to do the right thing for the greater good. Johnson has never at a single point suggested he got into this game for public service. His idea of heroic sacrifice is allowing someone else to raise his offspring.

That the pandemic music should stop when Boris Johnson of all people is prime minister is the darkest of cosmic ironies. We are being asked to put our trust – our lives – in the hands of a man whose entire career, journalistic and political, has been built on a series of lies. It is the work of seconds to dredge up Johnson columns about radical population control or Johnson buses about the NHS enjoying vast savings from the EU. Who knows which of these, if any, he ever really believed.

Time and again this week I have been reminded of that great line from last year's *Chernobyl* drama series: 'When the truth offends, we lie and lie until we can no longer remember it is even there. But it is still there. Every lie we tell incurs a debt to the truth. Sooner or later, that debt is paid.'

Johnson's 'fight them on the beaches' moment: true grit, or more shifting sands?

24 March 2020

As the welcome for long-overdue action on coronavirus subsides, let's put his address into Churchillian perspective

Well, we can't know if it felt as he had always imagined it might. But Boris Johnson has at last been required to deliver the type of speech he has been practising in front of his bathroom mirror since childhood. For future actors, it's their Oscar acceptance speech. For Johnson, it has always been Winston Churchill at war.

No living soul has sought comparison with Churchill more fre-quently, or at greater length, than Johnson himself. Huge amounts of Johnson's Churchill biography are an attempt to foreground faults in Churchill that might excuse those often cited as the author's own. The thinly disguised plea to be considered in the same bracket as his idol frequently spills over into unintentional comedy. Churchill, Johnson is at repeated pains to claim, 'might be thought of as a man whose love of lush language exceeded his good sense, who lacked that vital note of sincerity'. Might he, now. Elsewhere, I'm not saying that Johnson has been stung for years by criticism of his own uninspiring parliamentary orations – but he does go very far to point out that Abraham Lincoln received a poor notice for the Gettysburg address. Again: if you say so, hun.

So the nature of our prime minister's obsession with Britain's wartime leader, and what we might euphemise as the points of difference between the two men, tell us much about the individ-ual on whom it has fallen to steer us through this current crisis. Some of Johnson's supporters ardently believe he is going to turn out to be our Churchill; other Britons remain ever so faintly unconvinced.

Clearly, the first reaction to Johnson placing Britain in a form of lockdown on Monday night is: thank heavens he finally did it. It is something that many in the NHS and beyond have been demand-ing for a considerable time now. Better late than never, is the mes-sage from a huge number of voices in that quarter.

Still, once the giddy welcome for what should long have been the basics – clarity and decisive action – has subsided, we probably have to put Johnson's address to the nation into perspective. So try and imagine if, for an entire week before his 'We shall fight on the beaches' speech, Winston Churchill had been giving rambling press conferences in which he said stuff like: 'I want people to be able to visit our great beaches! I want to keep our great beaches open! I have to tell you that should my beach waffle prove demonstrably unclear to millions, then I may be forced to bring forward measures to lay the ground for some kind of beach fight . . .'

As it goes, the classic Churchill speech, made live in the House of Commons, was immediately recognised by political friends, bitter rivals and most of the great chroniclers of the age as a sensational piece of oratory and a true spine-tingler. Johnson's Monday-night pre-record was met largely with relief. Thankfully, his famous smirk had twitched out only one and a half times, reminding us that it isn't only a tell of his fundamental unseriousness (though it is often that). Sometimes, it is the psychological glitch that occurs when he is being tested far beyond his abilities.

Soon after he took office in 1940, concerned allies appointed a doctor to personally care for Churchill. A physician named Charles Wilson was dispatched to see the prime minister in his Admiralty House apartments. 'I have become his doctor,' remarked the disgruntled Wilson, 'not because he wanted one, but because members of the cabinet, who realised how essential he has become, decided that someone ought to keep an eye on his health.'

There have been moments in the past fortnight to wonder if the same could not be done for Johnson, only with a head doctor. The need to be liked is a common enough syndrome in clinical psychology, if rarely exhibited to the degree in which it has taken hold in this case. But when you're the point man for a nation in the early stages of a mushrooming pandemic, there is arguably going to be a line where this need tips over into something dangerous.

In due course – such a deceptively affectless phrase – we may discover how fatally that line was crossed for most of March. Our future selves may look back on this time as one in which, for all the seismic disruption, we had no idea how real it was going to get. Though snatches of horror stories are emerging from the hospitals, the first huge wave of them has not yet broken. When it does, that and the many waves that follow it will surely dominate tragically for months. With respect to those already suffering terribly, we are still in the very early stages of something that is about to become unimaginably bigger.

But there is a reason that dramatists are often interested in what latterly appears to be the calm before the storm. Think of the likes of the BBC's *37 Days*, which examined the complex currents at play before the outbreak of the first world war and gave flesh to the convincing perception that the world drifted insouciantly into disaster. It is why scrutiny – even in times of crisis – matters. You've heard of straight-to-DVD; for far too much of the past month it has felt as though some in power have been governing in a way we might call straight-to-public-inquiry.

Anyone who thinks, 'This is not the time for questions,' might note that it was only when the questions rose to fever pitch over the past few days that Johnson appeared nudged to act. Those questions, often from ordinary citizens, were born of true concern and a true sense of duty – on which the government does not have a monopoly. There will be more questions like them in the weeks and months ahead, and anyone trying to tell you they shouldn't be asked is a grifter. There is more than one way to love your country, and no member of the public should ever surrender the right to question what is in the public interest.

First the corona prince, now Johnson.
Who are their designated survivors?

27 March 2020

The trajectory is darkening, with Britain now a significant step nearer to being led by Dominic Raab

Here we are, then. TFI whatever day it is. It might feel unclear if you're suffering from a persistent cough or are just trying to hack up the red pill.

Unfortunately, return to the simulation is impossible. As I type this, both Boris Johnson and the health secretary, Matt Hancock, have tested positive for coronavirus, while the chief medical officer, Chris Whitty, is self-isolating. The prime minister says he is experiencing mild symptoms and will self-isolate in Downing Street, where he is continuing to helm the UK's response to the pandemic. Fatalistically speaking, this die was cast the second we learned he'd appointed Dominic Raab as his 'designated survivor'. Why lie about who we are, you know? Just activate whatever protocol installs a 'roid-fuelled salesman for Magnet kitchens (Esher branch), whose unbeaten monthly commission run will only come to a horrifying end if anyone checks the showroom freezers.

A quick process question, before we go on: does the designated survivor now require a designated survivor, and so on? I daren't turn on the news in case there's a political scientist extrapolating how few steps it takes for the model to get us to Prime Minister Russell Brand.

Johnson isn't the only ultra-high-profile sufferer, of course, after Prince Charles's diagnosis dominated Wednesday's headlines. It's thought experts considered contact tracing, but abandoned it when they realised the sheer multitudes of people involved in picking up after HRH even between reveille and the breakfast table. Happily, the presence of Covid-19 is not thought to make any material difference to Prince Charles's preferred domestic procedures. The royal toothpaste will still be squeezed on to the royal toothbrush by a key-worker servant, only they'll do it in one of the rubber-gloved laboratory boxes they use to handle Prince Andrew's bedsheets.

In the meantime, there continues to be a huge range of reactions to the suspension of life as we knew it. Americans are buying more guns, though mass school closures mean there are fewer favoured locations to use them. In the UK on Thursday night, millions stood on doorsteps or leaned from their windows to applaud NHS and care workers, a vastly moving moment confused only by the participation of many Conservative MPs and ministers who in 2017 not only voted against a pay rise for nurses, but loudly clapped its defeat – and whose funding priorities have left some frontline NHS workers threatening to resign over lack of protective equipment. The World Health Organization recommends the sort of full-body armour you'd want to attend dinner at Michael Gove's; current government largesse allows for a 'Kiss the Cook' apron and a cardboard Simon Cowell mask.

Then again, the coronavirus seems to be quite the learning experience for some. On Monday Tory MP Steve Double rose in the house to marvel that the crisis is 'teaching us that many people that we consider to be low skilled are actually pretty crucial to the smooth running of our country'. He asked the home secretary, Priti Patel, to review the government's new points-based immigration system 'to reflect the things we've learned'.

While many are optimistic we'll entirely remake society in the wake of all this, I'm not so sure. If it takes a once-in-100-years global pandemic to jolt people in public office into the realisation that nurses are actually quite valuable, it's pretty hard to scale up for the next logical step. You're essentially looking at an extinction-level event to nudge them into the headspace where we reward said nurses even slightly better. The manifesto page where you seek buy-in for your plan to increase public-sector pay just says, 'Re-route a fucking asteroid towards us.'

Elsewhere, it's hard to know what to make of the supposed humbling of Sports Direct Sith Mike Ashley and Wetherspoons taplord Tim Martin. Both men have U-turned on their commercial reaction to the government's coronavirus measures. On the one hand, it's the absolute bare minimum, staged solely out of fear for their future bottom lines. On the other, it could be the darkest harbinger yet. Indeed, if you've currently got the Book of Revelation open, you might have been expecting them. Two hoarse men of the apocalypse, gruffly locating some knock-off contrition. Give it a couple of days and pale rider Richard Branson will hove into view, offering to never sue the NHS again in return for a bail-out for his airline. Who knows how many villains the coronaverse has yet to reveal to us?

To recap the ones we are aware of, Martin enlivened Tuesday evening by releasing an occasionally coherent video in which he lurched round his kitchen with a mug and put 43,000 people out of work. I can't tell you it divided the critics. Even in normal lighting, Martin looks like he's holding a torch under his chin and telling you a ghost story about what's going to happen to you in one of his pubs. Then again, every night is Halloween night down the 'Spoons, and Martin always wears the same costume: coarse fisherman whose wife is missing after 30 years of coercive control. Neighbours say she planned to leave him.

Like I said, it's just fancy dress. But hats off to Britain, which seems to have realised that unless it moves to swift online justice, then Martin is the metaphorical fate waiting for all of us down a remote country lane. Following his monstering, Tim has decided that refusing to pay his staff for last week's work and telling them to try their luck at Tesco doesn't reflect the man he is at all. I'm sure he'll grow from this.

As for Ashley, he too apologised on Friday morning for being himself (I paraphrase), adding that his emails to the government were 'ill judged and poorly timed'. No doubt. And yet, it's decidedly awkward that the government made time to read whatever quarter-witted bile Ashley sent, but claims not to have seen the communication from the EU about getting in on their scheme to buy extra ventilators. Given that Matt Hancock specifically referred to the scheme on last week's *Question Time*, we have to ask: is there a tear in the bullshit–time continuum? Or did the government reject a major potential source of ventilators to own the libs? Alternate fan theories are available; do mark this story as 'developing'.

Finally, it took less than 48 hours of wielding new powers before Derbyshire police were grotesquely misapplying them by using drones to track individual or family groups of walkers in the Peak District and shame them on social media. They've come in for a lot of stick for it, but let's not throw the format out entirely. Could it not be repurposed? Given the looming hole in content schedules now that all TV production has been halted, why not release Mike Ashley in the very remotest part of the Peak District, armed only with a backpack containing a 4kg kettlebell (up from £9.99 to £14.99 on SportsDirect.com), a 12kg kettlebell (up from £29.99 to £39.99) and a £452 skipping rope? Derbyshire police could then track and film one man's desperate attempt to get back to civilisation. On the current, darkening trajectory, Ashley's bound to be something-in-line to designated survivor status. Plus, you've got to think next year's Bafta cinematography category would be theirs to lose.

The horror of coronavirus is all too real.
Don't turn it into an imaginary war

7 April 2020

Politicians may turn to platitudes about heroes or battlers or victories, but they can't disguise Britain's grim current reality

The language of war is baked into most of us, to one degree or another. Our new daily discourse runs deep with talk of field hospitals, frontlines, the battles against an invisible enemy. The shock of the news that Prime Minister Boris Johnson lies seriously ill in intensive care drew a tide of messages and well wishes from world leaders and other politicians, many of which invoked a kind of martial courage. 'You are a fighter and we need you back.' 'He is a fighter and will beat this virus.' Together 'we will be able to win this battle'. 'You fight for a swift recovery.' 'You are a fighter, and you will overcome this challenge.' I truly hope he does.

For his part, Dominic Raab – who will deputise for Johnson – was described as looking 'shell-shocked' last night, before this morning chairing the 'war cabinet'. According to the breakfast interview inquiries thrown at Michael Gove, it seems that one of the primary questions is whether Raab is now technically in charge of the UK's response to a notional nuclear attack. I suppose we have to treat this as a matter of vital pertinence, though like many people living through this once-in-100-years deadly pandemic, I'd have just three words for any nuclear power contemplating an imminent first strike at the UK: not now, mate.

As the news gets more horrifyingly real each day – and somehow, at the same time, more unmanageably unreal – I'm not sure who this register of battle and victory and defeat truly aids. We don't really require a metaphor to throw the horror of viral death into sharper relief; you have to think it's bad enough already. Plague is a standalone horseman of the apocalypse – he doesn't need to catch a ride with War. Equally, it's probably unnecessary to rank something we keep being informed is virtually a war with things in the past that were literally wars. 'Your grandparents were called to war,' runs one popular meme. 'You're being asked to sit on a couch. You can do this.' Unsurprisingly, given this level of bellicose confusion, we have already seen those who visit the park literally branded 'traitors'.

Perhaps most importantly, it should be said that people don't die from this ghastly illness because of a lack of 'fight', whatever that might mean. Patients don't 'lose' against coronavirus because they failed to smite it or to personally out-strategise it. In recent years there has been a growing attempt to actually listen to people with cancer and the language used around the disease, and a mountain of evidence indicates that they largely disdain and frequently loathe the characterisation of their sickness as a 'battle'. The absurdity of putting the burden of healing on the patient incenses many, who don't care to be told that they are 'winning their war' or remembered as having 'lost their battle'.

Writing on the death of Robin Gibb, Jenni Murray (herself a former cancer patient) righteously refused to characterise him as having lost any battle, instead stating the reality: 'he drew the short straw of a difficult disease'. Or think of the late, great Deborah Orr's withering refusal to tolerate this nonsense in her rules on how to talk to cancer patients. 'Funnily enough,' she twinkled menacingly, 'it's not comforting to be told that you have to go into battle with your disease, like some kind of medieval knight on a romantic quest. Submitting to medical science, in the hope of a cure, is just that – a submission. The idea that illness is a character test, with recovery as a reward for the valiant, is glib to the point of insult.'

Perhaps it would be better for us all if we resisted talking about coronavirus in this way. Last year, new research found that the ubiquity of military metaphors in cancer discussions could do more psychological harm than good, making people fatalistic about their treatment chances and encouraging the feeling that altering their own behaviours was beyond them.

In our current crisis, it is interesting how the language of war is used, and by whom. Without wishing to over-generalise about that innate desire to be a hero, women in public life seem to do it rather less. Health workers themselves do it even more sparingly. Easily the most powerful thing I have seen thus far in the coverage of the deepening virus crisis was a report screened on BBC News, which was given access to an intensive care ward at University College Hospital in London. The BBC correspondent framed his film entirely in terms of war. 'This is the frontline in a war,' it began. 'Every day some battles are won and some are lost.' That's certainly not a judgment on the excellent report; it may be a helpful way of communicating the desperation to many people. But it was notable that the hospital workers themselves never strayed into that kind of terminology. I can't shake the memory of the female ER worker talking about how impossibly difficult some doctors and nurses found the unique work of the Covid-19 ICU. I don't know how long she'd been on shift, but she spoke absolutely fluently and with absolutely no judgment. 'Some of our staff can't cope with it . . . not all of them can deal with it.' Not for her the veil of platitudes about heroes or battlers or victories. The grim bathos of reality is more powerful. I felt the lurch again reading a *Guardian* report about the desperate shortage of PPE in care homes, in which the executive chair of the National Care Association spoke plainly. 'Once you run out,' she said, 'you are down to Marigolds and bin liners.'

Oof. I wonder, incidentally, if I am alone in having felt the absence of any women in the government's 'war cabinet' of five top ministers, and whether we'd be hearing quite so much about wars and battles if there were more. I understand, of course, that this is where the cards fell – there are a whole six women in the cabinet, and ministers can only do the jobs that were put in front of them months before this crisis exploded. Even so, I feel the imbalance.

Then again, on Sunday night the Queen made an address to the nation that – to surprise in some quarters – ended up feeling powerful even to many of those who feel the Jedi mind trick of royalty does not usually work on them. Her Majesty certainly mentioned the war. But she provided something that has not been in ready supply from government podiums over the past few weeks, yet is arguably needed more and more as the darkness sets in: a strangely homespun oratory. Castlespun, whatever.

This was not the oratory we associate with soaring wartime speeches or martial inspiration. The callback to her first broadcast, made in 1940 to evacuated children, was particularly affecting. For all the second world war metaphors we've had over the past month, this was the first time the parallel was made explicitly with what war really means for the vast, vast majority, who don't regard it as a chance to be the hero of popular stereotype and earn their glorious mentions in dispatches. For them – for us – war is a state of fear, of seeing our children frightened, of being the victims of immense disruption, and of being separated or sundered from many of those we love. War is not epic poetry. Death is all around us; let's dispense with the endless conscription.

The truth about why Cummings hasn't gone: Johnson is too terrified to sack him

26 May 2020

The prime minister's decision is not born of loyalty to his lockdown-busting adviser – he just can't get rid of his ideas man

Perhaps on Sunday you watched the entire nation being lectured on what constitutes fatherly responsibility by Boris Johnson, a man who won't even say how many children he has and leaves women to bring up an unspecified number of them. Perhaps on Monday you watched the *Guardian*'s Rowena Mason being lectured on journalism by Johnson, a man sacked from a newspaper for fabricating quotes from his own godfather, and who blithely discussed helping a friend to have another journalist beaten up. Perhaps today you heard Michael Gove tell LBC he has 'on occasion' driven a car to check his eyesight.

If you *did* see these things, I can only direct you to the slogan flyposted all over Paris during 1968's civil unrest: 'DO NOT ADJUST YOUR MIND – THERE IS A FAULT WITH REALITY.' The term 'gaslighting' is much overused, but let's break the glass on it for the events of the past few days. As for 'indefensible' . . . well, I don't think that word means what you thought it meant.

Anyway. I see the latest science Dominic Cummings knows more about than you is optometry. Half an hour late on Monday afternoon – like he's Mariah Carey and not some spad in inside-out pants – the Islington-dwelling humanities graduate took to Downing Street's rose garden. There, he delivered the most ridiculous address to a nation since Tiger Woods stood in front of an audience, including his mother, and apologised to his wife and sponsors. The difference is that Woods had a problem with cocktail waitresses, while Cummings fucks entire public health messages in the middle of a deadly pandemic. Also, he's not remotely sorry.

By now you may be dimly aware that his wife showing coronavirus symptoms saw Cummings first return to Downing Street, then embark on what we might call an Odyssean project: a heroic 260-mile quest all the way to County Durham, breaking the spirit and letter of the lockdown rules he helped to write. I guess he just wanted to be a rule-maker, not a rule-taker. Then, he explained, he embarked on a 60-mile round trip to Barnard Castle, with his child in the car, to see if his eyes were so banjaxed that it was unsafe for him to drive. Which is . . . but no. I'm sorry, I just can't with that one. Hopefully he's at least nuked his car insurance premium.

Apologies for having to get tough with a guy who has always cultivated an image of himself as the Roy Keane of Westminster, even if that is like being the Clint Eastwood of the DVLA. But if Cummings and his wife didn't know what they'd done was wrong, why would they choose to write a lengthy article last month about their virus experience – full of personal family information – which omitted all of these dramas, all of these material facts. Or, as Cummings addressed these questions of what is unredeemable in the rose garden: 'I stress to people that they should not believe everything in the newspapers.' And I stress to people that by far the most inaccurate account of the period in question was in *The Spectator*, bylined Mary Wakefield and Dominic Cummings. As for his querulous domestic exceptionalism, you'd think they were the first parents ever to get properly ill in possession of children. Or child, in this case. God knows, it's not much fun. But, dare millions of us say, it is kind of what you sign up for – a reality not lost on the ICU nurse couple I heard on the radio, explaining about both of them being hit hard by Covid-19 and having to isolate with their own three children, without help.

Cummings's university history tutor once described him as 'something like a Robespierre . . . determined to bring down things that don't work'. Five years after his revolution Robespierre himself was deemed to be something that didn't really work, and was 'brought down', to euphemise the business of being relieved of your head in front of an ecstatic mob. I must say I found the footage of Cummings being screamed at in his street on Sunday distinctly disturbing when set alongside his account of his family's house having become a target for threats of violence. This is never right.

Part of what's disturbing is the vignette of a Britain Cummings himself did much to foment: grimly polarised, reflexively aggressive and running with an undercurrent of menace. His crowning triumph – the successful campaign to leave the EU – was a masterclass of stoking and exploiting divisions, unpleasantly emotive half-truths or untruths, and evidently considered itself above the law. I wrote last year about the dangerous folly of whipping up people-versus-parliament narratives, and how quickly those who imagine themselves to be on the side of the people can suddenly be reclassified as enemy politicians. But even I would have thought it too neat, too written, for Cummings to find himself on the wrong end of his sorcery as quickly as he has been. The thing about playing to angry mobs is that eventually they get angry with you. They came for Robespierre in the end too.

For all the draw of the Cummings character, though, the last few days are ultimately a terrible story about Johnson. 'Wash your hands, wash your hands,' the prime minister kept gibbering last night. He's certainly washing his hands of it all. All populists secretly hate their people, and Johnson is no different. But that 'secretly' is key. His decision to keep Cummings brings his contempt for those he is meant to serve into the open. He would rather endanger their lives by compromising a vital public health strategy.

But why? The thing about Johnson is that he desperately wanted to become prime minister, and he desperately wanted to have been prime minister. It's just the bit in between he struggles with. With Othello, it was jealousy. Macbeth: ambition. Lear: pride. Johnson: career liar, hollowed out by narcissism, who not even his friends would joke was motivated by public service. I guess it's the little things that trip you up, isn't it?

Anyone who imagines his defence of Cummings is born of loyalty is unfamiliar with the concept 'Boris Johnson'. This is actually a simple story: man with no ideas is too terrified to sack his ideas man. Or, to put it in the complex intellectual terms it deserves: some street heckler once shouted at David Hasselhoff, 'Oi! Hasselhoff! You're nothing without your talking car!' Cummings is the talking car to Johnson's Hasselhoff.

So here we are. Cummings stays, and only irresistible external events will make Johnson do the right thing. He himself is not capable. We have the highest death toll in Europe, we left the care homes to their fate, our test-and-trace blunders are an international embarrassment, and we didn't even save our economy. Johnson takes daily runs, but even in a crisis appears only once or twice a week to do some leadership.

This is the utter smallness of the man, and the tragedy for everyone stuck being governed by him. Perhaps the greatest tragedy is the acceptance. It would be nice to think we're not so beaten that we don't expect better than what he's given us. After all, lives literally depend on it.

Marcus Rashford is showing our failing politicians how to do their jobs

16 June 2020

People usually ask how many nurses you could exchange for one foot-baller. But one Rashford is worth a hundred ministers

Marcus Rashford is 22 years old and the reason desperate families will now continue to receive free school meal vouchers during the holidays. During lockdown, this prodigiously talented campaigner has started a charity that has raised millions to feed 400,000 children, partnered on a drive to counter homelessness and now wants to stop 1.3m British children going hungry this summer. Any other CV points – minor interests, hobbies, stuff like that? Ah yes, hang on: he also plays as a forward for Manchester United and England. Today, in a powerful plea that has succeeded in forcing a government U-turn, Rashford wrote: 'I don't claim to have the education of an MP in parliament, but I do have a social education.'

And we'll come to Gavin Williamson, the 43-year-old secretary of state for education, in due course. Suffice to say, Gavin has gone so missing in the biggest game of his career that the coastguard has called off the search and it has now become a matter for the Hubble telescope. As for the prime minister . . . shortly before Marcus Rashford was born to a single mother whom he idolises for her tireless work and sacrifices, Boris Johnson was writing that single mothers were producing a generation of 'ill-raised, ignorant, aggressive and illegitimate children'. Which, let's face it, means so much more coming from him.

For now, a reminder of where we were two and a half months ago. Taking the podium at a government press conference, even as Covid-19 was ripping silently through the care homes he'd later lie he'd put a 'ring of steel' around, Gavin's cabinet colleague Matt Hancock was very keen to show he had his priorities in order. 'I think the first thing that Premier League footballers can do is make a contribution,' Matt proclaimed. 'Take a pay cut and play their part.'

Well, there you go. It must have seemed such an easy win for politicians who know nothing about footballers, or indeed about football. Or, increasingly, about winning. Just a reminder of where the 'world-beating' UK currently is: we have the third-highest death toll in the world, the OECD has predicted we will have the worst-hit economy in the developed world, and we are on course for one of the slowest and most socially painful exits from lockdown. If this is world-beating, I'd hate to see us lose. I don't need to tell you that during this entire shitshow, under their exclusive management, the government has only suggested a single group in our society should take a pay cut: Premier League footballers.

To dispense with the more irrelevant end of the housekeeping first: Premier League players were going to take a pay cut anyway when Matt was going for his headline; they announced the 30% reduction within hours, and have since contributed in a vast and mostly unpublicised number of ways to social and charitable initiatives within their communities and beyond. But even if they had done absolutely none of that – genuinely unthinkable – imagine Matt Hancock, secretary of state for health in a time of pandemic, spending even one minute having a view on what footballers were doing. Because that actually happened. I know the buzzphrase is 'easy to say in hindsight', but on the basis that I wrote about it at the time, I'm going to have to go with 'easy to say in sight'. This is not a matter of retrospect – it was always a matter of spect.

As is the observation that what is happening right now to children – most particularly the vulnerable, but far beyond too – will be a disgraceful stain on this government. Schoolchildren in this country are in crisis. A fifth have done little or no schoolwork at home, with four in ten having no regular contact with teachers.

When Tory MPs are being besieged by constituents asking them where on earth the Nightingale-style plans for schools are, let alone the Nightingale schools themselves, then something has gone catastrophically wrong, for which Gavin Williamson at the very least should be taking a 100% pay cut.

Why has the government failed children so incredibly badly, in ways that will damage many of them for ever? Did they think people wouldn't notice? The negligence is so enormous that it demands several interlinked theories. For what minuscule amount it's worth, I have one for the set. The men – and it is almost exclusively men – who have stood behind Downing Street podiums for months telling us what a great job they're doing have a somewhat unreal understanding of what has been happening in the domestic sphere since lockdown, because this has never been how they themselves have lived. My suspicion is they have wives who have done huge and disproportionate amounts of household-running and child-rearing work for them, while they have climbed the greasy pole. This has insulated them from the realities of how others live, and consequently from forming anything like an informed appreciation of how they might currently be living under the privations of lockdown. What ends as the failure of a generation of children began simply as a failure of imagination.

That would certainly fit with the Sunday that Dominic Cummings spent in No. 10 not getting sacked. Then, you might recall, he contrived to persuade Boris Johnson and Michael Gove that driving to Durham was a rational and normal response to maybe having to do some childcare while ill. On the one hand, Johnson's government would have attempted to keep Cummings if he'd explained he'd driven to Durham in order to carry out a series of ritualistic sex murders. On the other, he had perhaps found two perfect individuals to sell this particular bridge to. Johnson and Gove have the air of guys who would genuinely think driving hundreds of miles in high lockdown was reasonable on the basis of something they would regard as a unique situation. Seriously, what else could Dom do? Certainly not his own childcare, like other human earthling parents.

At the end of the day, to fall back on a football commentary staple, it's guys like this who have failed schoolchildren and vulnerable children. The lives other families have been forced to lead during lockdown haven't felt within their purview, even when – in the case of Williamson – it is literally their official purview.

So we are left with a 22-year-old footballer having to point out the realities to men whose job it is supposed to be to know. The one thing people love to say about footballers is how many nurses' salaries their contracts could pay for. Oddly, nurses and footballers seem to be the only two currencies traded on this exchange – which must be to the great satisfaction of politicians. And yet, purely in terms of moral worth and strategic competence, how many Gavin Williamsons would you have to amass before you were even close to the value of one Marcus Rashford? How many Matt Hancocks? How many Boris Johnsons? Perhaps it's time to move the goalposts and ask those questions instead.

Chris Grayling's track record? There is no track; just a stretch of scorched earth

10 July 2020

His career has been a series of breathtaking failures. Yet he's just been touted as chair of the intelligence committee

News that Chris Grayling is intended to be appointed chair of the intelligence and security committee feels like a cosmic inevitability. There is simply no aspect of the British state that is regarded as too big to Grayl. In the event of nuclear devastation, almost certainly somehow caused by Chris Grayling, Chris Grayling would not simply survive, but there would be someone surveying the ash cloud and the onset of nuclear winter going: 'You know what, clearing this up looks like a job for Chris Grayling.'

Please don't ask by what arcane Downing Street process appointments such as Grayling's are decided. You are much better off imagining a wingbacked armchair with its back to the viewer, so that all that can be heard is a Mr Burns voice rasping: 'Grayling, you say. Remind me of his track record.' 'Well, put simply, sir . . . his record is that there is no longer a track. There's just a huge stretch of scorched earth, dozens of charred horse skeletons, and it's all overhung by a noxious pall so toxic it makes the Chernobyl exclusion zone seem like a visit to the Selfridges perfume counter.' 'Perfect. Prepare his office.'

What do you even call this way of parcelling out power to inept satellites? A wallygarchy? At least Putin's guys are competent. If one of them is ordered to take a company off the state's hands or boil someone in oil, they discharge the task competently and with the requisite amount of pride in their work. Chris Grayling would bankrupt the company and boil the wrong guy, and blow up the entire oil refinery in the process. He himself would walk from the conflagration unscathed – a sort of Terminator of shitness, who promptly receives a call on his mobile. 'Chris, old boy!' the chap on the other end of the line would say. 'Glad I caught you. How d'you fancy running something called a track and trace programme?'

Speaking of Vladimir Putin, the big focus for the intelligence committee is to finally publish the report into alleged Russian interference in UK politics. This document has been missing in one of those bureaucratic Bermuda triangles so beloved of transparent states. First it couldn't be published because the committee couldn't meet because we were having an election; and after the election they couldn't publish it because they hadn't convened the new committee. The report was sent to Downing Street last 17

October. Back then it was said the likelihood of its contents being a bombshell was fairly slim, as the security services had signed off promptly on its conclusions.

Alas, even accounting for the advent of the coronavirus, the sheer amount of time that has passed since that moment has fanned the flame of hope, tended in some quarters, that the Russia report contains a smoking gun – some sensational revelation, some neat explanation for whichever development in British political life over the past four years the hoper can't stomach any other way. We shall see.

For now, Grayling's ascent to chairman is expected to be a formality. I very much enjoyed last night's *Guardian* headline 'Grayling closes in on role as chair of UK intelligence committee'. 'Closing in' suggests a degree of targeted precision that Grayling's career does not. The only way Chris Grayling could close in on the intelligence and security chair is if he was actually attempting to close in on the keys to a holiday caravan in Rhyl.

Before he plays us some of his new stuff, then, let's take a moment to appreciate a few of Chris's greatest hits. I'm afraid I am wildly constrained by space, though lowlights include his time as justice secretary, during which he instituted a widely condemned ban on books being sent to prisoners and delivered hugely expensive yet rushed reforms to the probation service that contrived to significantly increase reoffending. The commercial arm of his department attempted to sell prison services to Saudi Arabia.

But it would be arguably at transport where his work ascended to the status of art form. He presided over the collapse of the Govia Thameslink and Northern rail services, of course, though his 'My Way' is surely the story of Seaborne Freight. This is the one where Grayling paid £1m to consultants and awarded a £14m contract to a firm for ferry services in the event of a no-deal Brexit. It swiftly emerged that the terms and conditions on Seaborne Freight's website were cut and pasted from that of a food delivery firm. In one section they pointed out: 'It is the responsibility of the customer to thoroughly check the supplied goods before agreeing to pay for any meal/order.' Grayling, alas, had failed to check Seaborne's goods before paying, and so it was that he only found out after losing £14m that the ferry firm . . . that the ferry firm . . . I'm so sorry, I can never believe I have to type this . . . that the ferry firm had no ferries.

When news of Grayling's latest mooted appointment broke, some people marvelled: 'How does he do it?' As though the tendency were something new. In fact, seeing men like Grayling continue to fail upwards is deeply traditional. Far from being an aberration, it is in keeping with the spirit of the political age: an aggressively misplaced nostalgia.

Indeed, there is an aspect of Brexit and the calibre of its ascendant personnel that has always felt karmic. Grayling's wildly overpromoted slapdashery is precisely the level of failure and incompetence you might have found in, say, the British Raj. Had he been born back in those days, you can absolutely see Chris dashing off a few catastrophic boundary changes for Louis Mountbatten or ruining a province, only to be rewarded with a bigger one. The difference is that we've brought it all home now. Having run out of other countries to do it to, Britain is now British-empiring itself.

'Over by Christmas': now where have we heard Johnson's new slogan before?

17 July 2020

Much like the prime minister's crass pre-cooked jokes at PMQs, this upbeat line feels prematurely delivered

Barely a week ago, the government launched its scheme to entice people back into cafes and restaurants, beneath the banner 'Eat Out to Help Out'. This is the sort of unforeseen innuendo that happens if you leave the sloganeering to people who – in some ineffable way – regard going down on someone as essentially leftwing.

In light of developments, that unfortunate slogan takes on more of a hectoring tone, as Boris Johnson mounts another podium to strongly suggest there will be a return to 'virtual normality' by November, 'hopefully in time for Christmas'. 'Over by Christmas' – another interesting slogan, there, from a government not even clever enough to realise it's not clever enough.

Either way, it's time for all redshirts to get back to their offices, if they can. Or, as Johnson's chief scientific officer said yesterday, there is 'absolutely no reason' to change the advice that people should work from home. These words came in a Commons committee appearance by Patrick 'Herd Immunity' Vallance, who, like Glenn Hoddle, now seems to think he never said them things. Vallance certainly seems to have missed the announcement from chancellor Rishi Sunak, who this week warned sluggish consumer units – 'people', in the old parlance – that the economic recovery would fail unless Britons got back into the shops and restaurants.

Please do enjoy the spectacle of the Conservative-run state commanding its populace to participate in capitalism. It's semi-optional, for now, though I'd like to think the participation drive will swiftly escalate into backbench MPs being instructed to motor round the streets of their constituencies with a PA system blasting out the message: 'YOU MUST RETURN TO THE MARKET ECONOMY.' Commuter commandants to be introduced by October.

Still, what's the worst that could happen? In fact, there is perverse good news for health secretary Matt Hancock, who has recently been looking like the central character in a short story about a man who starts haunting himself. According to a paper by two Oxford academics, it's possible that Public Health England has significantly overestimated the Covid-19 death statistics by including former sufferers who could have subsequently died of other causes. Hancock has ordered an urgent inquiry, which shows us that he CAN order urgent inquiries. The public inquiry into the government's fiascoid handling of the coronavirus is pencilled in for before winter – just not this winter.

Speaking of eccentric accounting methods, there are question marks over the spending announcements unveiled seemingly five times a week by Sunak. Some suspect the same money keeps being produced with elan, then produced again with a further flourish. Those who got to the sealed section in Adam Smith's *Wealth of Nations* will know that this is actually known as the Biscuit Mill model. It's based on an episode of *Bagpuss*, where the mice claim to have a biscuit mill, but in fact have only one chocolate digestive that they roll off their production line, wheel round the back, then roll off again, and so on. (Incidentally, I must confess that I myself have previously used this metaphor, making it a sort of meta-metaphor about the covert recycling of limited material.) The episode plays out with the mice eventually being exposed by Professor Yaffle. Who, in this latest case, is played by Paul Johnson of the Institute of Fiscal Studies. The director of the respected economic thinktank said on Thursday that Sunak's attempt to disguise old money as new money was 'corrosive to public trust', adding that 'the "Rooseveltian" additional £5.5bn of capital spending represents an increase of precisely zero this year on budget plans'.

As with Johnson's performance this morning and in recent days, none of it can really be said to fill one with confidence. Which, for a man whose sole political talent is supposed to be filling people with confidence, feels ominous. Johnson increasingly comes across as a public speaker of dazzling inagility. Even Theresa May murdered prepared lines more humanely. With Boris, the impression is of a man with a joke he'd like to make at some point during the next half-hour, waiting patiently for about 56 seconds, then losing all control and discharging it at the wrong moment. I wonder if it would help to think of something else entirely – cricket averages, say – or apply some kind of numbing agent before standing up to speak?

Consider the moment at prime minister's questions this week when Keir Starmer asked him if he had a message for the bereaved families of coronavirus victims. As a spectator, your only thought is: don't do the joke now. Just say a message for the dead people. But Johnson was powerless to resist himself. The leader of the opposition needed to decide which brief he was going to take, he began . . . *Don't do it now. Don't do it now. Don't do it now.* 'Because at the moment' – *please please please don't do it now* – 'he's got more briefs than Calvin Klein!'

There it is. Another premature ejaculation by the prime minister – as the promise of this all being over by Christmas may very well turn out to be.

Matt Hancock, could you honestly think of no one better to run test and trace?

18 September 2020

With the system in chaos, test-and-trace boss Dido Harding says the increased demand could not have been predicted. Yes, really

Do you remember Ye Olde Operation Moonshotte, an ancient promise by the elders of this government to test 10 million people a day? My apologies for the leading question. There are absent-minded goldfish who remember that figure, given it was announced by Boris Johnson's government barely three seconds ago. The only representative of the animal, vegetable and possibly mineral kingdoms who doesn't remember it is the prime minister himself, who on Wednesday told a committee asking him about it: 'I don't recognise the figure you have just given.' Like me, you probably feel grateful to be governed by a guy whose approach to unwanted questions is basically, 'New phone, who dis?'

Like me, you will be reassured by Matt Hancock's plan to throw another 'protective ring' around care homes. What's not to fear about a Matt Hancock ring, easily the most dangerous ring in history, including Sauron's Ring of Power?

Like me, you are probably impressed that the government is ordering you to snitch on your neighbours for having seven people in their garden, while whichever Serco genius is running testing as a Dadaist performance piece about human futility gets to live in the witness protection programme.

Speaking of geniuses, you probably feel relaxed to learn that Chris Grayling, who notably awarded a ferry contract to a firm with no ferries, is now to be paid £100,000 a year for seven hours' work a week advising a ports company. When I read this story I imagined his aides pulling a hammer-wielding Grayling off the pulped corpse of Satire, going: 'Jesus, Chris! Leave it – it's already dead! We need to get out of here!'

Elsewhere, testing supremo Dido Harding has surfaced in parliament. It was starting to feel like we'd see *Avatar II* in theatres before we saw Dido front up to explain this mushrooming fiasco. Her last appearance before a select committee was as head of TalkTalk – after two teenage boys hacked the network, resulting in 157,000 people having their personal details stolen. When she was appointed to head up the test-and-trace programme, Hancock explained he 'can't think of anyone better than Dido'. Then take another five seconds, Matt. Off the top of my head I can come up with Baroness Gemma Collins of *Towie* and Grandmaster Glitch from *Go Jetters*.

Still, here she comes again – Dido, Queen of Carnage, on hand to gloss the havoc. As she put it: 'I don't think anybody was expecting to see the really sizeable increase in demand that we've seen over the course of the last few weeks.' But, Dido: they literally were.

At least Harding is visible. Huge amounts of the malfunctioning system are now being run – badly – by unaccountable figures. Take firms like Deloitte, which ran logistics at the testing site at what we might call Chessington World of Misadventures. Hospitals felt forced to ask it to take over after the results of NHS staff were serially lost or misdirected. The pile of 2020 sentences I never expected to type is now Earth's tallest structure, but let's add another one: 'NHS commandeers Vampire Ride from accountancy firm charged with controlling spread of deadly pandemic.' (Seriously, stick a fork in me. I'm done.)

While Harding was defending the barely functional testing system, Jacob Rees-Mogg was telling the Commons that 'instead of this endless carping saying it's difficult to get [tests], we should be celebrating this phenomenal success of the British nation'. To which the only possible reply is four-lettered.

His own ma and pa clearly hopelessly overindulged Rees-Mogg, but millions of other parents just will not feel minded to take it from this rejected *Charlie and the Chocolate Factory* character. If there were any justice, Jacob would have been stretched into a mile-long liquorice lace by vigilante Oompa-Loompas, as they sang one of their trademark cautionary songs. Instead, he is somehow leader of the House of Commons. There, he speaks of what ordinary people 'should' be doing – with the air of a man who knows that if any of the Rees-Mogg progeny are sent home from school with a possible Covid symptom, it's not going to be him taking time off work to home-school them and wait for a test spot to open up in Manchester a week on Friday. There is zero uncertainty about childcare and loss of earnings in the Rees-Mogg household, where even the adults still have nannies. (At the age of 51, Jacob still retains the live-in childcare professional who was – formerly? – responsible for wiping his backside.)

Yet again, the overriding impression is of a government run by men for whom the domestic sphere is a mystery they have no wish to get to the bottom of. One of them driving hundreds of miles to Durham – just in case he got ill and still had to do his own childcare – sounds, to the other guys, like a totally reasonable thing to have done. Meanwhile, the big boss fails to be meaningfully involved in the lives of between 17% and 29% of his children (awaiting full data). If you can be persuaded it's normal to drive a 60-mile round trip with a child in the car to test your eyesight, then naturally you believe parents should think it fine to stick a five-year-old in their own vehicle and travel 400 miles to obtain what's necessary to get the child back to school and them back to work.

Either way, of *course* a government run by weirdo elitists didn't reflexively foresee that September – back to school, back to offices – was going to mean a huge surge in testing demand. This is the trouble when 'hardworking families' is merely a demographic you wish to appeal to, as opposed to who you are. Real-life 'hardworking families' could have told you in a heartbeat that September was the main event. THEY could have predicted it. Because unless someone else does it all for you, a huge part of parenting is about thinking ahead, planning, creating yet another routine that keeps the whole precarious show on the road – the endless foresight of it all.

Only this week Dominic Cummings was pictured slouching through the Downing Street gates carrying some archive letter written by US general Bernard Schriever pushing for continued investment in ballistic weapons technology. Cummings should hang around the school gates instead, where any amount of mothers who've seen all this shit before and didn't have time for it back then would be able to enlighten him in the simplest possible terms. Namely: 'Hey, squidbrain, I've got some "data" for you! Mind if I "special advise" you with it, only I don't have a window to put it in a 20,000-word blog? OK, here goes: I don't WANT you to build me a fricking missile defence shield, I don't CARE about the Manhattan Project, I think all your reading recommendations REEK of the business section of the airport bookshop, and I'm

NOT going to be accused of "carping" by guys who'd have a nervo if they had to change a nappy.

'You know what I want? A SWAB WITHIN A THIRTY-MILE RADIUS, YESTERDAY. Now spad THAT, genius.'

Only this government could miss the open goal of free school meals

27 October 2020

If it weren't so serious, there would be deep comedy in seeing Marcus Rashford run rings around Boris Johnson's lot

Will nobody think of the prime ministers? Everyone has a story of deprivation that has stuck with them during this pandemic, and mine is one from a selection offered by 'friends' of Boris Johnson, who were so concerned about his household finances a month ago that they went to the *Daily Mail* about it. We pick up the scene at a private gathering for some of these friends at the PM's country retreat, with Johnson holding court: "'Enjoy it,' he said before bellowing down the long dining table at Chequers: "Eat every scrap. I have to pay for this you know!"'

Like me, your tears may have spontaneously gushed at multiple such reports in recent months. If you missed them, let me summarise: a man who applied for a job which pays almost £160,000 a year, with hugely substantial benefits, is apparently feeling unable to manage on almost £160,000 a year, with hugely substantial benefits. Yet this is only the half of it. 'The food wasn't even very good,' Johnson's friend told the *Mail*, 'but the real tragedy is that Boris can't really afford to entertain on any kind of scale. I am not going to accept another invitation because it seems unfair that he should fork out to feed me when he hasn't got any money.'

Take a moment. I know I just did.

And so to the full-spectrum shitshow over free school meals, now decried by everyone from the government's own social mobility commission to its own MPs, albeit not enough for many of them to vote against it. The spectacle of Marcus Rashford running rings round any number of cabinet ministers is so painfully Manichean it has the flavour of a Nike advert, like that one in the Colosseum where Eric Cantona had to score the winner against Lucifer.

At Rashford's age – 22 – Johnson's chief interest in food distribution was limited to which bread roll to chuck first at a pleading restaurant owner. As a member of a university dining club that routinely trashed eating establishments for the fun of it, Johnson was arrested, along with other Bullingdon inadequates, over the smashing of a restaurant window with a pot plant. You can only imagine the condemnation – probably at ministerial level – that would these days be headed the way of football if a 22-year-old player was found to have done the same. And yet, this and many other incidents like it have proved absolutely no impediment to becoming prime minister.

If it weren't over something so deadly serious, there would be deep comedy in the now daily spectacle of Conservative politicians struggling to find the right words to deploy about an immensely impressive young black man whose day job is being extremely good at something that people actually like. Rashford scoring a stunning 87th-minute winner against Paris Saint-Germain last week, then coming straight off the pitch to tweet about child poverty feels like a Tory anxiety dream, the sort of psychiatric hazing exercise you have to pass before you get to green-light a bent property deal or shag a troubled 18-year-old researcher.

Boris Johnson says he 'salutes' Marcus Rashford. Nadhim Zahawi, who just voted against the job Marcus Rashford is doing, says, 'Marcus Rashford is doing an incredible job.' Matt Hancock says he's 'inspired' by Marcus Rashford. Which is nice. I mean,

Charles Manson was inspired by the Beatles. It's always important to remember that Matt Hancock kicked off this pandemic by using the heights of the Downing Street podium to declaim some cheap, easy and ludicrously irrelevant point about how Premier League stars needed to take a pay cut. Hancock, who should have taken a 100% pay cut months ago, is now excruciatingly reduced to playing nice. His interviews are so beaten it's like he's had trials for the Lib Dems.

There is increasingly vocal and widespread resistance to the school meals policy and the effect of the government's coronavirus response on already deprived areas of the north, even from the new crop of Tory MPs, many of whom didn't expect to win in last December's general election and consequently appear to have received the sort of rigorous vetting you might expect to have been lavished on a Ukip councillor or 1970s kids' TV presenter. And yet, Downing Street would like it to be known they are very relaxed about it all. According to what one No. 10 figure told *Politico*, the new MPs have simply been spooked by negative coverage and will soon 'toughen up'.

Let's hope they attain the toughness of serious elders such as Mansfield MP Ben Bradley. I find Bradley pretty mesmeric. He comes off as the government's dating coach, negging the voters while wearing a smirk usually seen on guys who can explain how, technically, paying nightclub entry counts as consent. In real life, Bradley spent the weekend agreeing with tweets suggesting that free school meal vouchers went straight to the 'crack den [and] brothel', adding, 'That's what FSM vouchers in the summer effectively did ...'

He somewhat belatedly deleted this tweet on the basis that 'the context wasn't as clear as I thought it was'. Perhaps someone in Downing Street reminded Ben that they're supposed to be looking like they give a toss about mental health these days? Addictions are not the most incomprehensible response to a range of despairs exacerbated by these times, and sneering in this brutal and crass way about them is a handy reminder of the difference between what some politicians nod along to and what they mean in practice. 'This week is mental health awareness week and it's really important that everyone feels comfortable talking about their mental health,' Ben was trilling at the requisite moment last year. 'I'm proud to be part of a government that has made it equal with physical health.' An absolute badge-kisser, there.

Where will Johnson's latest unforced error go? Some people stockpile loo roll or hand sanitiser; this government stockpiles U-turns. Most of its policies have the half-life of a particularly unstable radioactive isotope. It's explicitly a government of super-forecasters who can't see up to next Friday. Messaging is now so Dadaist that in the same week that they're fighting Rashford they leak the tale that they're planning to abolish quarantine for City dealmakers and hedgefunders, with one government source reasoning to the *Sunday Times*: 'It seems ridiculous that people who are coming to the UK for five or six meetings in a day and then flying out are forced to quarantine, especially when most of them come in private jets and have a chauffeur-driven car.' Hate to blindside them with another spoiler, but is that the thing which truly seems ridiculous?

You expect politicians to have been picked last for football, and there's no shame in that. Our trouble is that this crop of politicians were picked last for politics. This cabinet aren't the reserves or even the thirds – they're the ninths or 10ths or something, having been picked solely for their loyalty to Brexit, a project successive governments have spent the past four years proving is like deliberately relegating yourself to League One. That the pandemic music has stopped with a team of this calibre in charge really is the cruellest of timings, and, on current evidence, is only likely to get crueller.

We are all Johnson's exes now, led on by false hope and dishonesty

27 November 2020

You'd be forgiven for thinking we would exit lockdown into something better, but the prime minister's harsh tier system was our destiny

'Now is not the time', gibbered the prime minister, 'to take our foot off the throat of the beast.' Its throat? A lot of people feel like they've been living in the beast's colon for most of the year. Still, see you guys in tier 4 in January.

Incredibly, the above was not even the worst line of Boris Johnson's Thursday-evening press conference. Johnson is unaccountably celebrated as a brilliant orator but frequently spouts the sort of sub-inspirational shit you might see slapped on a photo of a crossroads on Instagram. This outing was a case in point, as the prime minister intoned: 'Your tier is not your destiny – every area has the means of escape.' Wow. I want to say '#makesuthink', but I'm going to go with: 'Then tell us what the means of escape is! Why does everything have to be a bleeding riddle?'

Unfortunately, the government doesn't even trust its own MPs enough to divulge what precisely will set your area free. And, as I mentioned last week, many of you will be quite bored with taking lectures in personal responsibility from a man who doesn't even take personal responsibility for an unspecified number of his own children.

For now: out of the frying pan, into the burns unit. Last month, before Johnson belatedly got around to announcing the national lockdown in a Halloween performance of quite terrifying ineptitude, over 50% of England was in tier 1. When the nation 'emerges' four weeks later, it'll be more like 1%. Boris Johnson has 99 problems, but the Isles of Scilly ain't one. Almost the entire country will now be in the toughest two tiers – which are themselves not the tiers you might have known and loved the first time round. There have been 'modifications'. Furthermore, there is the situation of areas such as Kent, which went into this lockdown in tier 1 but which Johnson has deemed will come out of it into an even harsher version of tier 3. Like Taylor Swift's, his tiers ricochet.

It is fair to say the reaction to yesterday's announcements is widespread WTF-ery. If you are able to follow all the news obsessively, these latest developments might not come as a shock. Since the beginning of our plague year, Johnson's failure to grasp any of the nettles at any of the moments they needed to be grasped has arguably long set us up for a bleak midwinter. And a bleak early winter, and a bleak late winter.

There's a reason the Office for Budget Responsibility places the UK on the naughty step of charts comparing not just European death tolls but also economic damage, despite the country having had to endure some of the most stringent restrictions in the continent. And it's not because it's 'just one of those things'. Johnson's government has fallen between every stool. Worse, they were so hell-bent on not having to learn from the first wave via any sort of inquiry that many of the mistakes have since been repeated in the second wave. If there is a third wave, expect yet another runout for all your favourites.

As I say, lots of hyper-engaged people may already feel they knew what 'the end of lockdown' would look like. If, however, your main preoccupation has been with keeping your head/business/life above water, you might have taken a very different signal from the government over the past few weeks, when you've had a second to pay attention. You might have assumed that the thing which followed the lockdown would be – how to put this? – less lockdowny. You might have assumed, what with all the deceptive performative fussing over Christmas and so on, that we would return on 2 December to something better than what we left on 4 November. You might even remember Johnson's successive promises to 'turn the tide' in 12 weeks (March) and a 'return to normality by Christmas' (July).

Alas, all of these little white lies are a function of Johnson's character. From the very start of this pandemic, the prime minister has confirmed he is temperamentally unsuited to delivering bad news. Instead, he has opted to deliver bad news hopelessly belatedly and good news self-defeatingly prematurely. The effect is to make people feel constantly cheated, even when the news is better than might have been expected, had their expectations been managed more fairly or reasonably. Hence why, up and down the country today, people feel led up the garden path. If they watched Thursday's Downing Street press conference, they will know to expect more of the same as we move forward. No sooner had Johnson explained how your tier wasn't your destiny than the chief medical officer for England, Chris Whitty, explained that even the new tier 2 would only hold infections level. Tier 1 would result in a rise.

Naturally, there is a certain irony in seeing Tory MPs who voted for Johnson now outraged to discover that he won't tell them the truth. Had you given a look to camera this morning every time an MP said something like, 'The prime minister needs to be straight with people,' you'd have had whiplash before breakfast.

Much worse are the ones still quietly making excuses for his character failings, like he's some special case. Even at his lectern, Johnson seems to cast himself as the chorus to events, as opposed to the guy who decrees them. All the sighs and the winces and the 'I wishes' – we are forever being encouraged to see things as happening to the prime minister, as opposed to at his behest. He lacks the leadership qualities required to own his response.

No doubt his last defenders would claim that Johnson is simply giving people hope. If so, then he is demonstrably going the wrong way about it. Johnson has become a specialist in dashing hopes falsely raised (by him). Yet hope is hugely important, now more than at any time this past year, and a better leader – even an adequate one – should be able to inspire without misleading.

Alas, Johnson continues to confuse giving people hope with placating them with fibs, only to let them down later, like he was always going to have to anyway. The pattern is not unfamiliar. There are women in several London postcodes to whom the prime minister once gave hope, only it later turned out he had been making false promises. Hang on to your lunch, but perhaps we're all those women now. We expect him to do this; we expect him to do that. So we became hopeful, after a fashion. When the time comes, of course, Boris Johnson doesn't think he can be reasonably expected to do the things he suggested he could – indeed, he protests that he never really suggested them anyway.

So, yes, this is the way he has always been. At the time of the leadership election, there were all sorts of open-minded Tories who voted for Johnson, apparently convinced the personal was not political. That was a misapprehension. Your tier might not be your destiny – but in his job, your character always is.

BILLIONAIRES: THE BEST OF US

If money's just a way of keeping score, then these guys represent the greatest winners on earth – and perhaps beyond. Certainly, a disproportionate number of them wish to leave our planet in their various spaceships and shuttles, a one-way journey we should all feel able to get powerfully behind. Wait – what? It's a return ticket? Oh. Well, that puts a very different light on things. How about they can re-enter Earth's atmosphere only if they pay full local taxes wherever they operate?

Dry eyes and an absent A-list as the new zeitgeist jettisons Philip Green

26 October 2018

Sexual harassment and bullying allegations may signal the end of an era for the Hawaiian-shirted colossus

'He reminds me of one of those guys from the 30s,' Simon Cowell once reflected of his friend Philip Green. 'Louis Mayer . . .' Ain't that the truth. When a couple of thousand people attended the Hollywood funeral of one of those other guys from the 1930s, Columbia Pictures' Harry Cohn, the comedian Red Skelton twinkled: 'It only proves what they always say – give the public what they want to see and they'll come out for it.' Sam Goldwyn made a similar comment about Mayer's funeral, but that one is thought to be apocryphal. For all his decades of unassailability, very few people attended the former MGM mogul's send-off.

I wonder if it will be the same for Sir Phil, whose legendary parties were once graced by the international A-list of his close personal friends: your Leonardo DiCaprios, your Kate Hudsons, your Gwyneth Paltrows. Until they weren't. Certainly, it feels that there isn't a wet eye in the kingdom at news that Green has been named in parliament as the businessman described by the *Daily Telegraph* as the subject of multiple sexual harassment and bullying allegations.

Though Peter Hain used parliamentary privilege to name the Arcadia retail tycoon in the House of Lords, it must be stressed that the original injunction against the *Telegraph* still holds, and these are merely allegations. As for allegations of what, over to the eye-catching release put out by Green himself on Thursday evening.

'To the extent that it is suggested that I have been guilty of unlawful sexual and racist behaviour,' this ran, 'I categorically and wholly deny these allegations.' As a shut-it-all-down statement, that does rather tend towards the intriguing. The *Telegraph* alleged 'immoral or reprehensible behaviour by someone in a position of power'. No one said anything about 'unlawful' – at least, not until Phil did. Furthermore, to which adjectives does that 'unlawful' apply? Clearly, he is denying he has been guilty of unlawful sexual behaviour; but is he denying he has been guilty of just unlawful racism, or of all racism, whatever that may be? We must hope Sir Phil breaks his silence again soon to clarify. Until then, we have only his recent utterances to go on. 'Am I a racist?' he demanded rhetorically this summer. 'The fact is that I've had a black chauffeur for the past 12 years.'

Naturally, Green's is unlikely to be the only rearguard action against the mushrooming fallout. The flighty celebrity class, who took all his hospitality (despite not being what anyone remotely normal would class as proper friends), will soon be rushing to distance themselves from their former host, even more than they did after BHS went tits-up. Expect the first 'Well, I'd heard the rumours' interviews within the week. Darling, there are off-gridders in the Andromeda galaxy who'd heard the rumours. Your mission is to convince us you somehow hadn't heard them when you were pictured in a PG60 T-shirt at his 60th birthday jolly to Cancún. Do you remember? There was a beach barbecue, at which the Beach Boys played.

It was once said that Louis B. Mayer was the greatest actor on the MGM lot, and there was always something of the dissembling showman to Green. A former boarding-school boy, his was a riches-to-even-more-riches story, and not the rags-to-riches one his barrow-boy persona appeared to imply. I am sure he would counter this hotly by saying that he built up a great British business. Except it's mostly owned by his wife, who lives in Monaco for tax reasons.

People say politics is showbiz for ugly people; Green treated retail as showbiz for people too ugly for politics. A shameless starstrucker, if you will, he rode the crest of that mid-noughties wave when it seemed the chatterati's only subject was celebrity. Or maybe celebrity and Islamist terrorism. You'd probably give the latter a look-in. Either way, it now feels as though the 2008 financial crash will be judged the more seismic event of its decade, and not 9/11, as people long thought. But the crash's impact was harder to read – indeed, it was misread and ignored for a long time – and turbo-capitalists such as Green were feted considerably longer than they might otherwise have been. Seemingly unaware he was on borrowed time, he bestrode the end of an era like a Hawaiian-shirted colossus.

There were the impossibly lavish parties, at which the theme always seemed to be *Après moi, le déluge*. But it was Green's decision to hire the zeitgeist supermodel Kate Moss to design for Topshop that turned him into one of a handful of household-name businessmen. He drank deeply of his own hype and soon formed a new and intense friendship with Simon Cowell, the leading impresario of the reality TV golden age – an age immediately succeeded by one in which the biggest reality star of that period now sits in the White House.

Given the boggling achievements of Donald Trump, Green and Cowell's own plans for domination now seem a timid failure of the imagination. But back then they were talked of as 'the new Disney'. There were reports they were going to buy ITV. There would be theme parks. They were going to make Caesar's Palace in Las Vegas the permanent global home of *The X Factor*. 'You have 20, 30, 40 million people tuning in twice a week,' explained Green to a journalist between bites of something or other. 'You bring two or three hundred million viewers to a venue – off we go! It's taking it up a peg. The rest of the world is part two.'

Only the terminally shallow could possibly have been convinced by him – and thus it was that one of David Cameron's early acts after becoming prime minister was to make Green his 'efficiency tsar'. (No one appointed more tsars than Cameron; if only there was some historical metaphor there for what ended up happening later.) Even as tax protesters – perhaps we should call them 'efficiency Bolsheviks' – were preparing to invade Green's Topshop stores to demonstrate against his tax avoidance, Green was farting out his official report into government waste. It was very simple, he thought, as such men often do. 'If I ran my business like this,' he scoffed, 'the lights would be out.'

And we shall come to BHS later. Back now to his report, in which Sir Phil concluded that the vast and complex apparatus of the state was basically just analogous to retail and could be fixed by such tactics as paying suppliers late. He also, somewhat amusingly, called for 'a mandate for centralised procurement'. So perhaps he was a bit of an unwitting Marxist after all. He wanted Alan Sugar to be the government's central procurer, incidentally.

But fortune's wheel was itching to turn. By the time of his 65th birthday – with BHS sold for a quid to some chancer, and a huge hole in its pension scheme – Philip Green's once-stellar party guestlist had been commuted down to Vernon Kay and Mike Ashley.

And that was mostly all we heard from Phil for a while – until just three weeks ago, when it seems he spotted an agreed promotion in his Oxford Street Topshop for an anthology of feminist writing and ordered it to be immediately torn down. In the light of events, perhaps that sort of lashing out would be best glossed by a psychoanalyst. One can only sketch the imaginary script for the notional encounter, but I am picturing the analyst saying: 'Soooo . . . . . . in the midst of spending a reported £500,000 on lawyers trying to suppress stories about your treatment of employees, you spied a small display to feminism in one of your stores. How did that make you feel?' At which point Phil might grope for his answer, and the shrink might ask: 'And why do you think that is?'

Why indeed? Certainly, he seemed to have had quite enough of the #MeToo movement earlier this year, judging by his comments to his unauthorised biographer Oliver Shah. 'Where's all this going to end?' Green wondered. Difficult to say. But if any future movie-maker wanted a way into so many of the biggest cross-currents of the age, they could do worse than alight on Sir Phil as a central character. It wouldn't be the adoring immortalisation he has always felt his achievements deserve. But for the public, it would be one way of recovering some of their costs.

Kylie Jenner: who'd want to be a matte lip billionaire?

7 March 2019

The 'self-made' littlest Kardashian has built a gigantic business in four years – but hate the game, not the playas

News that *Forbes* has named Kylie Cosmetics founder Kylie Jenner the youngest-ever billionaire at 21 has provoked fury and merriment in sadly unequal measure. I'm not going to get into the usual turbocapitalist caveats today – this is, let's face it, a showbiz column. But as an avowed Team Merriment member, I am all in favour of any business plan that just DARES anyone over the age of 30 to get it.

This is easily the most brilliant Kylie Jenner story since this time last year, when the littlest *Kardashians* star wiped $1.3bn off Snapchat stock with a single tweet suggesting she wasn't really feeling the app's new redesign. If you missed these deathless 18 words, they ran: 'Sooo does anyone else not open Snapchat anymore? Or is it just me . . . ugh this is so sad.' To repeat: ONE POINT THREE BILLION DOLLARS WIPED OFF.

But back to this week's news, and the attendant reminder that there will always be middle-aged haters. If your response to learning that someone built a billion-dollar business, in four years, out of a matte lip product is to gnash your teeth, then it's too late for you. You hate the playas, not the game. You have become old in the absolute dreariest of ways. There's no way back now. You're not going to end up as one of those senior citizens people describe as 'young at heart', or who have younger friends who find them fascinating and amusing and open-minded and who long to be in their company. You are going to be 'that guy'. And, yes, I instinctively feel you are a guy.

Watching the backlash, *Forbes* felt moved to clarify its assessment criteria with a statement on Wednesday. 'To be clear,' this went, '*Forbes* defines "self-made" as someone who built a company or established a fortune on her own, rather than inheriting some or all of it.' The publication has deemed this necessary as a key objection seems to be the description of Jenner as a 'self-made billionaire', on the basis that she derived some kind of familial benefit from the Kardashian brand (est. 2003). Well, of course.

But I'm not sure why, for a certain type, this is abhorrent in Kylie Jenner but admirable and almost confusingly arousing in the case of Rupert Murdoch, say, or Donald Trump. Both of these gentlemen inherited a huge amount from their fathers, who were already well established in the businesses into which the sons would follow. Why should they be idolised for what they did with familial advantage, but Jenner regarded as just a little madam who's no better than she should be? I can't think. But I expect to put my finger on it in due course.

In the meantime, we must always remember those analyses that suggest Trump would be as rich or richer than he is now if he had simply put the money he inherited from his daddy in an index-linked fund. Ought we really, then, to refer to Trump as a 'self-made billionaire'? In the circumstances, 'self-curtailed billionaire' might be more accurate. In some ways, Trump reminds me of the supposed mogul in *The Big Lebowski*, of whom his infinitely brighter daughter eventually remarks: 'No, no, the wealth is all mother's. We let him run one of the companies very briefly, but he didn't do very well at it.'

Perhaps the moral superiority of Trump and Murdoch lies in the fact that they did such lovely things with their money, while Jenner's lipliner that seriously won't bleed all day is judged ultimately too historically toxic and culturocidal to celebrate. In the manner you would revere, say, Fox News or the Trump presidency.

Much of the Kardashian output is not to my tastes, but tastes are beside the point. The Kardashians represent plenty of the troubling currents of the age – but they certainly didn't create them. This entire era for the family started with Kim being exploited by a man who sold her sex tape – and has ended with the ladies of the family bestriding . . . bestroding? . . . bestraddling an entire entertainment and retail empire. I don't know if they have purchased a family motto yet, but I would go with whatever is the Latin for: 'If you sexually humiliate us, we will do this with it.'

The Kardashian plotlines never do a lot for me, but the characters are magnificent in their way. I recoil-marvel at Kardashian materfamilias Kris Jenner, the world's hardest woman and the most assiduous Mother Ten Per Cent to all her girls. I often try to imagine the atomic female energy levels in the notional Kardashian mansion, into which wandering traveller Kanye West has somehow stumbled. (A bit like William Holden at the start of *Sunset Boulevard* – but a lot more out of his depth.) The readouts must be off the scale. With the level of it Kanye is exposed to on a daily basis, is it any wonder West's public outpourings have mutated from standard creative twattery to such things as calling for the amendment abolishing slavery to be repealed? Sleeping in a Kardashian house is like sleeping next to the Infinity Stones. You don't know what the radiation is going to do, but I think it's completely reasonable to expect that at the very least it would literally alter your DNA.

The other criticism of Kylie Jenner's story so far is that she is the very antithesis of the supposedly wholesome Horatio Alger myth that sustained American readers back in the good old days. If you don't know Horatio Alger, he was a late-19th-century author who penned many novels in which teenage heroes rose from poverty to 'respectability' through hard work and clean living. (Alger himself was financially imprudent and almost certainly a paedophile, but that's one for another day.) He updated his template over time to suit the changing tastes and desires of the public to whom he was trying to appeal – as did authors who came after him. The Alger hero became a literary type who by the mid-20th century was no longer making the journey from rags to respectability but from rags to riches. Meteoric rises were in.

Adjusted for inflation, then, I think it perfectly – perfectly! – conceivable that were Alger still somehow writing today, his protagonist might be a young, hypersexualised, athleisure-wearing woman who took her company from nought to a billion dollars by sheer force of, like, will? – and a refusal to be afraid to rethink the medium stippling brush. Alger was, after all, trying to appeal to a market.

In fact, Alger's novel *Tattered Tom* has a female protagonist, of whose susceptibility to the superficial the author seems decidedly in favour. 'Good clothes exert more influence upon the wearer than we might at first suppose,' he explains at one point. 'And so it was with Tom.' And so, perhaps, with Jenner, whose understanding of just what a 12-shade bronzing palette can do for a wearer is arguably not so abhorrently different.

Richard Branson's bailout plea proves there's no one more shameless

21 April 2020

Eyeing up the public purse from distant shores, Britain's Best-Loved Businessman™ is truly one of the global super-elite

Motorboating enthusiast Richard Branson is playing a particularly idiosyncratic game of Monopoly. He would like to mortgage his private Caribbean island. In return, you, the taxpayer, have to buy him Mayfair and Park Lane, all the greens, all the yellows, all the reds, and stick a hotel on every one of them. Also, if Richard lands on Super Tax or Income Tax, he doesn't pay them. And if he gets the Community Chest card saying 'Pay hospital fees', he refuses and sues the hospital. The only bright side is that he no longer operates out of any of the stations.

But perhaps we're getting ahead of ourselves. By way of a recap, the tycoon is seeking a reported £500m government bailout of his Virgin Atlantic airline, and has stated in a blogpost that he is willing to put Necker Island up as collateral to secure lending for his businesses.

Without wishing to ask the cursory amount of questions, is this the same island that seems to get virtually destroyed every couple of years? I do believe it is. So . . . nice try, hotshot. This feels like being offered the chance to underwrite Richard Hammond's car insurance. A quick archive trawl confirms that Necker has in recent years been struck by both a devastating fire and a devastating hurricane – which, if I were religious, would probably make me think God was a guy who believed in paying UK income tax. Either way, offering up Necker is arguably the most WTF-tinged piece of collateral action since that late-1980s moment when Australian entrepreneur Alan Bond bought Van Gogh's *Irises* at Sotheby's, using a loan from Sotheby's, for which the painting itself was collateral. Confused? Don't worry; the short version is that it ended badly, in a number of ways.

But back to the present day and Britain's Best-Loved Businessman™. You will note that there has been some debate as to whether the pandemic is quite the moment for a man who once sued the NHS, and who has not paid income tax in this country for 14 years, to request a taxpayer bailout. The way Richard sees it, judging by his lengthily defensive blogpost on Monday, is that he's lifted so many people up. And he has. Mainly women – and bodily. The sheer volume of archive photos of a guffawing Branson carrying some stilettoed lovely, usually in water, makes it a genre all of its own. If he ends up being unable to fly passengers, I almost feel he could personally heft every single one of Earth's promotions girls across the oceans, like an alarmingly veneered St Christopher.

'As you know,' Richard's appeal for funds continues, 'creating positive social and environmental impact has always been at the heart of this brand.' Richard? Richard? IT'S AN AIRLINE. I guess the galaxy-brained question is: can our rapidly heating planet afford NOT to bail it out? While you ponder that, I'd direct you to Richard's recent assertion that aviation will be carbon neutral 'sooner than we realise'. And I'd encourage you to speculate on how soon it will be before Richard requests UK or US bailout money for his Virgin Galactic enterprise, where space travel has been 'set to be a reality next year' for a good 12 years now.

Ultimately, it's hard to see Branson as anything other than the classic 'billionaire philanthropist' (is there any other kind of billionaire?) who declines to accept that the public finances would be in rather better shape if people like them contributed their fair share. Forgive me for repeating myself, but philanthropy starts with paying tax. With the best will in the world, it isn't enough to imply the only reason you operate out of a tax haven is because you like the weather.

Of course, Richard is very far from the only billionaire entity to act like this. Even the trillionaire firms, Amazon and Apple, do it too. Rather than contribute the full amount to various countries in the traditional way – like all the boring little nurses and teachers and ordinary people do – they get away with the absolute barest of minimums, then swoop in flashily with 'aid' initiatives, with which they can be personally associated when something's gone tits-up.

Take announcements from the likes of Apple CEO Tim Cook, who has made much of the fact that the company has donated millions of protective masks to US healthcare workers, but whose firm paid £3.8m in tax on UK sales of £1.2bn not so long ago. (And this is before you even get to the Amnesty reports and lawsuits, in which they are accused of aiding often lethal child labour in their cobalt supply chains in places like the Democratic Republic of the Congo. Can the kids get a mask, Tim? No? OK, final offer: a trowel instead of a stick?)

Instead of the coronavirus crisis bringing some kind of reckoning for tax-avoiding opt-outs, it is simply making the biggest culprits even more shameless. We look likely to be obliged to knit the tech firms ever more tightly into the fabric of our states, for instance, via tracing apps and the data-based arm of any exit strategy. Meanwhile, they are accused of using the pandemic to weasel out of what relatively little they already owe. Last week, industry lobby group TechUK – which represents firms including Apple, Amazon, Facebook and Google – announced that the government should 'look again' at the new 2% digital services tax and delay liability for a year to give these firms some 'breathing space'.

Well, of all the metaphors to go for right now . . . Let's hope they manage to catch a breath, even as they look guaranteed to emerge from the pandemic vastly richer and more powerful than before. For Branson, the days of being able to just style it out may be numbered.

The question every politician should be asking is: what does Mark Zuckerberg want with us?

19 February 2021

His fight with the Australian government is about more than Facebook and news – it's about the pursuit of power in a world where companies are stronger than countries

You can say Mark Zuckerberg puts you in mind of a lot of things. An e-fit of a man police would like to speak to in connection with supermarket food tampering. A pink and overscrubbed supervillain – Lex Loofah – or the classical bust of a Roman emperor who's paused the rollout of his hair feature and lists his hobbies as 'flaying' and 'indifference'.

Ultimately, though, the most alarming way of looking at the Facebook boss is just factually: he's the world's most powerful oligarch, selling the lives of 2.7 billion monthly active users to advertisers and actually modifying the behaviour of those users with a business model that deliberately amplifies incendiary, nasty and frequently fake and dangerous things because that's what keeps you on his platform longer. So, yes: considering all that, it's just a comforting cop-out to say, 'Ooh, Zuckerberg looks like the character in a movie who's just delivered the line "Leave no trace of the village."' Forget post-truth. Mark's basically post-metaphor.

Anyway, Zuckerberg is in the news along with News Corp boss Rupert Murdoch, in a heartwarming generational fight between billionaires for who gets to say: 'I'm not IN the news, shithead – I OWN the news.' In short, Murdoch (and other news publishers) have long demanded Facebook and Google pay for people linking to or discussing their content on their platforms, or including it in search results. Facebook and others have long resisted.

Having failed to thrash out the issue in the thrashing yurt at various barefoot mogul retreats, Murdoch effectively instructed the Australian government to shake down the tech firms to pay publishers for the sharing of links, or else stop allowing the practice. Yes, here he comes, Monty Burns-Unit, absolutely refusing to allow the trident to be prised from his claw by the Valley bros. This week, Google chucked him some undisclosed loose change just to shut him up, but Zuckerberg refused, turning off news sharing in Australia and removing most Australian media from his platforms, as well as pages run by state health departments, charities and others. Alas, there is an outcry, with the publishers seemingly not wanting the thing they said they wanted any more. It's one of those fights where you're rooting for the asteroid to end it.

Of course, Facebook is the galactic leader in PR crises. Over the company's short, unimaginably powerful existence, it has made so many monstrous cock-ups and on such grand scales that it seems reasonable to predict the full collapse of human civilisation will be immediately succeeded by a Facebook statement containing the words: 'We know we have more work to do.' It'll probably have been drafted by Nick Clegg, whose political endpoint was always going to be donning Earth's last crew-necked sweater and doing comms for the apocalypse.

There is widespread outrage around the world over what's happened in Australia, particularly from politicians still fighting the last war, specifically the one against Murdoch. Here's some free BREAKING NEWS, guys: you lost that one. And given the scale of your newer foe, well . . . the tech companies have grown so far past the stage at which, say, oil companies were broken up, or inquiries into Microsoft begun, that humanity should probably stick a fiver on you losing this one too.

The true tragedy, of course, is that these guys have so much in common. Rupert Murdoch recently received the Covid vaccination, which I read on Zuckerberg's platform means he's been injected with Bill Gates, a line of medical inquiry I hope to see enthusiastically taken up by anti-vax-adjacent Tucker Carlson on Murdoch's own Fox News. Can people this ideologically similar really be so far apart? Let's hope they can still put their differences aside to form some sort of Injustice League.

As for the rest of us, it's hard being told how beautiful it is to connect by Zuckerberg, whose smile hasn't connected with his eyes since 2014. If friends are so important to our common goals, how come he doesn't have any? Maybe commodifying friendship gives Mark the excuse for not partaking in it. You don't see crack dealers using their own product, as the saying goes.

People often claim you're frozen developmentally at the time you become famous, which presumably stunts Zuckerberg back at the stage he was in his Harvard dorm room. I can't believe a product created to rate women has ended up as what the business professor and tech commentator Scott Galloway calls 'the biggest prostitute of hate in the history of mankind'. Honestly, what were the chances?

In her book *The Boy Kings*, Katherine Losse chronicles her time at Facebook, from being one of the firm's earliest employees to eventually becoming the person Zuckerberg appoints to write in his voice. Losse's job was to impart Mark's thoughts on 'the way the world was going' to the company and the wider public. When I read the book, it was hard not to deem his personal philosophy non-existent. It's like he's never thought about anything, ever, other than computer science and personal power.

Naturally, Zuckerberg orders Losse to watch *The West Wing*. This was a while ago, of course, and it wasn't quite four years ago that Zuckerberg embarked on a US listening tour, taking in 'little people' locations like Iowa truck stops. This was widely interpreted as the start of a long run-up at a traditional presidential campaign. We haven't heard a lot of that talk recently, but it seems reasonable to believe that Zuckerberg has since realised the president is very much junior personnel – something Murdoch understood decades ago, as far as Australian and UK prime ministers were concerned. Never mind truck stops being for little people. Politics is for little people.

Of course, Zuckerberg is sometimes required to visit Washington and attend hearings, occasions for which Nick Clegg dresses the normally T-shirted statesman as the reluctant teenage best man at his mother's third wedding. But as he accrues more and more unprecedented global power, the question every single politician should be asking themselves, like, yesterday, is: what does Mark Zuckerberg want with us? They should have clicked long ago that he isn't remotely interested in news as an idea or service. In 2016, Zuckerberg summarily fired the team that curated 'trending' news topics and replaced them with an algorithm that promptly began pushing fabricated news, as well as a video of a man wanking with a McChicken Sandwich.

One of several essays Zuckerberg instructed Losse to write in his voice was 'Companies Over Countries'. She resigned without completing it, but not before having asked him if he could expand on the slogan. 'I think we are moving to a world in which we all become cells in a single organism,' came Mark's mild reply, 'where we can communicate automatically and can all work together seamlessly.' Wow. A vision of our future that has me immediately paging Morpheus. Was Murdoch . . . was Murdoch actually the blue pill all along?

In space, nobody can hear Jeff Bezos.
So can Richard Branson go too?

11 June 2021

News that the Amazon overlord is about to jet off has got the Virgin boss clamouring to get there first. You can do it, Richard!

It's famously impossible to take a bathroom break during a rocket launch, meaning Jeff Bezos will soon experience what it's like to be one of his warehouse workers. Or, as the Amazon boss put it last week: 'To see the Earth from space . . changes your relationship with humanity.' That's hugely encouraging. I feel like we're just one successful interstellar-wormhole-mission-to-a-distant-galaxy away from allowing employees to unionise.

Anyway, along with his brother, Mark, and an auction winner (bidding has passed the $4m mark), Bezos is headed for space next month – or at least for the edge of it. Kind of like the ring road of space, which is home to a thin atmosphere, two discount carpet shops and a powerful sense that you just mic-dropped the entire tax avoiders' WhatsApp group. Bezos announced that he'd be riding in his Blue Origin rocket via a mildly alarming video last week, in which a camera crew films a perfectly lit, remorselessly off-the-cuff chat between him and his brother. 'I really want you to come with me,' ad-libs Jeff to Mark. 'I think it would be meaningful.'

And why not? I trust the Bezos brothers have a normal, healthy sibling relationship, allowing Mark to use up their entire three minutes of zero gravity contemplating the big questions, such as: 'Remember when you cracked my head open?'; 'Did you know Mom messaged me last night to confirm I'm the favourite child?'; 'Someone who wants a space-wedgie says what?'; and 'Would you call your general look "Vin Diesel after dioxin poisoning"?'

But enough of the bros. Needless to say, my first thought on reading this news was: poor Richard Branson. Just think how long Britain's Best-Loved Businessman™ has been threatening to give us a 10-minute break by going into space. His Virgin Galactic operation has basically been issuing announcements that commercial space travel is 'set to become a reality next year' since seemingly around 1986. How dare Bezos pull this shit? It must have felt a lot like this when people started buying their U2 CDs from Amazon instead of a Virgin Megastore.

And yet it seems all is not lost for the Virgin boss, whose most notable recent appearance was popping up last year to ask for a bailout for his airline, on the basis that 'creating positive social and environmental impact has always been at the heart of this brand'. (To which the only possible reply was: it's an AIRLINE, you preposterous chancer.) Imagine my mirth to read, just days after the Bezos announcement, a report that Virgin Galactic is now scrambling to send Branson up on a suborbital flight two whole weeks before the Amazon overlord.

But of course. Of COURSE Richard can't cope with being the galactic Salieri to Bezos's galactic Mozart. I've said it before, but I'll say it again: men are incredible! As is the 21st century. It's wild to see the complex aspirations and vast rivalries of the 20th-century space race basically reduced now to a willy-waver between two taxophobic billionaires whose personality is 'disliking ties'.

As for whether the rumours are true, Virgin has declined to deny the report, saying gnomically: 'At this time, we have not determined the date of our next flight.' But if Branson were to galactically gazump Bezos, it would surely serve as a tribute to the awesome pettiness of humankind. I'm sorry – of mankind.

Not that there wouldn't be a woman involved, I'm sure. You always need at least one to serve as a prop in the obligatory picture of Richard guffawing away while carrying a lady in his arms. (Then again, in zero gravity women don't even need men to lift them up, which leaves us with one unavoidable philosophical question: in space, what is the point of Richard Branson?)

Clearly, the true banter option would be for fellow space-racer Elon Musk to somehow pop up above the Kármán line around the middle of next week, simply using the location as the backdrop for one of his cryptocurrency insults. But, failing that, the only way the whole race could be more dignified is if Branson himself bought the Blue Origin auction ticket, forcing Bezos to take him along at the same time, with the era-defining footage beamed back to Earth simply featuring the two billionaires attempting to pinch and scratch each other in slow motion, soundtracked with the historic words 'Not in the face! Not in the face!'

Jeff Bezos is on a quest for eternal life; back on Earth, we're searching for Amazon's taxes

10 September 2021

The tech overlord is reportedly investing in age reversal, which means so much more than a fair contribution to the UK's finances

On the one hand, it makes huge sense for Jeff Bezos to pour millions into a company seeking the secret to eternal life. Karmic reincarnation may only be an outside possibility. But Jeff should hedge against the likelihood that under that scenario, he's coming back as a Yemeni woman.

Further developments in fauxlanthropy for the Amazon overlord, then, who has decided that death is as inevitable as taxes. Which is to say: not at all inevitable for the likes of him. Bezos was this month reported to be a significant investor in Altos Labs, an age-reversal firm which is on the scientific quest for immortality. Among other expansions, it is thought the firm will now open a lab within the UK, which I think you'll agree means so much more to our nation than a fair tax contribution from Amazon. You know we'd only spend that shit on social care or the NHS or something, when Jeff can see it's far better to get people on ordinary incomes to pay extra for all that, so that guys like him are freed up to splurge their money on Earth's most preposterous midlife crises. How else to interpret the fact that this eternal-life news emerged in the very week it was revealed that despite Amazon UK's sales increasing by £1.89bn last year, the firm paid just £3.8m more corporation tax?

Anyway, you'll be aware that the old immortality game is already being played by a number of other tech bros, from Google co-founder Larry Page to Peter Thiel, both of whom have siphoned serious millions into the idea that 'death is a problem that can be solved'. Other figures have been linked to firms investigating the benefits of transfusing yourself with the blood of someone younger and poorer (I paraphrase, but only slightly).

Indeed, as he ascended to the astral plane of gazillionaire retirement this year, Bezos quoted Richard Dawkins in his farewell email to Amazon shareholders. 'Staving off death is a thing that you have to work at,' they learned. 'If living things don't actively work to prevent it, they would eventually merge with their surroundings and cease to exist as autonomous beings. That is what happens when they die.'

Far better to live on indefinitely – probably in a vast Lalique test tube – than to log off earthly existence and risk entry to the notional next world, where Bezos could easily be subject to retributive divine justice for all eternity. Or for the time it takes to get a call-back from Amazon customer service. Whichever is longer.

As for his other hedges, experience shows us that Bezos loves to make splashy charity announcements at times when he senses a kind of planetary disdain being levelled at him. A couple of months ago, he got straight off his little space rocket and declared that he'd be graciously parting with $200m to launch some new initiative called the Courage and Civility award, which will reward 'unifiers and not vilifiers', and 'never ad hominem attacks'. What can you say, other than: well, I should hope so, sir! To put things into perspective, Bezos's wealth increased by $13bn on the single calendar day before he popped to the edge of space for four minutes. Even allowing for the $5.5bn he'd spent on getting his space operation to that point, giving away a couple of hundred million dollars is the equivalent of someone on the average UK salary parting with about £1.30 for charity. It feels insufficiently ad hominem to suggest that Jeff is showing his arse; better to point out that you can actually see that arse from space.

Then again, he has long tended towards what Charles Dickens called 'telescopic philanthropy' – a convenient focus on faraway 'good causes', as opposed to the ones on his own doorstep which he could fix pretty much immediately. Incredible, really, that a man who steadfastly refused to pay so many of his workers a living wage could ever publicly utter the words: 'The only way that I can see to deploy this much financial resource is by converting my Amazon winnings into space travel.' Yet here we are.

It's best to think of Bezos as Phony Stark, the kind of off-brand superhero who could only be thrown up by a planet seemingly incapable of rising to the challenge of itself. We must hope the boffins do manage to grant him eternal life. At his current rate of personal growth, it feels like it will take Jeff that long to work out that charity begins on his home planet – and that philanthropy starts with paying tax.

2021: STOP ME IF YOU'VE HEARD THIS ONE BEFORE

Having catastrophically failed to take seriously the exact same thing he catastrophically failed to take seriously last time, the prime minister is forced to impose another lengthy lockdown as British citizens continue to die in their tens of thousands from Covid-19. The Conservatives continue to poll so exuberantly at around the 40% mark that it seems perfectly sane for the prime minister to order them to torpedo the entire parliamentary standards procedure to save some rulebreaker called Owen Paterson. Party on, people! Indeed, it eventually emerges that Downing Street staff HAD partied on throughout the various lockdowns, even as they imposed hugely severe restrictions to which everyone else was expected to adhere. What does everyone else do for fun? Well, absolutely safe in the knowledge that the age of actual wars has passed, they enjoy participating in the culture wars instead.

Britons want a bit of drama from their leaders – and Keir Starmer isn't serving it

5 February 2021

The lawyerly Labour leader may think the public want calm and competence, but has he met them lately?

Like all desperate thrill-seekers in this interminable lockdown, I was momentarily stirred to hear there were some handbags between Boris Johnson and Keir Starmer in one of parliament's corridors after prime minister's questions on Wednesday. Yes! Action! I briefly imagined the lightning exchange of cash bets as watching MPs behaved much like the hyped-up midnight crowd in one of those underground Chinese insect-fighting contests.

According to some reports, the Labour leader was 'puce' and 'rattled' when he confronted Johnson for accusing him of having called for the UK not to leave the European Medicines Agency. Alas, subsequent accounts featured a Labour MP denying he had had to hold Starmer back – and in any case by that stage the Labour leader had formally apologised for wrongly thinking that Johnson had claimed he had wanted to join the EU's vaccine programme.

Ah well. I guess it's fitting that the Labour leader has finally mildly lost his rag in a misunderstanding over the European Medicines Agency and the EU's vaccine programme. And no doubt he ran the full gamut of emotions from shirty to tetchy. Unfortunately, the fact Starmer had to apologise for having been the one in the muddle guarantees he won't take such a sensationally daring risk ever again.

All of which brings us to the question: where is the British public at with Keir Starmer? Speaking for myself, I would say that I definitely get he can give sober and detailed university lectures in archaeology. But what most of the movie needs to be, if enough people are going to watch it, is him successfully outrunning a massive boulder hurtling down the tunnel after him. Can Keir Starmer outrun a boulder?

As always in the Labour party, any leading man – it's always a man – has to deal with a lot of poison darts being blown at them by their own side. Thus, this week there has been much ranting that Starmer's Labour is planning to do one of those many political phrases I never understand, and 'wrap itself in the flag'. I'd rather it attached itself to some jump leads, but there you go.

That said, not hating your country isn't the deafening alarm bell that Jeremy Corbyn's OnlyFans subscribers seem to think it is. There are a lot of those people still trying to style out the fact that following *an actual nerve agent attack on British soil* their absolute boy literally suggested sending Russia a sample of the aforementioned chemical weapon 'so that they can say categorically one way or the other'. That was one of the moments at which the 2019 electoral bed was shat, and the inability of some to even discuss it, let alone have a serious WTF-laden laugh at it, is one of the reasons they have to fantasise the red wall was lost because of whimsical *Guardian* columns like this one. (I heard they talked of nothing else but my Boris Johnson insults on the doorstep.)

Whether Labour's so-called flag-and-family strategy will work, or even happen, remains to be seen. Either way, Starmer has a tendency to feel like the embodiment of the famously passionless, lawyerly answer Michael Dukakis gave in a 1988 US presidential debate when asked if he'd support the death penalty if his wife Kitty were raped and murdered. Though everyone knew he was against the death penalty, Dukakis's response was immediately held to be so emotionless as to have finished his campaign there and then. I keep wondering if Starmer comes across as another version of that answer.

After all, if the past few years have taught us anything . . . wait, if the past few decades have taught us anything . . . come to that, if a simple trip on the Friday-night bus has taught us anything, it is this: Britain is a majority-nutter nation, and we mostly want to elect politicians with something of the nutter to them. Sorry, but that's the reality.

As a voting body, our longest electoral affections have been reserved for the very biggest nutters. Thatcher and Blair: obvious nutters. Fast-forward to the present day, and Johnson: nutter. The message of the 2016 referendum was the euphoric nutting of David Cameron (non-nutter). In fact, let me posit that the reason Jeremy Corbyn – full nutter – did better than expected against useless anti-nutter Theresa May in 2017 was simply because he WAS full nutter, and the electorate was at some level strangely drawn to that.

Corbyn was always going to fall short, of course, because he was the wrong kind of nutter. He was not a kindred nutter. As for May, her campaign's obsession with control, competence and the avoidance of risk was anathema. She parked the bus (sometimes literally, at campaign events held in empty hangars). Nobody wants to watch that. Certainly, not enough did to prevent the result sealing her eventual fate down the line.

The worry for Labour is that, in its own way, watching Starmer is just like watching May, or maybe José Mourinho without the eye-gouging. Labour's shadow cabinet feels like a back six, or even a back eight. In fact, everyone on the pitch always seems to be tracking back. It's worth bearing in mind that the default preferred metric by which the England football side will always be judged by the fans is: did they play with enough passion? Did they play on even as their head bandage dripped with blood? Do they understand what it 'means' to pull on 'the shirt'?

Given all that, it's hard to surrender fully to Keir Starmer's apparent conviction that what the Great British Public™ are crying out for is calmness and competence, even if that's what we collectively tell the pollsters. I mean, we tell the doctors we drink 14 units a week.

Arguably, then, the riskiest position of all is this conviction that a technocratic dream of adequacy rocks the UK's electoral boat. It's certainly pretty to think so. But hand on heart, I suspect that even when the nutter of the day has cocked it up, what the nutter-addicted people are always really crying out for is just another nutter, a different nutter, a new nutter to bathe us in nostalgia for whichever previous nutters we currently yearn. The dopamine-mainlining era of social media has only turbocharged this. We now demand 20 nutters a news cycle – and get 40.

Or, to transpose this one into another arena entirely, have you seen the epic parish council meeting video that went viral this week? No doubt the Handforth parish council's many factional-isms and furies have still to play out, but I fear I can tell you right now who's ultimately going to lose the battle over whatever it is they're fighting about: Jackie Weaver. Why? Because she's not a nutter. Listen, I don't make the rules. But it's a long old road – and in a scientific eight out of 10 cases, the nutters inherit the Earth.

Johnson is subdued, but his dog is causing havoc. Are you thinking what I'm thinking?

23 February 2021

Forget the spad wars at No. 10 – the real drama is over Dilyn, the prime minister's sexually incontinent canine

'I won't be buccaneering with people's lives.' I think you dropped an 'any more', prime minister. But hey – let's not tell our sad stories. Last night was the big roadmap-out-of-lockdown press confer-ence, where Boris Johnson looked into our eyes and told us he just wanted to take things slowly. He respects us too damn much for anything else.

I know we're supposed to say, 'Better late than never,' but honestly, there is something slightly galling about being lectured by this guy on the next long weeks and months of serious caution. I'm not saying I want to tear the pants out of it – fine, I want to completely tear the pants out of it – but you can see why the pace of release feels confusingly slow to some people. This, alas, is inevitable when you're governed by a prime minister who doesn't like to set boundaries.

For pretty much the entire pandemic, right up until about 10 minutes ago, Johnson has been the teacher who wants to be cool. You know the type – messes his hair up and calls you 'mate'. High-fives you when you get a right answer but claims that, in many ways, there are no wrong answers. Tells you to call him by his first name. Deals with early speculative breaches in discipline by announcing he's not going to send you to the headmaster, mate, because he comes at this stuff from different angles. Tells you to rip out the introduction to your pandemic textbooks. Insists he's the same as you guys and totally gets what you're going through; in fact, he actually feels it more deeply. Claims to have been expelled from three schools as a teen. Says he hates teaching because he's 'about freedom'. Rides a dirt bike. Raps Cardi B. Chaperones a school trip where 47 pupils die.

So, yes, it was quite the spectacle watching Johnson come through Downing Street's *Sars in their Eyes* double doors and indicate that tonight, Matthew, he was going to play the calm, authoritative setter of boundaries. Sorry, sir, but don't act like you didn't kill half of year 11.

The question on many people's lips – who on earth is this guy and what has he done with Boris Johnson? – made it off the lips of the *Daily Mail*'s political editor, who inquired of the PM: 'What's happened to you? Have you become a gloomster?'

It was at this point that Johnson said the buccaneering thing, and something about 'the crocus of hope', and spring coming 'both literally and metaphorically'. He also claimed that 'if you'd told me a few months ago' he'd be able to unlock at even this pace, then 'I'd have struggled to believe you'. Righto. Was this the few months ago when you were saying it would be normal by Christmas? Or the few months ago when you were refusing to lock down, despite it being blindingly obvious that it was urgent and necessary, and that your failure to do it was going to cost thousands of lives and condemn us to months longer under the restrictions we're in now? Or the even fewer months ago when you were unlocking for Christmas? Or maybe one of the months in between? Or since?

Whichever it was, it's slightly unfortunate that at the same time Downing Street's training and makeover team are wheeling out this new, nerd-adjacent version of Johnson, the backstage machinations of his permanently dysfunctional court are spilling out in public. Disunity in his save-the-union unit has seen two resignations in the past fortnight, with one departed special adviser's allies claiming it was on Carrie Symonds's instructions that Johnson furiously accused him of briefing against Michael Gove. Meanwhile, Johnson appointed unelected Brexit negotiator David Frost as a minister, apparently to stop him from walking too.

Well now. I don't think we can pay the slightest attention to some unelected spads or unelected ministers criticising the prime minister's partner for being unelected.

Much more diverting is all the drama concerning Dilyn the dog, who is reportedly being used by Islington blogger Dominic Cummings 'to fight a proxy war against the PM's fiancée'. I can't believe that (a) a nation run like this has the highest death toll in Europe, and (b) Dominic has time for briefings, having by now surely been snapped up by one of the big Silicon Valley companies.

And yet I read that Cummings reportedly holds a grudge against the Jack Russell cross, after it humped his leg at a No. 10 away day. There is more – much more. The dog is said to have caused expensive damage to Chequers antiques, while according to the *Mail*,

'One visitor claims to have seen Dilyn "mount" a stool made from the foot of an elephant shot by US president Teddy Roosevelt.' A lot going on in that sentence, start to finish.

In the Downing Street garden, Dilyn is said to have cocked his leg on some spad's handbag. 'Dilyn is a much-put-upon animal who in a non-Covid world would have had his balls chopped off long ago,' a No. 10 aide explained to the *Sunday Times*. 'It's not his fault that he is a bit exuberant.' Right. Are we still talking about the dog?

And that was when it hit me. Maybe we're NOT still talking about the dog at all. In a very literal, very metaphorical sense – stay with this – is it possible that Boris Johnson's old larrikin spirit has transferred itself into Dilyn the dog?

Let's look at the evidence. We have a prime minister who suddenly appears vaguely housebroken. Meanwhile, we have a sexually incontinent dog who will fuck anything – even a trophy pouffe, or Dominic Cummings – and who is being extensively briefed against by factions unhappy with his performance. It's surely the classic body-swap comedy: 'When he ingests a plot device, a struggling UK prime minister ends up in the body of his own resourceful and appealing rescue dog – and vice versa!'

Think about it. It's literally (and metaphorically) the only explanation that makes sense. That wild thing you see in the photographs, dragging Johnson round his daily Buckingham Palace runs, is actually Johnson himself. It was Johnson who pissed on the lady's handbag – huge Bullingdon Club energy, let's face it – and it was Johnson who wrecked the Chequers furniture and had it off with an elephant's foot. The creature behind the lectern who's been trained to say 'data not dates' for a chocolate drop is actually Dilyn.

Look, I don't know the trailer line for a paranormal state of affairs that's going to have to divert me till June. 'Becoming a dog made him a man.' 'Can you teach an old prime minister new tricks?' But I do know that these types of movie transformation are always the route to self-examination, radical self-discovery and significantly deeper empathy – which is certainly the other one-way journey the prime minister should currently be embarking upon.

Never mind about the economy, Britain has a new luxury brand – Rishi Sunak

26 February 2021

As pandemic announcements go, the chancellor's second budget can't compete with his Instagram hoodie shots

Exchequer spokesmodel/gyoza-toting architect of Eat Out to Spread It About/the Conservative party's idea of a cool person. Wherever you were before you suddenly became powerfully aware of the existence of Rishi Sunak, it wasn't the place you wanted to be. Possessed of the ability to spark a bull run on cashmere with a single hoodie shot – and curator of a personal brand that could make Matt Hancock kick over a small wastepaper basket in a jealous rage – the chancellor will next week unveil his second budget. Hopefully he'll do it on his Insta Stories, and Conservatives who fail to declare themselves #hereforit will be relieved of the whip.

The many, many Treasury-produced leaks and trailers for the event have included a glossy video package in which Rishi videocalled Gordon Ramsay – or, as the branding had it: 'Rishi Sunak . . . In Conversation . . . With . . . Gordon Ramsay.' 'I am SUPER-excited to see you,' said the chancellor to the poorly rating TV host. 'Thanks for making time for me!' 'You're welcome,' replied Gordon graciously, amazingly managing not to pick Sunak up on the failure to chirp 'Yes, chef!' after his every piece of shit-hot economic advice.

Anyway, even though I tried to let the Rishi × Gordon crossover event relax me like an extremely expensive wellness experience, I couldn't help noticing after a while that this 'video call' was not single-camera. In fact, there was clearly a crew in Ramsay's home, as well as a two-camera unit in Sunak's office. I don't know if you've seen *Broadcast News*, but it felt a lot like the bit where Holly Hunter realises that when William Hurt interviewed the rape victim, he totally staged his weeping cutaway shots. What a ridiculous old cynic. William Hurt, I mean – not Rishi Sunak, who is obviously young and self-effacing. Hand on heart, it's increasingly hard to remember how we managed before multibillion-pound plague announcements were run through the Clarendon filter and finished off with that already iconic 'Rishi Sunak' signature. I wonder if the chancellor appends it to gratitude journal entries or notes left on the fridge for the help. 'Could you pick up my dry cleaning – Rishi Sunak.' 'Peloton engineer coming at 11am – Rishi Sunak.'

A lot of people think the classic self-posted Rishi Sunak image is the one of the chancellor working in his book-lined home study in the aforementioned cashmere hoodie. But it's actually the one he tweeted of himself doing a thumbs-up through the window of a high-end kitchenware shop, accompanied by the words 'I can't wait to get back to the pub . . . and I don't even drink.' Only the least imaginative elements of British society could look at it and think: 'Is this guy . . . is this guy maybe a prat?'

Whether he ever got his pint of kettles is unclear – see also his Nando's. Sunak claimed last summer that the reopening of Nando's was 'the good news we've all been waiting for', but for whatever reason tended to be photographed coming out of private members' clubs in Mayfair instead. But then, he's very clubbable. Not like a seal; just like a guy you want to have around. Take that press conference where he followed Boris Johnson by debuting his new catchphrase: 'Thanks, PM!' This was simply his way of confirming that he is a young, reasonably priced midfield signing who is absolutely without personal ambition and just wants to provide great service to the star striker. 'Thanks, PM!' 'Yes, chef!' That's what a team player looks like.

And you just know a team as close-knit as the Conservatives is rooting for him. I'm imagining some Tory party social mixer back in, say, 2018, where a buoyant Matt Hancock takes pity on this diffident nobody. 'Everything you've heard is true,' I picture him saying to Sunak. 'I DO have my own smartphone app. Take a look.' Sunak takes Hancock's phone and beholds the Matt Hancock app, wearing the genuinely admiring face he might also use for content in which he's shown unboxing a new *Star Wars* figurine. 'Wow,' Rishi grins, 'this is absolutely awesome!' Hancock: 'It's in the App Store and everything.' Sunak, still doing the unboxing face: 'You know what, I was having dinner with Tim Cook the other night. Let me put in a good word for you, see if the algorithm can give you a bump. All about eyeballs, isn't it, mate?' Cut to Hancock, whose eyeballs have turned to carbonite.

So, yes, I want you to know that I'm typing this column in the Rishi Sunak autograph font. But it's so much more than a font; it's a way of putting the best spin on stuff, making it all feel fresh and from the heart – like there's a different way to do things, if you'd only invite it in. In fact, just typing in the Rishi autograph font makes me see how fusty some political traditions are starting to look. Take the one that's endured for more than two decades now, where prime ministerial hopefuls with school-age children have felt obliged to ensure their kids partake of state education. But not our guy – and we have to assume people will admire his choices in that department.

Quite frankly, I don't want to go back to my Arial font, a place of artless phrases such as 'tax raid on pensions' and 'warning shot from Philip Hammond'. So let's just play out on a lightly upbeat positive by declaring that people underestimate Sunak as spectacularly badly as he underestimated the coronavirus for most of last year. Which, when you consider his many underestimations – that optimising for the economy and health were mutually exclusive, that society should be opened prematurely, that people should return to office commutes, that no one needed to quarantine when flying in from abroad, that people should eat out to help out (help out the virus, that is), and that an autumn lockdown was unnecessary – should show you just how very, very underestimated the luxury Rishi Sunak brand is.

Boris Johnson has a text addiction, and it's bad news for all of us

23 April 2021

The leaks of messages between the PM and inventor James Dyson may just be a distraction from the bigger issue: we're led by a man with no self-discipline and a very busy phone

Incredible that Boris Johnson's craziest ex is not actually someone he's had sex with. When you think of the sheer volume of fatal attractions that must be stored in the prime minister's phone, under decoy names like 'James Dyson' and 'Mohammed bin Salman', it seems extraordinary that the biggest bunny-boiler is alleged to be ex-spad Dominic Cummings.

Anyway, speaking of *Fatal Attraction*, you'll have seen the news that undead Cummings is rearing back out of the bath again like Glenn Close, except wearing trackie bums and a T-shirt reading 'My girlfriend – YES I HAVE A GIRLFRIEND – went to Los Alamos National Laboratory and all she got me was this lousy T-shirt'.

According to some concerted briefing efforts by Downing Street, the text-for-access lobbying leaks that have so adorned British public life over the past week are down to none other than the defrocked master strategist we once knew as Otto von Jizzmark. Cummings himself denies it, in a Friday-teatime statement that tends towards the thermonuclear. Just like Princess Di, he won't go quietly. But as one Downing Street source puts it: 'If you join the dots it looks like it's coming from Dom.' Righto. I've joined the dots, and it's just . . . a picture of a cock and balls? Somewhat poorly drawn. Is that what you're getting as well, Superintendent Hastings? 'More than anything,' the No. 10 source says, 'the PM is disappointed and saddened by what Dom has been up to.'

Ooh – 'saddened'. Ooh – 'disappointed'. It's very difficult to see how this government could be more comically grand about being this excruciatingly undignified. I really wouldn't rule out a day in the near future when the Downing Street communications department draws itself up to its full height and intones: 'The prime minister has entered a treatment facility to address issues in the area of sex addiction. It goes without saying that he expects the nation to respect his privacy at this difficult time.'

As I say, are we even totally sure the individual on the other end of Johnson's text exchange is the actual hand-dryer genius James Dyson? It might just be a pseudonym for whichever tech mompreneur/concert trombonist/basic Rixo-shopping Sloane is currently keeping Johnson on the boil. I mean, MAYBE it's a chat about respiratory aids, but maybe it's just some mad sex code. Roughly speaking, the following is what we're dealing with. Dyson, or rather 'Dyson': 'Would you like to see my ventilators?' Johnson, panting in whatever broom cupboard in which he's skiving off a Cobra meeting: 'Oh God yes show me your ventilators.' 'Sadly,' replies 'Dyson', 'you need to remove the tax barriers to see them.' 'I will fix it tomo!' judders the desperate Johnson. Say it. Say it. 'JAMES I AM FIRST LORD OF THE TREASURY.' There you go. Better out than in.

The only statement from Downing Street this week that I actually believe is the denial that cabinet secretary Simon Case ever told Johnson to change his phone number, the PM apparently having had the same one for more than a decade. Very wise advice. That phone's like the ghost containment grid from *Ghostbusters*. If you switch it off, extremely bad things will happen. Even if he's as mediocre a yes-man as he appears, Case will surely have worked out that the phone is basically the safest repository for innumerable entities who are best 'managed' rather than fully ghosted. Attempting to shut down the phone completely could result in a vast release of potentially fatal psychokinetic energy to the Sunday newspapers.

On the other hand, are there really even Chinese walls between the various forms of sleaze? And if so, who paid for the wallpaper on them? You could certainly leave it to Johnson to cross the streams of this week's two biggest news stories – lobbying and football. It emerged that the PM was lobbied by text by Saudi crown prince and human lumberjack Mohammed bin Salman over his family's blocked bid for Newcastle United. Hand on heart, this feels ominous. After all, Amazon boss Jeff Bezos once struck up a WhatsApp relationship with the de facto Saudi ruler, and the next thing he knew the *National Enquirer* had its hands on a cache of text messages and photos of him in his pants. Still, as long as there's nothing incriminating on the phone of Boris Johnson, I'm sure the Saudi crown prince having our prime minister's deets is what the government's shit-eater-in-chief Kwasi Kwarteng could call 'good' for a modern democracy.

As for where we go next with text-for-access, none of it will be good. Today's Cummings angle may be intended to serve as a distraction, but it is increasingly hard to separate Johnson's lifelong lack of standards from his administration's rapid shedding of them. Of COURSE someone as sexually incontinent as Johnson would lead a government as procedurally incontinent as his is, spraying around unmonitored access and promises of procurement favours to whoever's lucky enough to be given the eye.

And yet, a lot of senior government figures seem to take genuine pleasure in pointing at the polls and excusing any amount of obviously questionable behaviour as 'just Boris being Boris'. They're seemingly incapable of grasping that the entire executive taking on the character of this amoral and discipline-free man will end very badly indeed. It is precisely Johnson's lack of discipline and moral courage that has resulted in this country having both the highest Covid death toll in Europe and the most unnecessarily long economic shutdown and loss of essential freedoms. Gloating that the voters don't think they deserve better will not be the recipe for a great British future.

Matt Hancock, the one-time sex cop now busted for a dodgy clinch

25 June 2021

The health secretary once described lockdown-breaking hookups as 'a matter for the police'. After the exposure of his office affair, will he hand himself in?

Sorry, but the only thing I want to see Matt Hancock doing against the back of his office door is sliding down it with his head in his hands. But he can probably bank on not being sacked by Boris Johnson for having an affair. It would be like being sacked by Stalin for being slightly arsey to work with.

Even so, Hancock will be glad that the British Antarctic Territory has been added to the green list, just as he's been added to the shit list. The South Pole suddenly looks well worth packing his bags for. Temperatures are currently minus 87 but feel like minus 108, making it considerably less frosty than any of Matt's current climes.

That said, if Hancock does end up being resigned for this, it would fit with the general twilight mood in the UK's national story. Nothing says 'country that's going to make a massive success of itself' like a guy getting away with contributing to tens of thousands of unnecessary deaths but having to quit for a knee-trembler. It's like getting Al Capone for snogging.

So, then, to the health secretary's 'steamy clinch' with Gina Coladangelo, the lobbyist and long-term friend he took on as an aide last year (though initially did not declare it), and who was subsequently given a paid non-executive directorship at the Department of Health. Footage of this has somehow found its way from Hancock's office security cameras to the front page of the *Sun*, in a WORLD EXCLUSIVE that feels like a major bollock-drop for the newsdesk of the Matt Hancock app. Guys . . . what happened?

Quite how the paper obtained the source material one can only speculate, though I'm suddenly reminded of a quote last April from a Downing Street official, who remarked to the *Sunday Times*: 'There is not much love for Matt Handjob here.' Nor in the Department of Health, perhaps.

In some ways, the only thing you have to remember about Hancock – apart from the app and the parkour and the crying on telly – is that when Prof. Neil Ferguson was discovered to have broken lockdown rules in the conduct of a relationship, Hancock went on TV to fume: 'You can imagine what my views are. It's a matter for the police.' So, yes – a shame to see sex cop Matt Hancock busted for sex crimes. But a reminder that cancel culture always devours its children.

Anyway. To the many, many, many sentences your 2019 self would not have understood, do please add: 'BUT THIS WAS TWO WEEKS BEFORE THE BAN ON HUGGING WAS LIFTED!' Absolutely devastating to think that a full 10 days *after* The Clinch occurred, Hancock went on telly specifically to warn people thinking of hugging a loved one that they 'should do it carefully'. Turns out we could have hugged people really hard, with tongues. Unless they were our relatives, I think?

'I'm really looking forward to hugging you as well, Dad,' Hancock smiled into the camera in that same interview. 'But we'll probably do it outside and keep the ventilation going. Hands, face and space.' Honestly, did you ever? How can I possibly trust a politician to lecture me on how to cuddle after this?

Back to the present day, though, and an early statement from another of the health secretary's aides – disguised as an unnamed 'friend' of Matt Hancock – would only say of the sensational revelation that 'no rules have been broken'. Hancock himself has since said he accepts 'that I breached the social distancing guidance', which is one way of putting it, while this morning he had his honour defended by Grant Shapps. Which doesn't exactly feel like the Kitemark. Arguably, the only way this story could now be more dignified is if a 'friend' suggested that the health secretary had – out of an abundance of caution – used a tongue condom.

As for the media maelstrom, I know a lot of your tears might struggle to materialise, but we can at least remark mildly on what a category-five shocker Hancock is currently having. He's being serially stalked by blog-to-kill sniper Dominic Cummings, who released WhatsApp messages from last year in which the prime minister is shown calling Hancock both 'hopeless' and 'fucking useless'. There followed a somewhat excruciating mention in dispatches from the Queen herself on Wednesday. 'I've just been talking to your secretary of state for health,' Her Majesty was filmed saying to Boris Johnson. 'Poor man.'

And now all . . . this. As suboptimal career patches go, this is the crap UK version of the one when news of Bill Clinton's affair with Monica Lewinsky broke. The very next day the colonel charged with carrying the 'nuclear football' briefcase asked the president where the codes to open it were, and Clinton was forced to admit he'd lost them months ago. Tough week. Worse for Hillary and Mrs Hancock, though, obviously.

According to his Downing Street spokesman, Boris Johnson considers the matter of his secretary of state for health breaking his own health advice closed and has nothing more to add. Something for separated families to fume over as they read about Hancock pushing hard to delay double-jabbed people being able to treat amber countries as green. Meanwhile, I would say that however much the pictures may be amusing some, they probably ought to investigate the CCTV leak as a matter of urgency. It's obviously not great that footage from inside government ministries is being given or sold to third parties.

As for Hancock, I read this morning that his job is now 'hanging by a thread'. Luckily for him, that thread will probably turn out to be made of Spider-Man's super-strength web fluid. After all, it's difficult to escape the suspicion that at some absolutely elemental level, this is what Johnson wants from his cabinet. It's not just that the prime minister has had a lifelong hard-on for Ancient Times, when the Greek and Roman gods were grotesquely fallible and morally compromised, and when he could quite imagine a creature of his various infirmities and appetites sitting atop Mount Olympus. No, we can only conclude that Johnson wants Matt Hancock and Gavin Williamson and so on to be bad at their jobs, because it provides cover for his own professional inadequacies. Why else would you keep someone you clearly kept describing as 'fucking useless' as your actual health secretary at the time of an era-shattering pandemic? Why else would you keep someone who constantly and demonstrably fails children and young people as your education secretary at a time when they so desperately deserve better?

The answer, alas, is that by remaining in place, guys like them serve as useful human shields. And I don't see why it shouldn't be the same with these cheating scandals either. Johnson must be only too happy to be surrounded by the erring and the compromised, because now he has shag cover too.

We can't keep politics out of sport, but please keep politicians out of football

9 July 2021

As the government piggybacks on England's success at the Euros, remember how it took on footballers – and lost – in the pandemic

Did you see the prime minister in the fancy seats at Wembley on Wednesday? He seemed to have come dressed as a particularly brutal Matt Lucas impersonation of himself. As for the young lady standing to his left and smiling indulgently at him, it's nice that his . . . mum, is it? . . . takes him out for the day and buys him a football top. But I do hope there weren't tears in the car on the way home when Boris Johnson was told he wasn't going to be allowed to run on to the pitch and do one of his special footer kicks on Sunday. (There certainly wasn't a mask in the car on the way home, as photos of Johnson show, but I guess it's only the help that catches it that way, so . . . basically victimless.)

Politicians and the football, then. A marriage made in the realms of guaranteed ridicule. Yet still they come. Or, in the case of Lee Anderson, still they stay away. Lee is one of the breakout plonkers of the tournament, being the Ashfield MP who early on announced that he'd be boycotting all England games because taking the knee was Marxist or something. One of the great achievements of Gareth Southgate has been bubbling his squad so fastidiously that no player has yet found out they are being boycotted by Lee. Should this hermetic seal hold up to and including Sunday's final, analysts believe that ignorance will amount if not to bliss, then certainly to an extra yard of pace on every England forward.

Meanwhile, as England have progressed, Lee's self-sabotaging stance has brought increasing gaiety to the nation, with his latest media appearance a masterclass in a particular variety of male sulk. He still wouldn't be watching the first major final England have been in since 1966, he told LBC, but would instead spend the game 'unpacking boxes'. Thoughts and prayers with Lee. There does seem to be an awful lot to unpack with him.

It's quite something to think that the government went into the first lockdown last year attempting to score cheap points on footballers' pay. They are now exiting all restrictions desperately trying to piggyback on what footballers have brought to the country, despite Johnson having managed England's pandemic like Steve McClaren.

This, needless to say, does not tell the entire story of the government's encounters with football over the past year and a quarter. It all began last April with a pious little lecture from a guy by the name of Matt Hancock – remember him? At the time he was spouting off, Hancock was the health secretary still allowing hospital patients to be discharged to care homes without even being tested. Priorities, priorities. 'I think the first thing Premier League footballers can do is make a contribution,' intoned Matt from his Downing Street podium. 'Take a pay cut and play their part.' Incredibly, it would take a full 15 months for Matt himself to take a pay cut, but at least Certain Events mean we're spared his ministerial take on 'the Three Lions' now. I'm not sure I could handle a broadcast interview featuring Matt honking, 'I do believe it is coming home, but I urge people to bring it home responsibly!'

Next up for the government and football were two bruising clashes against Marcus Rashford (they lost both), and the awards of MBEs for services to charity to both Rashford and Jordan Henderson. Spring brought some posturing about the European Super League that seemed deeply questionable, coming as it did days after the chief executive of one of the clubs involved had visited Johnson's chief of staff for a meeting in Downing Street. And the curtain-raiser to this tournament was of course a load of mealy-mouthed failure among ministers to condemn the boo-ing of players taking the knee, apparently to stoke their horribly ill-advised culture wars. Today England players are reported to be planning to donate any Euro 2020 winners bonuses to the NHS should they triumph, and are already donating all their match fees. Why don't these pampered, selfish etcetera-etceteras do something worthwhile with their cash, like buy Boris Johnson some more gold wallpaper or another holiday to Mustique?

Arguably, then, the government has had an absolute shitter against football this pandemic. But instead of owning it – which Lee Anderson is at least doing in his mad, sad way – we now see ministers in full reverse-ferret mode. Thursday brought eight tweets of excruci-ating faux apology from the failed politician Laurence Fox, who now seems to regret his decision to tip all over England's 'woke babies'.

What is to be done to stop this? I believe that all politicians should simply be fitted with an electric collar for the duration of any tournament, which administers shocks of increasing intensity each time they mention the subject, and a full 300 megavolts if they deploy the words: 'It's coming home.'

That, of course, would be rather a mild sort of just deserts for Priti Patel, who is widely believed to administer the electrodes to a subordinate for bringing her the wrong coffee or for failing to be 'can do' about some plan to install artificially grown megalodons in the Channel to deter migrant boats. Patel was early out of the traps on the football front this summer, pointedly arguing that fans had a right to boo the team taking the knee and dismissing the practice as 'gesture politics'. Or, as Priti now puts it, in a tweet accompanying pictures of her baring her teeth in an England strip: 'Just brilliant. Well done Three Lions. Football's coming home.' Oh dear. It's not yet clear if football is coming home, but the chickens certainly are.

You can even read this morning that the government is wor-ried they might 'jinx' the final if they commit to a bank holiday to celebrate an England win. In which case, I think the message to them must be very clear. Namely: don't worry. PLEASE don't worry. Nothing you do, ever, at all, has any effect on it either way. None of it is for you, none of it owes anything to you, and nothing you say about it should be taken with anything other than a laugh and a cordial four-letter invitation to shut up, for ever. We can't keep politics out of sport, and nor should we seek to. The two are entwined and always have been, just not in the way the various blazers want. But we should always, always keep politicians out of sport – because the one thing you can absolutely guarantee is that no matter what happens on Sunday, they'll be painting footballers as the enemy again soon enough. Set your watch by it.

Owen Paterson was just the fall guy. This week's chaos was all about Boris Johnson

5 November 2021

The prime minister has faced multiple investigations. You can see why the obliteration of the standards commissioner might seem appealing

An edifying week in the government of Britain, a country run by the third prize in a competition to build Winston Churchill out of marshmallows. Yup, this man is our sorry lot: this pool-float Targaryen, this gurning English Krankie cousin, this former child star still squeezing himself into his little suit for coins. The sole bright spot for Boris Johnson is that furious Tory MPs are currently only comparing him to the nursery-rhyme Duke of York. Still, give it time.

On, then, to the unforced blunderrhoea of the Owen Paterson affair and its fallout. The sheer full-spectrum shitshow of it makes sense when you understand two things: the Carl von Clownewitzes behind the government's shameful 'strategy' for sweeping aside a vital democratic check on corruption; and the fact that for

Johnson, none of it was to do with Owen Paterson. The departing MP for North Shropshire was simply useful for the prime minister's personal goals – until he wasn't.

We'll deal with the second point first. By far the most consequential investigation currently approaching Kathryn Stone's in-tray concerns the man already investigated by the standards commissioner more times than any other MP in the past three years: one Boris Johnson. Once an Electoral Commission probe into the same business has reported, a parliamentary standards investigation is widely expected to look at the extravagant refurbishment of Johnson's Downing Street flat, how it was paid for, how the public was told it was paid for, when and in what order they were told it, what the PM's wet fish cabinet secretary (Simon Case) and pet fish 'standards adviser' (Christopher Geidt) were told – and a whole lot of other difficult questions that have the prime minister sweating like *The Silence of the Lambs'* Buffalo Bill on *Grand Designs*. Or like Theresa May in a field of wheat. Or simply like Boris Johnson being asked a straight question, to which the answer can't be, 'She's just a friend, I swear.' Take your pick.

It's odd – given his hideously negligent mismanagement of the pandemic – that many Westminster experts believe the flat refurbishment has the greater potential to damage Johnson with voters. But there it is. There's no accounting for taste, neither in red lines nor soft furnishings. Perhaps it's because most normal voters who simply want £840-a-roll gold wallpaper, handcrafted rattan backscratchers and so on pay for such things themselves when the bills are presented. More than seven months and a lot of press reports later, Johnson eventually reimbursed the taxpayer £58,000 for the flat makeover. But that isn't the end of discussions on the matter, and you can quite see why the obliteration of the standards commissioner ASAP might seem so appealing. (No. 10 insists the two are unrelated.)

Anyway, we move on to the personnel involved in this week's epic fail, with the ringleaders being Johnson himself, Tory chief whip Mark Spencer and leader of the house Jacob Rees-Mogg. I don't know if Johnson knows anything at all about classical history and the ancient world – he wears his learning so lightly, it's just impossible to tell – but I think you'd stop shy of hailing this particular brains trust as the third triumvirate. Even given how badly the second one turned out. Quite why Johnson, the Conservative party and, indeed, wider society continue to tolerate Rees-Mogg being in any sort of position of responsibility is anyone's guess. The justification that he has some kind of yoof 'following' feels desperately 2017, a relic of a time when this country's ruling class could afford irony. Lavishly inept, the Moggster convinces about as much as an English toff from an early-1990s American movie played by some beta Derek Nimmo. I can never quite understand why the Grenfell-victim-blaming, frontbench-lolling Rees-Mogg is so keen to cite his nanny in public. It's like someone defecating in the middle of your drawing-room floor while telling you which finishing school they attended. And if Nanny wishes to sue me for saying Jacob turned out atrociously, then I'd be very pleased to see her down the Strand for four days of courtroom fun.

As for Johnson's other *consigliere* in all this, Spencer, he's done an absolute Bismarck. The ship, unfortunately – not the diplomatic genius. His cunning plan to overhaul the standards regime has been shelled, torpedoed and scuttled, and is now at rest 15,000 feet under the Atlantic. It is genuinely beyond comprehension that Spencer failed to predict that opposition parties would simply refuse to support the government's new standards stitch-up: a committee chaired by John Whittingdale (who was himself once investigated by the standards committee over a trip to the MTV awards in Amsterdam with his girlfriend, a dominatrix sex worker). There may well be toe fungus with more of a tactical clue than Spencer. You can quite see how he is being wishfully lined up as the second fall guy of the week.

The first, of course, was Owen Paterson, who was absolutely bang-to-rights on the breach of rules, but who has clearly been through the most unspeakable tragedy and should have been handled thousands of per cent more sensitively and intelligently by his friends. However, none of those friends was Boris Johnson, who last indulged in male friendship sometime around the John Major administration. Johnson's very much the best man who lets you down on the morning of the wedding. 'Mate, is it today? Fuck! I'm an idiot. No, mate, can't do it. I'm still in Verbier. Gutted I won't be able to try to shag her at the reception now. Anyway, have a good one.'

All of which makes the prime minister's statement on Paterson's resignation one for the do-me-a-favour files. 'I am very sad parliament will lose the services of Owen Paterson,' this ran, 'who has been a friend and colleague of mine for decades.' Mmm. If that's the case, how come your friend reportedly only found you were pulling the rug out from under him when a BBC reporter phoned him in the supermarket, a U-turn which could realistically only lead to his resignation a few short hours later?

Let's play out with how the British prime minister spent the eve of this shameful vote. Johnson was having dinner at the Garrick Club with the long-term climate denialist Charles Moore, having left his own climate conference, incidentally, on a private jet. Also incidentally, Moore used to edit the *Telegraph*, after Johnson made his name in the paper, publishing his various fabrications about the EU. Incidentally – again – Johnson fairly recently sought to install Moore as chairman of the BBC. (Moore has, incidentally, previously been a licence-fee refusenik.) Still incidentally, Moore is a real friend of Owen Paterson's, and has been a significant advocate for his foolhardy defence . . .

We sadly have no space for any more of the incidentals, incestuous connections, hypocrisies and potential stitch-up attempts in this single meeting between two chaps in a men-only club. But then, all that really needs to be said is that this is Boris Johnson's Britain. We just live in it.

With a sleaze storm brewing in parliament, Boris Johnson seeks shelter where he can

9 November 2021

Absent from an emergency debate about MPs' outside earnings, the prime minister could instead be found skulking in a CT scan room

Hugely encouraging to find Boris Johnson treating Monday's emergency debate on sleaze like the birth of a lovechild. Which is to say, he was unfortunately washing his hair. Metaphorically, of course. I get a strong 'Mate, after eight weeks hair cleans itself' energy from the prime minister.

The House of Commons isn't going to clean itself, unfortunately, which makes it all the more regrettable that Johnson always feels the need to get away from his mistakes. By next year he'll have billed the taxpayer for a full-scale Fortress of Solitude, with the only locked-on certainty being that Kwasi Kwarteng will assure us the £38bn crystal cave is a non-story.

Yesterday, though, we had Anne-Marie Trevelyan defending outside earnings. The trade secretary didn't think the ability to maintain lucrative consultancies should be removed, she said in one interview, because it brought a 'richness' to the Commons. Jesus, Anne-Marie: YOU HAD ONE JOB. Unlike half the Tory backbenches, obviously, who have three jobs. Good to know that ongoing performance art piece Chris Grayling takes a full £100,000 a year from Hutchison Ports Europe, where I imagine his advice runs to: 'Quick one: did you remember to acquire some ports? Seems obvious, but I once ballsed up on this front with ferries.'

The latest emanation from the WTF files is the revelation that Torridge and West Devon MP Geoffrey Cox has spoken just once in a parliamentary debate since February 2020, and spent part of this year working and voting remotely out of the British Virgin Islands, where he pocketed £150,000 of his £900,000 extra-parliamentary earnings for advising the tax haven's government on Foreign Office corruption charges. I mean . . . just get an OnlyFans, Geoffrey. It's so much more dignified. Incidentally, it's nice to remember how many people wanged on about what a nice voice this #massivelegend had, back when he was a scenery-chewing attorney general for Theresa May. You can bet they feel pretty ahead of the curve now. They could get Cox to record their voicemail greeting for them. He's bound to be on Cameo. Indeed, perhaps that's the logical next step in democracy's voiding of its bowels: Boris Johnson charging a grand a pop to gibber 'Build Back Birthday!' for paying members of the electorate.

Amazingly, Cox is just one element in what's becoming a category 5 shitstorm for Johnson. There are honestly too many fronts to fit in here, from Johnson's own byzantine arrangements for paying for £840-a-roll gold wallpaper to the grotesque racket of Tory treasurers donating £3m and reliably ending up in the Lords. (Johnson has appointed a full 96 peers in less than two years, meaning the Lords itself now runs to nearly 800 members and is bigger than the entire EU parliament.)

All this is before we even get to Delyn MP Rob Roberts, who has somehow just been allowed to rejoin the Conservative party and sit as an independent in the Commons, despite an investigation having found he sexually harassed a junior member of staff. Mind you, I've very much enjoyed the gentlemen across Fleet Street who've been pontificating along the lines of: 'Can you imagine a sexual harasser in any other workplace simply being allowed to carry on working there?'

Yes, guys. I can.

ANYHOW. In the absence of Johnson, you might have ordinarily expected Monday's debate to be opened by leader of the house Jacob Rees-Mogg. As one of the architects of the catastrophic Paterson amendment, however, Rees-Mogg was evidently deemed too much of an oratorical liability. He and his fellow blunderer, chief whip Mark Spencer, could instead be found sitting boot-faced and silent on the frontbench like Crabbe and Goyle – a pair of not-very-hench men who knew their blond ringleader wasn't going to show up. At the dispatch box, honours were instead done by Cabinet Office minister Steve Barclay, a political entity I find it very difficult to have an opinion about one way or the other. Ever since he was appointed from the ether as Brexit secretary in 2018, Barclay has somehow always seemed a placeholder minister, who materialises only as a temporary proxy – the human equivalent of an apologetic parenthesis: '[Sorry, actual minister to follow later]'.

But look, Steve didn't exactly have great material to work with – and it should obviously never even have been his script. The bottler who should have done it had instead spent the morning at a hospital in Northumberland, floundering to the cameras that he couldn't get back in time. Boris Johnson is the most extraordinarily bad liar, which is really embarrassing for him considering how long he's spent practising. I heard that if you spent 10,000 hours doing something, you were supposed to be an expert in it. In which case, Johnson should be able to compete intergalactically in this particular discipline. He should be good enough to be Earth's tribune in the Bullshit Games.

Instead, we found the PM skulking in a radiology department, trying to change the subject to Covid. That in itself tells you quite how bad things are. Changing the subject to talk about something he's handled as badly as Covid has the ring of 'Can we talk instead about how I can't live on £160,000 and two free houses?' or 'Can we talk instead about how my wife's five years older than my daughter?' I suppose you have to concede the quality of the white goods he's hiding in has improved. He's graduated from a fridge to a CT scan machine.

Arguably the darkest news this week, though, is the discovery that the standards commissioner, Kathryn Stone, now requires increased security after threats against her. What a moment for pause. It was barely two weeks ago that some in the Commons were calling for 'David's Law', in memory of the brutally murdered MP David Amess, explaining that sky-rocketing abuse of members was being fuelled by the internet. And yet, what is abuse of the previously pretty anonymous standards commissioner fuelled by, if not some hugely unnecessary and disgracefully targeted attacks on her led by some MPs themselves? If only they'd spend a little less time on the second jobs, and a little more considering the duties and honour of the first.

In the meantime, Johnson has reminded his MPs he's a weak man masquerading as a strong one, which is why serving ministers are now giving quotes to *The Times* like: 'We put up with him as long as he's popular. As soon as he's not, we should get rid.' That time may not have come. But like a lot of MPs' second pay cheques, it increasingly feels like it's in the post.

What's the truth about lockdown-busting parties at No. 10? Don't ask Shagatha Christie

10 December 2021

The Met already seemed slow to investigate last year's reported festivities – then the prime minister promised to help out

Great to hear that a 57-year-old Downing Street man is keen to help the police with their inquiries into a growing number of potential misdemeanours at his address. Boris Johnson says that 'of course' he will tell the Met the truth about rumoured No. 10 parties, which pretty much guarantees they'll never get to the bottom of it. When you want Sherlock Holmes but have to settle for Elizabeth Holmes.

Still, here he comes – Shagatha Christie, trying to deduce what the hell has happened this week. Happy to help: the sphincter of his prime ministership has failed. Tory MPs whose inboxes now resemble something designed by Lulu Lytle are reminded that character is fate. There was simply no other place a Johnson government would ever end up but mired in rampant lies, chaos, negligence, financial sponging and the live evisceration of public service. To the Conservatives and media outriders somehow only now discovering this about their guy, I think we have to say: you ordered this. Now eat it.

To self-styled classics expert Johnson, meanwhile, we should extend our sympathies. Dude . . . worst last-days-of-Rome EVER?! Instead of bacchanalian orgies and high-end decadence, you're back on the nappies while taking blitzkrieg for some naff Secret Santa 'do' at which a press officer was reportedly handing out prizes to other press officers. Still, I hope the prizes were free girlfriends. Give them something they need.

We'll get to the parties and the gold wallpaper and the institutionalised mendacity in a minute, but while we're vaguely on the police, many have noticed a certain investigative sluggishness on their part over the number of Covid rule-breaching events that may or may not have taken place last Christmas in the very house where the government makes the rules for the rest of us idiots. Do you detect the same? If so, at least someone's doing some detecting. I know most crimes have now effectively been legalised by lack of investigation, but it would be nice to think the Met might at least be able to chase down potential law breaches in buildings that have multiple serving police officers in and around them at all times. Mind you, when you think of all the people who restrain themselves to death in police stations without any coppers seeing anything, you can quite see how officers might miss a big cheese-and-wine party just yards from their various sentry points. It all depends on the sightlines, no doubt.

Anyway: standards. Apparently, Johnson's current independent standards adviser, Lord Geidt, is considering quitting after it turned out the prime minister misled him in his investigation into how the welfare king and queen of No. 10 treated themselves to a load of hugely expensive stuff for their flat on other people's dime. Picture Boris and Carrie looking in their rattan mirror (Soane, price on application) and going: 'We DESERVE this.' If Geidt does walk, Johnson will have disgusted two standards advisers in just over 12 months. Two! I'm not going to twee this up with the Lady Bracknell quote – it doesn't remotely cover it. Try and imagine Lady Bracknell going back to Armie Hammer's place; now you're in the ballpark. In the meantime, Johnson's standards adviser is starting to look like the old al-Qaida number-three position. Dead men's shoes.

Speaking of shoes, other lockdown-breaking gatherings are being alleged, including one reportedly held by Carrie Johnson in the No. 10 flat last November, in the immediate wake of a Kansas farmhouse landing on Dominic Cummings. After this, milady seems to have thought the ruby slippers would pass automatically to her, but this week they are beginning to look more like footwear for Liz Truss. (Rishi Sunak's slippers are made of actual rubies.) Were journalists at any of these parties? That is a line of inquiry/rumour, reminding you just how incestuous the political–media complex is in this backwater country. I keep reading that a journalist is godfather to the Johnsons' son, Wilfred. Then again, maybe the prime minister has had so many kids it's like jury service. Every UK adult should expect to be called as godparent at some point. Either way, getting too close to politicians on any side of politics is always a mistake for journalists: you might think the access makes them a great contact, but the compromises and self-editing required to retain them means that ends up being just a lie you tell yourself.

And, by extension, your readers. Telling me the REAL story of the election only after it's been won or lost is for courtiers. Professional pride or your terrible social life. Pick a lane.

Staying with the subject of rigorous independence, though, what a hoot to learn that the entire investigation into Downing Street parties will be carried out by the cabinet secretary, Simon Case, a certified wet blanket whose earlier appointment procedure was once characterised by Dominic Cummings as: 'I brought in Simon Case . . . because I thought the prime minister is not listening to me.' Sorry, but why is the person deciding who should be subject to disciplinary consequences on a team he works closely with ALSO the person who decides what those consequences are?

Still, what a world. The sheer clusterfuckery of it this week means we've barely time to even discuss Johnson or his intervention in that ex-Marine's Kabul pet evacuation – a saga on which we'll slap the title 'The Animals Give Farthing Wood'. I'm kidding, of course. A lot of people anthropomorphise their animals. You know the sort of thing: 'My dog loves *Homes Under the Hammer*.' 'My guinea pig is sulking.' 'My cats are high-value Taliban targets.'

As for Dominic Raab, in any other week we'd have been boggling at the Foreign Office whistleblower's claims that as capacity for removals from Afghanistan tragically dwindled, the foreign secretary was asked to personally approve individual cases, but 'took several hours . . . to engage', then asked for the relevant files to be resubmitted in a different kind of spreadsheet. According to Raab, that's 'not quite right'. Not *quite*? Wonder how he did put it. Maybe: 'I'm not interested in appeals for desperate people and their children not to be murdered unless they're correctly formatted.' Previous flights of fancy in this column might have cast Raab as the kind of guy who owns a lock-up with a chest freezer. This underestimated him. I now realise he combines the calm psychopathy of a medieval steppe warlord with the fist-gnawingly obdurate 'desk hygiene' of a regional manager. Regional manager of either a photocopier firm or a forced resettlement programme.

Regrettably, though, space constraints must end our recap of the week here. But on it all goes, as Omicron closes in. We'll play out with a reminder that in a pandemic that has so far killed 146,000 of the Britons who these people are supposed to be in politics to serve, the absolutely vital public health message has now TWICE been most fatally undermined by people who worked at the very heart of No. 10 with Boris Johnson. That is absolutely a disgrace, and absolutely not a coincidence.

THE ROYAL FAMILY:
TROUBLE AT THE FIRM

'A 21st-century monarchy'. As oxymorons-to-avoid go, it's probably up there with '4th-century brain surgery'. It's fair to say the
House of Windsor suffers the odd setback in this period, from failing to end its marrying-an-American-divorcee hoodoo to Prince
Andrew's mother effectively having to sack him from a hereditary
position for being friends with an international paedo. The Queen
must have longed for the relative pleasure of the *annus horribilis*.
There's *horribilis*, and *horribilissimus*. And yet, the public, whether
or not they care to admit it, mostly devour every second of the mess.
'What the public is feeling is a sense of great drama,' Bloomsbury
Group diarist Frances Partridge noted tartly of the abdication in
1936, 'not at all unpleasant.'

After a toxic buildup to Harry and Meghan's wedding, are we entertained?

18 May 2018

The cast of thousands taking their piece of this wedding has been a sight to behold

After the week they've had, it's too fitting that Prince Harry and Meghan Markle are doing this thing in Windsor Castle's St George's Chapel, the official spiritual home to the Order of the Garter. The order was founded after the perceived embarrassment and shaming of a woman at court in 1348, through no fault of her own.

Legend has it (possibly erroneously) that Edward III's dance partner accidentally flashed her garter, to various looks askance, prompting Edward to take the garter upon himself and challenge the mockers with what would become his new order's motto: *'Honi soit qui mal y pense'* – 'Shame on him who thinks badly of this.' 'Those who laugh at this today', Edward added, 'will tomorrow be proud to wear it.' Note how an embarrassing incident was opportunistically embraced by the crown, promptly knit into its mythology and swiftly used to further its wider ends. Almost immediately, Edward was using the same line to shut down criticism of his dodgy claim to the French throne. Gotta admire the balls on him.

To the matrimosseum, then, where it has been revealed that Prince Charles will walk Meghan up the aisle in the absence of her father, who you might vaguely have heard is recovering from heart surgery in Mexico. We don't know too much about Mr Markle's 69-year-old understudy, but as all theatre critics will tell you, anyone forced to go on at the last minute is always 'a revelation'. Ideally, a star will be born, because the House of Windsor's going to need one in a few years. Charles will lead Meghan to Harry, who will then turn to the wider TV audience and bellow: *'HONI SOIT QUI MAL Y PENSE'.* Harry's tone? Same as the bit in *Gladiator* when a flashing-eyed Russell Crowe inquires of the Colosseum crowd: 'Are you nut entertained? ARE YOU NUT ENTERTAINED? IS THIS NUT WHY YOU ARE HERE?'

And is it? On the eve of a royal wedding whose final week of preparations has been several stripes of toxic, we must once again ask: what do we want out of these people?

'She makes him happy,' one member of the public explained to the BBC. 'And that makes me happy.' In the Kensington Palace gift shop, a woman buying a £39 mug with Harry and Meghan's initials on it told me: 'I love how down to earth they are.' A lady who had travelled from Florida confided beneath the whirr of a news helicopter: 'I just like weddings.'

Craig Brown has noted that when it comes to the royal family in the modern era, 'the trend is toward praising the unexceptional'. All of which leads him to the central questions of our modern relationship with the monarchy: 'If they are so ordinary, why are they so special? And if they are so special, why are they so ordinary?'

This unresolved conflict has been much on display this week, alongside the snobbery and the sycophancy, the cruelty and the casual racism. You can't move for people explaining that the miserable drama with Meghan's poor paparazzi-colluding father shows us that 'all families are complicated' – like we need telling that where the Windsors are concerned. Please. They've been bringing their own drama since for ever. The very fact Harry is marrying an American divorcee sets a low success bar, even by the standards of his clan. The last time the experiment was tried, the couple in question ended up in a Bois de Boulogne villa with a couple of mines' worth of diamonds but only Hitler on speed-dial.

Too soon? Very possibly. Royal nuptials do something funny to people who otherwise know that wedding details are almost comically boring. People who would normally need to be a bottle of lady petrol down before they cared what type of cake their friends are having are positively gripped by news that Meghan's will be a lemon sponge with elderflower buttercream. Other people declare their furious lack of interest like a mantra that needs repeating just the 900 times a day.

In Windsor, many were treating Royal Wedding Eve like it was an early flight from Stansted, where it's basically fine to have a pint at any time. 'We open at 6am tomorrow,' said the barmaid at the King and Castle, with a thousand-yard stare. Elsewhere on the lanes around the castle there were slightly more claimants to be 'official town crier' than there once were to be Anastasia Romanov. Police had taken the possessions of some homeless people for 'safe storage', making way for the royal superfans who wished to sleep on the same streets to get a great viewing spot for Saturday. And if you were a screenwriter trying to come up with a vignette to illustrate a country in heady thrall to a version of its past yet struggling to meet the challenges of its present, you'd probably ditch that one as being too on the nose.

Before we had culture wars, we had John Mortimer's insistence that the nation could still be divided into cavaliers and roundheads. We now live in an age of endless taxonomy – and anger – where people are forever identifying adversarially. Leavers and remainers, Somewheres and Anywheres, people who adore the royal family and people who can't stand them. (Confusingly, many of the latter demographic adore the royals at one artistic remove. They worship the Queen as played by Helen Mirren and can't get enough of *The Crown*.)

After the wedding of Prince William and Kate Middleton, which I covered for work, I returned home to find my husband had not seen one nanosecond of the proceedings, choosing instead to watch *The Sorrow and the Pity*, a four-hour documentary about Nazi collaboration in Vichy France. I mean . . . *eyeroll*. Someone later asked him if he hadn't even wanted to see Kate's dress, and he said, 'Her DRESS?' as though he'd been offered sight of her dental records or her GCSE essay on weather symbolism in *King Lear*. This time round he'll be at the Cup Final clash between Chelsea and Man United, Saturday's other gloriously militarised event where a perceived arriviste will meet the game's version of royalty. And that concludes the court and social engagements for my household.

There was no evidence of protesters in Windsor on Friday, though some are promised for Saturday. Extended opening hours may help. Elsewhere, though, a certain cultivated ennui about Harry and Meghan's wedding is the badge of someone who would like you to know they have better things to do with their time. Nothing new here. 'I have noticed in the press certain references to Princess Margaret wishing to marry someone or other,' Noël Coward sniffed grandly to his diary back in 1955. 'I really must try to control this yawning.' Within two weeks Coward was practically wetting his pants at the news that Margaret was not going to marry the someone-or-other (Group Captain Peter Townsend) after all. 'This is a fine slap in the chops for the bloody press which has been persecuting her for so long,' he thundered. 'It has all been a silly mismanaged lash-up, and I can't imagine how the Queen and the Queen Mother and Prince Philip allowed it to get into such a tangle . . .' On and on it goes, quite the opposite of a yawn, right down to his hope 'that they had the sense to hop into bed a couple of times at least, but this I doubt'.

He perhaps needn't have worried on that score. Back to the events of this week, though, where we must once again wonder how tangles are allowed to happen to the royal family. How could Kensington Palace's courtiers not have predicted many months ago that Meghan's father was a potential vulnerability who might need assistance in the eye of the media maelstrom in which he would find himself? Instead of farting out press releases about floral arrangements, someone from the palace should have raced to Tijuana faster than a teen on spring break and helped manage the situation. Instead, they have presided over the biggest strategic bollock-drop since the snap election.

With barely a week to go, perhaps the palace was congratulating itself that the worst press to befall this wedding was the news that having invited 2,460 members of the public inside the castle walls to 'share their special day', the couple weren't actually going to feed them or anything. Some suspected they were just backdrop for the TV pictures, the most displeased peasant extras since Buttercup's forced marriage to Humperdinck in *The Princess Bride*.

But now . . . well. The final countdown has been marked by such eye-covering TV moments as Meghan's half-sister raging that her father snapped because he had been relentlessly hounded by paparazzi. As she put it: 'I think there are examples in history of how dangerous that can be.' Ouch. Plotlines never go away in the House of Windsor, they just lie dormant for a couple of series.

Alas, there undoubtedly remains a persistent feeling among some courtiers that it is the commoners who bring vulgarity to the royal family, who are themselves always unimpeachable. Anyone who recalls Prince Andrew bellowing at John Travolta, who was dressed as a giant vegetable, during Prince Edward's dignicidal Grand Knockout Tournament will find that take hard to get behind. (Edward had earlier stormed huffily out of a press conference wearing a sweatshirt reading 'NO I JUST LOOK LIKE HIM'.)

There was much sympathy for Meghan over the business with her father among those camped out on Friday morning. 'It's terrible what they've done to her,' remarked one woman in a camping chair, who, it must be said, had still bought three newspapers to read about it all. 'She's tough enough to survive it though,' judged her friend.

None of this is new, naturally, having happened to various brides of Windsor before. Indeed, once you are 'in', it is your turn to take the reins and disparage the latest newbie and their ghastly family. Roy Strong's diaries feature one encounter with Princess Michael, who is keen to define herself against the then 23-year-old mother-of-one, Princess Diana. Strong recounts Princess Michael's thoughts: 'Droves of the household were leaving, and then there was the terrible mother, Mrs Shand Kydd . . .' (I don't know about you, but I never trust a take on terrible relatives unless it comes from someone whose own father was a Nazi SS officer.) 'Poor Prince Charles, who had bought Highgrove to be near his former girlfriend.' Can't bear it for the guy. Strong then moves on to quoting Princess Michael directly: 'Being rude to servants is the lowest thing you could do, and [Diana] does it.' The Kents, of course, will be neighbours of Harry and Meghan when they move into their 21-room marital apartment in the same quadrangle of Kensington Palace, so doubtless Meghan can expect a warm and supportive welcome there.

Looking at the form book, then, marrying into the Windsors has frequently proved a reverse fairytale. It starts with you becoming a princess, and unravels from there. Tied ends are loosed, and afters are not ever happy. Even so, the weddings themselves are a type of Restoration comedy, briefly and amusingly refreshing the view of the monarchy to something light, youthful and positive, and allowing many people to stave off the gathering realisation that the Queen is the last big-hitting link with the postwar consensus, and if she and Attenborough go in the same year, we'll have effectively lost the rights to our country to Sky.

We've already lost the rights to this wedding to the US news site *TMZ*, which has wiped the floor with their British counterparts in terms of scoops, in arguably the most shaming defeat since Yorktown. Certainly, since England capitulated to the US in the 1950 World Cup. Wasn't it OUR tabloids that used to go into hospitals and try to get stories off recovering patients? Wasn't it OUR tabloids that used to goad relatives into saying terrible things for money? Aren't WE the best at ruining lives? What happened to us, man? Perhaps another sort of changing of the guard has occurred.

Still, the cast of thousands taking their piece of this wedding remains a sight to behold. Incredible, really, that no one in our royal family has ever eloped. Couple of the Saudis have done it, obviously, and you get a bit of it in Thailand. But, at more than one moment this week, Harry and Meghan must surely have been tempted to run off to Vegas, a city of marginally less excess than one of Prince Charles's weekend journeys to stay with friends in Herefordshire.

Yet here we are. At some point on Saturday a 'body language expert' on some network's dime will divine from the specific manner in which Meghan Markle steps from her golden landau that 'she has a lot on her mind'. Body language will be just one of the ancient disciplines being brought to bear on proceedings. The erstwhile royal butler Paul Burrell has been handling etiquette and so on for ITV's *Lorraine*, though he's unlikely to furnish viewers with a digression on the etiquette of hiding a load of one's late employer's dresses in the attic and then betraying her secrets in a series of lucrative books.

Then there are all the bookies, of course, and the hundreds of broadcast technicians taping cables to the pavements all the way around Windsor Castle, in a 'Sleeping Beauty' metaphor I'm sure Kay Burley will be hacking through in due course. And all the American television anchors, and all the souvenir sellers, and the childhood bodyguards who've cashed in. And the security consultants, and the lip readers. (For William and Kate's wedding, the *Sun* had lip readers trained on various members of the royal family. An executive decision was taken not to publish what had been gleaned from Princess Anne as it was – how to put this? – not thought to fit with the otherwise positive and upbeat mood of the day.)

Then there's Liam Fox, declaring on Thursday that the wedding will boost the UK's trade ties with the US. There's Marks and Spencer, changing its name to Markle and Sparkle for three days, and all the many pubs holding royal wedding parties, and all the many pubs holding anti-royal wedding parties. Just two people getting married, then, trailed by a vast army of chancers and cheerleaders and chisellers and critics also taking their cut – including me, by the writing of this article. As that other medieval saying goes, it's all in the game, yo. And just look how long it's been played. Helluva drug.

For hire: the former royal hangers-on who are hounding Meghan

28 February 2019

Equerries, butlers, spiritual healers . . . Princess Diana's former employees have been busy offering their unique 'advice' to the Duchess of Sussex

Who is the absolute worst former Princess Di hanger-on? I know who you're going to say – and we will obviously get to him and the dresses in his attic. But hold that thought, if only because of the sheer volume of Diana's ex-'helpers' currently crawling from the woodwork to attack the Duchess of Sussex for her perceived missteps.

I say 'to attack' – what I mean is 'to offer candid advice as someone who's been there'. And by 'been there', I mean worked for Princess Diana, then sold her out after her death. And, in one case, attempted to contact her in a seance on pay-per-view TV, in a show hosted by Patrick Macnee, the former *Avengers* star.

By way of a quick recap, Meghan's celebrity friends seem to have paid for a hugely expensive baby shower for her in New York last week. This has precipitated a mass gnashing of teeth by people whose reaction to the various crises besieging their nations is neither fight nor flight, but asking questions such as: 'Why can't she see the grave danger of being friends with Oprah?' and 'Doesn't she KNOW that tights are protocol?' Thank you for being this invested, Texas! And Surrey, and stuff. Alas, it is always the cruellest irony that caring about the royal family in this particular fashion is literally the most vulgar activity there is.

Or is it? I don't know about you, but I always like to take lectures in vulgarity from former members of Diana's household, who have since farted out tell-all books with titles such as *Shadows of a Princess*. And even more recently, tell-nothing books like *The Meghan Factor*. In this spirit, let us welcome Patrick Jephson, a retired equerry but serving shitbag, who has taken to the *Daily Mail* to warn Meghan of where accepting freebies might lead. According to Patrick, there is always a hidden price attached for the free-riding royal.

'Favours must be returned,' he judges word-countily, 'obligations quickly multiply, and pretty soon royal free-riders are handing over their most precious assets: credibility and dignity, if not, please God, their lives.' Wait, wait, wait, what? Did we just read . . . yes, I rather think we did. Please God this heavily pregnant woman doesn't DIE 'pretty soon' in a chain of events sparked by Amal Clooney giving her a Moses basket.

While you digest the hysterical bad taste of Patrick's candid friendship, do please also consider Jephson's genuine affront that Meghan should have judged the 'support network' of royal staff – of the type he once was – to be surplus to requirements when planning this private trip. As he stiffly points out, this staff 'exists to protect her'.

Affecting words from the author of a book which claimed that a pink vibrator Diana brought back from Paris was 'never used for its designed purpose'. 'For reasons of her own,' sniffs Patrick of Meghan, 'it seems that she has outsourced her support operations, including reputation management, to a group of her friends.'

Madness! It can be only minutes before Oprah or Serena Williams feels so treacherous and grasping that they decide to pen a tell-all book about Meghan called *Shadows of a Duchess*. I assume that you haven't read Jephson's first book, which contains lengthy passages of character assassination of his deceased former employer, but his self-reflections are fairly priceless. 'If all this sounds rather over-principled,' he muses of himself at one point, 'then it probably was.' Yeah, if anything, he's too much of a perfectionist. When Diana eventually bins him off, he 'told nobody of my agonised thoughts except God'. And then the readers of *Shadows of a Princess*, which itself was serialised like a bastard in various global outlets.

It is up to you whether you find Patrick more or less hilarious than Princess Diana's former spiritual healer, Simone Simmons, whose psychic odyssey has taken her frequently to the newspapers. Simone gets perfectly furious if you call her a chancer, so let me simply say that about 18 months ago, she told newspaper readers that Princess Di had been in touch to say she'd have voted for Brexit. There hasn't been any further detail since – we don't know where Diana stood on the Malthouse compromise, for instance, or, indeed, whether the deceased Princess of Wales believes that Wednesday's votes have in fact made no deal a shade more likely than it was at the start of the week. But Simone is a charlatan radicalised anew by Meghan's mere presence in the royal family. 'I give their marriage two-and-a-half to three years,' she pronounced in October. 'I don't want to see him badly hurt,' she claimed, 'and Harry won't know what's hit him when it does happen.' Well, we've all read our fairytales. This is why you have to invite the 13th spiritual healer to the christening. Having said that, would the UK falling asleep for 100 years be the worst result at this point?

But, for now, we can avoid him no longer. As far as offering frank advice and admonishment to Meghan goes, there is, quite simply, no one to touch Diana's former butler – or her 'rock', as Paul Burrell prefers it. For many, Paul is a rock in the Gibraltar style: controversial, unappealing and perennially surrounded by gibbons. Either way, he has, over the years and by increments, recast his relationship with Diana so entirely so that he now speaks of having 'worked with' the Princess. They were basically joint CEOs. Following Diana's death, you may remember, Paul felt that the only way he could 'protect the princess's world and keep her secrets safe' was to bung as many of her dresses and other portable items into the boot of his car as he could and transfer them to the attic of Chez Burrell.

Why do I always imagine it was her 'roomier' dresses – maybe the maternity ones? I should say there is absolutely no evidence for the implication. Then again, once you stash a load of your former employer's clothes in your attic, you do arguably have to run the gauntlet of people like me imagining what you wanted them for. Were they allowed to simply gather dust, untouched in the Burrell loft next to the Christmas decorations and every back issue of *Silver Service Enthusiast*? Or were they . . . taken out from time to time?

We may never know. Just as we will never know the exact details of why the trial that arose from this misunderstanding was curtailed. All we have to go on is Burrell's record of a conversation he had with the Queen shortly after Diana died, in which Her Majesty apparently breathed: 'Be careful, Paul! There are powers at work in this country about which we have no knowledge!' To which Paul replied: 'Dude, you're married to one of them.' I'm sorry – that's a complete fabrication. But, in some ways, as credible as the next thing Her Maj was supposed to have said to him during this bilateral summit: 'No one, Paul, has been as close to a member of my family as you have.'

This week, Paul was claiming, in the course of disparaging Meghan, that the Queen had said: 'We are not celebrities, to be royal is something quite different.' Again, [citation needed]. According to Burrell, the baby shower 'can only spell disaster', 'it all seems very odd to me' and Meghan is 'handing every ammunition [*sic*] to shoot her down and she's not helping herself'.

No one helps himself like Paul, of course, who currently seems to be notching up twice-weekly advice to Meghan via various media appearances. Hard to pick a favourite, but let's play out with his ludicrous warning to Meghan just before Christmas that 'Sandringham is *Downton Abbey* on speed'. Sure. Base speed, if anything. Up for three days straight and horribly jittery. Walking aimlessly round the corridors at all hours with the other tormented night creatures. Asking Prince Edward if he's got any weed but saying no to the Valium because this one person you know knows someone else who had a heart attack by doing that and, yeah, basically the best thing is to just keep walking isn't it and see it out naturally and . . . Sorry, but no. Still, plenty more from Paul as and when we get it – feel free to stockpile your own downers accordingly.

Poor Prince Andrew is 'appalled' by Epstein. Let that be an end to it

24 August 2019

Perhaps a royal wedding for Princess Beatrice might offer a welcome distraction for a man-of-the-world under unfair scrutiny

It's basically your classic men-of-the-world vignette. Lying in business dress in the New York mansion of his friend Jeffrey Epstein, Prince Andrew is receiving a foot massage from a young, well-dressed Russian woman. Other men are in the room while this is happening, and they include Epstein (also being foot-massaged by a Russian woman) and the literary agent John Brockman, who runs a foundation connecting scientists and intellectuals with billionaires. As the young Russians work on their feet, Andy is complaining about his lot. 'In Monaco,' he says, according to Brockman's account, '[Prince] Albert works 12 hours a day but at 9pm, when he goes out, he does whatever he wants, and nobody cares. But if I do it, I'm in big trouble.'

Waa waa waa. What could be a more effective heartstring-tugger than 'other European princes have it better than me'? It's right up there with Chandler's line from *Friends*: 'My wallet's too small for my 50s, and my diamond shoes are too tight!'

The scene is recalled in an email revealed by Brockman's soon-to-be former client, the tech author Evgeny Morozov. He is one of many divesting themselves of any even tenuous Epstein association in the wake of the billionaire financier's suicide in a Manhattan jail earlier this month, as he awaited trial for sex trafficking, underage and otherwise.

But what of Andy? Under some scrutiny, he and ex-wife Duchess Fergie private-jetted away from Balmoral last week, then jetted on to the luxury bit of Sotogrande, where they are said to be gracing private barbecues. Briefings suggest, distractingly, that they might be getting back together. Andrew has been snapped on an exclusive golf course. His daughter Princess Beatrice might be getting engaged to her boyfriend. 'They're going to get married,' royal expert Ingrid Seward declared this week, divertingly. 'I was told by a member of the family.' So, on go the Yorks, now in sight of their second happily ever after.

Back to the foot-massage scene, though, where the chaps seem to have got on to Prince Albert's night-time freedom via the subject of Julian Assange. Brockman reports Andy saying: 'We think they're liberal in Sweden, but it's more like northern England as opposed to southern Europe.' Is the implication that Swedish authorities investigating sexual assault allegations are being illiberal?

Either way, you don't get all that nanny-state stuff on Epstein's private Virgin Islands property, reportedly known locally as 'Paedophile Island'. Or, as Buckingham Palace finally put it in a statement denying any impropriety on behalf of the prince: 'The

Duke of York has been appalled by the recent reports of Jeffrey Epstein's alleged crimes.'

I'm slightly sorry for the royal flunkies who had to issue this line, given that most of us are suffering eyeball strain from all the rolling we're doing. Even so, I do feel we need further clarification on what precisely the duke is appalled by. Is it just the 'recent reports'? Because if we're meant to believe that Prince Andrew is appalled by ALL of the crimes of Jeffrey Epstein – both the ones alleged and the ones he served actual jail time for – then allow me to treat this statement with all the dignity it deserves. To wit: BULL. SHIT. Bullshit Prince Andrew didn't know what sort of guy his friend was when he was snapped walking with the Tier 1 sex offender, after he got out of jail, in a photo the *New York Post* headlined 'PRINCE & PERV'. Bullshit he didn't know why his close friend WENT TO PRISON FOR A YEAR, so kept hanging out with him anyway. Bullshit if, as Brockman recounts, he lay on his back in that guy's house, with a Russian attending to his feet, talking over her head to men of the world about the nocturnal licence afforded to minor European royals, and he didn't know roughly what he was swimming in. Bullshit. I get we have to pay for Andrew's lifetime of jollies; but we don't have to have our intelligence insulted by him. I'm not even going to wheel out that old writing device where one says that Prince Andrew is either stupid or deeply compromised, and wonder archly which it is. Guys, he can be both! In fact, the one feeds the other.

The plain fact is that Andrew continued to be friends with Epstein even after he pleaded guilty to procuring an underage girl for prostitution. I guess it was the old she-said, he-said thing. Or, as the Palm Beach police chief put it: 'This was 50-something "shes" and one "he" – and the shes all basically told the same story.' Obviously, Epstein got away lightly with his grotesque plea deal, because 50-something:1 isn't the ratio you need. Even last year, they still needed 60 accusers to stop Bill Cosby. Donald Trump's

17:1 she–he ratio is nowhere near enough to keep him from the highest office on the planet.

As for where we go from here, perhaps a multimillion-pound royal wedding would indeed be helpful. It should be quite the opposite. Whereas Princess Anne pointedly didn't, Prince Andrew demanded all the titles and trappings for his two daughters – security details, civil-list money, full royal weddings – and was furious when denied some of them. Yet Beatrice and Eugenie still live like . . . well, princesses. So, instead of distracting from the miserable stories of the female attendees of various Epstein mansions, these gilded lives should throw them into even more shameful relief. They suggest the kind of man – and we've all met them – who has a two-tier view of the female sex. There is a world for their daughters, hopefully insulated from men like their friend Jeffrey, and then there is another for the girls who service their friend Jeffrey.

Yet decent, humane people know there aren't two kinds of women and girls – there are just women and girls. I'm reminded of the climactic line in *All My Sons*, where the wartime profiteer Joe Keller has been finally made – by his own son's suicide note – to see how his actions were responsible for the fate of so many other young men. 'I think to him they were all my sons,' Keller reflects. 'And I guess they were. I guess they were.'

And so with the girls in the stories that swirl around Epstein and his circle, which includes the duke: either broken or yet to be broken. But, ultimately, breakable. They are all daughters too, your Royal Highness. The Russian masseuse on your feet, the 17-year-old runaway on whose bare hip you have your hand in that fateful picture in London, the terrified 14-year-old who ran screaming from your great friend's house in her underwear, who you must have read about at the time, because I did, and I didn't even know the guy. And all the others. They are each someone's daughter, or they were once. They all once played at princesses and castles and imagined their own fairytale weddings. Funny how dreams die, isn't it – and who helps to crush them.

How badly must you do your job for your own mother to fire you? Ask Prince Andrew

22 November 2019

The Duke of York has been sacked, but he is unlikely to show up in the UK's unemployment figures

In a development that only someone of his preternatural self-awareness can have seen coming, Prince Andrew's family has decided he needs to spend less time with their brand. To put that into perspective, the Duke of York is widely agreed to have done his job so abysmally that a hereditary monarchy has had to resort to a version of meritocracy. The absolute infra dig of it.

The Queen's second son was summoned to a Buckingham Palace meeting on Wednesday, where it was revealed the Windsors were reducing the head count/making internal efficiencies/pivoting to video. People love to imagine the royal family are just like us, so this was just your standard meeting with your mother in which you're decruited and offered the chance to retrain as someone who does even less work for a dazzling fortune. A lottery winner, perhaps, or bitcoin thief.

We don't know exactly what Her Majesty said to Andrew, but as a piece of placeholder dialogue, it's probably best to imagine the Queen demanding his gun and badge, then barking: 'You're on traffic duty! Sex traffic duty.' It's a perverse kind of duty – then again, it appears to have been that way for a few decades now – but please resist the natural urge to see Prince Andrew as the true victim here. He is expected to pick up a zero-hours international golfing contract, and consequently will not show up in Britain's coercively massaged unemployment statistics.

So, yes, we must wait for those ventriloquisers at *The Crown* to get round to the full dramatisation a few series from now. The bad news is their failure to have bought in early to the character of Prince Andrew, a role they will undoubtedly need to cast in light of events. The good news is they can probably now get actual Prince Andrew to play it, given his revised schedule has more windows than Buckingham Palace.

Still, retiring in your 50s, having enjoyed a consequence-free career: if HRH does ever end up being interviewed by the police, he'll have some common ground with them. Some think a subpoena is a gathering possibility, with the former British consul-general in New York questioning Andrew's claim to have stayed with him and not Jeffrey Epstein in 2001, on one of the occasions Virginia Roberts Giuffre alleges she was trafficked to have sex with him. Meanwhile, lawyers for some of Epstein's victims are making repeated appearances on US TV to emphasise his legal and moral duty to be interviewed by the FBI about what he knows.

Not that the Duke of York ever seems to have realised how good he had it. Indeed, it's customary for royals to spend a significant amount of time being jealous of other royals who have it cushier than them. Prince Charles, for instance, has long resented Andrew's lifestyle-to-duty ratio. Meanwhile, Prince Harry is believed to resent Prince William for not being caught by the media in the same number of youthful japes/Nazi costumes/racist videos as he was. And so on and so on – because there's always a prince or princess who has it better than you. Violin sizes may vary. Informed royal sources suggest that while it was the Queen who formally removed Andrew from public duties, it was Charles – the 'shadow king' – pulling the strings. The P45 is unlikely to have pained Andrew's elder brother too much.

It felt inevitable by Wednesday in any case, despite various hints of rearguard actions as the fallout from the *Newsnight* interview mushroomed this week. My favourite was the suggestion that the prince could do another interview, to put right the omissions of the first. And in one sense, why not? God knows there were other places he could have gone – claiming to have caught porphyria from a sofa once owned by George III, for instance, or to have been chemically castrated in 'Nam. Then again, the interview-to-correct-the-interview does vaguely remind me of that answerphone scene in the movie *Swingers*. Having left a 'weird, desperate' message on a woman's answerphone, Jon Favreau's character leaves another to make up for it, which ends up being even more horrendous and excruciating. So he leaves another, and another, until the woman suddenly picks up the phone as he's leaving one and says: 'Don't ever call me again.' This, but with landmark TV interviews drawing a line under stories about your close association with an international child-sex offender.

And it really was a landmark, even accounting for the fact that, ever since George I, this has been a family widely recognised for its lack of intelligence. One of the sensational real-time revelations of the Emily Maitlis interview masterpiece was the fact that Prince Edward must have been the clever one. Andrew was fully scores of IQ points away from being bright enough to pull his gambit off, yet retained a stunningly misplaced faith in his own charm.

How? He and his far-from-estranged ex-wife were always a pair of rolling liabilities, with Fergie's decades of financial incontinence a worthy foe for even the royal family's vast coffers. Incredibly – and yet entirely credibly – she was in Saudi Arabia at Crown Prince Mohammed bin Salman's summit at the moment Andrew was recording his BBC interview. 'Everyone has been so nice here in Riyadh,' she gushed, presumably lucratively. 'I think that comes from good leadership.' What can you say? Other than never mind the bonesaws, and that there are few people in public life who have provided such a consistently baroque series of answers as the Yorks to the rhetorical question, 'How stupid do you actually have to be ...?'

On balance, then, we probably won't be seeing another Prince Andrew interview. It wasn't simply bad; it was the *Heaven's Gate* of royal interviews, basically killing the entire genre. Nobody ever made westerns like they used to after *Heaven's Gate*, and nobody in the royal family is going to be giving carte blanche to a BBC interviewer again in a hurry.

But the more famous thing about *Heaven's Gate*, of course, wasn't that it ended westerns – but that it ended its studio. Michael Cimino's monster flop effectively collapsed the entire studio that produced it, United Artists – and the question after Andrew's interview is how dangerous his monster flop is to the royal family that produced him. In the warp and weft of the UK's royal story, people are always looking for the incident about which they will end up saying: 'Well, in retrospect, that was the moment . . .' Some royal historians are already judging Andrew's interview as seismically as Edward VIII's abdication.

Maybe. Either way, it should always be remembered that the abdication crisis was hugely enjoyed by the public. As Evelyn Waugh noted in a 1936 diary entry: 'The Simpson crisis has been a great delight to everyone. At Maidie's nursing home they report a pronounced turn for the better in all adult patients. There can seldom have been an event that has caused so much general delight and so little pain.'

In contrast, events relating to Andrew's crisis have been very far from painless – despite his arresting failure to mention Epstein's victims. But it has certainly felt like a unifying moment for a divided nation, and that is surely worrying for the royal family. A YouGov poll found a mere 6% of people thought Andrew was telling the truth. This week, it has been hard to escape the distinct impression that people from all sides of various divides have come together to agree the prince was a true wrong 'un. And to ask each other if they really did actually hear a guy claim to be biologically incapable of sweating because he OD'd on adrenaline in the Falklands.

So it remains to be seen if this unprecedented Buckingham Palace containment strategy will work. What can be said with some confidence is that Prince Charles's forthcoming reign has long felt like a coach crash waiting to happen, and that this grotesque drama feeds into that. Along with David Attenborough, also 93, the Queen is perhaps the last consented-to link with the postwar consensus. *Après* her, the essential personnel are a complete shower.

This week, we caught a glimpse of the Windsors' potential exposure when the Queen departs the earthly realm. Members of the royal family are not too big to fail any more. That feels of a piece with our deeply fractured nation, in which so many institutions have revealed themselves as no longer up to the job. Shortly after the EU referendum, a French diplomat likened the British government to a cartoon character that has run off a cliff but not yet realised it: 'They're in the air now, but at some point they're going to look down and fall.' Those words ring uncomfortably true for much beyond government on this septic isle. All sorts of jigs are up, all at once, for a post-imperial country that has been running on its own fumes for decades. Things go along much as before, until – seemingly abruptly, but not really – they don't. What now for it all? I can't help thinking of that great bit of Hemingway dialogue from *The Sun Also Rises*. 'How did you go bankrupt?' 'Two ways,' comes the reply. 'Gradually and then suddenly.'

Whatever you think of Harry and Meghan, their media critics are far worse

16 February 2021

Self-appointed 'defenders of the royal family's honour' may want to have a good, hard look at themselves

Like a lot of middle-aged newspapermen, the only reason I lose my mind over anything Meghan does is because I care – truly care – about the dignity of the royal family. There is something deeply sacred and pure about the throne of Olde England, which will in due course be inherited by a man who fantasised about being reincarnated as a tampon. The newspapermen know the thing about the tampon because the man's phone calls were hacked, and then they published them. So, yes, if it falls to Fleet Street's noblemen to defend the honour of the crown against a Californian wellness bore, then so be it.

News that Meghan and her husband Prince Harry are expecting another baby is followed by news that they will appear on *Oprah*. Both of these pieces of news follow last week's news that the duchess had won her privacy case against the *Mail on Sunday*, which had published her private letter to her father. As you can imagine, this triple threat of tidings has caused some commentators to completely lose their minds.

Alas, no matter how ridiculous anything Meghan and Harry ever do is – and they frequently are ridiculous – it will never, ever be even a hundredth as ridiculous as the behaviour of those foaming at the mouth about it. Where do you start with people whose chief criticism of the couple is that they are privileged and largely talentless, and the only reason they're raking it in is because of their name? 'We've got a caller on line one who says that up till now the royal family's always been a meritocracy.' Can't believe they've denied talented grafters like Fergie's girls their chance.

As for the complaint that Meghan and Harry are using their association with the crown to enrich themselves, have we stumbled into the 11th century? If not, please catch up! It's always been this way. I guess Meghan and Harry's real crime is making money off TV companies as opposed to the backs of peasants or siphoning it out of the Empire. On a PR level, it would probably help the Sussexes tactically if they now partnered with a pirate slaver or commandeered an entire country's mining concessions. A series of tedious authored documentaries for Netflix is simply too grotesque a route to wealth.

As someone whose chief concern is the gaiety of the nation, I find the new power dynamics quite bracing. The sovereign grant paid by UK taxpayers to the British royal family is £85.9m, which is less than Netflix spends on a single series of *The Crown*. You have to remember that America is a place so gushing with money that even Duchess Fergie has found ways to get sprayed with it there. It's somewhere even Paul Burrell had his own TV show. He was a judge on something called *American Princess*, which taught US girls how to behave like a princess. I never watched it, but I hope one of the challenges was playing dead while Paul put a hoard of your more portable belongings in his car, then hid them in his loft. For 'safekeeping'. Truly, he was Diana's rock.

I like to think of Paul as a rock in the Alcatraz sense, in that you honestly can't escape him. He still pops up, seemingly biweekly, to offer a verdict about how Meghan 'isn't helping herself'. Like the newspapers and the media outlets, Burrell serves as a reminder that only certain people and organisations are permitted – usually by themselves – to make money out of royalty.

As it goes, I always thought Meghan was an ideal fit with the House of Windsor. Like them, she has several appalling and grasping relatives, and though they are not as innately classy as Prince

Andrew or the children of SS officers or anything, the no-good Markles gave obligingly car-crash interviews and obediently staged photos for the press. They are, in that sense, deeply Windsorian. Ultimately, the Markles seemed to understand it was their job to provide competitively priced content from which newspapers could profit much more handsomely than themselves. Just like the royal family Meghan and Harry have left behind on this septic isle.

Naturally, you can see why some small-pond UK pundits simply can't handle the Sussexes' move to America. It's a horrendous moment when you realise your competition for royal stories and interviews is no longer some necrotic dipsomaniac on a rival tabloid, but Oprah. Much UK media reaction to Meghan and Harry reeks of this gathering powerlessness. Though having less and less of a clue is certainly not limited to this matter. Face it, we're a country where one of the best ideas the government could come up with for hanging on to an independence-leaning Scotland was sending Prince Edward to live in it – a solution that treats Scotland like some Victorian attic. Maybe we should store some of Paul Burrell's dresses in Scotland.

We're a country where the guys leading the media charge against Meghan are so emotionally warped that the only way they can begin to release their feelings of social, racial and sexual resentment is by using a 94-year-old woman's feelings as a proxy. 'They have disrespected the Queen' really means 'They have disrespected this newspaper' or 'They have disrespected me.' So you keep hearing people saying, 'How could they do this to the Queen?' and 'It's the Queen I feel sorry for.' Why? She's not your grandmother. You don't know her socially. It doesn't count that you've been through her bins or covertly taken pictures of her breakfast table or whatever. And it hardly needs saying that she would find you, personally, absolutely detestable. I honestly wouldn't wet your pants about it, you know?

Yet the wetting of pants continues. The biggest cry this week is that Meghan and Harry do want publicity, but only the kind that suits them. They 'want it all their own way'. Um . . . yes? So does everyone. So do I. So, most pertinently, do you. You want people to care about only one human right, the right to free speech, unless it's Meghan and Harry, in which case they can't have it. You want people to think you're the greatest journalists in the world, even though you had the story of the prince and his paedo mate staring you in the face and preferred to run headlines like 'Is Meghan's favourite [avocado] snack fuelling drought and murder?' You want people to only remember the driver was drunk, even though there was a large number of paparazzi chasing Diana at high speed. You want to loftily declare you will no longer use paparazzi photos, then use them all the time, every single day. In short, you want the fricking fairytale. Well, guess what: EVERYONE ELSE WANTS IT TOO.

So if it looks to you like Meghan's getting it, and you're not any more, then you need to face the unavoidable takeout: you've been outmanoeuvred by an emotional wellness podcaster. It's like being out-strategised by kale. As people who care – truly care – about dignity, do just let the absolute indignity of that sink in.

The tributes to Prince Philip have revealed so much – about other people

14 April 2021

The no-nonsense duke might have hated 'All This', but that hasn't stopped an entire nation from pontificating about him

Day five of the period of national mourning for Prince Philip, and the consensus is that 'Of course, he would have absolutely hated All This!' This judgment is generally made as someone trowels on a bit more of This. Particular pride is taken by those who are producing the sort of anecdote to which the late Duke of Edinburgh would surely have remarked, 'Get on with it,' or 'Is there much more of this?' One MP's tribute began: 'You mentioned in your opening remarks the duke's interest in ties.' Prince Philip's tailor offered a detailed account of how his waist measurement had expanded only around three inches over several decades.

But normal things such as barbecuing are held to become absolutely wondrous when royals do them. In his exquisitely naughty Princess Margaret book, Craig Brown quotes one royal biographer typical of their genre: 'The Queen and Prince Philip drove themselves to the polo ground. Philip drove a station wagon, the Queen her favourite Rover. Sometimes, instead of changing into polo gear at the castle, Prince Philip was seen changing, quite uncomfortably, in his automobile, sitting sideways, pulling his breeches on. Then –' Then?! Then what? This had better be fricking incredible. 'Then he would stand up and fasten the belt . . .' We'll leave it there for space reasons. The point is: can you imagine this passage of almost hypnotic dullness appearing in a biography of anyone else famous on the entire planet, except for a member of the royal family?

We know that Prince Philip has gone to the good place because many MPs spent yesterday afternoon telling us this. But you can easily envisage a Sartrean short story in which a man is hellishly trapped in some windbag's anecdote about him changing in the front seat of a car, condemned to spend all eternity never quite reaching the moment when he can fasten the belt and exit.

The genuinely interesting tales from Philip's genuinely storied life could all be read last Saturday. Since then, the currents and crosscurrents of reaction have revealed rather more about other people – even other countries – than they have about him. I kept thinking of the *Friends* episode questioning whether there is any truly selfless good deed as Keir Starmer yesterday chose to lionise the duke's 'quiet virtues' and 'discipline', while Boris Johnson preferred to insist that a history of what might appear casual racism was in fact just a man 'trying to break the ice, to get things moving, to get people laughing'. Both men seem to have seen what they needed to see in Philip.

Remainers have made sledgehammer references to the Europeanism Philip brought to the UK, while others pointedly claimed he was a typical refugee. Some people were simply telling other people about themselves: 'I am someone who values duty and constancy', or 'I am the sort of person who is too grown-up and egalitarian for such things.' Others have yet to get to the bottom of themselves: 'I am weeping for a man who thought tears a sign of ridiculous weakness.'

There certainly have been many signs of weakness, such as the BBC news anchor for whom breaking news seemed to presage almost breaking down as she read the palace statement announcing the duke's death. Do buck up, madam! Others loved it, naturally. It got great reviews in MailOnline's comment section, where emotion was equated with a sense of occasion. Nigel Farage immediately decided the tribute from Prince Harry's foundation wasn't anywhere near emotional enough, claiming it evidenced 'contempt'. Do buck up, sir! Nigel and many others would have benefited from being packed off to Philip-era Gordonstoun, where they would have been forced to wake to cold showers and barefoot runs and to have this absolute wetness knocked out of them.

Meanwhile, the BBC's wall-to-wall Friday coverage has become the most complained-about event in British TV history – but a full 116 actual Britons also complained that the Beeb was making it too easy to complain about its coverage. Honestly. No one IN the royal family has ever been a tenth as mad as some people are ABOUT the royal family – not even George III.

Speaking of America, I enjoyed a report in the entertainment industry news bible *Deadline* – 'Blanket Coverage of Prince Philip's Death Proves to Be a Big Turn-Off for British TV Viewers' – which seemed to view the event simply as an unforced ratings catastrophe. I suddenly clicked that American showbiz being so resolutely on Meghan's 'side' is partly rooted in Hollywood's gorgeously atavistic commercialism. They must feel pure incomprehension that the royal family should have lost/driven away/ whatever one of their biggest box-office stars. In this reading, the Windsors are like a golden-age studio that has simply failed to hang on to a highly bankable performer. Ultimately, Meghan's self-exile was a talent-management failure – proper showbiz sacrilege.

Over here, the duke's death was one of those moments that neatly displays how social media has changed people's behaviour. The film critic David Thomson is brilliant on how the advent of Sky Sports changed how footballers carry themselves on the pitch. The explosion in camera numbers and angles has turned them into entirely different performers to their predecessors from simpler visual times. Footballers are now television stars – and their gestures and expressions have consequently become tailored to the medium, being predominantly for the benefit of its audience. As Thomson puts it, 'They know they are part of a system of close-ups and slow motion.'

Something similar has happened on a mass scale with social media. People are far more performative online, in accordance with their consciousness of being watched. My colleague Jonathan Freedland made me laugh recently when he noted how Twitter had turned everyone into the Archbishop of Canterbury, somehow feeling that every major news story requires them to issue an official statement. Huge numbers of people now regard themselves as bound to post the sort of formal reactions to Philip's death that were once the preserve of former presidents of the United States or the queen of Denmark.

I'm not talking about the sort of things you can imagine people saying conversationally to others back when not everything was pixels – 'I hadn't realised his sisters weren't allowed at the wedding,' or 'My mum met him at the WI and said he was lovely.' No, I'm on about this type of stuff: 'Hugely sad at the death of the Duke of Edinburgh. He was a modernising influence on the House of Windsor, and his prickly exterior hid passions few understood. My thoughts are with the Queen.' Why thank you, random 41-year-old dude from the internet, and welcome to the Pooter party. But really, this is the sort of pontification one formerly expected only from absurdly pompous people utterly devoid of self-awareness or public standing, such as newspaper columnists.

A nation of archbishops-slash-newspaper-columnists – yet another thing Prince Philip surely wouldn't have wanted. But then, neither royal fans nor royal detractors care entirely selflessly about what the royals want. Emotions are for us, not them. They are mostly required to serve as Rorschach blots, in which we see only what we wish and reveal only ourselves. Knowingly or otherwise.

They won't remind us, but the tabloids hurt Diana just as much as *Panorama* did

21 May 2021

The BBC makes a convenient scapegoat, when in reality all of us were part of the ecosystem that destroyed Diana

'It brings indescribable sadness', ran Prince William's statement on the damning report into *Panorama*'s interview with his mother, 'to know that the BBC's failures contributed significantly to her fear, paranoia and isolation that I remember from those final years with her.'

'Paranoia' – what a word to take you back. When Martin Bashir's Diana interview aired in 1995, the MP (and friend of Prince Charles) Nicholas Soames was roundly attacked for describing Diana as in 'the advanced stages of paranoia' and in the grip of 'mental illness'. It's fair to say his verdict didn't come from a place of total support. Soames has since expressed regret for it, adding that he wasn't a doctor. Now, Diana's elder son uses the same word – with few these days disagreeing over how cruelly she was driven to it – while her younger son absolutely refuses to draw some comforting veil over her state of mental health.

The conclusions of the Dyson report are a shameful stain on the BBC, deeply compounded by coming 26 years after the offence, by way of cover-up and whitewash. How completely stunning that former director general Tony Hall judged Bashir 'an honest and honourable man', when anything more than cursory scrutiny marked him out so clearly – and I'm not a doctor – as a complete wrong 'un. It feels particularly gracious that Prince Harry's own statement tacitly acknowledged the BBC for 'taking some form of accountability' and 'owning it'.

And so to people yet to take ownership of their own actions. I think we can live without today's preposterous moralising from much of Fleet Street, who know very well the terrible things they and others did on countless occasions to get stories relating to Diana or her wider family. 'Defund the BBC,' was last night's pontification from former *Sun* editor Kelvin MacKenzie, who once put Diana's covertly recorded private phone calls on a premium-rate line so readers could ring in and have a listen. And those were the good years. Half the stuff these guys did in pursuit of Diana stories is, mercifully for them, completely unprintable.

Alas, we will spend the next few days hearing of the BBC's shame from some of the most shameless hypocrites in human history. The tabloids may not like Prince Harry's reincarnation as a super-rich Californian wellness wally, but it does have the moral edge over pulling people's medical records and hacking the phones of murdered 13-year-old girls.

But, of course, few have rewritten their own history more than Fleet Street's Diana-watchers. The overnight timing of the Paris crash meant the early editions of the Sunday papers had already been printed and contained, as usual, large amounts of unfavourable stuff about whatever else Diana had been up to the previous week. 'Troubled Prince William will today demand that his mother Princess Diana dump her playboy lover,' ran an exclusive by the *News of the World*'s Clive Goodman, who probably scraped it from the 'troubled' schoolboy's phone. There were acres in similar vein across the titles. 'The Princess, I fear,' feared the *Sunday Mirror*'s Carole Malone, 'suffers from the "Open Gob Before Brain Engages" syndrome – a condition which afflicts the trivial and the brain dead.' When Diana's death was announced, the reverse ferrets were so total that it's genuinely quite a surprise the *Sunday Mirror* didn't next week salute itself as 'the paper that broke the tragic news Di was brain dead'.

As for the editors, the person they secretly canonised was the driver, Henri Paul. Because once it was discovered he was over the alcohol limit, then what happened to Diana in the tunnel couldn't have been anything to do with the ecosystem in which they (and the chasing paparazzi who supplied them) were such voracious feeders.

Twenty-four years later, a full-spectrum failure to acknowledge any of this means many of these same people now sit and venerate Diana in the course of slagging off her troubled son, Prince Harry (it's what she would have wanted). They know very well the pain and turmoil of Diana's final years, having been such a helpful part of it, yet cannot tolerate the understandably damaged child raised amid it.

And so it is that Harry is now locked in his own grimly symbiotic relationship with sections of the British media. He won't shut up, which is what they claim to want, but don't, because his every SHAMELESS! AND! DISGRACEFUL! UTTERANCE! drives traffic. Attacks on Harry do huge business, so they continue. He, in turn, can point to those attacks as continued evidence of persecution. (Indeed, his livelihood might end up depending on wounded, marquee interviews. I'm not sure that long-term ratings lie in the Sussexes' dull-sounding ideas for documentaries in which they themselves do not feature.) This is nearly as toxic a cycle as the one in which Diana was locked, and is unlikely to have a happy ending, or even a happy middle.

I once saw some old news footage in which the Queen and Prince Philip returned home from a royal tour after leaving their children for six months. A mere part of the welcome party, the unsmiling five-year-old Prince Charles waits dutifully, simply required to shake his mother's hand. Anyone claiming this was entirely normal 'in those days' has royal brain worms. Yet Harry's recent suggestion that neither he nor his father had an especially healthy childhood is regarded as some kind of grotesque blasphemy, mostly by people who would be quite happy to refer to the above vignette as child abuse were anyone other than the Queen involved. These days, what is expected of the royals has become so warped that it is perfectly standard to find MailOnline commenters fuming of Harry, 'How DARE he bring his mother into this?'

Which brings us to the final group not to own their own actions: the great British public. Millions bought insatiably into Diana's pain, and newspaper sales spiked for all the most obviously intrusive stories. The pall of blameless sanctimony that descended after her death was a stunning exercise in mass hypocrisy. People were simply incapable of imagining that they too had been part of the ecosystem, and those who pointed it out were demonised by deflection. *Private Eye* was monstered for its cover, which carried the headline 'MEDIA TO BLAME' above a crowd of people outside Buckingham Palace. 'The papers are a disgrace,' read one speech bubble. 'Yes, I couldn't get one anywhere,' ran its reply. 'Borrow mine,' went a third, 'it's got a picture of the car.' WH Smith banned the edition from its stores, while taking money for the papers hand over fist.

From Diana to Harry, damaged people do damaged and sometimes very damaging things. But it's important to remember, as far as the royal family is concerned, that the public likes it so much better that way. Royal pain sells far more than royal happiness. *Panorama* may have lied – but the sales tallies and the traffic figures and the ratings never do.

2022: 12 PARTIES, A WAR AND A RESIGNATION

Overshadowing the year is Russian president Vladimir Putin's monstrous assault on Ukraine and its people – the biggest conflict in Europe since the second world war. But the story of Downing Street's lockdown-busting bashes is formally fitted with its '-gate' suffix, and Partygate becomes the scandal that simply will not die for Boris Johnson. A report into the affair by the civil servant Sue Gray is delayed at the eleventh hour, when the Metropolitan police finally decide to investigate 12 parties in No. 10 and Whitehall. The prime minister is found by the police to have broken his own laws. As the cost-of-living crisis begins to bite, the Conservative party's succession plotting manages to be both hasty and dilatory, but the revolt finally boils over after it is revealed that Johnson knew about sex pest allegations against his deputy chief whip before he appointed him. On 7 July, Johnson resigns, sparking a leadership contest that will give the UK its fourth prime minister in just over six years.

Who's really leading Britain – Boris Johnson or the crazy-face emoji?

11 January 2022

Seemingly, no one at a potential 100-person boozy lockdown gathering was able to predict it would upset the general public

As a lot of people in Boris Johnson's life have discovered, there is a point where he has simply broken too many things for the relationship to be put functionally back together again. Is he at that point with the British public, or even with the Conservative party?

Many are getting a really addled whiff of Humpty Dumpty off the latest revelations that the prime minister himself attended a 'mass gathering' in the Downing Street garden during the first lockdown. This May 2020 BYOB drinks party, *to which more than 100 people were invited*, kicked off a mere 55 minutes after that day's designated cabinet minister had given a national press conference insisting that people in England could only meet one person from another household outdoors, so . . . what was the party theme? Let them eat cheese and wine? Come as the last scene in *Animal Farm*?

Spellbindingly, Johnson yesterday refused to even admit he'd been at the drinks party, his smile twitching and his eyes swivelling as he cowered in some vaccination centre and gibbered: 'All that, as you know, is the subject of a proper investigation by Sue Gray.' Had he been interviewed by Sue Gray? 'All that is a subject for investigation by Sue Gray.'

I'm afraid the only sane response to this is: what?! What are you even talking about? Did you or didn't you go to a big party in your garden, you smirking fibreglass toby jug? Or do you also have to wait for some veteran civil servant to tell you whether or not you put your pants on the right way round this morning? Honestly, mate, just MAN UP. Johnson's turn as 'prime minister' seems to have moved past the sarcastic air quotes phase. This feels a lot like government by the crazy-face emoji, tongue lolling out and one eye boggling bigger than the other. Any Tory MP who voted for this galaxy-class liar to become leader should remember they were wrong on probably the biggest call of their career and consider resigning before the next election to go and work for a charity/ arms dealer.

Speaking of manning up, I wonder if the organisers managed to find any ladies to attend this 20 May party? I mean, I'm not saying that people who do well under Johnson are mainly guys who spent a significant part of the past decade masturbating to *Game of Thrones*. No, wait – I am. But one of my favourite things about the one Downing Street cheese-and-wine 'work meeting' that we have an actual photo of is that the only two women I can see in it are Carrie Johnson and Gina Coladangelo. Remember, girls: if you want to work at the heart of government, you need to be either a man or in a relationship with a man who does. If you can dream it, you can do it!

Back to the BYOB party, though – sorry, I know you need flashcards to keep your rule-breaking Downing Street pandemic bashes in order – which was organised by Johnson's principal private secretary, Martin Reynolds. Apparently, Reynolds now wants to get back to the diplomatic service, and perhaps the Middle East, and there is some talk about him being made an ambassador. You know, like when you or I break the rules and mess up spectacularly at work, and they make us an ambassador.

Two days after the May BYOB party, the story of Dominic Cummings's rule-breaking trips to Durham and Barnard Castle broke, which you'd think would have given these people a lifelong unforgettable lesson in just how incandescent the public were about rule-breaking by the elite. (And yet, given all the Downing

Street parties which followed that Christmas, they somehow forgot it.) But in May 2020, who could have predicted that a potential 100-person boozy gathering could piss the general public off? Who could have predicted that people who'd watched their family members die on an iPad, then buried them with only permitted numbers of mourners at graveside funerals would have an issue with it? No one at the party, apparently. In which case, every single one of them is in the wrong job and should resign and go and work for a thinktank/be our man in Havana.

Incredibly, even the Met are finally 'in contact' with the Cabinet Office over the latest party revelation. So do settle down to another episode of this farce, which might be entitled 'NO RUSH, PLOD'. Yet again we have to ask: where were the multiple police officers who were stationed in and around the Downing Street complex when this BYOB party was happening? Did they notice at least 30 people having a booze-up, three hours after their force's official social media account was reminding people of the rules? If not, is it just possible they might be in the wrong line of work?

Smartphones mean most people can check photos to see what they were doing on 20 May that year. I note this party occurred fairly soon after a Met officer told me to stop playing cricket in the park with my children, on the basis that cricket is 'sport but not exercise'. Admittedly, I don't care to run singles (I see myself as the Chris Gayle of Kensington Gardens), but let's not forget how officious police forces up and down the land were at the time.

What so many hundreds of thousands of us will also never forget, alas, are our own darker stories: graveside funerals; Zoom funerals; funerals after which no gathering was allowed by law. Just weeks before 20 May a 13-year-old boy had died alone in a London hospital, separated from his family, who were also unable to attend his funeral because they were adhering to isolation regulations. Every single person at the Downing Street party would have known that story.

But I am afraid this goes even further than shame and deceit. It is increasingly unignorable that these serial exposés of No. 10 culture are taking place against a backdrop of growing conspiracism in this country. Significant numbers of people turned to online misinformation over the pandemic, and a lot of previously soft conspiracism is now calcifying in deeply concerning ways. More are being sucked down those rabbit holes all the time.

I say sucked, but every one-rule-for-them revelation amounts to a push. After all, when people repeatedly see the duplicity and double standards of those in command, is conspiracism really such an irrational response? The tragedy is that we will all end up paying for the breakdown in trust, both in ways which are already obvious, such as rising anti-vax sentiment, and in ways we cannot yet predict. But they are coming, and Boris Johnson's way of doing business has hastened them. How can we counter some people's conviction that The Man is lying to them, when the man is so often shown to be lying?

Never mind wine fridges, the Tory party is drunk on Kool-Aid

1 February 2022

Yes, Conservative MPs really are rallying around a PM who used a paedophile-based conspiracy theory as a figleaf

If you've ever wondered what Jim Jones's corpse would have looked like if it had spent three weeks getting bleached and bloated by a Guyanese river, it floated up to the House of Commons dispatch box yesterday at 3.30pm.

Let's begin with some real talk. The prime minister is under police investigation for multiple breaches of his own Covid laws. At least four gatherings or parties in which Boris Johnson was directly involved are being probed by the Met, including one in his private flat. In total, police are investigating 12 potentially law-breaking Downing Street parties which took place after the British people had been ordered – BY HIM – to live under the most restrictive rules imposed in peacetime. The Global Britain that Johnson promised saw him yesterday bin off a call to the Russian president, who is apparently on the brink of an invasion, so that he could explain to the Commons that he needs to wait for police officers to decide if he went to an illicit party in his own home. The Conservative MPs somehow able to make their peace with all this increasingly resemble cult members accepting the latest transparent lies and failures of a cult leader.

Suitcases full of Kool-Aid seem to have been wheeled into Johnson's meeting with Tory MPs last night. Two weeks ago, Birmingham Northfield MP Gary Sambrook was widely reported to be one of the leading lights of a plot to remove Johnson; last night he issued a dispatch from the compound in which he declared the PM to be 'the Boris Johnson we love and who has delivered'. Sorry, Gary, but wake up. This ends with a bungling Swat team going through the window and discovering the whole place is wired.

As for what Johnson said to his followers last night, he is reported to have compared himself to Othello, who he seems to think was 'always seeing the best in people'. Righto. To confirm: the country isn't just being run by a guy who can't even understand the plot of *Othello*, but by a guy who can't even understand the plot of *Othello* and is writing a book about Shakespeare. It's called not giving a fuck, Gary – look it up. That said, good to see the PM getting his excuses in early for shopping Desdemona to the cops for her Abba party.

And yet, for someone who normally puts the 'I am' into iambic pentameter, Johnson will still speak only in the first person plural when it comes to 'taking responsibility' for what his investigator

Sue Gray found to be 'failures of leadership'. What a tell. As he preferred it yesterday in his statement to the Commons: 'We must look ourselves in the mirror, and we must learn.' Who's 'we'? Face it, Gary – he's the least convincing man in the mirror since Michael Jackson.

In fact, speaking of paedos, the prime minister chose to use one as a figleaf. Such a Churchill move. When the hour for leadership came, Johnson opted to knowingly advance a grotesque and indefensible conspiracist lie that Keir Starmer, when he was head of the Crown Prosecution Service, failed to prosecute Jimmy Savile.

All Conservatives who regard themselves as decent need to ask if it's really that much of a leap from this sort of thing to some of the other paedophile-based conspiracies that are increasingly part of the dangerous undertow of global populist politics. If they're not up to confronting it, it will continue. On past form, the Met will spend months not getting to the bottom of things. Should any fines be issued, I'm sure Johnson will get some Tory donor to set up a blind trust to pay for his. He should start running a cash phone-line during PMQs, like a proper televangelist.

At least those who remember what the past two years were actually like – i.e. everyone – can be glad that Gray's update acknowledged something crucial. Yes, she stated, working at Downing Street during the pandemic was challenging. 'Those challenges, however, also applied to key and frontline workers across the country who were working under equally, if not more, demanding conditions, often at a risk to their own health . . . The hardship under which citizens across the country worked, lived and sadly even died while observing the government's regulations and guidance rigorously are known only too well.'

This is a vital counter to the frankly eye-popping number of anonymous exceptionalist briefings from Downing Street employees, which talk about the 'saviour complex' by which some staff were apparently gripped. Unsurprisingly, perhaps, no one has ended up being more elitist than the guys who swept to power promising to smash elites, but who turned out to regard themselves as miles above rules that were followed even *in extremis* by silly little people like the actual head of state.

It wasn't always this way. By chance, one of my children recently visited Bletchley Park, which, as you know, was the centre of the Allied code-breaking operation during the second world war, without which the war might not have been won. According to his guide, they only started serving beer at the end of a shift in 1944. To put that into perspective, by that stage there was a fourth rotor on the Enigma machine, meaning the number of possible combinations had leaped to truly head-frying levels, and the staff had been working round the clock at the facility for a full five years of global conflict, under the constant threat of bombing. Flash forward to 2020. When they were getting pissed at 6pm in the garden in May, the desk johnnies of Downing Street had been stewarding a peacetime lockdown for TWO EFFING MONTHS. I mean, if you can't do that without intravenous prosecco, then . . . buck up?! Run along and work in interiors PR? This is the same self-awareness-to-self-regard ratio as people who list their occupation as 'film producer' but haven't actually produced any films.

As things stand, insufficient numbers of Conservative MPs are prepared to wake up and smell the cordite. But all the Tories defending Johnson and skirting around these insults to ordinary people shouldn't feel alone in the world. They have as their spiritual cousins all those craven Republicans who now refuse to condemn Donald Trump, despite the fact that they know he is a liar and a crook, know that he cares only about himself and thinks that rules are for little people, and know that he regards even them with a mixture of amusement and contempt.

Backing Johnson in the face of all this is really not much different from scuttling down to Mar-a-Lago to pay obeisance and hoping you get smiled at. Come on – what's the worst that can happen?

The innocent have paid a high price for the Post Office scandal. The guilty have not

15 February 2022

It was the word of hundreds of Post Office workers against a faulty computer system. Guess who was believed?

Some stories feel so unbelievable that every time you think of them again, you have to sit with the basic concept for a few moments just to remind yourself how truly, staggeringly outrageous the whole business is. It's almost as if your head has to be got round it all over again, every single time you go there. I'm like that with the Post Office scandal, which as of this week is the subject of an active public inquiry.

In the spirit of rearranging our heads once more, let's do the brief summary: between 2000 and 2014, 736 subpostmasters and postmistresses were prosecuted for theft, fraud and false accounting in the branches of the Post Office they ran. Their lives – and the lives of thousands of others – were torn apart. They were financially ruined, put out of work, locally shunned, driven into poor health and addiction, saw their marriages destroyed. Some – from a 19-year-old woman to mothers of young children to all manner of others – were imprisoned for many months. At least 33 victims of the scandal are now dead; at least four reportedly took their own lives. But . . . they had done nothing wrong. *They had done nothing wrong.* The blame, in fact, lay with Horizon, a faulty computer system designed by Fujitsu and imposed on their branches by Post Office management.

It is currently being described as the most widespread miscarriage of justice in British history. And here's the kicker: many post office operators had been reporting problems with Horizon to the

Post Office right from the outset. The Post Office not only failed to investigate adequately, but demanded the staff made up the financial shortfalls personally and denied to the complainants that anyone else had similar issues. Up in the rarefied air of the executive suite was Paula Vennells, who took over as CEO in 2012. Under her leadership the Post Office prosecuted hundreds of subpostmasters. To this date – more than 20 years on in some cases – nobody from the Post Office or Fujitsu, or the civil servants charged with oversight, has been held accountable, much less faced criminal investigation themselves. Instead, victims' heads have rolled.

So that's the short version, but of course it all feels inadequate. Even simply listing every individual injustice in the sparsest possible terms would take far more space than I have available; at even cursory depth, every single story is utterly heartbreaking and utterly extraordinary. And to add to the sheer WTF-ery, these are *subpostmasters* we're talking about, often working meticulously for long hours serving small communities. It's backbone-of-Britain stuff – and the prison doors clanged shut on them.

Among other burning questions, then, the current inquiry will look at whether the Post Office bigwigs knew there were bugs and glitches in the computer system, but pushed ahead with the prosecuting and the life-ruining anyway. I don't want to unleash too many spoilers here – it's important that viewers get to experience the breakneck magic of a British public inquiry in real time – but let's just say that a high court judge in 2019 described the Post Office's approach as 'the 21st-century equivalent of maintaining that the Earth is flat'.

Other highlights of the story? You'll enjoy the episode covering the bit where Post Office CEO Paula Vennells gets a CBE in the year 2019 (TWENTY NINETEEN), and then gets made both chair of London's Imperial College Healthcare NHS trust and something called 'a non-executive board member of the Cabinet Office', presumably because the government thought it important to bring in our brightest brains from business. By way of an inspired satirical touch, Paula also moonlighted as an Anglican priest and as a member of the Church of England Ethical Investment Advisory Group. (She has since 'stepped back' from these positions.) In 2019, after the Post Office agreed to pay nearly £58m to settle claims, Vennells issued a statement saying, 'I am truly sorry we were unable to find both a solution and a resolution outside of litigation and for the distress this caused.'

Ah. Students of apology types may have identified this as the classic sorry-that-we-just-HAD-to-hound-you-into-court apology. It's a real pro move, and your inability to execute it is why you, an amateur, live in fear of losing your livelihood, while hotshots like Paula and co. take millions and get bumped up into first class on the gravy train, no matter how monstrous their screwups. For while the subpostmasters have gone through the sort of wringer that makes Kafka feel like a Disney musical, extraordinary compassion has been shown to the managerial class in all this, who have been showered with honours and directorships and bonuses throughout.

Elsewhere, it must be said that this sorry saga has not been the finest hour of much of the news media. Most papers and TV news outlets would now admit they horribly under-reported the Post Office story over the years, with all the running made by the likes of *Private Eye*, *Computer Weekly* and the BBC journalist Nick Wallis, to say nothing of the campaigning victims themselves, such as the heroic Alan Bates.

As for the wider lessons of the scandal, what a lot it says about a society crossing the threshold of the third millennium that *thousands* of entirely upstanding human beings were disbelieved in favour of trusting a computer. Actually believing in the confusion and anguish of that famously gangsterish demographic – British subpostmasters – was regarded as a wholly irrational act. This, I'm afraid, is a version of 'only following orders'.

And it's also, alas, the bit where those of us who cannot believe it happened simply have to look around us. Today, technology is deferred to, even in the face of human tragedy, far more than it was 20 years ago. Spool onwards in the timeline and you will find more and more examples of ways in which technology was deemed to know best. In 2015, it emerged that in one three-year period, 2,380 sick and disabled people had died shortly after being declared 'fit for work' by a computerised test and having their sickness benefits withdrawn. Today, bereaved parents are told that nothing can be done about the algorithms that pushed their teenage children remorselessly in the direction of content they believe ultimately contributed to them taking their own lives, even as a Facebook whistleblower recently said that the firm was 'unwilling to accept even little slivers of profit being sacrificed for safety'. At the time the Post Office scandal began unfolding, Facebook wasn't even a glint in Mark Zuckerberg's eye; now, many technology firms are more powerful than nation states. Back then, *Little Britain*'s Carol Beer worked as a bank teller or holiday rep; now, computer-says-no culture runs the world.

Just when No. 10 wants to be taken seriously, it creates Sir Gavin Williamson

4 March 2022

It's hard to believe Boris Johnson will really crack down on Putin's cronies when he's just knighted one of his own

To pick this precise moment to give Gavin Williamson a knighthood reveals much about Boris Johnson. Why doesn't the prime minister just give Gavin a gas field, or a bank, and make him honorary president of British Fencing? No. 10 probably felt yesterday was a good day to bury bad news. Instead, there was plenty of fury at the revelation that yet another useless person has been deemed sufficiently useful to Johnson to receive an honour. Sir Gavin joins Lord Lebedev and far too many others. Say hello to the wallygarchy.

Given the ever more horrifying events in Ukraine, this local reward for failure can obviously be regarded as a trifle. On the one hand, it doesn't exactly matter if Gavin Williamson is made a knight of some corner of an irradiated Europe. On the other, it's telling that at the very moment the occupants of Downing Street are trying to reach for moral stature, they remind you just how small they really are.

One major lesson of the horrors of the past eight days, since Russia's invasion of Ukraine, is that we are in a new era. That new era, for those of us with the immeasurable luxury of not being bombed into it, should involve a taking of stock and a moral reset. Values, standards and principles matter in liberal democracies. Some of ours have been allowed to become rather tattered. For instance, we can and must agree that public service is not merely the gateway to cronyism. We can and must agree that political parties being funded by people whose sources of wealth are shadowy is a dangerous and compromising situation that needs urgent remedy. We can and must consider what it means that we have allowed London to become the global capital of choice for laundering the illicit wealth foreign nationals have siphoned out of their own countries. In short, we can and must be better than we have been in many ways, and fast.

Yet knighting Gavin Williamson in the middle of all this suggests we have a way to go. I'm sure some galaxy brain will be on to explain how I'm oversimplifying things, but it does feel like it would have been so much simpler to NOT knight Gavin Williamson. How hard can NOT honouring the worst secretary of state in recent memory really be? It is suspiciously unclear what the man sacked as both defence and education secretary is being honoured for. Services to making Russia go away and shut up? Leaking from a top-level National Security Council meeting and consequently undermining the trust of the intelligence services (denied)? Presiding over an epochal failure of British children, from which significant numbers will never recover educationally or in terms of life chances?

Obviously, we know that the Johnson administration never particularly cared about the schoolchildren – Williamson was kept in post despite his catastrophic failings during the first lockdown and the exams fiasco that inevitably unfolded that summer. In the end, everything about the government's approach to an entire generation of children can be summarised by the fact that they reopened the pubs before they reopened all the schools. Yet Gavin could find focus when he wanted to. When Christian Wakeford crossed the floor to join Labour earlier this year, the Bury South MP claimed that Williamson had threatened to cancel a new school in his constituency if he did not vote against extending free school meals into the holidays for the poorest children – a conversation Williamson apparently does not remember having.

It's hard to believe a government that knows all this and still honours Williamson will do the right thing in other areas. Will they clean up the oligarchs to whom they have hitherto shown such sublime indifference or active encouragement, or will they just say that's what they're going to do? They do, after all, say a lot of things. Take the culture secretary. The last time I saw Nadine Dorries cry at work she was sobbing because Boris Johnson had pulled out of his post-referendum leadership bid. Yet here she was on Thursday, turning on the waterworks at the dispatch box, offering the BBC 'heartfelt thanks and admiration' for its reporting. Oh, Nadine. NOW you're a fan, is it? Because just weeks ago you were issuing tinpot threats on your Twitter about the BBC as we've known it being over. Weirdly, I don't see Nadine's precious Netflix dodging the bombs in a Kyiv basement in order to bring the world the news. (I should say that the Beeb is in Kyiv alongside many exceptional journalists from other UK broadcasters – a reminder that the BBC's unique funding model has always elevated our whole market. Rivals cannot compete for funding, so have traditionally competed on quality. And if you don't believe that, go and watch a range of American broadcast news for an evening.)

Anyway, amazing that it's taken actual war in Europe to make the actual culture secretary realise that maybe – just maybe! – the enemy is a station like Russia Today and not the BBC. Like I said, *maybe* Nadine has realised that. Notwithstanding her tears, I don't buy it myself. The one thing you can be absolutely sure of is that this government will be trying to cripple the BBC again in a few months, because at that point that particular position will suit them better once again. The Johnson administration doesn't do immutable principles. They only do expedience. In fact, it's occasionally hard not to see in Dorries a watered-down version of higher-skilled monsters, such as Russia's foreign ministry spokeswoman Maria Zakharova, who yesterday claimed the BBC was being used to undermine Russia's internal politics and security. She should speak to Nadine. I keep hearing from her and half the rest of the cabinet that the BBC undermines the UK's internal politics. I can never remember exactly why – I think it's something to do with on-screen-talent salaries or running stories about the government that they don't like.

Either way, the government now seems to be engaged in a number of hasty pivots. If these are genuine, then good. The time for a 'Let's not, and say we did' approach has passed. But on the form book, promises to make the British political family completely legitimate are unconvincing. This week, the prime minister has managed to knight one of his cronies and not do very much about any of Putin's.

A world-leading visa system? Tell that to Ukrainian refugees who can't get past Calais

8 March 2022

Russia's invasion of Ukraine called for a historic humanitarian response. What we got was the same old, same old: from nasty to useless

One of the things people often say when they see a colourised photo from the past is how vividly it brings history to life. The type of historical images we are more accustomed – and perhaps more inured – to seeing in monochrome are made breathtakingly new in colour, and this or that photo from the second world war is given such immediacy that it feels like something more relatable from our present.

Yet for the first time yesterday, I saw the technique work in the other direction. When an image of the vast, desperate crowds at Kharkiv train station was flying around, an ITN cameraman posted the same picture but in black and white, and it instantly felt 10 times more arresting. Happening right now was a tableau straight from Europe's dark past – thousands of tightly packed people massed on a station platform and trying to flee, their number vastly exceeding the available space on the trains. Perhaps we know how to read this picture better when we literally see it in black and white.

Nearly 1,700 miles away in Calais, alas, another image surfaces. This is a piece of printer paper taped to a wall, perhaps by some cursed emissary of the British Home Office, which reads: 'NO VISAS DELIVERED IN CALAIS'. For the exhausted Ukrainians who find it, two sparse instructions follow: 1. Type in a long and unwieldy URL to fill in a form. 2. Go all the way to Paris or Brussels to apply for a visa.

Why are we like this? In the words of Alf Dubs, who arrived in the UK on the *Kindertransport* in 1939: 'Shouldn't we be ashamed of ourselves?' Why – yet again – does the Home Office respond to a crisis in a manner that appears to run the full gamut from nasty to useless? Contrary to all manner of contradictory spin from No. 10 and the home secretary, 'world-leading', 'tailored' and 'bespoke' solutions and innovations are not making things easier for Ukrainians in their time of need. Instead, the inevitable humanitarian crisis caused by Russia's invasion of Ukraine seems to have taken those who should have known better by surprise. Boris Johnson's administration is admirably tough on war but shamefully weak on what we know is its timeworn fallout.

At the time it was reported that Poland had taken 800,000 refugees, the UK had accepted a mere 50. Which, to put things into perspective, is half the number of people you'd invite to a Downing Street bring-your-own-bottle party in the middle of a lockdown. Outraged by this dated inaccuracy, the Home Office yesterday corrected the record to show that a whole 300 visas had now been granted to fleeing Ukrainians. Which is three BYOB guestlists, and a mere 2.7% of the number of refugees who arrived in Berlin last Friday alone.

The UK is reduced to preposterous sleights of hand, attempting to make a virtue of what amount to bars to entry. Yesterday, the Home Office was trumpeting having 'the first visa scheme in the world' to launch post-invasion, studiously ignoring the huge number of countries that have waived the need for visas entirely to tackle the crisis. 'I am not going to be drawn into this,' breezed Foreign Office minister James Cleverly. 'Because really this is a team sport, and we're pulling together as a team on this.' The numbers indicate we're not. We're letting other countries do the pulling together, while we sit in the boat and pontificate about the view.

Shambles is the kinder reading. The suspicion is that the system is functioning as designed – that these problems are not happening *to* the Home Office and the government of which it is part, but *because* of them. Both No. 10 and the Foreign Office slapped down Priti Patel's mooted plan to allow easier access for all those fleeing Ukraine. Other secretaries of state either offer pointed assistance to the Home Office or wash their hands of its operations. This morning, Ben Wallace volunteered Ministry of Defence personnel support; yesterday, Liz Truss sniffed: 'It's really a matter for the home secretary exactly how the visa process works.'

Can one of them – any of them – just get it together on this front? In the years and decades after the second world war, many nations in Europe and beyond looked back on their actions and came to the painful realisation that they could and should have done more in various ways, not least in accepting refugees. As images of exodus are now reminding us, history is never in the past. History is now. It will be to our enduring shame if we don't try much harder to be on the right side of it.

Never a police officer around when you want one – unless you're an oligarch

15 March 2022

When squatters occupied Oleg Deripaska's house in Belgravia, there was no talk of a lack of resources

Didn't you love the pictures of a column of Metropolitan police officers running towards Oleg Deripaska's house like it was a five-storey Greggs? Here they come, trotting with intent, a phalanx of shirt-sleeved, riot-shielded protect-and-servers who may or may not be available inside of six weeks next time your house is burgled.

To recap, four protesters yesterday occupied a house in London's Belgravia that is supposedly owned by the Russian aluminium magnate Deripaska (now on the UK's sanctions list). They unfurled some banners inviting Vladimir Putin to fuck himself and so on, before being removed by the largest Met police presence you'll see outside of a women's vigil for someone murdered by a Met police officer. Territorial support group, police negotiators, police climbers, riot police . . . you name it. And, my darlinks, one's rarely seen so much hardware. The only big guns they left back at the station were the surface-to-air questionnaires.

There were at least eight vans and two squad cars, as well as a JCB, which for some reason was not being driven by Boris Johnson. Surely the prime minister should have just piloted it through the wall of the Belgrave Square house, then emerged from the driver's cabin for the cameras, gurning the words 'GET SANCTIONS DONE'? Absolutely no sense of occasion.

Alas, despite all these expensive resources, the incident drew a viciously self-satirising statement from Deripaska's spokeswoman. 'We are appalled at the negligence of Britain's justice system shown by Boris Johnson's cabinet in introducing the sanctions and colluding with the sort of people who raid private property,' she fumed. 'It's truly a disgrace that this is happening in a country that is supposed to respect private property and the rule of law.'

Now come, come, madam – this isn't a 'raid on private property'. It's a 'special operation'. As for the response to it, that is *multiples* more police than anyone normal in London could ever hope for. To put it in perspective, it's about the volume of hardcore law enforcement you could expect if a woman in Red Square held up a small piece of paper that didn't even say 'No war', but simply said 'Two words'.

But, look, before we go any further, I'm not saying that the protesters don't need to be removed from the property. Of course they do. However, as the author and kleptocracy expert Oliver Bullough remarked: 'There must be 20 police officers outside the Belgrave Square property occupied by anarchists, which is I reckon approximately 20 more than ever checked the provenance of the money that bought it.' Also, not sure we can get completely behind the spokeswoman claiming to be 'appalled at the negligence of Britain's justice system'. Join the queue. If the oligarchs have an issue with 'Britain's justice system', perhaps they should spend less time clogging it up? Honestly, they're never out of it, with their libel suits and their in-group spats and their full-spectrum lawfare.

Still, an Englishman's home is his castle, and an oligarch's home is – oh, hang on. I'm just reading some more of the spokeswoman's outpourings, and apparently this isn't even his home. Deripaska says it is owned by 'some family members'. I must say, it's really great to see Oleg supporting British investigative journalism, even with all the stuff he has going on in his life right now. Where this type of guy is concerned, it normally takes really dogged reporters a year to discover who owns the shell company that owns the shell company that owns the shell company that owns the house.

Furthermore, we must thank Deripaska or Some Family Members for enabling another great British pastime – looking askance at what people have done to their houses. After all, we lay our scene in Belgravia, one of various areas of well-heeled London that a previous social class of occupants judge has 'completely *gone*, I'm afraid'. Or, rather, completely *gorn*.

In many ways I'm all for a new breed of horror moving in. Ring the changes, you know? But it's funny to think that Deripaska's house was once owned by politician and category-5 diarist Chips Channon – who, incidentally, was not held back by self-doubt in his interior design vision. As he wrote of a new scheme for the Belgrave Square dining room: 'It will shock and stagger London.' And, naturally, they talked of little else in the East End. Anyway, Edward VIII and Mrs Simpson came to dinner there one night in 1936 and, according to Channon, 'The doors were flung open . . . and there was a pause as everyone's breath was taken away by the beauty of the dining room.' Flash forward to 2022, and my breath was also taken away by the video shot yesterday by the protesters from inside the historic house. Blond wood floors and a glass banister? Literally worse than the abdication.

The occupiers were eventually arrested, despite attempts to settle in for longer. According to reports, when they caught sight of some people looking out of the windows of the house next door, one called over: 'We are your new neighbours. We'll come over tomorrow with some brisket.' (Brisket! A slightly surreal detail. Isn't the offering of cliché a cup of sugar – or, in this locale, a cup of green juice? Perhaps the protester is American. Like Chips Channon.)

As for the Met, this is without question another great look from its spring collection, fresh from being found last week to have breached the rights of the organisers of the Sarah Everard vigil. Winter, meanwhile, was enlivened by its declaration that it does not investigate 'historic crimes'. Maybe yesterday's alleged crime found itself in a liminal time zone – strictly speaking, it was not historic, being ongoing, and therefore could be investigated by as many officers as were available, minus the ones serving WhatsApp suspensions and whatnot. And yet a friend recently observed a burglary in progress, and no squad car came because of what he was told was a lack of available resources. When he followed up, he was invited to make an appointment to discuss the incident so officers could gather a statement.

In the end, then, I can't help feeling Monday's ridiculous tableau in Belgrave Square is symbolic of a wider discombobulation, as Londongrad struggles with the pivot to this new era. A whole lot of compromised institutions, from the legal profession to the police to the politicians, are going to require a significant reset if we truly do mean to stop enabling some of the worst individuals in the world at the expense of pretty much everyone else. Nothing wrong with being polite, of course. But, both literally and metaphorically, we really don't have to fall over ourselves running to assist these people.

Nazanin is grateful, but is she grateful enough? I don't know, but the trolls will tell us

22 March 2022

If she had been docile, the freed Iranian hostage Nazanin Zaghari-Ratcliffe might have silenced her critics. Instead, she had a few questions – so the ingratitude police are on the case

To Britain, where a woman who hasn't said a word for six years is apparently talking too much. Are you a man who's got a massive view about how a hostage should behave after a lengthy incarceration? Are you 90% throbbing forehead vein? Do you like your prison victims pliant and super-obsequious about having spent pretty much their young daughter's entire life as the cell guest of a theocracy? If so, we really, really want to hear from you! And I have a feeling we're going to! Could you possibly stow your two-litre caramel latte in the cup holder, handbrake-turn on to the hard shoulder, punch in the phone-in digits and then give a masterclass in how relaxed and unthreatened you are by the decadent western spectacle of a woman speaking her mind?

Encouragingly, because some British people like to put their mouth where their arse is, the above call to arms has been answered. By mid-morning today, #sendherback was trending on Twitter (further bolstered by those so horrified by the hashtag they felt the need to repeat it). Down the phone lines and across the internets, many people are simply not happy with Nazanin Zaghari-Ratcliffe's failure to react to her belated release like she's just won Miss World in 1957. You know the playbook: deeply indebted tears at a flow volume that won't disrupt the mascara; silence broken only by a pledge to work with children and animals. British children and British animals, just to be on the safe side.

And yet, having spent a lot of time at her press conference yesterday thanking a large number of individuals and organisations who played a part in her eventual release, Nazanin did mention the fact it took just the five successive foreign secretaries before something repeatedly promised to her actually happened. And it is this that seems to have caused a huge number of four-wheel-drive prams to be emptied of all toys.

Of course, you get a few wishy-washy ignoramuses disagreeing. 'If trying our best took six years,' reasoned Jeremy Hunt, 'then we must be honest and say the problem should have been solved earlier.' Sorry, Jeremy, but what on earth do you know about the situation?! Wait. Hang on – my producer's telling me Jeremy was literally one of those five foreign secretaries. OK, well . . . thanks for dialling in. But we'll have to cut you off now because I've got a 56-year-old man from Aldershot on the line, who once told a BT customer service representative that she was as bad as Hitler and is now marvelling at the absolute cheek of Nazanin. I've got a guy who thinks masks were fascism strongly suspecting that the ayatollah had a point about this bird. I'm kidding, of course. But one does sometimes wonder if this whole generational cohort is becoming coddled. Nobody tells them to shut up and buck up. Nobody tells them to get some perspective and ring off. It's just possible we're raising a generation of entitled middle-aged men who think their every needy opinion has to be listened to.

As far as genuine real-life examples go, I saw one individual who characterised Nazanin's wry difference of opinion with Richard Ratcliffe over the merits of the Foreign Office response as 'disrespect[ing] her husband'. Over on Nick Ferrari's show on LBC, a chap called Jason seemed outraged that Nazanin 'didn't come across as a sort of victim', adding, 'It would have been nice for her to say thank you.' (She did, at length – but perhaps it was too much for Jason to actually watch the thing.) Ferrari appeared to partially agree, remarking: 'There might have been a degree more gratitude.'

Aha! There it is. Gratitude. I'm never sure whether it means 'being thankful' or 'not being uppity'. However, I can tell you it heralds some important Venn diagram news: the people sticking it to Nazanin for not being 'grateful' enough are the same people who boo footballers for taking the knee. Yup, just like the old knee-taking, it all comes down to 'gratitude' – the UK's sole remaining virtue after the others were sold off to oligarchs and Middle Eastern sovereign wealth funds.

And, you know, I hugely admire people who have whittled down their entire emotional range to a single, extremely compact sentiment: the idea that people should be grateful. Other people, obviously – not them. After all, how can they be grateful when there are ungrateful people out there? Stands to reason. They're so ungrateful about a world that contains ingratitude that they have to ring a phone-in and lose their shit about it. Look what you made them do.

Indeed, this whole line of criticism reminds me of a particular genre of *Daily Mail* column, of which I'm a keen student. Consider Stephen Glover asking rhetorically: 'Couldn't Afua Hirsch summon a smidgen of gratitude?' Or Amanda Platell deploring Stormzy's mention of Grenfell at the Brits one year, asking: 'Can't you show a scintilla of gratitude, Stormzy?' The argument is always that 'this country' has given people like Stormzy a good life, and they should shut up complaining.

And yet, why should it be only – how to put this delicately? – people like Stormzy who should show gratitude? Why can't it be, say, newspaper columnists? To pluck an example from the air, Amanda Platell – not born here, incidentally – spends the rest of her columns complaining strongly and occasionally erroneously and distastefully about people and events in the UK. Meanwhile, Stormzy – born here, incidentally – doesn't seem to get to have similarly strong and occasionally erroneous and distasteful views about people and events in the UK. Why? If nothing else, a newspaper columnist telling people to be grateful is like a fisherman telling people to be vegetarian. We're literally in the complaining game, Amanda! Stop cocking up the business model!

I can't help feeling something similarly ironicidal is happening with Nazanin, where a woman is already having her freedom of speech policed by people who think they're absolute defenders of it. I mean, not to state the fist-gnawingly obvious here, but isn't the whole point about liberating someone from the clutches of some backward theocracy that you don't then immediately go and tell her to know her place? Isn't the point that you tell her to say whatever the hell she likes, how she likes, and don't wet your big-boy pants about it? You don't have to agree with her. But you don't get to tell her what to say, much less to say nothing at all. And if the home counties hardliners don't like it, maybe they could #GoAndLiveInIran?

The good news: Johnson's on the way out. The bad news: look who's on the way in

8 July 2022

One ridiculously graceless 'resignation' speech later, here are the top Tory gorgons competing to control the sunlit uplands

Boris Johnson is leaving office with the same dignity he brought to it: none. I've seen more elegant prolapses. Having spent 36 hours on the run from what other people know as consequences, Downing Street's Raoul Moat was finally smoked out of his storm drain on Thursday, having awoken that morning with what one aide described portentously as a 'moment of clarity'. I mean, he'd lost 57 ministers? And been booed everywhere, from the steps of St Paul's to the cricket? Hard to know how much more clarity could have been offered to this big-brain, short of a plane flying over Downing Street trailing a banner reading 'U WANT PICKING UP IN THE MORNING, PAL?' This is the version of *Jaws* where the shark eats the mayor, and the entire beach is rooting for the shark.

They got Al Capone on tax evasion; they got Al Johnson on evasion. Character is fate, and the prime minister was undone by his lifelong pathological inability to tell the truth. Johnson's ridiculously graceless 'resignation' speech ran the gamut from pettiness to miscast victimhood – a sort of Bozzymandias, where the vainglory stood in painfully unfortunate contrast to the fact it was all lying in ruins around him. As the boos threatened to overwhelm his delivery, it was clear that what would satisfy the crowds was him being made to do a walk of shame, like some Blobby Cersei Lannister. (Same hairdo.) Failing that, he should have been wheeled out of Downing Street in the booze suitcase.

I saw that preposterous old tit David Mellor running towards a TV camera to claim Johnson's downfall was a tragedy 'worthy of Shakespeare', which makes you realise just what a writer Shakespeare could have been if only he'd realised making Falstaff king would have been the banter option, and the best way to not Get Agincourt Done. Watching Johnson fail to play Henry V for the past three years has been like watching the lift-music version of Laurence Olivier have a crack at the role. The sort of prime minister who makes people leave reviews like 'Amazon, why is it not possible to give zero stars?'

Still, Johnson always said he didn't want to be a one-term prime minister. He will now not be a one-term prime minister. We'll return to him later – but first, let's have a look at some of the runners and riders competing for control of the sunlit uplands. Remember: make like Perseus, and only look at them in your rear-view shield.

Ben Wallace: Ben once fumed on Twitter that Michael Gove would be Theon Greyjoy 'by the time I am finished with him'. Then again, maybe it would actually be quite popular to run on a promise to relieve the Conservative party of its penises.

Suella Braverman: Literally might as well run for leadership of Starfleet. Or Mensa.

Liz Truss: The risk is that Liz looks quite sane next to Suella, in the same way that Marilyn Manson would look like a 10 next to the Demogorgon.

Rishi Sunak: Along with Sajid Javid, once described *The Rise of Skywalker* as a 'great night out', and therefore should be immediately disqualified on grounds of judgment. Failed even to persuade his own wife to pay him tax – though that's not mentioned in the campaign video he's just dropped, which goes big on something called 'paytriotism'. Currently joint favourite, naturally.

Penny Mordaunt: The other current favourite, reinforcing the notion that the less you know about these people, the better they look.

Sajid Javid: How madly overvalued is British political commentary? Well, we elected a newspaper columnist to run the entire country, and Javid's resignation speech was routinely described by professionals who apparently watched it as 'powerful' and 'devastating', when he fluffed his big lines and was more wooden than the Commons' panelling. Still: a chance to give his previous non-dom status the attention Sunak's wife's non-dom status deprived it of when it emerged earlier this year.

Tom Tugendhat: Will be hoping the Conservative party could learn to be as pleased with him as he frequently appears to be with himself.

Nadhim Zahawi: One of three secretaries of state for education to have served under Johnson this week alone, Zahawi accepted his current position of chancellor with suspicious alacrity, considering it was like being promoted to ship's purser on the *Titanic* 10 minutes after the ballroom had filled with water. I can't wait to find out more about Zahawi's business dealings – and feel we certainly shall.

Jeremy Hu: Sorry, I got bored before I finished typing his name. Arguably an electoral problem.

Grant Shapps: The spreadsheet king of Welwyn Hatfield, but could split his vote with one of his many aliases.

Steve Baker: Living testament to the ancient Conservative principle that they've always got a worse idea up their sleeve. Should wrestle with the question of how his just God can permit him.

Priti Patel: Somehow yet to realise it won't take a wave machine to sink this boat.

Kemi Badenoch: Absolutely deplores the obsessions of Twitter, in that very specific way of people who spend several hours a day on it.

Back to Johnson, though, whose farewell speech demanded a single facetious question: 'Will you be having a leaving do, mate?' The answer, amazingly, is: yes. Apparently, one of the reasons why Johnson wants to cling on as caretaker, taking no big decisions, is because he and his wife are having a huge belated wedding party at Chequers later this month. Liggers to the last.

The outcry has forced them to seek a new venue – but only because they were found out. It's like some especially grotesque version of the butterfly effect. How many Britons' lives will be affected, probably for the worse, by some dead duck's determination to hang around for his wedding party? In the worst economic crisis for generations, how might some struggling people's existences be made worse by this guy's attempt to sneak past Theresa May's number of days in office? What care, precisely, is being taken by this caretaker?

Wedding parties, days-in-office here or there – what desperately small and pathetic ambitions these are. And how accurately they reflect the psychopathic political character of a man who never had a single belief in anything other than his own advancement.

If you want a mildly consoling glimpse of Johnson's long prime ministerial afterlife, once his memoirs have sold (and sold well), picture him being slapped awake by his handlers in some six-star Malaysian spa hotel, then trundled down to the conference ante-room to sit with other speakers, like Al Gore and some sex case from the World Bank, before going on stage to do his 500th rendition of The Speech. £120,000 a pop; *Raging Bull*-style weight gain and gnawing despair come as standard.

Ultimately, though, the disappointments and desolation are all ours. It was Johnson's world; we now have to live in it. It's quite sweet that people still talk of a 'realignment'. I don't mean to cavil, but what the hell is 'aligned' here? The UK will have had four prime ministers in just over six years. It's a rolling mess, a joke to much of the world. The only thing you can really align yourself with is the view that it can always get even worse and even more chaotic. Send in the clowns. Ah, don't bother. They're here.

ACKNOWLEDGMENTS

'Acknowledgment' seems like far too lukewarm a word for how I feel about the people who have contributed to the making of this book. I do not merely acknowledge but SALUTE the tireless work and good humour of the entire crew at Faber, most particularly my editor Laura Hassan, a stone-cold goddess who threw down for me at every turn, as did the splendid Mo Hafeez in editorial. My unending thanks, too, to Sophie Portas and Hannah Turner in publicity, Jess Kim in marketing and Anne Owen in pre-press. You gals are all amazing, and you couldn't have done more for me. So, too, with Sara Talbot, Sarah Davison-Aitkins, Mallory Ladd and the dedicated Faber sales team. Hope it's not a massive bomb for you all, obviously. Pete Adlington created a cover that I never would have dreamed of, while Matt Crockett's photographs mean he simply has to do all my holiday snaps from now on. Sorry, Matt – you're a victim of your own success. I enjoyed all my interactions with the brilliantly forensic and marvellously amiable copy-editor Ian Bahrami, while Sean McTernan lawyered my favourite way: with lawyerly restraint. Huge thanks, too, to Pedro Nelson in production and my eagle-eyed proofreader/indexer Mark Bolland, whose index is an actual work of art (unlike what it glosses).

I bow down to my super-agent, Karolina Sutton, who is exactly the person I want batting for me every time, which she'll know means EVERYTHING coming from this obsessive consumer of all books, articles, TV shows and films about agents.

At the *Guardian*, I thank my editor Kath Viner for continuing to let me bang on every week and rolling her eyes indulgently at several of the more off-colour jokes. Thanks, too, to her predecessor, Alan

Rusbridger, for hiring me in the first place and backing me time and again down the years; plus, I know he must miss our regular pay rise negotiations more than he can say. Elsewhere, I owe a huge debt to Ian Katz, also formerly of the *Guardian*, for first thinking it might be fun to let me cover a general election. I absolutely know I wouldn't have kicked on and found the way I wanted to write about politics without that opportunity. Thank you, my friend. Meanwhile, a wonderful parade of section editors and subs, from Sport to Comment to G2, have played their role in every column in this book, helping and encouraging me so much. Hey, it takes a village – in which I'm basically the village idiot. And I'm sending a massive air-kiss to the *Guardian* legal department, with whom – as you might imagine – I've shared some very, very precious moments over the years. Guys, when one of you recently said, 'The best person at legalling Marina's column is Marina,' I felt (a) quite emosh, and (b) like I'd finally completed the game. However, I will continue to send my copy to you 'just in case'.

There would certainly be no book without the countless news reporters, photographers and TV crews on whose work my opinion columns are based. They do all the hard yards, then I just waft in at the end and dispense some whimsy. Speaking of which . . . for fun times on the road, thousand-yard stares at party conferences and a WhatsApp group that just won't quit, I send big love to sketch-writers present and past John Crace, Michael Deacon, Tom Peck and Rob Hutton. Your jokes are always better than mine. As are those of the brilliant Matthew Norman, who taught me how to do pretty much anything good that's in here – most especially that there don't have to be any rules.

I am grateful to Stephen Frears for approximately one million walks, during which these matters and many others were discussed. To Will Smith, for making me think I could do new things. To Elaine Clifton, London's greatest maximalist. And to Marlyn Lorenzo, for so many years of kindness and love.

Acknowledgments

I owe so much to my most beloved parents, whose lifelong kindness and support have meant the world to me, to the point where I feel too overwhelmed to write about it. Where would I even start? Thank you, both, for everything, for ever; also, for participating in a number of extremely melodramatic arguments about Brexit. To my sisters, who are my best friends: your dismissal of most of this book's subject matter is the sole correct perspective.

The book could only be dedicated to my husband Kieran, who has given me endless faith, advice, laughs and praise, even when I've written something sensationally useless. So: pretty often, let's face it. Kieran, I know you told me to absolutely not put you in the acknowledgments or, indeed, anywhere near the book, so I hope this feels maddening and, ultimately, quite disappointing.

And finally, I want to thank my three children, whose answers to the eternal question 'What am I going to write about today?' are always great ideas, like 'Pokémon', 'Me' or 'Hitler'. Actually, the time you played Monopoly really loudly next to my desk for two hours during lockdown while I was trying to write about Richard Branson gave me the intro to that column (page 343) – and there are countless other pieces of fun in here for which you are the total inspiration. I'm sure you'll never get round to reading this book, my darlings, but I do want you to know it's for you. It's all for you, always.

INDEX

Collins, Gemma, 322
Colston, Edward, 275
Computer Weekly, 434
Conley, Sean, 195
Conrad, Joseph: *Heart of Darkness*, 215
Conservative party: age profile, 106;
BBC, hostility to, 437–8; blackmailing
MPs claim, 437; Brexit appointments,
36–7; buying support, 208; cabinet as
ninths or 10ths, 328; as cultic, 428–9,
430–1; Downing St parties, 384–7,
388, 425–31, 440; DUP pact, 96;
elections as psychosexual, 225; ERG
coup fails, 171–4; executive assumes
Johnson's character, 369–70; and female
voters, 45; hardmen of, 155, 156, 157;
and immigration, 150–3; Johnson's
expulsions, 230–1; oligarchs fund,
436; Paterson affair, 377–8, 380, 383;
from post-truth to post-shame, 164;
principles v. expedience, 438; pubs
trump schools, 437; rehabilitating knife-
wielders, 248–9; school meals policy,
312, 326–7, 437; sleaze debate, 381–3;
steals Labour policies, 103–4; stockpiles
U-turns, 328; 'straight-to-public-
inquiry' government, 299; stupidest
cabinet minister, 162; 'third triumvirate',
379; 2019 electoral intake, 249; two
class A drugs, 221; v. nurses, 301–2; *see
also* Brexit; Covid
CONFERENCES: 2017, 102–8, 109,
112, 170; 2018, 164–71
GENERAL ELECTIONS: 2015, 202;
2017, 92–8, 103, 109, 151, 203; 2019,
230, 238–41, 244–50, 327
LEADERSHIP CONTESTS: 2016,
21–33, 38, 163, 437; 2019, 162, 163,
168–9, 219–26; 2022, 449–51
Conservative Way Forward, 154
conspiracies: and Alex Jones, 76; Covid,
192, 347–8, 428; paedophile-based,
430; as response to government
duplicity, 428; Starmer/Savile, 430;
Trump paradox, 195; and unhealthy
democracies, 192–3
Cook, Tim, 345, 366

Cooney, Ray, 258
Corbyn, Jeremy: and antisemitism, 39–40,
148, 149; appearance, 218; Blair-style
self-belief, 147–8, 149, 150; and Brexit,
207–8, 212, 215, 292; Cameron's final
PMQs, 34–5; 'don't know' outpolls,
170–1; on footballers' wages, 119–20,
121; as full nutter, 359; general election
(2019), 238, 250, 358; and IRA, 218;
Johnson on, 93; on Johnson and fridge,
247; merch, 43; nuclear beliefs, 92;
portrayal in media, 43–4; rise to power,
42; and Russian nerve agent, 358;
soundtrack, 95; as 30-year project, 250;
Tories blank, 202; as Tory antagonist,
103
Corbyn, Piers, 243
Cosby, Bill, 404
cosmetics, 339–40, 341, 342
Costner, Kevin, 42
Coulter, Ann, 86
Courage and Civility award, 354
Couzens, Wayne, 277–8, 280
Covid: Brexit policy repurposed, 294;
business response, 302–3; care homes
scandal, 138, 306, 311, 312–13, 322,
375; conspiracy theories, 192, 347–8,
428; cruise cancellations, 75; designated
survivor, 300, 304; and Djokovic,
137–8; Downing St parties, 384–7,
388, 425–31; 'Eat Out to Help Out',
318–19, 364; economic damage, 330,
370; essential terms lack definition,
294; EU ventilator scheme, 303; family
tragedies, 427; 'freedom day', 142;
government press conferences, 293,
312–13, 360–2, 363, 425; Hancock,
and hugging ban, 370–3; military
metaphors, 304–7; need for Johnson
psychologist, 298–9; no women in 'war
cabinet', 306–7, 323–4; 'Operation Last
Gasp', 295; Operation Moonshot, 321–
2; 'over by Christmas' hope, 319, 331;
police response, 303; PPE shortage, 301,
306; quarantine in City, 328; Queen's
address, 307; and schools, 313–14, 437;
tech giants exploit, 345; test and trace,

INDEX